31358

31358

PETER the GREAT

HENRI TROYAT

Translated from the French by Joan Pinkham

E. P. DUTTON   NEW YORK

This book was originally published in France
under the title *Pierre le Grand* by Librairie Flammarion.
Copyright © Flammarion, 1979
English translation copyright © 1987 by E. P. Dutton
All rights reserved. Printed in the U.S.A.

First published in the United States in 1987 by
E. P. Dutton, a division of NAL Penguin Inc.,
2 Park Avenue, New York, N.Y. 10016.

Library of Congress Cataloging-in-Publication Data

Troyat, Henri, 1911–
Peter the Great.

Translation of: Pierre le Grand.
Bibliography: p.
Includes index.
1. Peter I, Emperor of Russia, 1672–1725.
2. Soviet Union—Kings and rulers—Biography.
3. Soviet Union—History—Peter I, 1689–1725.
I. Title.
DK131.T713   1987   947'.05'0924 [B]   86-19694

ISBN: 0-525-24547-2

Published simultaneously in Canada by
Fitzhenry and Whiteside Limited, Toronto

W

Designed by Dana Maller

10 9 8 7 6 5 4 3 2 1

First American Edition

Contents

SIXTEEN PAGES OF ILLUSTRATIONS FOLLOW PAGE 176.

Translator's Note

As readers of M. Troyat's three earlier biographies of Russian czars know, his books contain a wealth of extracts from historical documents—official decrees, private letters, diplomatic dispatches, contemporary memoirs, and so on. Naturally, no matter in what language these texts were originally written, for his French readers M. Troyat gives the extracts in French. That fact poses special problems for the English translator, and I want to explain briefly how I have dealt with them in this book.

For most of the quotations from documents written in Russian, German, Dutch, Swedish, English, et cetera, I had no choice but to translate directly from M. Troyat's French. Double translation inevitably entails some loss of authenticity, and I can only hope that here it has not resulted in any distortion of meaning. Occasionally, however, I was able to bypass the French when, for example, I could find the original English of an account by an English visitor to Russia, or a contemporary English translation of the memoirs of a German diplomat. In such cases, the source of the passage in question is indicated in the notes.

One series of quotations for which I used an existing English translation requires special mention. Chapter 11 contains a number of long extracts from Russian documents relating to the trial of the Czarevich Alexis. These documents appeared, along with others, in the "Manifesto of the Criminal Process of the Czarewitz Alexei Petrowitz," which was published in St. Petersburg in 1718, immediately after the pronouncement of the verdict. In that same year the Manifesto was translated from Russian into French "by the Czar's express orders," and in 1723 the French translation was in turn done into English. It is from that version by an anonymous translator (contained in Volume II of Friedrich Christian Weber's *The Present State of Russia*) that I have taken the quotations from the Manifesto that appear in this book.

There are many discrepancies (although none of great substance) between the English texts presented in the Weber volume and those given by M. Troyat in French, and I have no way of judging how faithful the English translation is to the Russian original. Nevertheless, so far as I know, Weber's book remains the authentic English source for the documents in question. I therefore judged it best—with M. Troyat's permission—to adopt that version rather than to make a new translation of my own. Trusting that the eighteenth-century language and style of the unknown English translator will give the reader some flavor of the time, I have made no changes in his text other than to modernize the spelling and punctuation.

Much of the same source material used by M. Troyat has, of course, been mined by other biographers and translators. Hence many of the quotations given in this work also appear in other books, though often in quite different renditions. When I found in one of these other versions a turn of phrase that I liked better than my own, I have gratefully adopted it, and I hereby acknowledge my debt to my predecessors.

I also want to express warm thanks for the generous assistance of my friend Professor Andrée Demay. Her mastery of both French and English and her scholarly knowledge of the eighteenth century have helped me to resolve many difficulties throughout the book.

J.P.

1
Violence in the Kremlin

When his wife died on March 14, 1669, Czar Alexis Mikhailovich gave vent to so much grief that the members of his entourage thought the deceased would never be replaced. Besides, who could succeed the beautiful Maria Miloslavskaya, who was said to have been something of a witch and to have had a cloven hoof? Sensual and prolific, in twenty-one years of marriage she had given her husband five sons and six daughters. It was true that three of the sons had died one after the other and that neither of the remaining two, Feodor and Ivan, had a strong constitution.* Feodor was no fool, but he seemed so frail that the weight of the imperial mantle would crush his shoulders. As for Ivan, his father could not but shudder at the idea of abandoning the throne of Russia to a degenerate, epileptic adolescent afflicted with a pendulous lip and rheumy eyes. Of the daughters, the only one worth mentioning was Sophia, who was intelligent, cunning, energetic,

*Alexis Mikhailovich's daughters were Eudoxia, Anna, Catherine, Martha, Maria, and Sophia. Sophia was born in 1657, Feodor in 1661, Ivan in 1666.

3

and stout. But the Czar rebelled at the notion of a petticoat in the order of succession. He had to have more sons, with strong bones and clear heads. He was distressed that his bed was empty. In mourning the departed, he was no longer sure whether it was the companion of his nights or the reliable procreator whom he regretted losing. All things considered, he was not so old—just forty— and he was still capable of begetting a child. A pious, indecisive, indolent, cautious, peaceable man, it took him a long time to admit to himself what he wanted. Then suddenly, after two years of widowerhood and prayer, he made up his mind. For the greatness of Russia, he must remarry. A portrait of the period shows him stiffly robed in heavy brocade strewn with rubies, emeralds, and pearls, wearing a conical cap edged with sable and surmounted with a cross, the scepter in his right hand, the globe in his left, a solid, thickset, bearded man with a scarlet mouth under a drooping mustache, stern eyes, and a strong nose. Plainly a man who, though he may fear heaven, has not renounced the world.

As soon as he made known his intention, the court was seized with wild excitement. According to time-honored tradition, the Czar was to choose a bride from among the most beautiful and deserving maidens, who would be summoned for the purpose to the Kremlin in Moscow.* In keeping with the custom of the *smotriny,* or "viewing," a throng of candidates from the great and petty nobility, escorted by their parents, arrived on the appointed day: September 14, 1670. Tall or short, blonde or brunette, pretty or plain, young or not so young, decked out in splendor or modestly dressed, they all had in common virginity, good health, stolid virtue, and an ardent hope of being chosen. They had no sooner reached the palace than they were herded into the *terem,* † where expert ladies examined them from every angle, questioned them, undressed them, felt them all over to determine if they were worthy of the imperial favors. Not even the most intimate parts of the body were exempt from these investigations. The young ladies

*There was a kremlin (*kreml*), or central quarter surrounded by fortifications, in other old Russian cities as well: Pskov, Rostov, Novgorod, Nizhni-Novgorod, Astrakhan, etc.

†*Terem:* gynaeceum, apartment in which the upper-class women of old Russia lived an almost cloistered life.

who were judged unfit were immediately expelled. The rest were led in a twittering flock to the dormitory. There they waited in a fever of excitement for the visit of the master of the house, who would decide their fate. Whispers, prayers, quivers of anticipation —then the door opened. It was he, the bearded Czar, the all-powerful widower, Alexis Mikhailovich. Each girl dreamed of being the one to console him. Accompanied by a physician, he walked between the rows of beds, glancing over the candidates as though not seeing them. Suddenly he stopped in front of a certain Natalya Naryshkina and held out to her a handkerchief embroidered with gold and pearls. Natalya lowered her eyes. She would be Czarina.

Actually, the Czar had known this young woman for a long time. He had met her at the home of his friend Artamon Matveyev, head of the *prikaz** of ambassadors, a man of some education, famous for his library, for his chemistry laboratory, and especially for the extraordinary fact that he had a Scottish wife. This innovator was interested in Western ideas, and he had not wished his charming ward, Natalya Kyrilovna Naryshkina, the daughter of a poor and obscure provincial gentleman, to live behind the closed doors of a *terem*. She was allowed to sit at her guardian's table even in the presence of guests and had captivated Alexis Mikhailovich from their first meeting. Tall, with a mat complexion, black eyes, long lashes, and a modest demeanor, she radiated piety, honesty, gentleness, submission. To be sure, she was twenty years younger than the Czar. But the splendid visitor was not troubled by the difference in age. Quite the contrary, he counted on her freshness to reawaken his torpid senses. He had been tired of late and felt faint at times, symptoms that would no doubt be cured by the touch of a young girl's skin. He had made a concession to custom by summoning all the boyars' daughters to the Kremlin for the *smotriny*, but he knew in advance the name of the one who would come into his bed.

The marriage was celebrated on January 22, 1671. Overnight the numerous and demanding Miloslavsky clan, who owed their

---

*Prikaz: a government department in old Russia. In addition to the *prikaz* of ambassadors, there were *prikazy* of war, finance, justice, etc.

dominant position to the late Czarina Maria, gave way to the no less numerous and demanding Naryshkin clan, who were related to the new Czarina Natalya. As they changed places, the arrogance of the newcomers was equaled only by the silent hatred of those whom they supplanted. But the Czar was enchanted with Natalya's gaiety and her discreet coquetry. He was not the only one to appreciate the young woman's charm. The Patriarch Nikon took a fancy to her and was always at her heels. This holy man had the reputation of being both the scourge of heretics and an insatiable ladies' man. Another of the beautiful Natalya's admirers was a courtier of humble extraction, Tikhon Streshnev. It was said that the Czar closed his eyes to the attentiveness shown his wife by these two gallants, among others.

On May 30, 1672—the year 7180 according to the calendar then in use in Russia*—she gave birth to a son. The child was given the name Peter. While no one yet ventured to call him Peter the Great, the astrologers who were consulted all predicted a glorious future for him. Not only had his star appeared in proximity to the planet Mars, but there was another portent: on the day of his birth the army of Louis XIV, led by Condé and Turenne, had made ready to cross the Rhine. According to the experts, this military event was a sign that the infant had before him a great career as a victorious warrior.

The Czar, overjoyed, gave thanks to God, pardoned some condemned prisoners, forgave the debts of debtors to the state, had vodka distributed by the barrel, and gave a gargantuan feast for four hundred guests. The banquet, consisting of 120 dishes, ended with a sickening apotheosis: for dessert, a gigantic eagle made of sugar candy, a duck, a canary, and a parrot done in caramel and, last, a Kremlin built out of multicolored confectionery, complete with walls, towers, cannon, foot soldiers, and cavalry. While the guests, who were already stuffed to bursting, made a last effort to choke down a few sweets, acrobats, dancers, and cymbal players did their best to distract them from the contents of their

*In Russia at this time years were counted starting from the presumed date of the creation of the world. May 30, 1672, according to the Julian calendar, corresponds to June 10, 1672, on the modern Gregorian calendar.

plates. During the days that followed, the boyar Artamon Matveyev, in deference to European customs, organized theatrical performances at his own house and at the palace. Most of the plays were performed in German by German actors recruited from the capital's colony of foreign craftsmen, but as a daring innovation, the scholar-monk Simeon Polotsky, tutor to the Czar's children, wrote for the occasion two plays in Russian: *The Prodigal Son* and *Nebuchadnezzar.*

What most delighted Alexis Mikhailovich was that, for once, his offspring looked strong and healthy. All his other children had shown from infancy signs of ugliness and degeneracy. This one was a model of vigor, beauty, and liveliness—all it took for the palace scandalmongers to call into question Peter's paternity. Some of them insinuated that the Czar, weakened by age and sapped by illness, could not have produced in his decline a son of such flourishing health. They even named the true father: Patriarch Nikon—a giant, a force of nature, a violent, authoritarian, and brilliant man—or else the shrewd, energetic Tikhon Streshnev, who was very close to the sovereign and to Natalya. Many years later Peter, tormented by doubt as to his paternity, was to ask the question suddenly during a banquet. Pointing to Count Ivan Mussin-Pushkin, he cried: "That man, at least, knows that he is the son of *my* father.* But *I* don't know exactly whose son I am!" And bounding toward Tikhon Streshnev, he went on in a drunken voice: "Tell me the truth, are you my father? Obey! Speak out without fear or I'll strangle you!" "Sire," replied Streshnev, "I know not what to say to you—I was not the only one." Then Peter hid his face in his hands and staggered out of the room.†[1] The suspicions that were to gnaw at him all his life never even crossed the mind of the man who considered himself his progenitor.

Natalya soon gave Czar Alexis Mikhailovich two more children

---

*Ivan Mussin-Pushkin was the illegitimate son of Czar Alexis.

†The question of Peter's paternity has never been settled definitively. It is true that as an adult he was over six feet six inches, like Patriarch Nikon; it is also true that he was intelligent and strong-willed, like Streshnev, that he did not resemble Czar Alexis Mikhailovich either physically or mentally, and that according to contemporaries the Czarina had many lovers. But all those facts do not add up to proof. After all, Peter would not be the first man of genius to have been fathered by a mediocrity.

—two lovely, healthy daughters a year apart.* Better yet, she created an atmosphere of cheerfulness and simplicity around him that helped him, despite his weariness, to carry on his work as sovereign. Impressionable, irresolute, and wavering, it pained him whenever he had to impose his will. During his reign he had to struggle against the schism in the Church, the Cossacks who revolted under Stenka Razin, the Turks, the Poles, the Swedes, and his own boyars, who did not always understand his wish to imitate Western ways. He dreamed of carrying out reforms, yet yielded to the traditionalists as soon as they accused him of trying to destroy the sacred heritage of Russian customs. At forty-seven he was worn out trying to govern the country whose pieces he had patiently put together. Stricken with scurvy and dropsy, he died during the night of January 29–30, 1676, not without having commanded in a faint voice that after his death the crown should pass to his son Feodor, who was barely fifteen.

The *Zemsky Sobor*—the assembly composed of the Duma (council) of boyars, the Holy Synod, and a few officials from the most important *prikazy*—met at once and, in obedience to the wishes of the deceased, chose as czar Feodor, the brother of Sophia and Ivan and half brother of Peter. On June 21, 1676, the Dutch representative Van Keller, who had witnessed the coronation, described the ceremony as follows: "The great personages and the courtiers were all superbly dressed in stuffs of gold and silver; in many cases their coats and tall hats were very richly embroidered and loaded with quantities of pearls. Prince Michael Dolgoruky threw great handfuls of gold and silver coins to the people. The place swarmed with folk of all sorts shouting at the top of their voices, wishing the prince every kind of good fortune, whilst in their eagerness to pick up the coins some were trampled to death."

Hardly had the bells celebrating the accession of Feodor III fallen silent, hardly had the mead dried on the mustaches of the boyars invited to the coronation feast, when the great housecleaning began. Since the mother of the new Czar was Maria Miloslavskaya, Alexis Mikhailovich's first wife, the whole Miloslavsky tribe

*Feodora (1673–1678) and Natalya (1674–1716).

returned to the palace in force to drive out the Naryshkin tribe, to which the Czar's widow and his youngest son Peter belonged. First the victors accused Artamon Matveyev, an upright minister and Czarina Natalya's guardian, of having caused the death of Alexis I by practicing black magic. Did not the accused possess a chemistry laboratory and books on algebra? That was enough for him to be imprisoned, tortured, and exiled to Siberia. As for Natalya, she barely escaped being relegated to a cloister. She was merely sent, along with her son, Peter, to Preobrazhenskoye, a village near Moscow.

The boy, who was tenderly cherished by his mother, was still only a little tot with curly dark-brown hair, big black eyes, and chubby pink cheeks. A sturdy child, quick in movement and in thought, he was curious about everything, open to everything. What a contrast to his half brother, Czar Feodor III! The very young sovereign was gentle, thoughtful, cultivated; he spoke Latin and Polish; he wrote verses on occasion. But he was scrofulous and sickly, and the duties of his position seemed to be too much for him. He entrusted the management of public affairs to his sister Sophia's lover, the magnificent Prince Basil Golitzin. In addition to his talents as a lover, which were highly valued by the Czarevna Sophia,* Prince Golitzin had talents as a statesman, which were highly valued by the Czar. But Feodor, after two consecutive marriages,† was having increasingly frequent episodes of illness and bemoaned the fact that he had no male offspring. The only son his first wife had given him had died in infancy shortly before her. The daughter born of his second wife had also died. His blood was thin. Who would succeed him? His brother Ivan, who was going on sixteen but whose mind was deranged and who had to raise his eyelids with his fingers to distinguish the objects around him? Or his half brother Peter, who was lively, eager, and intelligent but not yet ten? Should he decide on the basis of the law of primogeniture or on the basis of health and brains? Feodor hesitated but leaned strongly toward Peter. All eyes in Moscow were fixed on the Krem-

---

*The Czarina was the Czar's wife, the Czarevich his son, the Czarevna his daughter or sister. As the daughter of Alexis I, Sophia was the Czarevna.
†In 1680 he had married Agatha Gruschevskaya, who had died the following year; his second wife was Martha Apraxina.

lin, where amid the greatest mystery the future of the country was being forged.

This Kremlin was a citadel with crenelated walls, built in the center of the capital by the Muscovite princes of former days for defense against enemy armies and popular uprisings. Here lived the Czar and the Patriarch; here beat the heart of the nation. At great moments in history, it was to this sacred place that the crowds streamed to give vent to their joy, sorrow, or wrath. A fortress in time of war, the Kremlin was open to all comers in time of peace. Starting at dawn a throng of visitors of every sort passed through the gates, removing their hats in the presence of the holy images hanging over them. The carriages of the boyars made their way with difficulty through the press of common people. There were peasants with petitions to present, crippled beggars, monks come to see the Patriarch, clerks running from one government office to another, arrogant archers, cake sellers, pickpockets, sightseers staring up at the buildings, public scribes ready to compose on the spot a petition or a love letter. This motley, noisy crowd flowed around the buildings of stone and wood, an incredible mixture of the sacred and profane. Within these walls all styles of architecture were jumbled together—Gothic, Byzantine, Italian Renaissance. The buildings were nested one inside the other like children's toys. In the main square, amid dozens of chapels and little churches, rose the Cathedral of the Annunciation, the Cathedral of the Assumption, the Cathedral of the Archangel. The palaces themselves looked like churches, with their domed roofs, colored tiles, and the riotous ornamentation of their façades. Round about stood other large buildings housing the treasury, the armory, and the innumerable services of the Czar's household—kitchens, coach factories, laundries, bakeries, woodsheds, and stables that accommodated up to forty thousand horses, including some valuable purebred Arabians.

Inside the dimly lit palaces silence reigned. The walls of the low-vaulted, smoky rooms were decorated with frescoes or hung with leather or silk. On the pillars gold and vermilion were mingled in fanciful arabesques. A few oil lamps flickered here and there in the corridors. It was in this stifling atmosphere that the court around Feodor III anxiously awaited reports from the sickroom.

Groups formed on the basis of kindred ambitions. People plotted in low voices behind an arras, placed their bets on Ivan or on Peter, trembled, and hoped, for the accession of one or the other to the throne would mean the rise of his supporters and the downfall of the opposing faction. Ivan, the son of Maria Miloslavskaya, had behind him the whole Miloslavsky clique, and Peter, the son of Natalya Naryshkina, all the Naryshkins. At the head of the Miloslavsky faction the fat Czarevna Sophia was busily at work. Taking advantage of Feodor's illness, she never left his bedside, kept his young wife away from him, and, on pretext of caring for him, poured into his ear the most self-interested advice. Since he was a Miloslavsky, she said, he must designate another Miloslavsky—that is, his brother Ivan—to succeed him. If by aberration he designated his half brother Peter, it would be Peter's mother, Natalya, a Naryshkin, who would assume the regency during the child's minority. He could not betray his own flesh and blood that way. It was unfortunate that Ivan was retarded, but Sophia stood ready to protect and advise him. Would she not make as good a regent as Natalya?

There was no doubt that Sophia had the makings of a leader of men. Highly educated, with a quick and crafty mind and a sharp tongue, she had no intention of settling for the unobtrusive role usually played by Russian women in the *terem. Her* domain was the whole palace, the outside world. It was as if the awareness that she was ugly, far from moving her to modesty, exalted her ambition. The Franco-Polish diplomat La Neuville wrote that she had "a deformed body, monstrously fat, a head as big as a bushel basket, hair on her face, and ulcers on her legs." He added: "Her mind is as sharp, subtle, and political as her figure is broad, short, and gross, and without ever having read Machiavelli or learned about him, she has a natural grasp of all his maxims."[2] At the age of twenty-six she looked forty. This virago was possessed by an unbridled sensuality. Although passionately in love with Basil Golitzin, who was her official lover, she permitted herself indiscretions with officers of the *streltsy* corps.* In the first days of spring in 1682, Feodor III's strength was failing rapidly. On April 27 of that year,

Strelets means "shooter" or "archer." The plural is *streltsy.*

at four in the morning, he breathed his last. It was said that earlier he had called for a blackberry tart. Had it been poisoned? Some persons insinuated that Sophia had hastened her beloved brother's end by indulging his taste for sweets. In any case, after a reign of six years, the Czar expired without having designated a successor.

While the bells of the Kremlin tolled the knell, echoed by the other bells of the city, the new Patriarch, Joachim, much at a loss what to do, left the death chamber and called an impromptu meeting of the *Zemsky Sobor* in a room in the palace. The boyars, ecclesiastics, and officers who had been assembled in haste were called upon to reply on the spot to the prelate's question: Since the late Czar had not chosen his heir, was it Ivan or Peter who should assume the crown of Russia? The Patriarch added: "Let him among you who allows himself to be guided by his passions suffer the fate of Judas!" By a large majority the assembly acclaimed Peter. Outside, however, the people, who had come running at the sound of the bells, crowded at the foot of the "Red Steps,"* a monumental staircase interrupted by broad landings. With the richly dressed members of the *Zemsky Sobor* behind him, Joachim showed himself at the top of the staircase, announced the result of the election, and asked the crowd if they were satisfied with this choice. He was answered by a roar of joy: "Let Peter Alexeyevich be our Czar!" After which the multitude dispersed to spread the good news and get drunk on vodka.

Joachim returned to the palace, blessed little Peter I, aged ten, and supervised the installation of the astonished child on a throne that was too big for him. All the persons present filed before the young monarch to swear allegiance and kiss his hand. Sophia, swallowing her rage, had to bow like the others before the boy, who was trying to sit up straight. Calmly he watched the slow succession of venerable faces. Most were familiar to him. But he found that today all the courtiers wore an air of unaccustomed solemnity. They had put on their finest garments. Narrow caftans

*In old Russian, the word *krasny* could mean both "red" and "beautiful." One could therefore say in English either "Red Steps" or "Beautiful Steps," "Red Square" or "Beautiful Square."

of gold or silver brocade over which their beards spread wide, Persian sashes knotted under the stomach to accentuate the curve of the paunch—a proper source of masculine pride—and red leather boots with upturned toes. No women, except for the Czarinas and Czarevnas in ceremonial gowns. They stood with their heads bowed and, as was only correct, with tears in their eyes. Natalya couldn't believe her good fortune. Here she was, Regent. In the midst of the conflicting sentiments of those around her—triumph and hatred, fear and hope—she was all gentleness, innocence, and futility. She did not act; she submitted to events and prayed that all the discord around her son Peter would at last subside. Behind her stood the greedy, frivolous men of the Naryshkin clan, openly triumphant. To them would fall the juicy plums of office!

But the massive and terrible Sophia was still to be reckoned with. Having tasted the life of a free woman at her brother Feodor's side, caring for him and advising him, she refused to contemplate a return to the *terem,* that gynaeceum of another age where the daughters and sisters of the czar vegetated in a life of chastity, idleness, gossip, prayer, fasting, and the interpretation of dreams, seeing no man except the Patriarch or close relatives. A physician was admitted to their bedside only in extreme cases. Then the room was plunged into darkness and the doctor would take the patient's pulse through a piece of gauze. In church, to which they made their way by secret corridors, the czarevnas, like the czarinas, were hidden from the eyes of the faithful by curtains of red taffeta. As their rank prevented them from marrying one of the czar's subjects, no matter how high he stood in the social hierarchy, and since they could not betray their religion by marrying a foreign prince, they usually had to settle for a future of solitude and prayer. But Sophia wanted to live, to love, to dominate. Especially because she now had at her side a man who satisfied her physically and intellectually: Basil Golitzin. With him she devised the plan of revenge. The two lovers won over to their scheme the Czarevna's uncle, Ivan Miloslavsky, called the Cruel, the brothers Ivan and Peter Tolstoy,* the monk Sylvester Medvediev, as erudite as he

---

*Peter Tolstoy was an ancestor of the great novelist.

was mad, and Prince Ivan Khovansky, a mighty warrior who was vain and daring. It was on him that Sophia was counting to rally around her the formidable band of *streltsy*.

The *streltsy* (that is, archers or harquebusiers) were a creation of Ivan the Terrible. They were divided into twenty regiments of a thousand men each, most of whom were stationed in Moscow. In former days they had distinguished themselves in glorious campaigns, but for a long time now they had enjoyed their exceptional position without risking their lives in the service of the state. Free soldiers, housed, outfitted, and paid by the public treasury, they were harquebusiers from father to son and jealously defended the privileges that set them apart from the regular army and the Cossacks, whose pay was much lower than theirs. They administered themselves and had their own commander, who was always a boyar of high rank. Installed with their wives and children in districts reserved for them alone, they had even been granted the right to engage in commerce and industry without being licensed or taxed. In exchange for these advantages, they policed the streets, formed the sovereign's honor guard, and put out fires. These troops of insolent, avaricious janissaries were especially proud of their uniforms: a brightly colored caftan (red, blue, purple, or green according to the regiment), a red sash, a tall velvet hat trimmed with sable, yellow boots of supple leather. For weapons each carried a harquebus, a saber, and a halberd. The inactivity of the *streltsy* completed the collapse of discipline in their ranks. Soon they became nothing but bands of hardened troopers who, faced with a faltering state, thought they had a right to do whatever they pleased. Allegedly the defenders of order, they often made common cause with the fomenters of disorder. Although sheltered from cares of any kind, they shouted louder than the common people who, with entire justification, protested the weight of taxes and the corruption of officials. Under the reign of the indolent Feodor III they were already holding assemblies, openly discussing political and religious questions, criticizing the throne and the Church, and accusing their own leaders of misappropriating funds.

When Peter I ascended the throne these vociferous troopers threatened to revolt unless the Czar punished their colonels who, they said, robbed them and made them work on Sunday. The

Regent Natalya, in a panic, called back from exile Artamon Matveyev, who had been so wise an adviser to her husband. But Matveyev was slow to return, and time was pressing. To appease the *streltsy* the Regent, on bad advice from the Duma of boyars, decided to condemn the colonels, without making the slightest investigation. In front of the troops the accused officers were beaten with rods on the calves of their legs until they had restored the money demanded by the plaintiffs. The beatings went on for several days, for two hours at a time. "They broke many rods while beating the poor unfortunates," wrote a witness. "The *streltsy* crowded into the square and acted as judges; the punishment was stopped only when they cried, 'Enough!' Certain colonels whom they particularly detested were beaten twice a day."[3] Finally the humiliated officers submitted and emptied their coffers. The horde of praetorian guards shouted for joy. Natalya and the Naryshkins thought they had warded off the danger. In reality, they had only encouraged insolence and paved the way for insurrection.

Sophia and her accomplices followed the events with fiendish interest. They met at night at Ivan Miloslavsky's house, decided which of the Naryshkins and their friends would have to be eliminated to clear a path to the throne, and summoned paid spies and assigned them precise missions. These spies, one of whom, Feodora Rodmitsa, was a confidante of Sophia's, slipped into the districts where the *streltsy* lived, stirred up the malcontents, and told them that the Naryshkins had poisoned Feodor III, that they were mistreating the Czarevich Ivan and threatening to assassinate him, that Ivan had not renounced the crown, and that furthermore, Peter I was not the son of Alexis Mikhailovich but of Streshnev or Patriarch Nikon. A hired thug, dressed like a Naryshkin, molested the wife of one of the *streltsy* and fled, an incident that exacerbated their anger. Others of Sophia's agents distributed money, buying consciences that were only too ready to be bribed. All was ready for the bloodbath. But before going into action Ivan Miloslavsky waited for the arrival in Moscow of his worst enemy, Artamon Matveyev, whom he had sworn to destroy and whose name he had set at the head of the list of victims.

At last Artamon Matveyev returned from exile and entered Moscow. He had taken only a few steps in the Kremlin before he sensed the catastrophe that was brewing. But it was too late to reverse the situation. On May 15, 1682, Ivan Miloslavsky launched the offensive. His emissaries infiltrated the districts of the *streltsy* and spread the rumor that the Naryshkins, having assassinated Czar Feodor III, had now assassinated Czarevich Ivan. Immediately nineteen regiments of the praetorian guard rose up in arms shouting, "Death to the traitors!" They sounded the alarm, downed floods of vodka to strengthen their nerve, threw off their multicolored caftans, and appeared all dressed alike in their red shirts with sleeves rolled up to the elbows, like workmen getting ready for a cleanup. Brandishing pikes, halberds, and sabers, pushing and pulling cannon, the roaring tide swept toward the Kremlin. Orders were given to close the heavy gates of the citadel. But the guardhouses were already overwhelmed. The first waves of *streltsy* were battering the walls of the Faceted Palace. Inside there was panic. To show the rebels that they had been deceived, Natalya, half dead with fear, agreed to appear on the Red Steps flanked by little Czar Peter I and Czarevich Ivan. Behind her stood Patriarch Joachim, Artamon Matveyev, Michael Dolgoruky, and other boyars, members of the Duma.

"Here is Czar Peter Alexeyevich, here is Czarevich Ivan Alexeyevich," she cried. "God be thanked, they are alive, and in their house there are no traitors." While his mother addressed the crowd Peter was finding it hard to master his terror. Why were the faces of all those people down there so full of hate? Against whom? What had to be done to make them go away? Taken aback by the sight of the two children, the *streltsy* fell silent, hesitated, lowered their arms. A few archers made bold to climb the first steps of the staircase and question Ivan:

"Are you really the Czarevich?"

"Yes," stammered Ivan.

"Have they done you any harm?"

"No harm."

Sensing the shift in the wind, Artamon Matveyev descended the steps and harangued the *streltsy* in a rough but kindly manner. He reminded them of their past victories and exhorted them to remain faithful to Czar Peter I, who had been chosen honestly. Patriarch Joachim spoke in turn, calling upon the soldiers in the name of the Almighty to withdraw, since they had seen for themselves that the Czarevich was alive and well. The crowd, sobered, undeceived, stood wavering and muttering, as if ashamed that they had been enraged over nothing. Just when the match seemed won, Prince Michael Dolgoruky, commander of the *streltsy,* decided to exploit the first advantage and humiliate the rebels who had dared defy the power of the state. Shouting insults, he ordered them back to their quarters and threatened them with the worst punishments for insubordination. This ill-timed intervention was the spark that rekindled the dying fire. The janissaries stood dumbfounded for a moment, then rushed upon Michael Dolgoruky in a rage and hurled him to the foot of the stairs. The bulky, heavy body fell upon pikes that pierced it through and through. The *streltsy* finished hacking it to pieces on the ground with their halberds. The sight of the blood flowing from the open wounds whetted the fury of the assailants. Now they went after Artamon Matveyev, whom Natalya tried vainly to protect by throwing her arms around him. Torn from the Regent's embrace, he too was pitched down over the heads of the crowd like a sack of laundry, skewered on pikes and cut to pieces amid howls of delight: *"Liubo! Liubo!* (That's good! We like that!)" repeated the tormentors. They rushed into the palace looking for the Naryshkins and the forty-six "traitors" whose names appeared on the blacklist drawn up by Sophia and Ivan Miloslavsky. In their wrath they spared neither the royal apartments nor the altars of the inner chapels. They broke down doors, searched chests, ripped open mattresses, smashed furniture, tore and stained the hangings with their bloody hands. Outside alarm bells were ringing, two hundred drums were tirelessly beating, drunken voices were demanding further executions.

Natalya, terror-stricken, pressed little Peter against her side. What were his feelings at the sight of this butchery? According to certain witnesses, he was terrified. According to others, he displayed a courage beyond his years. No doubt the truth was that in the midst of the carnage he felt a mixture of awestruck repulsion and sick attraction. Ever afterward the spectacle of human suffering, of human madness, was to hold an irresistible fascination for him. By imperceptible degrees the horror of violence led him to the taste for violence. Numbed, petrified, subjugated, he let himself be dragged along by his mother, who tried to escape the soldiery by taking refuge in a room in the Faceted Palace.

Meantime, the *streltsy* had recognized Athanasius Naryshkin, one of the Czarina's brothers, who was hiding in the Church of the Resurrection of Christ. They dragged him out by the collar from behind the altar and cut his throat on the parvis. Next it was the turn of an innocent young man, Feodor Soltykov, whom the frenzied demons mistook for a Naryshkin and cut to pieces. But their chief enemy, Natalya's older brother, Ivan Naryshkin, was nowhere to be found; with a few other boyars he was hiding in the room of Peter's eight-year-old sister, Natalya. Exasperated and not knowing whom to turn on next, the *streltsy* brought the mutilated corpse of Michael Dolgoruky to his father, an old man in his eighties, to delight in his dismay. He received them in bed—he was semiparalyzed—offered them a glass of beer, and sent them away. After they had left, he said to his sobbing wife: "Do not weep. They have eaten the pike, but his teeth are still intact"—a proverb meaning: "We will yet find the strength to take revenge." A malicious servant ran to report these words to the praetorians, who retraced their steps, hauled the wretched man out from under his covers, cut off his arms and legs, finished him off with their halberds, and threw his body onto a pile of manure in the courtyard.

Night was coming on. The *streltsy,* weary of slaughter, dispersed after posting guards at all the strategic points. But the terror went on in the city. Isolated groups forced their way into the richest houses, looted, and tortured. The common people of Moscow, meanwhile, took no part in this revolt. For the lower classes it was a palace affair that didn't concern them. Why should those who lived in the basement get mixed up in what was happening on the upper floors? In vain did the harquebusiers open the prisons: the prisoners remained in their cells. They had been placed there, they said, by an order of the Czar and only an order of the Czar could release them. As for the serfs employed in the great houses, instead of taking sides against their masters, they reasoned with the rioters: "Your heads will fall on these stones. What will you gain by these uprisings? Russia is a big country, you cannot make yourselves masters of it."[4]

At dawn the next day, May 16, the alarm sounded again, and

on orders from Ivan Miloslavsky the *streltsy* returned to the Kremlin. As on the day before, they demanded Ivan Naryshkin, whom they considered the head of the accursed clan. Weren't people saying that as a piece of bravado he had dared to place upon his head the sacred crown of the Czar? But Ivan Naryshkin, hidden in a closet under mountains of mattresses, once again escaped all searches. Time and again the shouting harquebusiers ran past the hiding place where he crouched breathless, his heart pounding. To make up for their disappointment, they stabbed, beat, slashed, burned with hot irons the "suspects" whom their comrades brought in from outside. Thus the German physician Stepan Gaden was put to torture because dried serpents had been discovered at his house. But this small fry was not enough to satisfy the demands of the *streltsy*. They must have Ivan Naryshkin in person. If he was not delivered up to them, they swore to kill all the boyars. Their furious shouts reached the ears of Natalya: "Give us Ivan Naryshkin! We will not leave until you do!" With calm treachery Sophia said to her young sister-in-law: "Your brother will not escape the *streltsy* forever. Are we all to perish to save him?" Natalya agreed that by trying to save her brother she ran the risk of sacrificing many innocent lives, including, perhaps, that of the son she adored. For if the rioters did not have their way they would be tempted to turn on Peter in reprisal. The boyars surrounding the young woman implored her on their knees. She had to choose, no matter how much it cost her. At last, yielding to the entreaties of those around her, she sent a message to Ivan saying that he must make his way by a roundabout route to the Cathedral of the Holy Savior, where she would wait for him with Sophia. Perhaps in that consecrated place her tears and prayers would move the *streltsy* to pity.

Ivan Naryshkin, a lighthearted young man who had always lived a carefree life, understood the sacrifice that was expected of him and accepted it with stoical serenity. Having reached the cathedral without being seen, he made confession, took communion, and said to his weeping sister: "My only desire is that my blood should be the last to be spilled here." The boyars, who were increasingly afraid for their lives, urged him to show himself on the parvis. They pushed him out by the shoulders. He stepped forth resolutely, holding an icon of the Virgin pressed against his chest. Natalya still hoped that this holy image would stay the hands of the executioners. But no sooner had he appeared before the mob than they threw themselves upon him. Seized by the hair, dragged to the ground, clubbed on the head, spat upon, he was first subjected to torture. Then, as he refused to confess to the crimes of which he was accused, they thrust his body through and through with pikes. He was still breathing when the butchers, drunk with cruelty, cut off his limbs. The head, arms, and legs were fixed on stakes. Yet no one thought of harming Natalya. At most, a few shouts broke out directed at her: "To the cloister! To the cloister!" It seemed that the last slaying had momentarily assuaged the appetite of the multitude. With angry mutterings and derisive laughter they dispersed, leaving the boyars frozen with fear, the Czarina in despair, and Sophia secretly satisfied.

On the following days there were a few more summary executions and some looting, but the storm had spent its force. Already, families were authorized to remove the corpses piled in the square. Most of the bodies were so mutilated that it was hard to identify them. The first person who dared to take advantage of the permission granted was Artamon Matveyev's black servant. He gathered up the shapeless remains of his master in a sheet and took them back to the house.

To secure the gratitude of the murderers, Sophia distributed to them the goods of their victims, granted each a reward of ten rubles, raised their pay, and sent away the boyars whom they disliked. But while she thus ingratiated herself with them, she also reminded them, through her emissaries, of the final goal of the operation. On May 23 the praetorians, duly recalled to order, appeared again outside the Kremlin, and a delegation headed by their leader, Prince Khovansky, demanded of the princesses and the Duma that henceforth the power be shared between two Czars: Ivan and Peter. "If anyone opposes this measure," said the *streltsy*, "we will take up arms again and there will be a great disturbance." Natalya and Sophia convoked the Duma, and the frightened boyars hastened to endorse the outrageous demand. To justify their cowardly decision they invoked historical precedents: Joseph and Pharaoh, Arcadius and Honorius, Basil and Constantine. Thus, they explained, if a war broke out, one of the Czars could lead the army while the other remained in Moscow. But Sophia was not to be satisfied with this half measure. She wanted her brother Ivan, the imbecile, to have a right of precedence. Two days later the *streltsy* came back with their halberds, and the boyars, again assembled, proclaimed that Ivan would be *First Czar* and Peter *Second Czar*. Finally, on May 29 the same *streltsy* shouted their demand that because of Ivan's poor health, his sister, the Czarevna Sophia, be named Regent. Once again the boyars of the Duma bowed submissively to the will of the militia. The former Regent, Natalya, was now only a broken woman in mourning, trembling for the future of her son.

Having attained her goals, Sophia gave a banquet for the *streltsy* and filled their glasses with her own hand. In order to guarantee them protection against any subsequent prosecution, on June 6 she delivered to them a letter of pardon, which congratulated them on the action they had undertaken "in the name of the Holy Mother of God." In Red Square a stone column was erected engraved with the names of the victims and an indication of their alleged crimes. On June 25, 1682, in the Cathedral of the Assumption, in the presence of the Patriarch, eight metropolitans, four archbishops, two bishops, and eight archimandrites, there took place the strange coronation of the two Czars of Russia, one of whom was a sick adolescent oblivious to the proceedings and the other a terrorized child. They were seated side by side on twin thrones of gilded wood encrusted with precious stones, which had been ordered from Holland. Although they were dressed in matching caftans made of cloth of gold trimmed with lace and fur, the audience was struck by the contrast between their faces. Czar Peter, very tall for his age, had a hard, gloomy look. He moved his head with a nervous tic. It was said that this convulsive movement dated from the bloody days of May. Those who knew him well said that he could not forget the scenes of torture he had witnessed and that sometimes in the middle of the night he woke up screaming. Seated next to him with vacant eyes and half-open mouth, Ivan seemed lost in an inner dream. The solemn chanting of the choir rose toward the two children. All eyes were fixed on them, the incarnation of the future. But Sophia already knew that it was she who was the true head of the country. Never before in the history of Russia had a woman held such power. Actually, it was not Ivan and Peter whom the Patriarch had just crowned but she, she who had no right to the eminent role she was assuming and yet whose cunning and determination had enabled her to remove from her path czarinas, aunts, and older sisters and to push herself—enormous, insolent, violent—into the first rank.

2
The
Regency

*C*ould it be that it was easier to seize power than to exercise it? As soon as Sophia had won her victory she asked herself the anxious question. The corpses had hardly been removed from the square when she and her lover Basil Golitzin had to confront the formidable problem of the sectarians. Profoundly religious, the Russian people had been shaken to their roots by the reforms of Patriarch Nikon, who under the reign of Czar Alexis Mikhailovich had dared to correct the mistakes in the manuscripts of the Holy Books. There were many who refused to renounce the errors of their fathers, consecrated by tradition. Whole colonies of Raskolniki, or Old Believers, had been established almost everywhere in Russia. The dissenters didn't want to base their faith on anything but the old texts, despite the inaccuracies of the translation done long ago from Greek to Russian, and would observe only the old customs denounced by the present Church. Thus they forbade their adherents to say *Iisus* (Jesus) as the priests taught, since the copyists of the past had spelled the name of the Lord *Isus*. They insisted that the word "hallelujah" should be repeated in prayers twice and not three times; they consigned to the wrath of God those who made the sign of the cross with three fingers, in the modern way, instead of with two;* they refused with horror to attend the Orthodox churches, called the popes (the village priests) swine, and predicted that if Christendom continued on this path it would be consumed by fire from heaven.

Other religious brotherhoods were created throughout the country, linked by a common concern to deny the authority of the official Church. Some sectarians slept in coffins, others flagellated each other, still others condemned themselves to eternal silence, castrated themselves, cut one another's throats, or locked themselves up in a house with their families, set fire to piles of straw, and perished in the flames singing hymns to be sure of entering paradise. Under pressure from their fanatical parents, children would say: "We will go to the stake; in the other world we will have little red boots and shirts embroidered with gold thread; they will give us all the honey, nuts, and apples we want; we will not bow down before the Antichrist."[1] Soldiers were sent to prevent these autos-da-fé. But their arrival only precipitated the madness of the fanatics, who would throw themselves by the hundreds into the purifying flames. The most reasonable of the schismatics sought refuge in the forests, organized themselves into autonomous communities, and lived soberly by their labor, refusing the aid of the priests and professing among themselves the faith of their ancestors. Thus Russian heresy included a whole psychological spectrum, from the demented excesses of some to the quiet protest of others.

Moreover, even the faithful who obeyed the teachings of the regular Church were above all attached to the outward forms of religion. Their faith was inseparable from its external manifestations. The genuflections, the signs of the cross, the repetition of prayers, the fasts, pilgrimages, touching of relics, the long periods of standing before icons seemed more important than the feeling that inspired them. The almost mechanical performance of certain gestures supported the exaltation of the soul and often took its

---

*The sign of the cross made with two fingers symbolized the duality of Christ's nature, while made with three it symbolized the Holy Trinity.

place. Superstition mingled with piety and added to it a delicious sense of pagan mystery. People did not eat pigeon because the Holy Ghost was represented by a dove. They feared the evil eye, believed in spirits of the house, the lakes, streams, forests, interpreted every dream, every omen, consulted visionaries and sorcerers, venerated village idiots who conversed freely with God. Thus the "New Believers," steeped in magic, illuminism, and primitive idolatry, were quite prepared to understand the "Old Believers" and to pardon them their strange customs. The schism spread among the people and even in the army. The Raskolniki proliferated, especially in the ranks of the *streltsy.* To win their support, Sophia had given them for commander Prince Ivan Khovansky. Very soon she realized how unwise she had been. Khovansky, a vain and authoritarian old man, nicknamed "the Braggart," was worshiped by his men and encouraged them to affirm openly, in Moscow, the superiority of the old faith over the new. Not long after the coronation of the two Czars, rampaging soldiers led by the defrocked priest Nikita entered the Kremlin and swarmed onto the parvis in front of the Cathedral of the Archangel near the Red Steps brandishing icons, holy books, and halberds. Climbing onto a wooden platform, Nikita insulted the Orthodox clergy, shouted that the churches were nothing but stables and cow sheds, and exhorted the good Russian people to demand the reestablishment of the old liturgy.

Frightened by the memory of the days of May, Patriarch Joachim sent a priest to admonish the janissaries. He was greeted with blows. A few stones flew overhead. Ivan Khovansky urged Sophia to order the Patriarch to go to Cathedral Square to calm the crowd. Sophia refused. But she consented to receive a delegation of *streltsy* in the presence of the upper clergy, in the great hall of the Faceted Palace. As soon as Khovansky transmitted the invitation to his men there was a general scuffle. Everyone wanted to attend the meeting. They ran shouting and laughing, roughing up a few popes and monks on the way. The two young Czars were absent. But the Regent was there, with the Czarina Natalya and Basil Golitzin. The sight of the Czarevna Sophia, Patriarch Joachim, and the principal boyars made not the slightest impression on the angry *streltsy.* They scarcely bowed before the two thrones, arrogantly ignored the ecclesiastics and high dignitaries, and, on orders from Nikita, opened their books, arranged their icons, and lit their tapers to sanctify the impure place. While Patriarch Joachim tried gently to explain to them the necessity for the corrections that the various councils had made in the sacred texts and the liturgy, they gesticulated, danced in place, and made the sign of the cross in their own way. Defying the head of the Orthodox Church, Nikita cried: "We have come so that the divine service may henceforth be celebrated as in the time of Czar Michael Fedorovich, according to the old books. . . . We demand that the priest use seven and not five hosts, that the sign of the cross be made with two fingers and not with three, that prayers be offered before the eight-pointed crucifix, which is the one on which the Savior died, and not before the four-pointed crucifix of the heretics. . . ." "Mind your own business," retorted Patriarch Joachim. "It is not for you, men of humble station, to judge religious questions; the archbishops see to those."[2]

At these words Nikita, beside himself with rage and foaming at the mouth, insulted the prelates, who drew themselves up in their rich cassocks, rolling their eyes in alarm. Was it going to come to blows? Already fistfights had broken out here and there. A few shouts rose from the crowd, no longer addressed to the Patriarch but to the Czarevna herself. "It's time you retired to a convent! You've disturbed the country's peace long enough!" The hall was divided into two unequal parts. On one side, occupying almost all the space, was the yelping mass of Old Believers; on the other, backed up against the wall, a few persons who held power, conscious of their powerlessness. The sea of heads surged and tossed. The candle flames wavered in the confined atmosphere. As night was falling, Sophia judged it prudent to announce that in view of the lateness of the hour the meeting was suspended and that a decision would be made within the next few days. So saying, she closed the session and withdrew, followed by the Patriarch and the chief boyars. After she had left, the Raskolniki poured out into Cathedral Square brandishing their books and their holy images, crossing themselves with two fingers, and shouting victory.

Losing no time, Sophia summoned nonsectarian representatives of all the regiments of *streltsy*, explained to them, with tears, the danger in which the Church and state were being placed by their misguided comrades, and begged them to support her in her struggle against heresy. They answered: "We are not for the old belief. That's not our business. That's up to the Patriarch and the Holy Synod." Reassured, she gave them vodka and money and lauded their courage. They withdrew fortified and ready for a police action within their own ranks. A few days later they arrested Nikita and the other ringleaders. Nikita was beheaded in Red Square. His acolytes were exiled or imprisoned.

This extreme measure did not provoke the uprising that Sophia had feared, but neither did it bring the dissident *streltsy* to any show of repentance. Emboldened by the admiration of his soldiers, old Prince Ivan Khovansky openly preached insubordination. To them, he was the true master of Russia. They called him *batiushka*, "little father," and melted with happiness when he called them *dieti*, "children." "My children," he told them, "because of you the boyars are threatening me. I don't know what to do anymore. Do as you think best!"[3] Thus he prepared their minds for another rising.

On September 2, 1682, Sophia received an anonymous letter warning her that Ivan Khovansky was planning to have her executed, along with the two Czars and the Czarina Natalya, by the *streltsy*, who were devoted to his cause. It is probable that this letter came from Ivan Miloslavsky, an open enemy of the old prince, and that it had no basis in fact. But Sophia, who was only too happy to have a pretext, pretended to believe in the existence of a real plot, warned the boyars of the danger threatening them all, and suddenly left Moscow with the two Czars, Basil Golitzin, and the court. Shortly thereafter, having arrived in the village of Vozdvizhenskoye, she sent Ivan Khovansky a very gracious message inviting him to join her so that they might discuss the affairs of the country. Khovansky's pride was flattered and, refusing to believe in a trap, he set out with his son Andrei and an escort of thirty-six *streltsy*. While they were preparing to make camp twenty-five versts from Moscow,* a strong detachment of soldiers encircled the little

*A verst is a little more than one kilometer, or about two-thirds of a mile. —TRANS.

group at Sophia's orders, disarmed them, and brought them to the main square of the village, where the scaffold had already been built. No investigation, no debate, no tribunal. The sentence had been long since prepared. A *diak* (secretary) read it out in a thundering voice: "Prince Ivan, you have always done as you pleased without consulting the Czars; you have distributed state funds to people who did not deserve them; you have allowed the *streltsy* to invade the royal apartments with gross insolence. . . . Your evil intentions with regard to the sovereigns have been revealed, your treason is unquestionable: consequently, the Czars condemn you to death." The same punishment lay in store for Ivan Khovansky's son. Despite their protestations of innocence, both were beheaded on the spot. Their thirty-six bodyguards met a similar fate. On this same day, September 17, the Czarevna received the congratulations of her entourage on her name day, St. Sophia's.

When the *streltsy* in Moscow learned that their commander, their "father," had been executed, they rose up in arms, occupied the Kremlin, seized Patriarch Joachim, spent the night drinking, and then wondered if they ought to march against the boyars' troops or stay where they were and await the assault. From different sides disturbing news reached them: Sophia's agents had roused the whole country against the troublemakers, and a large army of nobles, with their serfs, was preparing to attack the capital. A letter from the Czarevna to the Patriarch, intercepted by the rebels, confirmed this information. The arrogance of the janissaries promptly gave way to tearful terror. They who had thought to rule Russia now pinned their only hope on the Regent's clemency. They dispatched a delegation to her to assure her of their submission and begged Patriarch Joachim to intercede on their behalf. Three thousand harquebusiers, with ropes around their necks, carrying executioner's blocks and axes, set out with their families for the Monastery of the Holy Trinity, where Sophia was waiting for them.* She received them on September 27, early in the morning, without the two Czars but surrounded by her boyars. While the wives of the *streltsy* wailed with grief and rent the garments on

*The great Troitsa-Sergeyevsky Monastery, founded by St. Sergius of Radonezh in the fourteenth century, is located some forty miles north of Moscow.—TRANS.

their breasts, the guilty men prostrated themselves before the Cza-revna. The metropolitan whom Patriarch Joachim had sent at the request of the mutineers implored her to be magnanimous. She yielded to his counsel, not from charity but prudence. One must never reduce the vanquished to despair—that would only give them a taste for revenge. Seated on a throne before the praetori-ans, Sophia announced that she was prepared to consider the incident closed. All their lives, she said, would be spared. But she posed conditions for this extraordinary reprieve: the *streltsy* must return the weapons they had stolen from the arsenal, they must stop making arrests without an express order from the sovereigns, and they must swear never again to rebel against the authority of the state and the Church. Moreover, the honorific title of *palace infantry* would be withdrawn for misconduct, the commemorative column erected in Red Square would be destroyed, and the least reliable regiments would be relegated to the border towns.

On November 6, 1682, the two Czars and the Regent, sur-rounded by boyars and escorted by tens of thousands of men, made their entrance into a pacified Moscow. The *streltsy*, who on that day had orders to present themselves without arms, pros-trated themselves with their foreheads in the mud as the proces-sion passed. Order was reestablished. Sophia was triumphant. And little Peter, gazing upon the bent backs on either side of the street, became aware of the beneficial effects of firmness in cases of popu-lar insurrection—drown the rebellion in blood and pardon the survivors as soon as the danger was averted. The young Czar was to remember this lesson all his life. As the child took his first steps he was already wading through horror, violence, and lies. On every side he saw gaping wounds in men's bodies and festering evil in their souls. In the midst of these wild beasts, only his mother had an innocent face. But she was lost in dreams, while he had a consuming need to act, to command, to create. Like the half sister he feared and detested. And with good reason: hardly was she reinstalled in the Kremlin when she made a decision that allowed of no appeal. Her brother Ivan would remain in the palace with her, while Peter would be sent with his mother to the village of Preobrazhenskoye.

Being now rid of one Czar out of two, the greater part of the *streltsy,* and the most troublesome elements of the Old Believers, Sophia made ready to run the country with Basil Golitzin. The members of her entourage compared her to Semiramis of Babylon or Elizabeth of England. She chose as her model Pulcheria of Byzantium, Empress of the East. Without respect for the two weak crowned heads whom she overshadowed, she insisted on being called "Great Sovereign," "Very Christian Czarevna," and "Autocrat," took her place beside Ivan at official ceremonies, and had her portrait engraved in Holland wearing the crown of Monomakh.*

But the rarefied air of the summit didn't make her light-headed. Her first decisions were firm and wise. As early as December 30, 1682—seven weeks after she had returned to the capital in force—twelve of the twenty regiments of *streltsy* left, by her order, for distant garrisons. It was with bowed heads that the once-proud harquebusiers set out with their wives and children on the snow-covered route to exile. Farewell to the good old days of privileges, carousing, and insolence! Those who remained in Moscow were disciplined, reliable troops. Incompetent or untrustworthy officers had been replaced. To head the praetorian guard as successor to the decapitated schemer Ivan Khovansky, Sophia designated Feodor Shaklovity, a *diak* of the Duma, energetic, fierce, and shrewd. Henceforth she was to rely on two men for support in governing: Golitzin and Shaklovity. Her political decisions were inspired by generosity one moment and authoritarianism the next. Thus, while recommending that Huguenots who escaped from France after the revocation of the Edict of Nantes be welcomed with every possible consideration, she hunted down sectarians and ordered that recalcitrants be given to the flames. While talking with Basil Golitzin about improving the conditions of serfdom, she issued a ukase providing that serfs who had fled be returned to their landowners. And while authorizing foreigners to worship according to their faith, she imposed on her own people a single official religion. Her wish to be tolerant was continually stifled by the necessities of absolute power. Nevertheless, like her father, Alexis Mikhailovich,

*The crown of Vladimir II (1053–1125), called Monomakh from the name of his maternal grandfather Constantine IX.

she was attracted to the West. She read a great deal; she wrote plays that were performed at the palace; she herself, it is said, acted in comedies; she had Molière's *Le médecin malgré lui* translated into Russian; she introduced into aristocratic circles a degree of politeness "in the Polish fashion."

But the great thing in her life was her consuming love for Basil Golitzin. The tall, good-looking man had never let himself be put off by the unattractiveness of this fat, shapeless woman with the domineering look in her eye. He served her in her bed and at her desk with equal ardor. Oddly enough, this stud was also an intelligent, refined, capable politician. Foreign visitors who came into contact with him were captivated by his elegant manners and quick mind. He would receive them in his palace with its sculptured ceilings and show them his picture gallery, his library, his geographical maps, classical marbles, Venetian mirrors, and French furniture, holding forth delightfully all the while in Latin or Polish. His model, he declared, was Louis XIV, "whose noble inclinations corresponded to his own." According to the diplomat La Neuville, Prince Basil Golitzin intended to "people the deserts, make the beggars rich, transform the savages into men, the cowards into heroes, and the shepherds' huts into stone palaces." His program for government comprised, among other measures, the freeing of the serfs, the creation of a regular army, the opening of the frontiers with Western countries, the sending of young men abroad to complete their education, and the proclamation of all sorts of freedoms, including freedom of religion. There was no harm in dreaming. Sophia, at his side, permitted herself to dream too. Her liaison with Golitzin was known to the courtiers and even to the people. She flaunted it as if to show her defiance of the shameful condition of women in Russia. But that didn't mean that she was prepared to make a change in the misogynist tradition of her contemporaries. Having turned her back on the *terem* and its prisoners, she was content to demonstrate by her daily conduct that common laws could not be applied to an exceptional being. The fact that her favorite had a wife and child did not disturb her. If need be, she would send Princess Golitzina, née Countess Hamilton, to a convent, where God could console her for having been abandoned. Should she marry her lover after having had the

Church pronounce a divorce? She thought about it sometimes. But she realized that she would never be able to have him anointed czar, for that would mean changing the dynasty. So what was the point?

In external affairs as in domestic matters, Sophia's policies were based on the advice of the munificent Basil Golitzin. Following the example of his predecessors, he envisaged expanding Russia's territory to the west and south. The country could not survive (always the same problem!) unless it acquired outlets to the sea. But it would be senseless to provoke Poland, which was at the height of its power, or the Sweden of Charles XI, whose army intimidated the world. There remained soft, mad Turkey. And it so happened that John Sobieski, John III of Poland, had just beaten the Turks and Tatars at Vienna and was inviting Sophia to participate, along with the Polish, Austrian, and Venetian forces, in the final destruction of the Ottoman Empire. An excellent opportunity to secure ports on the Black Sea. But before they would agree, the Regent and her lover demanded important concessions. By the Treaty of Moscow (April 21, 1686), Poland ceded to Russia as the price of her cooperation the city of Kiev, cradle of the Orthodox faith, the vast open spaces occupied by the Zaporozhe Cossacks of the Ukraine, and the province of Smolensk as far as the Dnieper. "Never did our ancestors conclude so glorious and advantageous a peace," Sophia proclaimed in a manifesto. "The glory of Russia resounds to the ends of the earth." And in the same burst of enthusiasm she decided that Basil Golitzin would be the one to command the army. An incomparable lover, a consummate diplomat, he must also be a brilliant leader in war. In vain did he argue his lack of competence in military affairs; she persisted in her determination and appointed the Scottish general Patrick Gordon to assist him.

As soon as he was out in the field Golitzin realized that his fears had been justified. His army's advance was slowed down by heavy, useless convoys. Between the Dnieper and the Isthmus of Perekop they ran into a gigantic conflagration. The Tatars had set fire to the steppe, and an area 250 versts long and one hundred wide was in roaring flames. Suffocated by the smoke, men and horses were unable to move. Golitzin resigned himself to retreating, only too happy that the enemy, likewise hampered by the fire, didn't try to pursue him. On July 11, 1687, the Russian troops, 150,000 strong, crossed the border again in disorder. To quiet the general discontent, the Cossacks accused their hetman,* Samoïlovich, who was forthwith judged and exiled to Siberia. To succeed him they elected his worst detractor, Mazeppa. Although there had not been a single battle in the area, the losses were evaluated at forty thousand men burned, asphyxiated, or in flight. Sophia's pride would not let her believe in defeat, and she welcomed her favorite as a victor. While he had expected blame, he received jewels, medals, and fifteen hundred peasants. The officers and men were rewarded proportionately. But the feigned rejoicing could not deceive public opinion for long. The men who had returned from the expedition recounted their misadventure in whispers. At court as in town, everyone knew now that the alleged victory was a cover for the most ridiculous failure. This national humiliation was aggravated by news of the Polish advance in Podolia and Moldavia and of the successes of the Venetian fleet off the Peloponnesus.

By 1688 the Khan of Crimea had retaken the offensive, laying waste part of the Ukraine and threatening Kiev. Sophia decided to order a second campaign. Blinded by love, she refused to consider any other commander for the army than her beloved Basil Golitzin —this time, she was sure, he would give the measure of his military genius. No one in Moscow shared her opinion. Before he left for the border, Golitzin found in front of the door of his palace a coffin with the inscription: "Try to be more successful."[4]

At last in the spring of 1689 he found himself before the fortifications of the city of Perekop. Instead of assaulting it, he parleyed with the Tatars, who were playing for time. Supplies failed to arrive in the Russian camp, rations were short, heat and sickness decimated the ranks. Although he was secretly demoralized, Golitzin noted in his letters to the Regent a few brilliant actions that, he said, would assure the final success of the enterprise. That sufficed to make Sophia exultant. *"Batiushka,"* she wrote him, "my all, may God grant you long years to live. This day

---

*Hetman: the elected chief of the Cossacks.

is particularly happy for me because God, our Lord, has glorified His name and the name of His Mother through you, my all. Never has divine grace manifested itself in so striking a manner, never did our ancestors receive such evidence of heaven's favor. Just as God used Moses to take the people of Israel out of the land of Egypt, He has used you to lead us across the deserts. . . . What can I do, oh my love, to reward your great labor as you deserve, oh my joy, oh light of my eyes? Can I really believe, oh my heart, that I shall soon see you again, oh my whole world? . . . If it were possible, I would bring you back to my side in a few instants. . . . Your letters all arrive, fortunately, by the grace of God. The bulletin on the battle of Perekop reached me on the eleventh. . . . How can I show my gratitude to God, to the Holy Mother, to the merciful St. Sergius, worker of miracles? . . . The medals are not ready yet; don't worry about them; as soon as they are ready I will send them to you. . . . So far as the army is concerned, you may decide everything as you please. . . . How can I ever reward all of you, and first of all you, my light, for the trouble you have taken? If you had not gone to such great pains, no one could have done what you have done."

And she officially confirmed her satisfaction in a message to the commander in chief, drawn up in the name of the two Czars: "By your action the savage and eternal enemies of the holy cross and of all Christendom have been so forcefully overthrown, defeated, and put to flight that in their horrible despair they are destroying their impure habitations and burning all the villages and hamlets of Perekop."

The truth was that the Tatars, far from fleeing, were pursuing the retreating Russian army. The horsemen of the steppe harried the rear guard, which broke into a rout. Wagons and cannon were abandoned on the spot. Twenty thousand dead, fifteen thousand prisoners—that was the cost of the debacle. But once again Sophia refused to believe in such total defeat. "You will win because I wish it," she had said to Golitzin before he left. She could not reverse her judgment now. The returning "heroes" were therefore greeted with Te Deums, triumphal arches, cannon salutes, and pealing bells. Again honors and rewards rained down upon commander in chief, officers, and soldiers, who could not understand why. Golitzin found himself the recipient of three thousand rubles, a gold cup, a caftan made of cloth of gold trimmed with sable, and several well-populated villages.

It was true that along with these presents he received the news that he had been replaced in the Regent's bed. During his absence Sophia, who was of a gluttonous temperament, had given herself to Feodor Shaklovity. Relieved of his duties as a lover, Golitzin nevertheless retained his functions as political adviser and head of the *prikaz* of ambassadors. The people detested him, but he took no notice of that. There were some who accused Sophia of being "a harlot, a whore." It was said that she had had children by her different favorites, that she had fooled the nation with her talk of victory when the Russian army had been beaten hollow, and that Basil Golitzin had allowed himself to be bought off with Tatar gold. Golitzin was soon responsible for another defeat, this time of a diplomatic nature, when he signed the Treaty of Nerchinsk with China, ceding to that country both banks of the Amur River. The Siberian river, which was perfectly navigable and had belonged to Russia for more than thirty years, thus passed to the Chinese and formed the new border between the two states.

Few people in the Kremlin understood the grave strategic consequences of abandoning the river. In any case Sophia, who was kept informed of the negotiations, scarcely paid any attention. Having acquired a taste for power, she found it harder and harder to be merely Regent. Though Peter had been banished with his mother to the village of Preobrazhenskoye, he represented a threat to her. Sooner or later the day would come when, having reached his majority, he would demand the right to rule. She would be ousted, sent back to her obscure life as a woman. The *terem*, the convent. . . . Never would she accept such a downfall after so much greatness. Born to command, to govern, and to love, she must fight to protect the extraordinary opportunity she had won, fight with determination, and, if necessary, with cruelty. Ivan the degenerate was no obstacle. But Peter? How could she remove him permanently from the political scene? To be sure, she could have him quietly assassinated. Her new lover, Feodor Shaklovity, advised her to do so. But she hesitated. She was torn between vague scruples of conscience and the ambition to reign alone at last as autocrat of all the Russias. To her, Peter was a half brother, still half a child, and half a czar. . . . The days passed, and this time the woman who already had so many severed heads to her credit did not dare to give the fatal order.

3

Peter
or
Sophia?

Having been driven out of the Kremlin by the Regent, Peter and his mother had installed themselves in a modest house in the village of Preobrazhenskoye near Moscow. "This habitation," Berkholz, chamberlain to the Duke of Holstein, was to write later, "resembles a Norwegian presbytery. I would not give a hundred pieces of silver to acquire it." The old house was perched on a hill, and from its windows could be seen an undulating plain, fields of barley and oats, meadows with tall grass, leafy copses, the cupolas of a few churches surrounded by dark log huts, and the shining curve of the Moskva River. Here one was far from the palace and its intrigues.

The exiles lived all the more simply because the Czarevna Sophia was stingy about their allowance. In order to make ends meet, the gentle Natalya sometimes had to appeal in secret to Archimandrite Vincent of the Monastery of the Holy Trinity. The few courtiers around the young woman wore gloomy expressions. In the dark, low-ceilinged rooms they endlessly rehearsed their grievances against the Regent and her bad advisers, deplored the disastrous course of events, and prayed God to right the injustice done to His true servants. In this oppressive atmosphere of regret, defeat, piety, and threadbare ideas, Peter was suffocating. To relieve his boredom he sought distraction in studies and games.

Actually, his studies were chaotic. When he was little he had had for a tutor the Scotsman Menesius, then the *diak* Nikita Zotov, who had been especially assigned to teach him "the art of letters." On hearing of his appointment Nikita Zotov had burst into sobs and declared himself unworthy to educate "such a treasure." Naturally lazy and a drunkard, he consumed even more alcohol to give himself the courage to instruct his great pupil. For whatever it was worth, he taught him to read the Bible, to write without worrying about spelling, and to sing hymns. Peter's notebooks have been preserved: he has difficulty forming letters, runs words together, and spells phonetically, but his goodwill is evident. For relaxation after his labors, Nikita Zotov would recount to him, between bumpers of vodka, the wars fought by his father, cite the names of victories, extol the virtues of the Russian army. These tales inflamed the boy, as alcohol inflamed the narrator. He too dreamed of covering himself with glory in combat. His first toys, the list of which may be seen at the Museum of the Arsenal, were flags, drums, knives, hatchets, and miniature cannon. Surrounded by boys of his own age—the sons of boyars, grooms, or valets—he played war. He would shoot wooden bullets against the walls of a convent and assault a fort that he and his comrades had built on an island in the Yauza River.

In 1687 Prince Jacob Dolgoruky, who was returning from a diplomatic mission to Paris, brought back to Peter, at his request, an instrument "with which one can calculate distances without approaching the place oneself." Enchanted by the astrolabe, Peter lamented the fact that he didn't know how to use it. No one around him was able to enlighten him. Finally they dug up a Dutchman named Franz Timmermann who understood the object. Natalya promptly engaged him to work alongside Nikita Zotov as Peter's science teacher. Under this new instructor the boy learned the rudiments of arithmetic, geometry, artillery, and fortification, all jumbled together. To be sure, the notions he acquired in this way were heterogeneous and superficial. But his intellectual appetite was insatiable. He was consumed with the need to know all about everything. Later he was to boast that he had learned how to practice fourteen trades. For the moment, he was delighted just to pick and choose at random in the orchards of knowledge. His desire to possess an astrolabe was only one of a hundred manifestations of his boundless curiosity. Having discovered in a boathouse, with this same Timmermann, a half-rotten English boat that had belonged to his great-uncle Nikita Romanov, he decided to have it repaired under the direction of the Dutch carpenter Karsten Brandt. The old carcass of planks was patched up, fitted with a mast, a sail, and a tiller, and launched with great ceremony on the Yauza River. Then, to have more room to maneuver, it was transported to the great Lake Pereyaslavl. It was to become "the grandfather of the Russian navy." On board this boat Peter learned from Karsten Brandt the science of navigation. From the first lessons, he was seized with a passion for sailing. Accustomed to dry land, he found inexpressible happiness in gliding over the water. The pliant movements of the boat, the subtle interplay of the wind blowing where it would and the sail capturing and utilizing it, the creaking of the hull, the lapping of the waves, the lightness with which he skimmed over the water, and the flat, liquid odor that enveloped him were all intoxicating. He was drawn irresistibly toward wider and wider spaces, toward limitless horizons, toward the sea that he had never seen. He had Brandt build two little frigates and three little yachts. While still a child he dreamed of a great fleet—this, in a country that possessed just one port, Archangel, lost in the icy mists of the White Sea. Was it some atavistic reversion to his Varangian forebears that expressed itself in this fascination with seafaring?*

Peter's discovery of sailing didn't prevent him from taking an interest in maneuvers on land. At sixteen he was no longer content to command regiments of urchins throwing stones and riding bareback through the fields of Preobrazhenskoye on the little horses of the region. His playmates had grown up with him. They made up an eager, laughing band, the *poteshnye,* or "amusers."

---

*The Varangians were Scandinavians who, under Prince Rurik, established a monarchy and a dynasty in Russia in the ninth century.

Now Peter recruited others from among the valets, falconers, and stableboys who had had nothing to do since the death of Czar Alexis. Some young nobles joined them: a Buturlin, a Boris Golitzin. . . . To outfit these battalions of merry lads Peter sent to the arsenal in the Kremlin for military uniforms, weapons, powder, lead, drums, and flags. He borrowed horses from the *prikaz* of the stables. He organized a central administration for the regiment, appointed officers and noncommissioned officers. Every day his *poteshnye,* in dark green uniforms, trained in the meadows, playing at war. Attack, counterattack, flanking maneuver. Peter insisted on performing all the military functions himself, starting with those of the drummer. He wanted to know the work and concerns of the soldier as well as those of the captain. From month to month the laughable little army grew in size. Nothing to fear from such scatterbrained boys, thought Sophia: while Peter amused himself with mock battles, he could not be dreaming about the conquest of power. The longer he was left to games of make-believe, the more surely removed he would be from political reality. Peter, however, seriously planned to transform the play regiments into shock troops. He needed competent instructors to teach the art of warfare to the new recruits. Where could he find them? Without hesitation the young Czar turned to *Nemetskaya Sloboda,* the German Settlement.*

This suburb of the capital, on the banks of the Yauza, a small tributary of the Moskva River, was a sort of segregated district in which all foreign nationals, Protestant or Catholic, who had come to seek their fortune in Russia were required to live. At first a simple village with little wooden shanties, the German Settlement soon became a place of calm, elegance, and Western civilization. Brick houses, flower beds, straight tree-lined avenues, fountains—what a contrast to the oriental disorder of Moscow! It was a European enclave in the heart of old Russia. Here lived not only Germans but also Italians, Englishmen, Scottish victims of Cromwell's

*The name is derived from the Russian word for Germans, *Nemtsy,* meaning "those who are mute," i.e. who do not speak our language. The inhabitants of Moscow had so dubbed the first German residents, and since most Russians did not distinguish between the different foreign languages, the word soon came to be applied to foreigners of all nationalities.

persecutions, Dutchmen, Danes, Swedes, and even some French Huguenots who had preferred exile to conversion. Of course a few adventurers had slipped into the lot. But for the most part these immigrants were honest, capable, highly enterprising people. Some of them bore great names. Their piety and sense of family helped to preserve harmonious relations among the different elements of the little cosmopolitan society. Different by birth, language, and religion, they were nonetheless welded into a single block by the consciousness of being aliens in the midst of Russia. Their numbers steadily grew. They excelled at the most varied trades: there were doctors, apothecaries, engineers, architects, painters, schoolteachers, merchants, goldsmiths, astronomers, army officers. Their children regularly attended the schools they had established. Lutherans and Calvinists had their churches and their pastors.* They maintained constant correspondence with their countries of origin. The English ladies sent to London for books and trinkets. The Dutch representative Van Keller—a rich and respected man—received a weekly courier from The Hague who brought him news of the outside world. The immigrants in the German Settlement, therefore, were often better informed on European events than the Regent herself.

Moreover, almost all members of the diplomatic corps took up residence within this privileged perimeter. Many a Russian nobleman came there seeking a breath of Westernism, and some even invited immigrants into their homes to teach their children from books in Polish, German, English, or Latin. At first the professors would have to take these books away after the lesson, for it would have been unseemly for a boyar to keep books in a foreign language under his roof.[1] But this restriction was soon forgotten, and more than one noble family took pride in possessing a library that included works printed beyond the borders.

The influence of the German Settlement even made itself felt on the furniture of the great Russian houses. In residences that had formerly been filled with wooden benches, carved chests, and long tables of polished oak there now appeared armchairs upholstered with tapestry, gilt side chairs, pedestal tables with inlaid tops,

*The Catholics did not yet have a church.

clocks. The murals that had used to decorate interiors were supplanted in the taste of wealthy owners by paintings and engravings on religious subjects. Finally, yielding to European fashion, the Russians bought mirrors—though these, being still considered dangerous to morality, were covered with a curtain. A lady raised the curtain only for as long as necessary to adjust a diadem or apply her makeup and let it fall immediately afterward. For oddly enough a Russian woman, otherwise so reserved, made heavy use of cosmetics. Her face would be thickly plastered, white for the complexion, red for the cheekbones, black for the eyebrows. The most affluent had their cosmetics sent from abroad; the others used cooked beet juice to color their cheeks.

Nevertheless, Russian ladies lived like recluses, far removed from the currents of society. They didn't even dream of envying their sisters in the German Settlement, who enjoyed an unheard-of freedom of manners. On holidays over there, the immigrants entertained as families, women and men mingling; they organized masked balls and attended performances by itinerant actors. Their favorite dance was the old German round, *Grossvatertanz.* Couples turned, smiled, and chattered to the sound of the music. They drank beer, laughed, and behaved as if they were in Berlin or London or Amsterdam.

All this novelty fascinated the young Peter. Since he had reached the age of reason there were three things in the world that attracted him: war, the sea, foreign lands. To learn about life he looked to the gentlemen of the German Settlement. It was there, he thought, that he would find the necessary instructors for his regiments of *poteshnye.* He was not mistaken. At his invitation foreign officers, including the Baltic Baron von Mengden, flocked to Preobrazhenskoye. They taught the *poteshnye* campaign service, arms drill, gunnery. Gradually the village became a little garrison town. Two regiments were constituted in this way, bearing the names of their billeting places: the Preobrazhensky and the Semeonovsky. A rough sense of fraternity united these young men who were scarcely out of adolescence. After they had played at war they would get so drunk that they rolled under the table. Whether drilling or carousing, the Czar was in no way distinguished from his companions. Peter thought no more highly of young Prince

46

Boris Golitzin than of a brave and clever rascal by the name of Alexander Menshikov, who had been a pastry cook's assistant. Indeed, the latter soon became his confidant, his most trusted friend.

Peter was sorry every time he had to leave Preobrazhenskoye and go to the Kremlin—officially he was still the Czar—to fulfill the duties of his post. There, seated on the throne beside Ivan, stiffly robed in a heavy brocade gown, wearing a crown that crushed his temples, and constrained by protocol to the immobility of a statue, he would receive ambassadors, preside over interminable banquets, listen with boredom to wordy speeches. As early as 1683 Kaempfer, secretary to the Swedish envoy, wrote to Stockholm:

"The two Princes were seated on their thrones, the younger [Peter] with an open countenance, his wonderful beauty heightened by his graceful gestures. Every time someone addressed him the crimson blood mounted under his eyes, so that had we been in the presence of a young lady of ordinary rank and not of an imperial person, we should all have fallen in love with her. When the moment came for the Czars to rise to inquire after the health of the King of Sweden, the younger did so with such alacrity that the master of ceremonies held him back until his brother was ready to take part in the conversation." Five years later it was the Dutch resident Van Keller who wrote to The Hague: "Taller than all the courtiers, the young Czar draws the greatest attention to his person. His intelligence and his knowledge of military affairs are developing as auspiciously as his physical qualities. . . . We are assured that he will soon be able to exercise sovereign power. If this change in the state comes about, we will see many questions take on a different aspect."[2]

As soon as he was freed from these tiresome court duties, Peter would enthusiastically plunge back into the virile atmosphere of Preobrazhenskoye. Boyars visiting from Moscow looked with dismay upon the goings and comings of this athlete with the wild mane and sparkling eye who ran with his pipe in his mouth, jumped over ditches, shouted orders, and handled a musket, sword, or ax among a cohort of young men most of whom were of humble extraction. In the view of these haughty observers, the Czar, a veritable Byzantine divinity, should remain in his palace

47

aloof from the world and show himself to the people only on solemn occasions and in the midst of quasi-religious pomp. By mingling with the soldiery Peter, they thought, was lowering himself to the level of common mortals and betraying his historic role. The reports they made to Sophia reinforced her reassuring conviction that her half brother was not so eager to reign.

As for Natalya, she was worried about her son's wild ways and the company he kept. She wanted to sober him down, bring him to reason, get him settled, and on the advice of the Naryshkin clan she decided to have him marry a young and pretty person from the middle ranks of the nobility, Eudoxia Lopukhina. Eudoxia was twenty and he was seventeen. He offered no resistance. After all, his brother Ivan had been married also, three years earlier, to Prascovia, the daughter of the boyar Soltykov. The weddings of czars, Peter thought, were only annoying but necessary formalities. He had first experienced the pleasures of lovemaking with servant girls at inns. They sufficed him. When he led the timid Eudoxia to the altar, on January 27, 1689, he already knew that she would not hold him either by her submission or by her caresses. After two months of "honeymoon," he could stand it no longer and escaped to go sailing on Lake Pereyaslavl, while his young wife sank into numb and weary waiting. On April 20, 1689, he wrote to his mother: "My beloved mother Czarina and Grand Duchess Natalya Kyrilovna, bless your son Petrushka so that he may succeed in his work. I should like to have news of your health. Thanks to your prayers, we are well. The lake has melted and all the ships, except for one big one, have been freed from the ice. But we need rope, and in this I beg your kindness, to give the order to the Artillery Department to send us seven hundred fathoms. They must be sent immediately, for the work is held up and our stay here is prolonged. Meanwhile, I ask your blessing." And later, again to his mother: "Hallo! I wish to know how your health is and to beg your blessing. Here everything is going well. I repeat that the ships are in good condition. Your unworthy Petrus." As for Eudoxia, the neglected wife, she sent a short note to the freshwater sailor: "To my master, the object of my joy, Czar Peter Alexeyevich. May your health be good, my light, for many years. I beg you, don't be too long in returning. —Your little wife bows before you."

But Petrushka didn't pay much attention to his "little wife." Back at her side, he was less concerned with sentiment than with politics. The rumors that reached him from Moscow proved that Sophia's ill will toward him had only grown over the years. During his childhood he had accepted being kept on apron strings by his half sister, but he could no longer tolerate it now. One of his advisers, Boris Golitzin, even assured him that the Regent was determined to do away with him.

On July 8, 1689, he had to attend a religious ceremony in the Cathedral of the Assumption in the Kremlin along with Czar Ivan and his whole family. After the service Sophia wanted to take part in a procession that was traditionally reserved for men. Peter indignantly objected. Ignoring his remonstrances, she showed herself to the crowd carrying an icon, like an authentic sovereign. Peter was furious, left the procession, and returned to Preobrazhenskoye. A few days later, on learning that despite the humiliating failure of the second Crimean campaign, Sophia was welcoming Basil Golitzin and his "glorious generals" with transports of enthusiasm and showering them with rewards, he flatly refused to receive the "conquering hero."

Sophia understood that Peter had begun an open struggle with her. The reports of her agents mentioned the growing popularity of the young Czar among the Muscovites and the dissatisfaction of certain boyars over the reverses the Russian army had met with. Moreover, she was beginning—a little late in the game—to worry about the growth of the battalions of "amusers" at Preobrazhenskoye. Volunteer informers ran back and forth between Moscow and the village where Peter was anxiously waiting to see what would happen next. At the urging of her lover Shaklovity, Sophia called together the commanders of the *streltsy* and revealed her plan to them: on the night of August 7–8, 1689, they were to surround Preobrazhenskoye and massacre Czar Peter's amateur soldiers, his officers, advisers, servants, and foreign friends, his mother, and his family. As for Czar Peter, he too would be killed or at least put out of the way of doing harm. As a reward for his devotion, each *strelets* would receive twenty-five rubles. The commanders of the janissaries promised the Regent that this bloody operation would be carried out properly and with dispatch.

But during the night of August 6–7, two conscience-stricken *streltsy* left at a gallop for Preobrazhenskoye. They arrived toward midnight, woke Peter, and warned him of Sophia's intentions. At their first words he gave way to terror. The memory of the carnage of May 1682 perpetrated by the same men had made such a deep and terrible impression on him that at the mere idea of once again confronting those hordes of butchers in red shirts he was shaken with tics and lost his senses. Leaping out of bed, he didn't even think to warn his mother or his wife but ran barefoot in his night-shirt to the stable. There he threw himself on a horse and shouted to some servants to bring him clothes in a nearby wood where he was going to hide. Shortly afterward they joined him in his leafy retreat, helped him to dress, and galloped off with him at top speed toward the fortified Monastery of the Holy Trinity.

Behind the high surrounding wall, with its battlements and its nine towers, rose the painted, gilded cupolas of thirteen churches. Here lived a large population of monks, novices, and servants. Several times in the past the monastery had heroically resisted the assaults of the Poles. It was a strong refuge! Peter reached it at six o'clock in the morning, his body aching all over and his mind in disarray. He was carried to bed. But he was too overwrought to sleep. With his face convulsed and tears in his eyes, he told Archimandrite Vincent of the attempt that was going to be made on his life and demanded that measures be taken to defend him. Fortunately, his best supporters were already hastening to join him, and, surrounded by the officers of the Preobrazhenskoye camp, he plucked up hope again. In reality, he was of such a nervous, impressionable temperament that he hadn't the strength to withstand the shock of events. It was only by a prodigious effort of will that he found the courage he needed, carrying decisiveness and action to extremes in order to triumph over his inborn timidity.

At the end of this fateful day of August 7 his mother and his wife appeared. Their frail support was no comfort to him. On the other hand, with what joy he watched as there gathered under his windows his faithful amateur soldiers, the *poteshnye,* and one regiment of *streltsy* that had long since been won over to his cause!

While Peter was bolstering his spirits with the sight of his troops, Sophia, who mistook the situation, was laughing at her rival's shameful flight. Still, she hesitated to attack the stronghold of the monastery. Her attempt at surprise having failed, it seemed the better part of wisdom to use cunning to obtain the Czar's surrender. She therefore invited him to come to Moscow, where they would discuss the situation calmly as brother and sister. Peter refused, instead sending a messenger to order all the *streltsy* to disobey the Czarevna and rally to his side.

Each of the two parties was trying to buy up as many regiments as possible. In the urgent bargaining the smallest squad counted; a single musket changing sides could be enough to tip the balance one way or the other. Couriers from the Kremlin and from the monastery galloped past each other along the roads bearing promises, threats, propositions, injunctions. Sophia guessed that some of the praetorians whom she had thought faithful were wavering, and she addressed them from the top of the Red Steps, promising them gold if they served her, punishments if they betrayed her. Despite her eloquence, her words did not seem to touch an audience grown suspicious from too many mortifications. Called upon to choose between a legitimate young Czar who considered himself a soldier among soldiers, and an illegitimate Regent who had just rewarded her lover for a second time despite his responsibility for two bloody defeats by the Tatars, the *streltsy* debated within themselves, hesitated, and secretly leaned toward simplicity, male solidarity, and the law. The very next day a few detachments left Moscow in secret for the Monastery of the Holy Trinity. The movement gained momentum, the military quarters emptied out, and the number of followers around Peter grew. On September 4 the foreign regiments, commanded by General Gordon and Colonel François Lefort, slipped outside the walls of the capital by night and were welcomed by Peter with delirious joy.

Now he no longer doubted that he had reversed the situation. In a burst of optimism Sophia sent Patriarch Joachim to him to preach reconciliation. But instead of exhorting the young Czar, the Patriarch sided with him. Sophia then decided to go to Holy Trinity herself and give her half brother a good talking-to. Ten versts from the monastery she was stopped by armed men who ordered her to turn back. Peter, she was told, refused to see her. She returned to Moscow champing at the bit, only to be confronted on

September 6 with the intransigence of the last *streltsy* whom she had thought she could still count on. They demanded that she deliver up to them her lover and adviser Shaklovity, so that they might take him to the Czar. Since he was responsible for all the trouble, they said, he would be the best victim to offer in atonement. After having punished him according to his crimes, Peter would be appeased and would perhaps pardon the other agitators. As Sophia refused this deal, the *streltsy* threatened to unleash a new riot bloodier than the preceding ones, and she gave in.

On the next day, September 7, Shaklovity, abandoned by the Regent, was taken to the Monastery of the Holy Trinity and put to torture. He confessed that he had had some evil thoughts but denied that he had intended to do away with Peter. This restriction did not suffice to save his head. Condemned to death, he was decapitated on September 11, along with other ringleaders. Basil Golitzin, thanks to the intervention of his cousin Boris, was merely exiled to a village at the edge of nowhere, in the great North, where he would have one ruble a day to live on with his family of five. There remained the case of Sophia. Peter wrote to his brother Ivan:

"Dear brother, lord Czar Ivan Alexeyevich, to you, to my little sister-in-law, to your wife, to your posterity, greetings! . . . By the grace of God, the government of Russia was bestowed upon both of us, in the assembly of our Holy Mother Eastern Church, in the year 7190 [1682]. . . . There was never any question of a third person's sharing power with us. Nevertheless, our sister, the Czarevna Sophia Alexeyevna, by her own will alone has taken over the conduct of our government, contrary to our desire and that of the people, and you know how patient we have been. Today a scoundrel, Fedka Shaklovity, and others, his accomplices, taking advantage of our benevolence, have plotted against our life and that of our mother, which has just been confessed after interrogation and torture. At present, my brother Czar, now that we have reached our majority the time has come for us to govern by ourselves the State which God has entrusted to us. Let us not permit a third person, our sister the Czarevna Sophia, to share our title and to meddle in affairs that we two should administer together, between men. . . . Lord and brother, let your paternal kindness allow us to appoint upright judges and to replace the bad ones so as to bring peace and rejoicing to our country. When we are reunited we will settle all that; as for me, lord and brother, I am ready to revere you as a father. . . . Written in the midst of cares by your brother, Czar Peter, who wishes you good health and bows before you.''

Too weak-minded to reply to a letter of this importance, Ivan hunkered down, kept silent, and waited for the storm to pass over. So Peter sent to Moscow the boyar Ivan Troyekurov, a companion from the earliest days, with orders to inform Sophia that she was to withdraw to the Novodevichy Convent, which had recently been built near the capital. Stricken, mortified, she understood that she had lost the match. No doubt she regretted that she had not had Peter assassinated when he was only a child, instead of sending him with his mother to Preobrazhenskoye. In politics, kindheartedness rarely paid off. But Peter was showing himself merciful in turn— he could have condemned her to death. After all, Sophia thought, she was getting off cheap. Her brother Ivan made no move to restrain her, so she set out for the convent, with a mixture of bitterness and relief. Her name was henceforth excluded from all official acts. A cell would be her realm.

On October 6, 1689, Peter, victorious, left for Moscow followed by his court, his boyars, his "amusers," and his *streltsy.* At the gates of the city the people crowded around to acclaim him. The bells of "forty times forty churches" were in full peal in honor of his return. On all sides heads bowed as the procession passed. Peter, who had trembled like a leaf during the night of August 6–7, now relished the intoxication of revenge. His brother Ivan, who was waiting for him in the Kremlin on the parvis of the Cathedral of the Assumption, took a step forward, supported by two boyars, and fell into his arms. The crowd screamed with joy and wept with emotion. They saw before them a radiant giant with a sunburned complexion and sparkling teeth giving the ceremonial embrace to a sick man. Peter was seventeen years and four months old.

4

The German Settlement

When Peter took stock of what he had accomplished during the last months of 1689 he had reason to be satisfied with himself. Having narrowly escaped death, he was now at the summit of power. Sophia was in a convent paying for her audacity in having tried to secure the throne for herself; her chief supporters had been beheaded or exiled; the army, including the *streltsy,* had been restored to discipline; the people were calm, satisfied, trusting; and poor Ivan, living forgotten in the depths of an apartment in the Kremlin, devoted all his time to his wife, who was deceiving him, and to his daughters, who were probably not his.* The foreign diplomats expected that now that Peter had a free hand he would take firm command of the ship of state. The Dutch resident Van Keller wrote: "As the Czar [Peter] has much intelligence and shrewdness, while at the same time he knows how to win the affection of all and shows a pronounced liking for the military, heroic actions are expected of him, and people foresee the day when the Tatars will find their master at last."

*One of his five daughters, Anna, would become Czarina in 1730.

But Van Keller could not have been more mistaken. Having waged this desperate struggle for power, Peter had no wish to exploit his advantage. It was as if the superhuman effort had drained him of ambition; or rather, as if he did not feel ready to assume the responsibilities he had desired. Young and bursting with energy, he was inclined to warlike games, drinking bouts, and affairs with maidservants—not to politics. He hated paperwork. As soon as he could, he would escape from the Kremlin—a dark, solemn, gilded cavern swarming with monks and courtiers—to run about the streets, drill his troops, or steer a ship on Lake Pereyaslavl. For the management of the state he relied on his mother, the weak, ignorant Natalya. She was assisted by a trio of boyars, Patriarch Joachim, and the Duma. The whole lot were fiercely reactionary. At the urging of the Patriarch, the foreigners Peter liked so much were accused of heresy; groups that studied the Bible and discussed religion were condemned; the Jesuits were expelled; the German mystic Kuhlmann was burned alive in Red Square. . . .

Intolerance was the order of the day, and while it made Peter angry, he did not think it necessary to intervene. On rare occasions, in the midst of his many occupations, he would visit his wife. Eudoxia, an exemplary product of the Russian *terem,* was a nice, insipid little person who knew how to read and write, blushed at anything, was always praying, believed in dreams, accepted every superstition, and responded to her wild husband with more sentiment than passion. She called him "my joy," "my heart," "my light," "my little paw," and yielded submissively to his demands in the hope of having a child.

Although Peter's forays into the conjugal bed were few and disappointing, Eudoxia became pregnant, and on February 19, 1690, gave birth without mishap to the Czarevich Alexis.* To Peter the birth of this first son was a gift from heaven, the assurance that his line would not die with him. Excessive as was his wont, he shouted for joy, roared with laughter, twisted the wrists of his young wife in a burst of gratitude, drank vodka, had the cannon fired, and immediately afterward abandoned the exhausted

---

*In 1691 Eudoxia was to give birth to a second son, Alexander, who would die six months later. A third son, born in 1693, died the same year.

mother and the wailing infant to resume his life as a bachelor in the welcoming houses of the German Settlement, where other women, more willing and more experienced, awaited him. Nevertheless, he returned to the Kremlin for the obligatory banquets in honor of the happy event. The whole city shared in the rejoicing. In the palace and in hovels people drank with equal enthusiasm. "Since the birth of the Czarevich they have done nothing but feast and carouse on as grand a scale as possible," wrote Van Keller. "Mardi Gras has further increased the frenzy of the festivities. As these diversions are almost always accompanied by much havoc, there have been disorders, brawls, and crimes. . . . Many persons were very ill used and came to a sad end. . . . It would be desirable to put an end to such days dedicated to Bacchus, for decent people cannot walk the streets without being constantly set upon or insulted, although in certain places in the city armed guards have been posted to prevent the violence of the drunkards."[1]

The festivities in honor of the birth of the Czarevich were hardly over when Patriarch Joachim died.* In his testament he solemnly called upon the Czar to give up associating with foreigners, to relieve them of all commands in the army, to destroy the Protestant churches in the German Settlement, and to punish with death all attempts at conversion. The fiery prelate's recommendations were only an expression of the general aversion for these people come from elsewhere, who spoke an incomprehensible language, prayed in a shed, did not worship the Holy Virgin, and —horrors!—ate a weed called *salad,* "just like cattle." Far from obeying the injunctions of the deceased, Peter proposed to appoint as his successor a cultivated man with a liberal turn of mind, the metropolitan of Pskov, Marcellus. But Czarina Natalya, who did not share her son's liking for European culture, followed the advice of the clergy and gave preference to the metropolitan of Kazan, Adrian. Many reasons were given for passing over Marcellus, from the fact that he spoke "barbarous" tongues (such as Latin and French) to the fact that his beard was not long enough.

Angered by this decision, another example of time-honored blindness, Peter once again felt the need to shake off the tutelage

*On March 27, 1690.

59

of the all-powerful clergy. The Russian church, with its vast treasure, its innumerable tax-free lands, its own system of justice, its
peasant serfs and fortified monasteries, formed a state within a
state. The Patriarch, elected by the Holy Synod with the approval
of the Czar, was a dignitary independent of the sovereign and
accountable to no one. He had at his orders the metropolitans,
archbishops, bishops, monks, and popes. Monks were celibate and
generally educated; the popes—married, penniless, filthy, and ignorant—were not trusted by the people, who looked upon them
not as guides but merely as officiants with fine voices and solemn
gestures. To show the primacy of spiritual power over temporal,
on Palm Sunday in Moscow the czar would appear in the religious
procession leading by the bridle an ass ridden by the patriarch.

Peter refused to follow this humiliating custom. He would not
be seen walking with bowed head, like a chastened penitent, in
front of a donkey on which the chief prelate was lounging in his
richest chasuble. Similarly, he would not renounce his friendships
with the people in the German Settlement. The xenophobia of
Joachim, Natalya, and the boyars of the Duma made everything
that reminded him of old Russia even more insufferable. He
wanted to escape from the ancestral customs that weighed him
down like a heavy garment smelling of incense and mildew. He felt
he was rebelling against the Russian past when he openly dined at
the home of Major General Patrick Gordon. Fifty-five years old, the
descendant of a good Scottish family, Gordon had enlisted in the
Russian army, fought in Sweden, Germany, and Poland, participated in Basil Golitzin's two unfortunate campaigns in the Crimea, acquitted himself honorably of several trade missions to England, and lent Peter instructors to organize his play battalions. At
the time of the coup against the Regent, it was he who had persuaded the foreign officers to join the Czar at the Monastery of the
Holy Trinity. Since that day he had become Peter's friend and
adviser, valued for his chivalrous character, his knowledge of
Western ways, and his austere virtue, which was not without a
touch of pedantry.

Another friend and adviser of the young sovereign was the
Swiss François Lefort, who had also rallied to the monastery at the
critical moment. Lefort was a restless adventurer who had served

under different flags before landing at Archangel and enlisting in the Russian army. Thirty-five years old, almost as tall as Peter, he had little education but spoke fluent French and broken Russian, Dutch, German, Italian, and English, and had traveled in so many lands and seen so many adventures that listening to him one would have thought he was half a dozen different persons. His eventful life had reinforced his natural gaiety, daring, and enthusiasm and his taste for luxury and debauchery. He was tireless, excelled at all physical exercises, rode wild horses superbly, could outshoot anyone with a musket or a bow, and drank like a sponge without showing any effect. Peter felt more at ease at the home of this extraordinary, prodigal bon vivant than anywhere else. Here he took delight in smoking, getting drunk, shouting, arguing, brawling. The banquets usually lasted for three days and three nights. Gordon would leave the gargantuan feasts with a heavy head and an upset stomach, but Lefort and the Czar, still in fine fettle, would declare themselves ready to start over at once.

Peter was so pleased with these receptions that he invited his Russian friends to them, and, as the house became too small, he had it enlarged and decorated at his expense. After one of these parties a foreign guest wrote: "For four days General Lefort feasted and entertained His Majesty magnificently, along with all the chief noblemen of the country and all the principal foreigners and their ladies, numbering two hundred persons. Besides the magnificent banquets, there were balls every day, beautiful music, very curious fireworks, and every day twenty salutes from twelve pieces of cannon. His Majesty has had a very beautiful room built that can hold fifteen hundred men, but hung with such splendid tapestries and so superbly worked in sculpture, the whole being gilt, that it could pass for a veritable imperial chamber, and one of the finest. Our monarch has made him a present of fifteen great tapestries of silk richly worked in gold, but of extraordinary size and so skillfully done that it is wonderful: they are valued at fourteen thousand crowns. The general is very magnificently furnished, with silver plate, weapons, jewels, paintings, mirrors, and tapestries, everything being very cunningly made and of great price; a great number of servants, a score of fine horses in the stable, and a permanent guard of twenty men at his door."[2]

The "ladies" who attended these feasts, "Scotswomen with delicate profiles, Germans with dreamy eyes, or buxom Hollanders,"[3] had nothing in common with the modest recluses of the Muscovite *terems*. The wives and daughters of foreign craftsmen, merchants, or officers, they wore dresses that showed off their figures, spoke freely, laughed heartily, sang songs from their countries in chorus, and when the orchestra struck up a dance tune, abandoned themselves in the arms of their partners without false modesty. Some of them were generous with their favors and not above accommodating an admirer on a handy table. The one whom Peter found most attractive was none other than his friend Lefort's own mistress: Anna Mons. The daughter of an immigrant from Westphalia, she called herself Anna Mons de la Croix because it sounded more aristocratic. Her father, Johann Mons, ran an inn in the German Settlement. She had been serving drinks there with her sister when she drew the attention of Lefort.

Anna Mons was completely uneducated, collected recipes for witchcraft, made no secret of her greed, and flaunted her vulgar manners, but she was pretty, lively, spontaneous, laughing, and desirable. What a contrast to the pious, boring, moaning Eudoxia! Lefort, a cheerful believer in sharing the wealth, yielded the young woman to the Czar who wanted her so much. Anna Mons was delighted to be moving up in the world, and expected that her promotion would bring her sumptuous gifts. She was soon disabused. Her new lover was stingy with his money if not with his caresses. He took her roughly, selfishly, like a trooper, and rewarded her only with trinkets. At least, in the beginning. Then, gradually, he increased the number and value of the presents. She received jewels, an estate including 295 peasant farms, etc. The Czar no longer bothered to hide the affair. He was proud of it, presented his mistress to foreign diplomats, and took up with the shabby parents of the former waitress. That didn't prevent him, incidentally, from deceiving her with chance partners during an orgy or spending the night in a brothel in the German Settlement, where he was known to the inmates as "Herr Peter." But always he came back to Anna Mons as the best source of pleasure.

In reality, he loved women for the satisfaction of his sexual needs, but he had no esteem for them, no respect, no sentimental interest in them. He despised them in proportion as he desired them. To the suppers in mixed company at Lefort's, he often preferred freewheeling stag parties. On these occasions the guests, following the Czar's example, would lose all restraint. The feasts were called "battles with Ivashka Khmelnitzky,"* and indeed the drinking bouts often did degenerate into battles "so formidable," wrote Kurakin, "that many persons died." It sometimes happened that the Czar, maddened by wine, would fall upon one of his companions with his fists or unsheathe his sword to run him through. The other guests would have great difficulty restraining him. At other times he would be content to slap a man who had contradicted him or to snatch off his wig. But usually, notwithstanding the great quantities of alcohol he consumed, he kept a cool head. While all around him bodies were slumping, faces grinning, and tongues wagging, he would observe the scene with a keen eye and take note of the revelations that, in the general euphoria, one or another of the guests would make between hiccups. It was his way of discovering the secrets of the men around him. Carousing became for him a means of governing.

Peter's liking for drunken disorder was accompanied by a liking for displays of light and noise. His friend Gordon, who knew something about pyrotechnics, had taught him how to make fireworks. To justify his new passion, the Czar invoked the necessity of accustoming the Russian people to the sound and smell of powder. In reality, he was as happy as a child to preside over these artfully combined explosions. He took every opportunity to send up rockets and compose emblematic pieces. He would run from one emplacement to another brandishing blazing matches, criticize the amateur pyrotechnists, and, his face blackened with powder, laugh as he watched sheaves of sparks fall open in the sky over Preobrazhenskoye. He was so reckless in pursuing this explosive activity that accidents ensued. On February 26, 1690, Gordon mentioned in his journal the death of a gentleman who had been felled by a spent rocket weighing five pounds. A similar misadventure occurred again a few months later. This time Timmermann's son-in-law had his face burned and three workers were killed on

---

Khmelnoy means "drunk."

the spot. But these were trifles compared to the risks run by the Czar's companions in the maneuvers he imposed on the former *poteshnye*. He had had a miniature city, Presburg, built on the Yauza. It included a small fortress, a barracks, a court of justice, administrative offices, and a little port with a fleet of boats lying at anchor, all for the sovereign's military amusements. The troops were divided into two camps, with foreigners as officers, Russians as noncommissioned officers. Although he was the master of these armed forces, Peter wanted to be only a soldier among the others and took his place in the Preobrazhensky regiment as an ordinary sergeant.

Perhaps it was to harden himself, to strengthen his weak nerves that he plunged so frantically into simulated warfare. Cannon thundered, grenades exploded, shots were fired on all sides, and the infantry advanced in line, with banners unfurled, to the sound of fifes and drums. On June 2, 1690, Peter, who was leading the assault with naked sword, suffered facial burns from the explosion of a grenade. A little later the same thing happened to Gordon. Several officers were wounded in a hand-to-hand skirmish. In October 1691, during one of these melees, which Gordon called "the field ballet military," Prince Ivan Dolgoruky was mortally wounded. Peter was saddened by his death, but it did not turn him from his purpose. On his instructions two armies of twenty thousand men each were to meet each other in October 1694 in a gigantic sham battle. One of these armies, commanded by Feodor Romodanovsky, would defend the artificial town of Presburg while the other, with an equal number of troops under the command of Buturlin, would besiege the enemy positions. It was to be the "Kozhukov campaign." To add a comic note to the performance, Peter decided that Romodanovsky would take the title of king of Presburg and that Buturlin would be king of Poland. The fury of the assailants was equaled only by the determination of the defenders. Lefort, who took part in the operations, later wrote: "They threw grenades, a kind of pot or jug filled with more than four pounds of powder. . . . There was the greatest fury. . . . In the attacks on a ravelin I had my face and ear burned. They feared for my eyes."[4] The Czar said to Lefort: "I am sorry for your misfortune. You kept your word when you said you would die rather than leave the field. I have nothing to reward you with now, but one day I will do it."

The losses sustained by the two armies in the course of these maneuvers were estimated at twenty-four dead and eighty wounded. The defeated "king of Poland" was taken prisoner and dragged with his hands tied behind his back to the camp of the "king of Presburg." Having received the surrender of his unfortunate adversary, the "king of Presburg" gave a banquet for all the participants. After this formidable shindy, Peter felt that he had tempered himself at last. When would he see real battlefields?

But he wanted to be as strong on water as on land. He had not forgotten his beloved boats. At his orders the Dutch carpenter Karsten Brandt engaged twenty workmen and set up shop with his crew at the edge of Lake Pereyaslavl to build a fleet. Near the shipyard—a spot two days' journey from Moscow—were hastily built a church and a one-story wooden structure as simple as a foreman's lodgings. The windowpanes were made of mica, but a two-headed eagle with a crown of gilded wood was displayed over the door. It was there that the carpenter-Czar would come to stay sometimes. Dressed as a worker, he wielded ax, hammer, and plane with cheerful frenzy, making the chips fly around him. He liked working with wood and associating with rough men who were masters of their trade and taught it to him without concern for his rank. Occasionally a band of merry young fellows would come to join the Czar, bringing wagons loaded with casks of wine, beer, and mead or kegs of brandy, and accompanied by ladies of easy virtue. That was the recreation. Immediately afterward Peter would go back to work.

In February 1692 he became angry because his mother wanted him to return to Moscow to receive the ambassador of the shah of Persia. But soon the lake seemed to him a wretched puddle unworthy of his great dream. He had to have "the real sea." Natalya, knowing how reckless her son was, begged him to give up his proposed trip north. He stood firm but promised not to go on board any ships—he would be content, he said, to watch maneuvers from afar. In July 1693 he left with a suite of one hundred persons, including Lefort, Romodanovsky, Buturlin, a priest, and two court dwarfs, for Archangel near the Arctic circle, the only port in his realm where he could breathe the sea air. When he arrived he was so enchanted with the gray waves breaking, the mist on the horizon, the swarming mass of sailors on the quay, and the commercial activity of the city, where all the merchandise of Europe was piled up, that he could no longer contain himself and forgot his promise.

In no time he was dressed as a Dutch sailor and on board the yacht *Saint Peter,* scudding along in the wake of other boats heading out to sea. A sharp wind whipped his face. Heavy waves shook the deck under his feet. Standing beside the helmsman he dreamed of the day when the Russian colors would fly over these vast empty spaces where as yet only foreign flags had been seen. As soon as he returned to Archangel he decided to create a fleet of warships. A first vessel of no great size would be built in Russia by local workmen; another, a forty-four-gun frigate, would be ordered in Holland from the burgomaster of Amsterdam, Witsen. In the meantime, learning that her intrepid son had ventured on the waves to the very approaches of the Arctic Ocean, Natalya wrote to him, entreating him to return to Moscow. She even had a letter sent to him in the name of her three-year-old grandson Alexis: "Greetings and good health for many years, my dear father, Czar Peter Alexeyevich. Come back to us soon, you who are our joy, our sovereign. I ask this favor of you because I see how sad my grandmother is." At last Peter reluctantly started back.

In Moscow he found his mother ill and was worried. He had a deep affection for her, a religious veneration. In his eyes she was the sole being in the world whose love was not sullied by any calculation. In spite of the care lavished on her by the court physicians, she died on January 25, 1694. Peter's grief was as violent as a summer storm. He howled, wept, prayed. But on the third day, with Natalya scarcely laid to rest, he supped at Lefort's in gay company. He needed wine, noise, the smiles of Anna Mons so as not to be overcome with mourning. Sadness, he thought, was a graver illness than the one his mother had died of. It was a man's duty to taste all the pleasures of the earth, not to stare obstinately into the hole that had just been dug in it. Already on the fourth day he returned to his passion for shipbuilding and wrote to Feodor Apraxin: "Although my sorrow is still fresh, I am writing to you about the affairs of the living: I am sending you Niklaus and Yan to build a small boat. Let the necessary wood and iron be delivered to them; let 150 dog-skin hats be made and as many pairs of shoes of different sizes. . . ."

In the spring he received a letter from Witsen informing him that the man-of-war ordered in Amsterdam would arrive in Archangel in July. Peter wanted to be on hand to welcome it. On May 8 the Czar and his usual retinue left Lake Pereyaslavl on twenty-two big, flat-bottomed boats and headed north along the rivers. On May 17 the flotilla, coming up the Dvina, passed Kholmogory and entered Archangel, greeted by salvos of cannon. How could he pass the time while waiting for the Dutch vessel to arrive? Drawn by the heave and spray of the sea, Peter could not sit idle. With a few close friends and a priest he went on board the yacht *Saint Peter* and decided to sail to a monastery on Solovetsky Island. When the boat was already 120 versts out of Archangel, a violent storm arose on the White Sea. The sails were hastily lowered. Buffeted by enormous waves, the *Saint Peter* cracked at every joint. The sailors were in despair. Foreseeing shipwreck, the most experienced among them gave up the struggle and commended their souls to God. The Czar's friends sobbed and wrung their hands before the priest, who blessed them. The Czar made confession, received communion, and took the wheel. This time he mastered his nerves. It was almost as if he were exalted by the fury of the elements. His determination heartened the crew. On the advice of the pilot he steered the yacht toward Unskaya Gulf, to take shelter from the tempest. The successful maneuver was hailed as a miracle. When Peter set foot on solid ground once more, with his own hands he hewed a ten-foot cross out of wood and carved an inscription on it in Dutch, to prove that he knew the language of seafarers: "This cross was made by Captain Peter, in the summer of 1694." Then, lifting the cross onto his strong shoulders, he carried it to the shore alone like an athletic Christ and planted it at the place where he had landed.

Upon his return to Archangel he celebrated with song, gunpowder, and copious supplies of wine the divine favor that had preserved his life. He was often to be seen drink in hand, sometimes with his friends, sometimes with the sailors of the port. "He takes more pleasure and satisfaction in talking with our compatriots and gazing upon our ships than in anything else," wrote Van Keller. At last, on July 21, 1694, the frigate *Holy Prophet* appeared off the coast in full sail. In the city cannon thundered, bells rang, Peter danced for joy. He seemed not twenty-two years old but twelve. Never had he received a more beautiful present. Climbing on board he admired the marvel close up; he liked everything, the superstructures and cabins, the sailors and ropes, the cannon and the casks of French wine. Straightaway he dictated a letter to the burgomaster of Amsterdam, who had sent him the *Holy Prophet:*

"*Min her!* By the present letter I can tell you only this, that Jan Flamm [the pilot] has arrived in good condition, carrying forty-four cannon and forty sailors. . . . In this hour of happiness I am not disposed to write but rather to do honor to Bacchus, who is pleased to close with his vine leaves the eyes of him who would wish to write you a more detailed letter."

And he signed in Flemish, out of friendship for his correspondent: "*Schiper Fonshi Psantus Profetities.*" Which was no doubt supposed to be: "*Schipper van Schip Sanctus Propheties*" (Captain of the ship *Holy Prophet*). At that moment Holland won his devotion heart and soul. He adopted for Russia the Dutch flag of red, white, and blue in horizontal stripes, changing only the order of the colors.[5]

But he also had to organize the hierarchy of this newly founded navy. Peter gaily distributed ranks and functions. Romodanovsky, although he knew nothing about navigation, would be the admiral; Buturlin, who was equally ignorant, vice admiral; Gordon, rear admiral. As for Lefort, having lived for a long time on the shores of Lake Geneva, he was just the man to command the first man-of-war of the Russian fleet. Peter himself remained a mere captain, just as he was a simple bombardier on land. This deliberate modesty in reality hid a deep sense of pride. True greatness scoffs at titles, clothes, and settings, he thought. All his life he was to affect poorer lodgings and poorer dress than the gentlemen of his court, so as to show that his power owed nothing to the external signs with which other monarchs too often surrounded themselves for fear of not being respected. He was a curious mixture of buffoonery and seriousness, of drunken abandon and sober application. Between binges he would examine maps, pore over treatises on artillery, study the construction of oceangoing vessels, and have Gordon translate the manual of maritime signals for him. Or he would read foreign newspapers and the intercepted letters that were communicated to him by the head of the postal service, Andrew Vinius, son of a Dutch immigrant, who had been converted to the Orthodox faith. Attentive to world events, he gradually became persuaded that Russia, which was in an unfavorable position geographically, would never be able to breathe freely and develop harmoniously until she had broken the iron collar that was choking her. As he slowly turned the terrestrial globe his glance was irresistibly drawn to two points: the Black Sea and the Baltic. There was only one way to gain access to them: war. But notwithstanding the military maneuvers of the last few years, he did not feel ready. Physically and mentally, he still belonged to the world of games. Besides, his advisers recommended caution.

Many Russians had joined the group of foreigners who in the beginning had made up Peter's usual circle. The most conspicuous was the giant Menshikov, the former pastry cook's assistant, who had never opened a book but who looked so dashing in his Preobrazhensky regiment uniform! Come from the lowest level of society, he had an alert mind, a gift for sharp repartee, unbounded ambition, a taste for luxury, and a blind devotion to his benefactor. It was whispered that he was Peter's "favorite." According to some the Czar, though he loved women, was not above making an incursion into the other camp if occasion presented itself. A contemporary, Berkholz, cites the presence at court of a pretty youth, an ex-lieutenant, who was there only "for the pleasure" of the sovereign. Later, at Peter's request, the Saxon painter Danhauer was to paint a portrait of one of his pages in the nude. Villebois wrote that the Czar was subject to "fits of passion in which age and even sex were of small importance to him."[6] In his correspondence Peter called Menshikov "the child of my heart." He dragged him everywhere and heaped titles and gifts upon him as he would upon a mistress.

Also at Peter's side were three ministers charged with current affairs. Gabriel Golovkin was thin, distinguished, sanctimonious, and cunning. It was said that he was such a penny pincher that when he came home he would hang up his long red wig on a nail so as not to wear it out. Feodor Golovin was a cultivated, level-headed, hardworking man of whom Leibniz wrote that he was "the wittiest and most intelligent of the Muscovites." The third, Prince Prozorovsky, austere and pious, always made the sign of the cross before opening a door, for fear that a heretic might have touched the handle before him.[7] Others revolved around this triumvirate: Prince Romodanovsky, a great lord, upright, hard, and cruel, had the privilege of being called "Majesty" by the Czar himself. The real sovereign closed his letters to the mock sovereign with the words: "Your Majesty's very obedient slave, Peter." Romoda-novsky lived amid Asiatic magnificence and counted five hundred persons in his retinue. In the courtyard of his palace visitors were greeted by a tame bear holding in his paws a vessel full of peppered vodka, which they had to drain to the last drop before crossing the threshold. Boris Sheremetev, descendant of an illustrious line of boyars, was considered "a worthy gentleman" by the English am-bassador, Whitworth, but Peter, while he respected the man's in-tegrity, found him a deadly bore. Peter Tolstoy, on the other hand, was a model of spitefulness and deceit of whom the Czar said with a laugh: "When you have anything to do with Tolstoy, you have to put a stone in your pocket so as to break his teeth before he devours you." Once, touching Tolstoy's forehead, he cried: "O head, head! If I didn't know you were so clever, I'd have had you cut off long ago!" Another "clever" companion was Peter Shafirov, the son of a mercantile agent, a Polish Jew who had converted to the Orthodox faith. As a clerk in a draper's shop, this plump, stocky, unctuous little man had attracted the Czar's attention by his education and his gift for languages: he spoke six. Peter made him an assistant to Golovkin, who needed a polyglot secretary. For Shafirov that was the beginning of a dizzying ascent to sinecures and honors. Other advisers crowded around the sovereign: Yagu-zhinsky, Matveyev, Dolgoruky, Kurakin, Buturlin, Tatishchev. . . . Some were of very noble lineage, others came from the lowest classes of society. Whatever their background, Peter treated them all in the same way, at once rough and friendly, suspicious and naïve. For the time being he hardly knew what to use them for. Most of them had titles and no real functions. He would gather them together for tumultuous banquets at Lefort's house. Some who were old or had delicate constitutions were reluctant to participate in these drinking sessions. But one could not refuse an invitation from the Czar if one valued his place. Despite his repugnance, the courtier would have to laugh and drink on order, amid the thick smoke of pipes, the smell of stale wine, and the gyrations of the dwarfs, dressed as clowns, who besieged the table.

Soon the disorganized revels were no longer enough for Peter. He wanted to give them a permanent, official, institutional form and at the same time to make them more amusing and irreverent, so he founded the "Burlesque Conclave" or "Synod of Fools and Jesters," designed to celebrate the cult of Bacchus with frequent and abundant libations. At the head of this company of drunkards he placed the biggest drunkard of all, his former tutor Nikita Zotov, who was awarded the title "Prince Pope" or "Prince Patriarch." To enable him to play this role, Zotov was given a salary of two thousand rubles, a palace, and twelve servants, all of whom were stutterers. During the "ceremonies" he wore a tin miter and carried a tin scepter, spewed forth incoherent speeches in which obscenities alternated with quotations from the Bible, and blessed the company that knelt before him with two long Dutch pipes, hitting them on the head with a pig's bladder. Then he would give them, as an icon to kiss, an indecent statue of Bacchus. He would dance before them, staggering and belching, tucking his sacerdotal robes up over his bandy legs. The Prince Pope was surrounded by a college of twelve cardinals and a great many mock bishops, mock archimandrites, and mock deacons, all inveterate guzzlers and gluttons.

The Czar himself played the archdeacon. He attended all the meetings and drank more than anyone else. With his own hand he drew up the statutes of the order, established the hierarchy of its members, and specified the smallest details of the sacrilegious performances. The elect, having donned the red robes of cardinals, had to go first to the house of the Prince Pope, called the *Vaticanum,* to thank him and do him homage. Four stutterers would show them into the consistory where the throne of His Very Holy Buffoonery stood behind piles of casks. The first question asked of the newcomer would be not "Do you believe?" as in the primitive

Church, but "Do you drink?" The Prince Pope would add: "Reverendissimus, open your mouth, swallow what is given to you, and you will tell us wonderful things." Vodka would stream down the throats of the novices and their initiators, and then they would march in procession to the house next door, where the conclave was to be held. Peter, in the garb of a Dutch seaman, would lead the way beating a drum. Behind him came the Prince Pope, seated on a cask drawn by four oxen, surrounded by bogus monks, and accompanied by an escort of goats, pigs, and bears.

A spacious gallery furnished with couches awaited the members of the conclave. Beside each couch stood a big barrel cut in two, one half for the refreshments, the other for the guests to relieve themselves in. It was forbidden to leave the couch until the end of the conclave, which lasted three days and three nights. Servants, dwarfs, and buffoons relentlessly plied Their Eminences with drink, provoking them to the filthiest language. Among these official clowns were some who were fools "through natural infirmity," whom the sovereign found highly amusing, and others who were fools "for punishment," condemned to simulate lunacy because they had performed their former functions unsatisfactorily. All were in costume and vied with each other making faces, while at their signal the "cardinals" bent their elbows and drained one glass after another. Vodka, wine, beer, mead—everything went down mixed together. Soaked in alcohol, sweating, panting, eyes starting from their heads, the hapless conclavists insulted each other, wept, rolled on the ground, vomited on their masquerade costumes, or fought with each other in fits of idiotic rage.

The Czar also drank but kept a clear head. Circulating among the drunks he applauded their senseless behavior and encouraged them to degrade themselves still further. "At all the entertainments given by this Prince," wrote Villebois, "when wits began to be muddled by wine he was in the habit of walking around the tables and listening to everything that was said; and, when one of the guests let fall a remark that it was important for him to look into under calmer circumstances, he would note it down so that he could make use of it at the right time and place."[8] On Christmas night, and on some other holy days, Muscovites would be dumbfounded by the sight of a sacrilegious procession passing through the streets. The Prince Pope appeared astride a barrel drawn by twelve bald men. He was wearing his tin miter and a chasuble embroidered with playing cards. The "cardinals" followed him in comical cassocks, mounted on oxen and brandishing bottles. Then came other "dignitaries" in sleighs drawn by pigs, bears, and dogs. All these people were bawling out blasphemous litanies. They stopped in front of the richest houses to be served drinks. Who would dare to refuse? But among the common people as among the nobility, an insidious rumor was spreading: could the Czar be the Antichrist?

Eudoxia, learning that these public outrages to religion were inspired and directed by Peter, wept, regretted that Natalya was no longer there to reason with her son, and prayed God to enlighten the Czar. But in vain did she entreat her husband to renounce his demonic practices: he would laugh and push her away. She was a bore. He himself probably didn't know what the institution of the Prince Pope and the drunken cardinals meant to him. To be sure, he was glad enough to debase the Orthodox patriarchy, whose authority rivaled his own in the country. Had he not already refused to lead Patriarch Adrian's ass by the bridle? Now he was carrying insolence to new heights. Nevertheless, he remained a Christian by conviction. He respected the Church, provided it kept to its spiritual role and did not encroach upon the prerogatives of the government. As for the Pope, that strange head of the Catholics, to Peter he was only a distant personage in a bizarre costume who had not the slightest influence on Russia. One could therefore make fun of him like any other carnival figure without offending God.

In his fondness for huge farces, the Czar harked back to the ribald tradition of the Middle Ages, mingling the sacred and the profane, mocking kings, popes, and abbots, sometimes speaking blasphemy without ceasing to tremble for the salvation of his soul. It was in his nature to want to shake up everything around him. And first came the old Russian customs, popular and religious. He liked the Protestants because they dared to innovate in matters of faith—only they did so gravely and soberly, while his own negation took the form of gaiety, caricature, and folly. Wasn't he mocking himself when he declared himself the subject, the slave of "His

Majesty" Romodanovsky? So why shouldn't he mock the Patriarch and the Pope? You had to laugh until you split your sides and drink until you lost your senses. Any pretext would do to break the monotony of the daily routine. The mind was always sharper after a good bender. Peter was not far from thinking that political genius and the capacity to hold liquor went hand in hand in great men. A primitive colossus overflowing with strength and vitality, he obeyed elementary instincts as old as man. Everything about him was complicated, confused, obscure, violent. He was bursting with health and eccentricity. But never in the course of these bacchanals did he forget that he was Czar.

It may even have been that at the moment when his companions thought him sunk deepest in drink, he conceived his best plans. One of the ideas he found most tempting was to resume hostilities against Turkey. He would like to succeed where Sophia and Basil Golitzin had twice failed. His brother Ivan, a pale phantom, was not strong enough to oppose his designs. Nor was anyone around him. Yet he hesitated. How could he tell whether he was still only a captain fit for the drill ground or already a real warrior?

5
War Against Turkey

*A*lthough Peter was preoccupied with his maneuvers at sea and on land, his drunken orgies and his love affairs, he could not but realize that the situation of the country was deteriorating. Domestically, both nobles and common people were criticizing the Czar's frivolousness, his infatuation with foreign advisers, his pointless military games, and his indecent attacks on the Church. Laziness and disorganization reigned among servants of the state. Bandits swarmed in the countryside and even at the very gates of Moscow, robbing, holding captives for ransom, murdering with impunity. The police were overwhelmed. And the Duma, to which the young sovereign had hitherto abandoned the management of affairs, was too weak and divided to make the smallest decision. Among the boyars who had rallied to Peter's cause in 1689 there were now some who regretted the days of the Regency. No doubt Sophia had had her faults, but at least she had governed.

In external affairs the situation was even worse. In 1692 twelve thousand Tatars had pillaged Nemirov, carried off thousands of prisoners, both men and women, and captured all the horses.

These incursions into Ukrainian territory were frequent, and the inhabitants of the threatened regions begged the Czar in vain to protect them. Seeing Russia's inertia, Mazeppa, the new hetman of the Cossacks, was perilously close to an alliance with Poland. France was negotiating with the Grand Vizier for custody of the Holy Places. Already Catholic priests had taken the Holy Sepulcher, half of Golgotha, the Church of Bethlehem, and the Holy Grotto from Orthodox monks. Dositheus, Patriarch of Jerusalem, wept for shame and dreamed of a holy war. To mark his contempt for a weak nation, Sultan Ahmed II, who had officially informed the other European sovereigns of his accession, had not deigned to announce it to the two Czars of Russia.

Peter swallowed every insult without turning a hair, then suddenly awoke. He opened his eyes, looked around in surprise, shook himself as if suddenly coming to maturity. Lefort had conceived the plan of taking Peter on a journey across Europe, to show his Swiss and Dutch compatriots how he had prospered in the Czar's service and the friendship and esteem with which his master favored him. The Czar, he said, being always curious about anything new, would learn much of value from his visits to the most advanced and best-equipped countries in the world. Peter was quickly won over to the idea, but he didn't want to appear abroad as a second-rate sovereign who had no claim to fame. Before setting out he had to raise himself to the level of the greatest kings of the West. He would not agree to leave home until he was respected and feared beyond his borders. To achieve that, he needed the laurels of war. Urged on by Lefort, he abandoned games for the real thing.

On January 20, 1695, in the depths of winter, he promulgated a ukase ordering mobilization against Turkey. But while turning back to Golitzin's project, he changed tactics. Instead of trying to break through at Perekop, he chose as his objective Azov* on the estuary of the Don. This city, which was strongly fortified by the Turks, defended both the mouth of the river and access to the Black Sea. To deceive the enemy, Sheremetev carried out a diversionary attack with 120,000 men against the Turkish fortresses at

*The ancient Greek colony of Tanais.

the mouth of the Dnieper. At the same time a small army of 31,000 men, including all the new regiments, the Czar's artillery company, the *streltsy,* the court militia and city militia, marched on Azov. This latter force was commanded by three generals: Gordon, Golovin, and Lefort. It might have been another maneuver in the mock siege of the miniature fortress of Presburg.

"We had a good time under the walls of Kozhukov, and now we are going to play under the walls of Azov," Peter wrote Apraxin. With his usual penchant for disguise and farce, he took the pseudonym Peter Alexeyev, insisted on being treated like an ordinary artillery captain, and wrote to Romodanovsky, whom he had once dubbed king of Presburg: *"Minher Kenich,* * Your Majesty's letter, dated from your capital of Presburg, has been delivered to me, a favor from Your Majesty for which I am bound to shed the last drop of my blood, for the which purpose I am now setting out. —Bombardier Peter."

When at last they arrived under the walls of Azov, the three commanders in chief—Gordon, Golovin, and Lefort—could not agree. Bombardment of the city made no dent in the enemy's resistance. The first assaults on the outworks were disappointing. Against Gordon's advice Peter ordered a large-scale attack for Sunday, August 5, 1695, and asked for volunteers, promising great rewards. Not one soldier, not one *strelets* stepped forward. The artificial engagements on the drill grounds at Presburg had hardly prepared them for real combat. But 2,500 Cossacks of the Don offered themselves for the cause. Plenty of troops were added despite the lack of enthusiasm of the regiments chosen. The attack, ill prepared and badly led, was repulsed with heavy losses. Peter then decided to use mines instead of cannon to breach the outer defenses. But the mines either didn't explode or, when they did, killed more Russians than Turks. By a miracle, however, one of the devices made a big enough hole in the wall for the attackers to pour through. Despite the fury of their attack they were thrown back. Other operations were even worse failures. The only trophies the Russians brought back to camp were a flag and a cannon captured from the Turks.

*No doubt he thought he was writing in German *Mein Herr König.*"

It began to rain. The river overflowed, flooding tents, wetting the powder, turning the trenches into mudholes. After 196 days of siege, the council of war decided to retreat by way of Cherkassk. The Tatar horsemen harried the rear guard and massacred those who fell behind. Cold set in after the rain. Lacking supplies and warm clothing, soldiers died by the hundreds. Wolves attacked the survivors. It was an even greater disaster than the one that had been attributed to Basil Golitzin.

But like Golitzin of whom he had been so critical, Peter presented himself in Moscow as a conqueror. When he made his triumphal entry into the city, a Turkish prisoner in chains (the only one, perhaps!) walked at the head of the procession. The Te Deum was sung in the churches to give thanks for the imaginary victories. The losses suffered by the army were officially attributed to the treachery of one Jacob Jansen, who was supposed to have betrayed the secrets of the Russian strategy to the enemy.

The public was not deceived, however. Nor, for that matter, was Peter. But far from overwhelming him, this humiliation only made him pause and reflect. For him there was no such thing as a lost cause—there were only lessons one had to profit from so as to turn the situation to one's advantage. While all around him detractors were recalling the prophetic words of Patriarch Joachim warning against foreign advisers and heretical generals, he coldly analyzed the reasons for the defeat. The fortress of Azov, which could not be taken by land, would have fallen, he thought, under an attack by sea. The inferior vessels of Lake Pereyaslavl were good only for amusement: what Russia needed was a real navy. Very well then, he would create one. And fast!

At Peter's instigation, the Duma of boyars gave orders to build a fleet of warships. The whole country was called upon to contribute to this project. Every landowner who possessed more than ten thousand "souls" was required to pay for one ship, fully equipped and armed. Even the monasteries would have to deliver their quota in proportion to the number of serfs they owned. The Czar's family alone was to furnish nine ships. The problem of manpower was solved with exemplary determination. Captains, pilots, sailors, and shipwrights were hired abroad. When they arrived at Voronezh, the place selected for the great shipyards, some of them were appalled at the living conditions and ran away. They were caught and brought back. The ordinary workmen were assembled by massive requisitions in Russia itself: blacksmiths, carpenters, joiners were torn from their forges and benches and sent by forced march to the banks of the Don. To perform the unskilled labor, thirty thousand muzhiks were swept up in raids on the surrounding countryside, despite the entreaties of their families, and herded into Voronezh like cattle. Nor was there any lack of materials. They were assembled with the same brutal exercise of absolute power. Seven thousand trees—oaks, pines, lindens—were cut down in record time in the vast forests of the region, while in warehouses throughout Russia government agents seized the iron, copper, tar, rope, canvas, nails, and hemp necessary to fit out the ships. To command the future fleet, which was still on blocks, Peter appointed an entire general staff: the Swiss Lefort was admiral, Lima, a Venetian, was vice admiral, and Balthasar de l'Osière, a Frenchman, rear admiral. The Czar himself would settle for the post of captain-pilot. But for the moment there was no question of putting out to sea. In the shipyards of Voronezh Peter had rolled up his sleeves. Mixing with the workmen, he was busy with ax, plane, plumb line, hammer, and compasses. He built with his own hands the swiftest and most elegant of galleys, christened the *Principium*, able to carry two hundred men. "As God ordained for our ancestor Adam, we eat our bread in the sweat of our brow," he wrote the boyar Streshnev.

While he was at the shipyards a courier brought him painful news: his half brother, the sickly Ivan, had died suddenly in Moscow on January 29, 1696. So now he was sole Czar of Russia. He had been so in fact ever since Sophia had been relegated to a convent. But the disappearance of the discreet companion of his childhood saddened him. He sighed and returned to work with redoubled zeal. For the moment nothing else mattered but the beautiful wooden frames with their exposed ribs, held up on stays. The workers, underfed and ill housed, died by the dozens. Others were brought, under threat of the knout. The foreign engineers got drunk and quarreled. Deluges of rain flooded the terrain. But Peter was not discouraged. To complete his navy he sent to Archangel for two men-of-war built in the Low Countries, the

Apostle Peter and the *Apostle Paul.* Since the rivers were frozen, the two enormous vessels were hauled to Voronezh over the snow and ice. The construction work begun in the fall of 1695 had been carried out so expeditiously that by May 1696 twenty-three galleys and four fire ships were launched amid noisy fireworks and libations. At the head of the fleet that sailed down the Don toward the sea was the galley *Principium* commanded by Peter—or rather by Captain Peter Alexeyev, as he insisted on being called henceforth. The land army, which was to cooperate with the naval forces in taking Azov, was placed under the command of Generalissimo Alexis Schein, assisted by General Gordon.

The first naval engagement turned to the advantage of the Russians. Having dispersed the Turkish boats anchored off Azov, the Czar's fleet blockaded the estuary to prevent supplies from reaching the city. Again the siege began, with its inaccurate shelling, feeble musket fire, and ineffectual explosions of mines. Peter wrote to his sister, the Czarevna Natalya: "Hello, little sister. I am well, thank God. To obey your letter I do not go near shells and bullets; but the shells and bullets come near me. Will you please tell them not to?" Finding it impossible to penetrate the enemy's defenses, the generals became discouraged and assembled the junior officers and men to ask what they thought was the best way to get into the city. Some *streltsy* suggested they try the method that Vladimir the Great had used long ago to conquer Kherson: to build a huge mound of earth against the ramparts and thus dominate them. Fifteen thousand men labored night and day at the gigantic embankment. As they worked they were raked with grapeshot by the Turks, who took easy aim from the top of the walls. Losses were high. Would they have to give up Vladimir's stratagem? At this point arrived various Austrian officers and engineers who had left Vienna four and a half months earlier. They advised against continuing the embankment and found the enemy's range with such precision that under the bombardment the Turks soon had to evacuate the corner bastion. The besieged were running out of supplies and ammunition. On July 17, 1696, the Cossacks of the Dnieper made a bold surprise attack and won the outworks of the fortress; on the eighteenth at noon the citadel surrendered; on the nineteenth the Turkish soldiers came out from behind the walls with weapons, wives, children, and baggage; the deserter Jacob Jansen, who had gone over to the enemy during the first campaign, was delivered into the hands of the victors; finally, the Bey presented the keys of the city to the generalissimo and took ship with his retinue for the open sea. The Russians entered Azov. Most of the houses were in ruins. Peter had kept his word. On July 20, glowing with happiness and in a facetious mood, he wrote Romodanovsky: "*Min Her Konih!* Learn, Your Majesty, that God has blessed the armies of your kingdom. Yesterday Your Majesty's prayers and good fortune caused the men of Azov to surrender in despair. . . . Written on board the galley *Principium*—Piter."

Having strengthened the defenses of Azov, Peter installed a garrison of eight thousand men and set out for the return journey. From Cherkassk he wrote to Vinius that he was counting on him to set up arches of triumph in Moscow in honor of the victorious army. Vinius replied asking for a month's time in which to decorate the city. Mastering his customary impatience, Peter decided to make a visit to some ironworks in the Tula region, which would give Vinius time to prepare the festivities. It was not until September 30 that the procession made its entrance into Moscow. They were welcomed by a gigantic arch of triumph topped with a double-headed eagle, surrounded with flags, and decorated with allegorical figures and flattering inscriptions. One golden streamer bore the words: "Return of the Emperor Constantine." Another: "Victory of Emperor Constantine over the Emperor of Rome, the pagan Maxentius." And still others: "The strength of Hercules and the courage of Mars," "Honor to the brave warriors of the sea," "Honor to the brave warriors of the land." There was a huge painting on canvas representing a Turkish pasha and a Tatar chief in chains, with the god Neptune saying: "I congratulate you on the capture of Azov and I submit to your will." From the top of the arch of triumph Vinius was shouting into a megaphone verses welcoming the admiral and the generals. In the parade, which advanced slowly to the sound of bells, artillery salutes, and shouts of joy, were to be seen the grotesque Prince Pope Zotov seated in a carriage holding a saber in one hand and a shield in the other, gifts from Mazeppa, Admiral Lefort followed by his flag, Vice Admiral Lima, and Rear Admiral Balthasar de l'Osière, Generalissimo Schein, General Golovin, General Gordon, trumpets, kettle drums, priests holding icons aloft, sixteen banners that had been taken from the enemy and that soldiers were trailing in the mud, Tatar prisoners in chains, all the regiments that had participated in the action and—in disgrace on a wagon—the traitor Jacob Jansen, wearing a turban, bound to a gallows, and flanked by executioners, with a placard on his chest reading "Scoundrel" and over his head another reading "Apostate of four religions, he is hated by the Turks and the Christians."*

All Moscow was on hand to acclaim its army. The cheers swelled as a simple naval officer passed, marching behind the magnificent carriage of the admiral. This officer was very tall. His rugged face shone with joy and determination. He was wearing a uniform of coarse German wool and carried a boarding pike on his shoulder. His hat was decorated with a white plume. No need of a crown for people to recognize the Czar. True to his penchant for farce, he traversed the city on foot, while his generals took their ease in carriages and at the head of the procession rode the king of clowns, the Prince Pope, the drunkard Nikita Zotov.

As rewards for their outstanding deeds, the military commanders received medals, estates, and serfs; the soldiers a few pieces of gold. The chief victors assembled at Lefort's for a banquet. They drank, danced, shot off fireworks. The artillery salvo that punctuated the final toast was so violent that it shattered all the windows in the German Settlement. In the midst of the uproar Peter was thinking about what was to follow. While for most of his companions the fall of Azov marked a happy ending, for him it was only an episode in the war with Turkey. Access to the Black Sea was still shut off, Turkish forts still prevented Russian ships from passing through the Kerch Strait. So he must accelerate the building of warships, hire more skilled workmen, and even—a revolutionary notion!—send Russian gentlemen abroad to learn the art of navigation. Thus fifty personages of high birth were summarily ordered to leave the country. Twenty-three of them bore princely titles. Some were heads of families. No matter! Let them leave wife

*Jacob Jansen, born a Catholic, had converted to Protestantism, then to Orthodoxy before becoming a Moslem.

and children to obey the wishes of the Czar, let them travel at their own expense, each accompanied by a single orderly, let them settle in Italy, in England, or in Holland and learn afar everything that Russia needed to know in order to become the most powerful state in Europe!

When these sentences of exile for educational purposes were announced, there was despair in aristocratic circles. But no entreaty could make Peter relent. Young or old, the future students had to pack their bags to go live among the heretics. They would not be permitted to return to Russia until they had obtained a certificate of proficiency from their instructors. If they came back prematurely, all their property would be confiscated by the Czar. When it came time to part, the abandoned wives wore blue gowns as a sign of half-mourning. But Peter, ready as usual to set the example, declared that he himself was prepared to leave the country as part of a great embassy, to visit the Western nations, learn about scientific progress there, and try to secure military or diplomatic cooperation against Russia's hereditary enemies. Now that he had defeated the Turks at Azov, he could hold his head high before his brother sovereigns.

6

The Great Embassy

Peter was aware that in planning the "Great Embassy" abroad he was breaking with ancient tradition. Until now only one Russian prince had ever ventured beyond the borders of his native land: in 1075 Iziaslav, Grand Duke of Kiev, had paid a visit to Emperor Henry IV at Mainz. Since that time the Muscovite sovereigns had stayed home and their subjects had been strictly forbidden to stick their noses outside. For a Westerner, to travel abroad was a means of satisfying legitimate curiosity; but for a Russian, even to think about crossing the frontier was already an act of treason. Here anything that moved was suspect. In the *Account of the Three Missions of Mgr. de Carlisle* (1672), we are told: "It is forbidden for Russians to leave the country, else they would learn about the customs and ideas of other peoples and might think about breaking the chains of their slavery."[1]

On December 6, 1696, when the Czar announced his plan to the Duma, most of the boyars reacted with consternation. Was it meet for a great monarch to leave his domain and the influence of the Orthodox Church to go wandering about in the lands of the

Catholics and Protestants? Should he stoop to eat the bread of foreigners? Notwithstanding the timid remonstrances of the aristocracy and the clergy, Peter held his ground. He wanted to form alliances and to learn trades—the better to conquer the infidels at the first opportunity. For this purpose the Great Embassy would go to Amsterdam, Berlin, Vienna, Rome, Copenhagen, Venice, and London, everywhere except France, since Louis XIV supported the Turks and was trying to have his own candidate installed on the throne of Poland.

There were three ambassadors. Lefort assumed the functions of first envoy, seconded by Feodor Golovin and Prokofy Voznitzin. Each of the three was accompanied by twelve gentlemen and two pages. With them went thirty-five "volunteers" whose mission was to learn from the foreigners. Among these "volunteers" was one Peter Mikhailov. Behind the false name hid the Czar. In this way he accommodated both his fondness for hoax and his natural shyness. Lost in the crowd he would direct operations, observe, learn without making himself known. It was forbidden on pain of death to reveal his presence to anyone. The surveillance of the mails would be increased. Letters intended for the sovereign would be addressed to Peter Mikhailov and would contain no expressions of excessive respect. The private seal that Peter Mikhailov would use for his correspondence during the journey represented a ship's carpenter surrounded by his tools, with the inscription: "My rank is that of a student and I need teachers."

The embassy would also include three interpreters, an equerry, four chamberlains, physicians, surgeons, cooks, priests, two goldsmiths, six trumpeters, a swarm of servants, seventy soldiers from the Preobrazhensky regiment chosen for their height, four dwarfs, a monkey, and a merchant assigned to look after the great quantities of sables that were to be sold to cover expenses in case the chests of gold ran out. Of course they would also take along bills of exchange for each capital city, the crown diamonds, and the Czar's drum. For nourishment they would take huge wagonloads of flour, salmon, caviar, smoked fish, honey, and vodka.

Carriages and wagons were ready for the departure when on February 23, 1697, Lefort gave a farewell banquet at his house in the German Settlement. In the middle of the festivities two *streltsy* asked urgently to see the Czar and revealed to him that they had gotten wind of a plot against his life. The leader of the conspirators was supposed to be a colonel of the *streltsy*, Ivan Ziegler, a former supporter of Sophia's. He was said to have won others of the praetorians to his cause, as well as the son of the boyar Pushkin, the officer of the crown Alexis Sokovnin. Mad with rage, the Czar rushed from the room, ran to Ziegler's house, had him arrested and put to torture. A complete confession resulted, which the culprit's accomplices, interrogated in turn, confirmed. They had indeed intended to kill the sovereign, to punish him for his "anti-Christian conduct." After his death they would have had his young son Alexis ascend the throne and recalled Sophia to the regency.

Peter was shattered. Would he always find behind his back vindictive *streltsy* who resented him for his reforms and regretted the good old days of the Czarevna Sophia? A hastily established tribunal condemned Ziegler and Sokovnin to be dismembered and beheaded, the others simply to be beheaded. But this classic punishment was not enough to satisfy the Czar. The Russian people needed stronger images, he thought, to keep them in line. He gave orders to disinter the remains of Ivan Miloslavsky, who had been dead for twelve years but whose memory was linked in his mind with the terrible revolt of the *streltsy* in 1682. On March 4, 1697, the body, three-quarters decomposed, was dragged by pigs to the place of execution, cut into pieces, and placed underneath the scaffold in an open coffin. On the platform the executioners proceeded to dismember the conspirators. Slowly they cut off arms, legs, heads. A red juice flowed through the cracks between the boards onto the boyar's corpse. Thus past and present conspirators were joined together in infamy. All Moscow watched with bated breath as the putrefied remains were watered with fresh blood. When the butchery was finished the executioners arranged the severed limbs around a stone pillar bearing iron plaques on which were engraved the names of the accursed. Their heads were fixed on pikes at the top of the column. It was forbidden to remove these piles of flesh. They lay rotting, giving off a nauseating smell that drove away passersby. To be on the safe side, Peter exiled all the culprits' relatives to remote provinces and took advantage of the opportunity to banish his wife's father and uncles from court on no definite grounds.

It had taken him not ten days to put things in order. Restored to good spirits, he made the last arrangements for his departure. In his absence the administration of the state would be entrusted to a Council with three members. Prince Romodanovsky, with trusted troops, would guarantee the safety of Moscow. The *streltsy*, who were always making trouble, would be sent to the frontiers without their families.

The Great Embassy left Moscow on March 10, 1697. Its credentials, issued in the Czar's name, were drawn up in solemn terms: "Very powerful lords, our great and puissant Majesty the Czar desires that you receive this letter with respect. And we ask you, when our great plenipotentiary ambassadors reach your borders, not only to receive them with their retinue and to render them the honors due them, but to grant them audience when they request it. . . . Written in our Czarist court, in the great city of Moscow, this eighth day of the month of spring, in the year of creation 7205."[2]

Thus, in accordance with his subterfuge, the Czar pretended to be personally absent from the delegation. Nevertheless, his jealously guarded secret was soon known at foreign courts. The coded dispatches of their ambassadors arrived before the mission set out. There was astonishment in Amsterdam, in Vienna, in London. Since Peter wanted to go unnoticed, they would pretend not to know who he really was. But what a strange thing for a sovereign to do! Really, these Russians came from the ends of the earth and had notions that defied common sense!

The Great Embassy, composed of 250 persons, made slow progress over the roads full of potholes where carriages and wagons sank in the mire. The landscape, pounded by rain squalls, was dismal, the inns fleabags. But Peter remained in great good humor.

It was only when they reached Riga, in Swedish Livonia, that his spirits were dampened. A few cannon were fired off to salute the convoy as it entered the city, but otherwise the welcome was rather cold. The members of the mission, who should have had a palace at their disposal, were lodged in simple houses of the townspeople. And the governor, Count Dahlberg, claimed illness to avoid receiving them personally. "I have not visited them," he wrote to Charles XII, "and I have not invited them to the castle, thinking either step unnecessary, for they are not accredited to my King, and the governors who preceded me acted no otherwise with other ambassadors under the same circumstances. . . . We pretended to be unaware of the Czar's presence, so as not to provoke his ire. No one in his retinue dares speak of it, on pain of death."

Peter, who insisted on remaining incognito, nevertheless felt that the local authorities were too cavalier with the official representatives of Russia. But he had come not to be honored but to see. He and his companions nosed about everywhere, questioned Swedish officers, drew sketches, made notes of figures so insistently that the inhabitants of Riga were offended and wondered if these people were diplomats or spies. "The Russians climb elevations to study their location, go down into moats to measure their depth, even make drawings of the principal works," Dahlberg reported to his king. In the end he denied his over-curious guests access to the citadel. Peter was furious and wrote to Vinius: "Here, we have been treated like slaves; we have had plenty to see but nothing to eat." At the end of the letter he added in invisible ink details that, had they come to the attention of Count Dahlberg, would have enraged the haughty governor: "There are 2,780 soldiers here. We have visited the city and the castle, where soldiers were stationed in five places: one thousand men in all. The city is well fortified, but the surrounding wall is not finished. At certain points in the city there are sentinels who prevent anyone from passing. The people are not very prepossessing."

Peter's ill humor was dissipated at Mitau, where the reigning duke, Frederick Casimir of Kurland, a personal friend of Lefort's, received the Great Embassy with pomp and cordiality. But in this pleasant city there were neither fleet nor port nor shipyards, and the Czar was in a hurry to learn. He went to Libau and there found the Baltic, which he called the Varangian Sea, heaving under a storm and struck by bolts of lightning. Yielding once again to his love for sailing, he decided to make the journey to Königsberg by boat while his companions traveled by land. Impatient with the bad weather that delayed his departure, he whiled away the time drinking with the sailors of the port, who took him for a Russian captain sent by the Czar to outfit a corsair.

When he finally reached Königsberg, ahead of his embassy, he began by taking artillery lessons from Colonel von Sternfeld. At the end of his period of apprenticeship, the colonel was to give him a certificate reading as follows: "I have given the man Peter Mikhailov daily instruction in both theory and practice. In both these studies he has surprised everyone, making so much progress and acquiring so much knowledge that he may be considered and honored everywhere as a careful and courageous master artificer. For these reasons, we extend to all, great and small, whatever their grade or rank, the humble, pressing, and kind invitation to recognize the said Peter Mikhailov as an accomplished bombardier and an expert and prudent artificer."

Proud of his new skill, the "bombardier Peter Mikhailov" was waiting only for the arrival of the ambassadors to organize a display of fireworks in honor of his host, Frederick III, elector of Brandenburg.* At the last minute the elector sent his apologies by Count Kreyzen and Provost Schlacken. Peter received the two messengers at table in the presence of the boyars and one of his dwarfs. He was drunk and sentimental and from time to time leaned over to kiss Lefort with manly roughness. Hardly had the elector's envoys taken their places, at his invitation, when his expression changed. His features were convulsed by anger. He pounded his fist on the table and shouted: "The Elector is good, but his advisers are devils! *Gehe! Gehe!* (Get out!)" And seizing one of the unfortunates by the throat he pushed him out, repeating: *"Gehe! Gehe!"*

Nevertheless, he did not hold this contretemps against Frederick, who received the mission with much fanfare. Soon the Russians and the Brandenburgers were trying to outdo each other in magnificence. For official visits the ambassadors donned brocade caftans strewn with pearls and precious stones. They had diamond buttons on their robes, and their hats, ornamented with the double-headed eagle, were also trimmed with diamonds. Next to them in his modest green uniform "bombardier Peter Mikhailov" looked like an orderly—which was exactly what he wanted. Especially since, despite his incognito, the elector treated him like a sovereign, even pretending not to be offended by the bizarre be-

*Later Frederick I of Prussia.

havior of this harebrained eccentric from the northern steppes. "Bombardier Peter" strode through the streets of Königsberg jostling the passersby, who cleared a path for him in fright. One day he stopped a noblewoman by shouting "Halt!," grabbed the watch she was wearing on her bodice, looked at the time, and went off, leaving the poor lady ready to faint. Another time he snatched off the wig of Frederick III's highly respectable master of ceremonies, threw it in a corner, and demanded that the courtier bring him women. One evening when he was having supper with the elector a servant dropped a plate and broke it on the marble floor. At the noise Peter leaped up, shouted, drew his sword, and made a few passes with it, fortunately wounding no one. He was calmed down by a promise that the offender would be whipped.

In spite of these aberrations, Peter had long political conversations with the very strict, dignified elector. Frederick III had it in mind to conclude a treaty of defensive alliance against Sweden. But Peter was evasive, because for the time being all his attention was focused on affairs in Poland. The death of John Sobieski had left two major candidates for the crown: the Prince de Conti, supported by France—that detestable ally of Turkey's—and Sobieski's son, the elector Frederick Augustus of Saxony, supported by Russia. Peter told anyone who would listen: "I would rather see the devil on that throne than Conti!" He sent the Polish Diet a letter announcing that he would intervene militarily if they made the wrong choice, and he backed up his words by ordering Romodanovsky to advance with his army to the Polish-Lithuanian border. To get a "free decision" out of an assembly, he thought, nothing was so effective as the presence of a few soldiers at the door of the conference room. Obliged to pronounce themselves under threat, the Polish lords came out with contradictory votes. Frederick Augustus seized Cracow and imposed his will, while the Prince de Conti, defeated, returned to France.

Having won his case, Peter continued on his way to Holland without stopping in Berlin. In Koppenbrügge (Hanover) he was invited to dinner by the electress Sophia of Hanover and her daughter Sophia Charlotte, electress of Brandenburg. He hesitated a long time before accepting, because the description he had been given of the two women was not reassuring. The mother, he had been told, was a ruin of flabby flesh who had replaced all her missing teeth with squares of wax. The daughter, aged twenty-nine, was apparently pretty, educated, and mischievous, and her two-year stay at the court of Versailles had given her French manners. She had read everything, was a friend of Leibniz's. As Peter rode in great pomp to the reception, he wondered which of the two was more to be feared, the worldly chatterbox or the toothless witch. Seated between the two women, who were observing him like some strange animal, he was at first very embarrassed. *"Ich kann nicht sprechen* (I cannot speak),'' he told them, covering his face with his hands. He ate with his fingers, in a slovenly way, dripped sauce on himself, didn't know how to use a napkin. But he soon yielded to the sparkling charm of his young dinner companion and entered into conversation with her. Sophia Charlotte was astonished by Peter's naturalness, his enthusiasm and quick repartee. She had expected to meet a crude muzhik, and now she was pleased to see a slender, vigorous, broad-shouldered young man of barely twenty-five, who was half a head taller than the giants in his bodyguard and had an energetic face with a round forehead, large black eyes under arched brows, and a fleshy mouth darkened by a small brown mustache. "He may have had no one to teach him how to eat properly," she noted, "but he has a natural, unconstrained manner and a lively mind." And: "He is at once very good and very bad. He is a perfect reflection of his country."

The meal lasted four hours. The Czar and Sophia Charlotte exchanged snuffboxes as a token of friendship. When Peter rose from table, quite his cheerful self again, he insisted that according to the custom in Moscow all courtiers should stand and drain their glasses four times at a single draught to the health of the Czar, the two princesses, and the elector. He then listened graciously to Sophia Charlotte's Italian singers and ordered drinks to be poured for them to reward their talent, but confessed that he had no taste for music. "Perhaps you prefer hunting?" asked Electress Sophia of Hanover. "My father was fond of hunting," Peter replied, "but as for me, I prefer sailing, shooting off fireworks, and building boats!" And he proudly showed the two women his calloused hands.

The evening continued with a ball. They danced until four in the morning. Peter wanted to put on gloves for the occasion, but none could be found in his baggage. He therefore stepped boldly forward with bare hands. In his enthusiasm he felt as if he were at a gathering in the German Settlement. The nobles in his suite were mystified when they felt under their fingers the whalebone corsets of their dancing partners. Were the ladies' ribs so near the surface? "These German ladies have devilish hard bones!" Peter exclaimed. He summoned one of his fools and as the assemblage did not appear to be amused by the fellow's contortions, drove him out with a broom. The ten-year-old Princess Sophia Dorothea he liked so much that he picked her up by the ears, kissed her on both cheeks, and set her down again, having ruined her coiffure. But no matter what he did the two electresses were delighted. "He is a completely extraordinary man," wrote the mother. "It is impossible to describe him or even to imagine him without having seen him!" And the daughter was so much of the same opinion that reporting her impressions in a letter to Fuchs, she left unfinished a very suggestive sentence: "That's enough of all this to tire you; but there's nothing I can do about it; I love to talk about the Czar, and if I followed my inclination I would tell you more than . . ."[3]

When Peter left Koppenbrügge he sent Sophia Charlotte four sable skins and three pieces of damask that the princess didn't know what to do with: they were just big enough for upholstering chairs.

On the evening of August 7, 1697, Peter, having left most of his suite behind, arrived in Amsterdam with Menshikov, four boyars, and an interpreter. But instead of stopping in the great commercial and industrial city, he hired a boat and had himself taken to Zaandam, a little port he had heard about in Russia from his friends the Dutch carpenters. As soon as he set eyes on the town with its shipyards, windmills, melting-houses for whale oil, and workshops for the manufacture of clocks and ship's tackle, he was charmed by the bustle in the streets and the prosperity of the inhabitants. On the banks of the canal leading to the sea he chanced upon a fisherman who turned out to be a certain Gerrit Kist who had been a blacksmith in Voronezh. Peter hailed him, embraced him, asked him to keep his identity secret, and without more ado moved in with him. In the little wooden house he had two rooms, a stove, and a mattress stowed in an armoire with folding doors.* No one to serve him; he meant to make his own bed and cook his own meals. The better to get inside the new part he was playing, he bought the sort of clothes worn by native boatmen: red jacket, collarless justaucorps with big buttons, wide knee-breeches, conical felt hat. Thus attired, "Master Peter" (*Peterbaas*) or "Carpenter Peter of Zaandam" went off to wield ax and plane in the shipyards. But he took time out to stroll the streets and visit sawmills, roperies, oil presses, and workshops for precision instruments. Everywhere he went he asked questions and took notes. In a paper factory he took over the press from which sheets were being drawn and performed the delicate task perfectly. While downing numerous mugs of beer at an inn he concluded the purchase of a small boat. He repaired it, fitted it with a mast and sail, and went to try it out on the Zaan River. When he returned to port he was beset by a crowd of curious onlookers. Had he been recognized? A certain Cornelius came up and stared at him open-mouthed, so insistently that Peter slapped him. "Bravo!" shouted the spectators. "Now you've been knighted!" Peter went sailing on other occasions, sometimes with feminine companionship. "The Czar has run across a peasant girl in Zaandam who has taken his fancy, and on holidays he goes out in his boat alone with her to make love, after the manner of Hercules," says the unknown author of a letter preserved by Leibniz.[4]

The inhabitants of Zaandam had soon realized that the Russian giant was a nobleman of the first importance. One of their compatriots had sent them a description of the Czar from Russia: "Tall, with a head that shakes, his right arm in constant motion, and a small wart on the right cheek." No possible doubt: it was he! Now the Dutch were so curious about him that he could no longer go anywhere without being followed by a troop of staring citizens. They came to watch him work at the shipyard or steer his yacht. They gathered in front of his house. The burgomaster was obliged to post guards to keep the crowd away. At the end of a week in

*This cottage still exists. Protected by brick walls, it is open to the public. Visitors have included Grand Duke Paul of Russia, Joseph II, Gustave III, Alexander I, Napoleon and Marie Louise, Alexander II, the poet Zhukovsky, and other notables.

Zaandam Peter packed his bags in exasperation, boarded his frail boat, and, despite the bad weather, set sail for Amsterdam again.

Not long after, the Great Embassy joined him there. As the procession passed, a noisy throng crowded around to admire the ambassadors all dressed in gold and glittering with pearls and diamonds in their state carriages, the twenty-four Haiduks* carrying silver axes and big scimitars, the court lackeys in scarlet livery, and in the last carriage the solitary giant in the uniform of a junior officer who people said was the Czar. The municipal authorities did the honors. He visited the town hall, went to the theater to attend a ballet, *The Charms of Armide,* and a comedy, *The False Lawyer,* drank heavily at interminable official dinners, applauded fireworks as a connoisseur, and participated enthusiastically in a mock naval battle. But despite all the festivities he retained his interest in serious work. He asked his new friend Burgomaster Witsen, with whom he had once corresponded about the purchase of ships in Holland, to arrange for him to work in the great shipyards of the East India Company. His wish was quickly granted. Under the name of Peter Timmermann he was engaged as a carpenter in Ostenburg. He took lodgings in a foreman's house and every day at sunup hastened to the shipyard to work with ax, plane, and adze and to help carry beams. Sometimes he would sit down exhausted on a log, rest his ax between his legs, wipe the sweat from his forehead with the back of his hand, and inhale the good smell of wood, pitch, tar, and brine. "We are working here not out of necessity," he wrote to Patriarch Adrian, "but in order to learn the maritime arts and to be able on our return to triumph over the enemies of Jesus Christ and by His grace to become the liberators of the Christians. That is a hope that I shall never cease to cherish until my last breath."

Thus while devoting himself to his favorite task, he never lost sight of politics. Every post brought him letters from Moscow. He kept informed about European affairs. When he learned about the Treaty of Ryswick, which was such a relief to the Dutch, he guessed that Louis XIV was only playing for time. "Here," he wrote Vinius, "the idiots are rejoicing and the sensible people are not, because

---

*Attendants dressed in Hungarian semimilitary costume.—TRANS.

they know that the Frenchman is deceiving them and that there will soon be war again." He discussed his political concerns with his companions, but he didn't want any of them to be idle. He divided up all the "volunteers" among various shipyards and workshops to learn manual trades. Some worked as carpenters, others specialized in manufacturing sails or assembling rigging, still others studied navigation. In a few months the Czar obtained from his employer, Gerrit Claes Pool, the following certificate:

"Piter has shown himself a good and skillful carpenter in the construction of the hundred-foot frigate *Peter and Paul,* which he worked on from start to finish. In addition, having under my guidance made a thorough study of naval architecture and the drawing of plans, he has, I think, fitted himself to practice those arts."

But soon he had to lay down his tools to go to The Hague, where the Great Embassy was to be received in audience by the members of the States General. Time and again on the way Peter ordered his carriage to stop so that he could measure a bridge, visit a windmill, or question the workers in a sawmill. In The Hague he refused to sleep in the sumptuous apartment that had been prepared for him and went to an inn where one of his servants was already asleep on a bearskin in an alcove. He awoke the man with a kick. "I want your place," he said. The representatives of the States General who were present at the scene exchanged looks of consternation. After this incident they were not surprised when the Czar, persisting in his pretense of traveling incognito, refused to take part in the solemn reception and asked to be left in an adjoining room from which he could see everything without being seen. Unfortunately, other people had had the same idea. Annoyed at having company in his hiding place, he decided to leave. But in order to do so he had to cross the audience chamber, so he demanded that the members of the States General stand facing the wall while he passed. The forty-eight deputies protested, saying that etiquette forbade them to turn their backs on a sovereign. When the Czar appeared they arose as one and bowed. He threw them a withering look, pulled his wig down over his nose, and stalked furiously toward the door. After this unfortunate interruption the ceremony continued with all due pomp. The three Russian ambassadors were dressed one more splendidly than the next:

caftans of cloth of gold lined with fur, tunics of black satin with the double-headed eagle embroidered in gold on the back. Feodor Golovin delivered a long speech in Russian that was translated by an interpreter. Lefort offered his hosts six hundred pairs of sable skins. The members of the States General promised to examine the Great Embassy's proposal concerning the possibility of the Low Countries' supporting Russia against the Turks, the affairs of Poland, and the use of the port of Archangel.

Peter, meanwhile, was so busy he scarcely knew what to do next. Insatiable and unmethodical, he ran here and there, visited shipyards, saw the whalers return from Greenland, studied the technique of printing, attended Professor Ruysch's anatomy lectures, and, when showed the perfectly preserved corpse of a child, thought it so beautiful that he embraced it effusively. He took the noblemen of his suite to the anatomy hall of the celebrated Dr. Boerhaave, the Theatrum Anatomicum, to witness a dissection. Looking at the inert body whose arteries had been laid bare, he had a sense of exultation in the presence of the mystery of the human machine. As two of the boyars did not seem to share his fascination, he forced them, we are told, to bite into the muscles of the cadaver.

He wanted to know everything about the articulation of the bones, the system of veins and arteries, the functions of the major organs, the production of the humors. Notwithstanding his incompetence, he resolutely participated in operations and bought a kit of surgical instruments that thereafter he took with him wherever he went. Having seen a tooth puller at work in a public square, he was suddenly fired with enthusiasm for the art, learned the rudiments as quickly as possible, and acquired all the necessary instruments. Henceforth he looked upon the 250 subjects in his retinue from a different angle. They became his patients and were obliged to submit to a close inspection of their mouths. If any tooth looked dubious to him, he pulled it out. The roars of the unfortunate victims, far from restraining him, only increased his determination. His herculean strength was a great help to him in his labors. It was not unusual for him to get carried away and remove a piece of the gum as well. No one dared protest these assaults by the sovereign. Some people considered it an honor to have had a tooth extracted by him. One might hope that a promotion would come of it, or even friendship. All his life Peter was to consider himself an excellent dentist. He kept the teeth drawn from his courtiers in a little bag and often examined the collection proudly. Each tooth recalled a face convulsed with pain.

The same hand that wielded the scalpel or the forceps also handled the burin. He took advantage of his stay in Holland to learn the elements of copper engraving. Obviously, all the notions he acquired in this way were superficial and unsystematic. His voracious intellectual appetite—a mixture of restless curiosity, caprice, and sudden impulse—stemmed from Russia's cultural backwardness. He wanted to become a one-man walking encyclopedia so that he could impart his freshly acquired skills to his compatriots: it was as much for them as for himself that he was making this hasty inventory of Western knowledge.

When he returned to Amsterdam he resumed his labors as a carpenter, celebrated, glass in hand, a victory of the Russians over the Turks, and impetuously embraced the burgomaster at the launching of the ship *Amsterdam,* which he had worked on. But he decided that he had learned everything he could from the Dutch and that for advanced studies in shipbuilding he must go to England.

King William III, whom he had met in Utrecht and in The Hague, sent him his personal yacht escorted by three ships of the line. The Czar was so moved on parting from Lefort that the members of his entourage were astonished. "They embraced each other so hard," wrote the general's brother, "that they both began to weep in the presence of a number of persons."[5] Leaving most of his retinue in Amsterdam and accompanied only by Menshikov and a few boyars, Peter set sail on January 7, 1698. Knowing his guest's tastes, the king had appointed as his guide the Marquis of Carmarthen, a redoubtable consumer of brandy and gin who could have shown Lefort a thing or two in that line. In London the travelers were received in a magnificent house situated at 15 Buckingham Street. As was his wont, the Czar disdained the beautiful chamber intended for him and moved into another, more modest one with three of his servants. When William III entered the cramped little room to greet his guest, he was choked by the stench and asked that the window be opened despite the cold. A few days later Peter paid him a visit at Kensington Palace. There he never glanced at the paintings, tapestries, and precious furniture and was interested only in an anemometer. At his request the Marquis of Carmarthen showed him the Academy of Sciences, Oxford University, Windsor Castle, the Woolwich Arsenal, the Tower of London "where they imprison good English folk," the Mint, the Observatory, a coffin factory, a cannon foundry, shipyards, docks, and so on. Intrigued by the English parliamentary system, Peter secretly witnessed a session of the House of Lords. Wishing to remain unobserved, he perched in a gutter on the rooftop and peered in through a skylight to see the king on his throne and all the great men of the kingdom on their benches. Following the debates with the help of an interpreter, he told his companions: "It's good to hear subjects speaking the truth openly. That's something we must copy from the English!" Did he really think so, he who tolerated no opposition, no sharing of power?

In a laconic journal kept by one of the Czar's traveling companions there occasionally appears the notation: "We stayed at home and were very merry." A euphemism for a grand Russian-style drinking bout. One day Peter, who was fond of monstrosities of all kinds, had brought to him a woman who was seven and a half feet tall; when she held out her arm, he passed under it without bending his head. But it was another woman who captured the Czar's fancy: the actress Laetitia Cross. He amused himself with her but when it came time to pay for the lady's favors he proved so parsimonious that she broke out cursing. When people advised him to be more generous he replied: "For five hundred guineas I find men to serve me well with their minds and hearts. This harlot served me indifferently with what she has to give, which is worth less."[6] He won back the five hundred guineas—the wages of love —by betting on a boxing match and backing one of his grenadiers against an English pugilist.

Peter was delighted with the services of the Marquis of Carmarthen, who was both his cicerone and his drinking companion, and for twenty thousand pounds granted him the privilege of exporting to Russia three thousand barrels of tobacco. To be sure, he was a smoker himself, but he was aware that the Russian Church opposed the use of "the devil's weed." When his advisers expressed some anxiety lest Patriarch Adrian object, he exclaimed: "Do you think I don't know how to make a priest obey me?"

In England he met another ecclesiastic, Bishop Burnet of Salisbury, who had been assigned to take him to religious services and explain the dogmas of the different churches. The prelate observed the impatient visitor disapprovingly and noted in his memoirs: "He is a man of a very hot temper soon inflamed, and very brutal in his passion; he raises his natural heat by drinking much brandy, which he rectifies himself [i.e., which tendency he tries to correct] with great application: he is subject to convulsive motions all over his body. . . . He wants not capacity and has a larger measure of knowledge than might be expected from his education, which was very indifferent. . . . He is mechanically turned and seems designed by nature rather to be a ship-carpenter than a great prince. This was his chief study and exercise, while he stayed here: he wrought much with his own hands, and made all about him work at the models of ships. . . . There was a mixture both of passion and severity in his temper. . . . After I had seen him often, and had conversed much with him, I could not but adore [i.e., wonder at] the depth of the providence of God, that had raised up such a furious man to so absolute an authority over so great a part of the world."[7]

Peter soon tired of London and moved to John Evelyn's house in Deptford on the Thames, near the royal shipyards. There he was not content to use an ax and drink beer with the local workmen. He consulted the most qualified engineers and seamen and filled his notebooks with hasty notes. "I would have remained a carpenter all my life if I had not studied in England," he said.

As always with Peter, the studies were complemented by orgies. In the evening, after the day's work, the Russians abandoned themselves to such excesses that the neighbors listened with terror to their shouts and laughter. They slept anywhere, ate anything at any hour, respected neither furniture nor paintings. When John Evelyn regained possession of his house after three months of occupation by the Czar and his suite, he was horrified: the doors and windows had been taken down and burned, the hangings had been torn down or soiled with vomit and spit, precious parquet floorboards were smashed to pieces, masterpieces of painting were riddled with bullet holes (every portrait having served as a target), and flowerbeds were trampled as if a regiment had camped in the garden. Evelyn had the police draw up an official statement of the damages: they came to 350 pounds sterling. The royal treasury reimbursed the owner in that amount without anyone's making the slightest remonstrance to the illustrious visitor. Quite the contrary: William III declared he was so happy to have received such an excellent guest that he asked him to pose for the court painter Sir Godfrey Kneller. He would keep the portrait, he said, as a souvenir of their meeting.* In addition, he begged the Czar to accept as a gift the frigate *Royal Transport,* which he had already sailed on English waters. In exchange, Peter gave him a big uncut diamond, wrapped in a bit of dirty paper.

At the end of April 1698, Peter was back in Holland, where the Great Embassy was waiting for him. The request presented to the States General for help against the Turks had not been granted as expected. Moreover, the health of Charles II of Spain was rapidly declining. There were going to be great upheavals. He had to take defensive measures. Off to Vienna! When the Russians departed there were many sighs of relief. "The state and our little town have been relieved of—delivered from—this visit that was so celebrated, such an honor, so extraordinary, and so onerous," wrote Noomen. And indeed, the cost of the visit had come to 300,000 florins instead of the 100,000 allotted for it in the budget.

The journey to the capital of the Holy Roman Empire lasted three weeks. At the gates of Vienna the long convoy of carriages had to wait for a column of troops to pass, and Peter was furious. Determined to remain incognito, he was nevertheless wounded by this lack of respect. It was not he they were insulting but Russia. As soon as he had had his first contacts with Austrian diplomats he understood that the emperor was in no hurry to receive him, especially since the Czar intended to present himself at the palace as an ordinary private person. At last he was given an appointment at the Palace of the Favorite. Thither he went wearing a dark caftan, a poor cravat around his neck, a gilt sword at his side, and

*It now hangs in Kensington Palace.

no sword knot. Lefort went along to act as interpreter. A servant showed them in, not by the main entrance but by a little side door, had them climb a spiral staircase, and preceded them down a gallery. In the presence of Leopold, who appeared in all his majesty, Peter was suddenly flustered and kissed his hand. He kept nervously taking his hat off and putting it on again until his interlocutor begged him to keep it on his head. After fifteen minutes of commonplace conversation, the Czar withdrew, in a rage. But when he went out into the garden he saw a Venetian gondola on a pond. With childish glee he jumped into the boat and rowed it over the water, leaving the Austrian chamberlains flabbergasted.

Some time later the emperor received the Great Embassy at last. Peter hid among the boyars of second rank. Respecting his wish to remain anonymous, Leopold raised his hat slightly and asked Lefort: "How is our beloved brother, the Czar?" Lefort replied imperturbably: "When we left His Majesty in Moscow, he was in as good health as one could wish." The audience was followed by a state dinner. In the banquet hall the heat was stifling and the ambassadors, bundled up in their caftans of fur-lined brocade, were sweating profusely. Defying etiquette, they withdrew for a few minutes to change. In the course of the meal six different wines were served. Lefort asked the emperor for permission to give a taste of them to his "friend," a "simple volunteer" who was standing behind his chair. The "volunteer," of course, was none other than the Czar. Once again the emperor bowed to the peculiar wishes of his guest who, it seemed, was comfortable only in disguise.

Nevertheless, Peter visited the empress and the imperial princesses; he met Prince Eugene of Savoy and the king of the Romans, Joseph, Leopold's son.* On St. Peter's Day he attended a religious service in the church of the Jesuits and immediately afterward lit a display of fireworks with his own hands. "There was much drinking," he wrote to Vinius, "and several couples got married in the garden." The emperor, not to be outdone, invited the ambassadors to a costume ball. Peter appeared as a Frisian peasant; the emperor and empress came as innkeepers. The innkeeper drank

*Later to become emperor.

the health of the Frisian peasant, and vice versa. The dancing went on until dawn.

Despite these festivities, Peter had to admit that on the diplomatic level, the results of his journey were quite negative. The Treaty of Ryswick was hardly signed and Europe was already preparing for another war, over the Spanish succession. The Dutch and British cabinets were focusing all their attention on that part of the world. The Austrians saw no reason to support Russia's claims, at least for the time being—they were even determined to negotiate with Turkey so as to free up all their troops for the West. Peter, whose plans for a crusade against the infidels were frustrated, began to think that it was not to the South that he should strike but to the North. Accordingly, he turned his attention from the Black Sea to the Baltic. He had been so coldly received by the Swedes in Riga! Such a proud people ought to be taught a lesson. By imposing the elector Frederick Augustus of Saxony as king of Poland, he had withdrawn that country from French influence and had laid the groundwork for an alliance against Charles XII. A good point for Russia.

Another good point: the recruitment of foreign experts. In the course of his travels Peter had been able to hire many reliable men who would come to Moscow and, he expected, do much to educate and advance his people. Among them were the excellent naval officer Cornelius Cruys, who would be made an admiral, Captain John Perry for the building of canals, Captain de Villebois, twenty-three commodores, thirty-five lieutenants, seventy-two pilots, fifty doctors, three hundred forty-five sailors, four cooks, and assorted craftsmen—six hundred forty persons in all. They were accompanied by a large quantity of equipment packed in two hundred sixty chests marked with the initials P.M. (Peter Mikhailov). In the jumble of hardware were muskets, pistols, cannon, sailcloth, drawing compasses, mariner's compasses, anchors, cork floats, three coffins, eight blocks of marble intended for a future school of fine arts, a stuffed crocodile, and the honorary doctorate that Peter had been awarded by Oxford University.

Obviously, the cost of the journey, including the purchases, had been very high: the figure mentioned is three million rubles. The trip had lasted eighteen months, but not for a moment during this long ramble through the lands of science and good manners had Peter neglected the affairs of Russia. Everything he saw and heard brought him back to his native land, so remote, so crude, so threatened. He inquired after the construction of forts in Azov and Taganrog, followed events in Poland, and even concerned himself with Russian influence in China. "You tell me," he wrote Vinius, "that an Orthodox church has been built in Peking and that many Chinese have converted. That is very good, but for God's sake proceed cautiously and gradually in this matter so as not to anger the Chinese rulers or offend the Jesuits, who have been established there for a long time."

To complete his survey of Europe and to study the building of galleys at first hand, he had wanted to go from Vienna to Venice. The preparations for departure were already well under way when an urgent message reached him from Moscow: the *streltsy* had revolted again. Beside himself with anger, the Czar cried: "The seed of the Miloslavskys has sprouted again!" And taking an abrupt leave of the Austrian court, he jumped into a post chaise and sped toward Russia. Lefort and Feodor Golovin followed him at a short distance. The rest of the Great Embassy stayed where they were, awaiting instructions. In the light, jolting vehicle Peter could hardly master his impatience. He was torn between the desire to get back to his capital as soon as possible and the fear of compromising the diplomatic results of the journey by racing home. His concern for internal politics commanded him to return in haste; his concern for external politics commanded him to take his time. The call of the motherland was the stronger. When the house is on fire, first you have to save the walls; the garden can wait. Peter rolled day and night without stopping, straight for Moscow. Thirty horsemen were his only escort. He didn't even see the countries he passed through. He was straining toward a single goal: to annihilate the *streltsy*. In his mind they had taken the place of the Turks.

7

The Revolt
of the
Streltsy

On the way Peter learned fresh details about the revolt of the *streltsy*. Sent away from the capital as a punishment after the conspiracy of 1697, these men, accustomed to the peaceful life of Moscow, had been unable to endure the hard conditions of guard duty on the Turkish and Polish frontiers. Separated from their wives and children, badly fed, badly paid, and badly treated, they had seized upon the Czar's departure for foreign lands as an opportunity to return home in force. At the end of March 1698 four regiments of *streltsy* who had been transferred from the South to the West had sent to Moscow a delegation of 175 soldiers to demand the return of the entire troop. They had immediately made contact with the Czarevna Sophia in Novodevichy Convent and she, it was said, had encouraged them to play for high stakes.

Terrible news spread like wildfire throughout the army: the Czar had died in a distant land, the boyars wanted to eliminate the Czarevna Sophia and the Czarevich Alexis, the pagans in the German Settlement were conspiring to seize power and sell Russia to the heretics. Inflamed by these reports, the regiments of *streltsy* marched on Moscow. Their goal was to impose their will on the boyars and to put Sophia back on the throne. At first Peter had berated Romodanovsky roundly for his weakness in dealing with the rebels' demands: "Why didn't you order an investigation?" he wrote. "May God be your judge. . . . You think I am dead because the mail is late; you are afraid and you dare not take any action. No one is dead, thank God, we are all alive. Why are you so frightened, like an old woman? Is someone any the less living because a messenger goes astray? I expect nothing good to come of such cowardice!"

But when he reached Cracow he learned from other messages that the revolt had been crushed, thanks to the intervention of the regular army under Gordon. Wishing to avoid bloodshed, the Scottish general had first gone with a small escort to the camp of the mutineers and promised them their lives if they would lay down their arms and deliver up their leaders. They had rejected this proposal with screams of hatred and had prepared for combat. Artillery fire had soon overcome their resistance. Fifty-six ring-leaders had been hanged on the spot and 1,956 rebels thrown into prison. Order had now been restored. Moscow was calm under the stern surveillance of Romodanovsky. The Czar could prolong his travels if he liked.

Thus reassured, Peter decided to postpone his investigation of the affair and to go to Rawa near Lemberg to confer with Augustus II, the new king of Poland. The *streltsy* would get what was coming to them; they would keep.

The meeting with Augustus II was an explosion of friendship. The two monarchs were in agreement on everything: immoderate drinking, love of the army, and the necessity of forming an alliance against Sweden. In token of cordial relations, they exchanged clothes and swords. After three days of carousing and talking politics Peter continued his way home.

He arrived in Moscow at six o'clock in the evening on August 25, 1698. He didn't bother to visit his wife or even to pay his respects to the icon of Our Lady of Tver or the relics of the national saints but avoided the Kremlin entirely and hastened to the German Settlement, to his mistress Anna Mons's house and then to Lefort's. There he spent the night drinking with comrades in arms.

Early the next morning he began to receive the boyars who had flocked to pay him homage. He greeted them very affably, congratulated Gordon on his bold action, recounted his travels, spoke of his conversations with Augustus II, and then suddenly, brandishing a pair of scissors, cut off Generalissimo Schein's beard. The generalissimo stood dumbfounded, wondering what he had done to deserve this disfigurement, but the Czar was already attacking the hairy chin of Romodanovsky. All the boyars received the same treatment, except for Streshnev and Cherkassky. Tufts of hair lay strewn on the floor; the Czar roared with laughter as he clicked his shears, the noblemen looked at each other aghast. For the first time since adolescence they felt cool air on their chins. They were filled with a religious fear. Only recently, in a pastoral letter Patriarch Adrian had again condemned shaving: "It is not fitting to change the face of man. . . . The Savior Himself, our Christ, wore a beard. Similarly, the holy apostles, the great prophets, Constantine the Great, Theodosius the Great, Vladimir the Great all had beards and kept them as God-given ornaments. . . . Do you think it looks fine to shave your beard and leave only the mustache? It was not men whom God created like that but dogs and cats. . . . To shave one's beard is not only a horror and a dishonor, it is a mortal sin. . . . Orthodox men, do not give in to this diabolical inclination! . . . Where will you stand at the time of the Last Judgment: with the saints whose faces are adorned with beards or with the shaven heretics?" These words still echoed in the ears of the gentlemen standing astonished and shorn. But one could not resist the Czar's will. If he had taken an aversion to beards, it was because in his eyes they represented the prejudices and superstitions, all the dark past of a people that he wanted to drag into the light of the West.

When they went home the boyars had to face their weeping wives, who were not to be consoled at seeing them deprived of the noblest attribute of manhood. Five days later, during a banquet at Generalissimo Schein's, the Czar, who was in high good humor, commanded a twenty-five-gun salute and ordered his favorite clown to attack the beards that remained. The clown grasped handfuls of hair and cut into them, contorting his body the while. Those who had already been through the ordeal roared with laughter at the dismay of those whose turn it was now. At the next meeting—a feast with music and dancing for five hundred persons at Lefort's—Peter could admire with satisfaction the smooth cheeks of his companions. The faces of the Russians now resembled those of the Germans or Dutch. But their hearts? On that score, the Czar thought, there was still much to be done.

But it was not to play with scissors that he had rushed back to the capital. It was good to cut off the beards of friends, better to cut off the heads of enemies. Having been informed of the results of the investigation of the rebellion, he felt that the interrogations had not been conducted seriously enough and that it was important to prove that Sophia and her clique were responsible for the conspiracy.

This time he wanted to crush the *streltsy* once for all and put his half sister beyond the possibility of doing harm. And trust him to use a heavy hand. He appointed a commission of boyars, presided over by the terrible Romodanovsky, to question and judge the accused. For this purpose fourteen torture chambers were prepared with all the necessary apparatus. The guilty men, 1,714 of them, chained in the monasteries and prisons of Moscow, were taken to Preobrazhenskoye in batches of 130 and divided among the different torturers. The interrogations began on September 17 —Sophia's name day!—and lasted from six to eight hours a day. Sunday was a day of rest. Thirty bonfires were kept burning at all times on the perimeter of Preobrazhenskoye. As soon as a *strelets* refused to answer a question or denied the obvious facts, he was put to torture. Hanging by his wrists, he was given the knout. From thirty to forty blows an hour, the whistling lash cut his flesh to the bone. When the victim fainted, the doctors revived him. If he persisted in silence, his tormentors gave him the strappado, thrust burning brands into his flesh, burned his feet, tore him with red-hot pincers, broke his ribs with tongs. In the end the executioners grew weary of working over these pieces of bloody meat, and the judges and clerks went distracted amid the shrieks and death rattles. Only one man among them all seemed indefatigable: Peter. He attended all the tortures, intoxicated, so it seemed, by the smell of blood, pus, roast flesh, and excrement. He asked questions himself, insulted and struck the human rags who had scarcely strength to speak. Patriarch Adrian presented himself holding up in both hands the miraculous icon of the Virgin and begging him to have mercy upon the *streltsy* who had strayed. Peter exclaimed angrily: "Why this icon? Get out of here and go back to your place. Know that I venerate God and the Holy Mother as much as you do, but know also that my duty is to protect the people and to punish the criminals who conspire to ruin them!"

On September 30, 341 *streltsy* were taken two by two in carts to the place of execution. Tattered, haggard puppets, they staggered at every jolt. In their hands they held big lighted tapers. Wives, mothers, children ran after the carts uttering heartrending cries. At Pokrovsky Gate the convoy stopped in front of the Czar, who was on horseback. He had put on the Polish uniform that Augustus II had given him and was surrounded by a group of clean-shaven boyars. Also present were many officers and the entire diplomatic corps, who had been summoned the day before. A crowd of common people stood at a distance. The Czar had a clerk read the sentence condemning to death the "robbers, brigands, insulters of the cross, and rebels" of the *streltsy* regiments. The executions began: 201 of the condemned were hanged; 100 others, from fifteen to twenty years of age, were given the knout, branded on the right cheek, and sent to Siberia; 40 of the most important were taken back to prison to undergo further tortures.

This was only a first stage. When the judges and executioners had regained their strength, they went back to work. This time they questioned not only the *streltsy* but their wives and the princesses' maidservants. One of these servants gave birth in the midst of torments. Others were buried alive, according to ancient custom.[1] Peter went to visit his half sister Sophia to interrogate her in person. She denied having had anything to do with the plot. Her sister Martha admitted only that she had spoken to the ex-Regent about the forthcoming arrival of the *streltsy*, who were still devoted to her cause. And the *streltsy* too, despite the sufferings inflicted on them day after day, said little that advanced the inquiry. There was no proof that Sophia had been the soul of the conspiracy, and yet the Czar was convinced that she was responsible for it. From October 3 to 18, 772 *streltsy* were beheaded, quartered, or hanged. One hundred ninety-five of them were strung up on gibbets under Sophia's very windows in the garden of Novodevichy Convent where she was imprisoned. In the clenched hands of 3 of the corpses, the executioner had placed a copy of a petition that the mutineers were supposed to have addressed to the Czarevna. Peter could no longer restrain his appetite for vengeance. He wanted to drown in blood the memory of these revolts that had haunted him from earliest childhood. In front of the horrified ambassadors, he himself seized the ax and struck. Several contemporaries—the Austrian diplomats Korb and Guarient, the Frenchman Villebois, and others—attest the fact.

There is nothing surprising in Peter's having wanted to roll up his own sleeves. For him all activities were of equal value. He took pride in demonstrating that he excelled in the most diverse trades. Just as he meant to be a skillful sailor or carpenter, so he meant to hold his own with professional executioners. When he brought the blade down on the neck of a condemned man, he was only doing a job conscientiously. The spurting blood left him unmoved. To him, suffering was a natural phenomenon. His interest in the task he was accomplishing was not sadistic but scientific. He was not punishing, but operating. When he had finished, he felt the satisfaction of work well done, just as when he came back from the shipyard.*

At his order the corpses were to remain where they were for five months, swinging from gibbets or lying in the snow with limbs scattered. The approaches to the Kremlin were strewn with headless bodies that gave off a foul stench despite the cold. Hundreds of heads planted on pikes were prey to crows. At the sight of these shapeless leather balls without eyes or noses, with straw-colored hair, passersby gravely crossed themselves. In the beginning of 1699 the tribunal resumed its work in ten torture chambers. Another 137 men hanged and 285 knouted and branded with a red-hot iron. On February 3, 1699, General Lefort's nephew wrote

---

*Certain authors have been shocked at the idea that the Czar could have beheaded a number of persons with his own hands (five according to Korb, eighty-four according to Kurt Kersten, some hundred according to Villebois, etc.). They claim that the reports of contemporaries were based on gossip and should be dismissed so as not to tarnish the image of the great man. It seems to me that, quite the contrary, Peter's violent, vengeful nature and his tendency to carry everything to extremes make it very probable that he participated directly in the executions, as memoirs of the time relate.

from Moscow: "Today there are condemned to death three hundred more of those unfortunates who wanted to send us to the other world. His Majesty has ordered that all foreigners should be there to see them executed. They are the last. All the others have already received their sentences."[2]

After they had been left on display for a long time, the decomposed corpses were finally piled onto carts and sent to different cities in the provinces, where they lay in heaps in the public squares for the edification of the people. Later they were buried in mass graves. Over each stood a column with an iron plaque on which were engraved the crimes of the deceased, whose heads were fixed on stakes.

As soon as the executions were over, the sixteen regiments of *streltsy* were dissolved. The men were sent away from Moscow and forbidden to move without a passport or to take service again in the army. Wives and children of the offenders also had to leave the capital, and people were forbidden to give them shelter or work: let them become beggars, let hunger and cold complete the task of the executioners.

As for Sophia, since her guilt had not been proved, Peter merely forced her to take the veil in Novodevichy Convent, to which she had already been relegated. Stripped of her titles and confined to a narrow cell, she became Sister Suzanne, a nun like the others.* Martha, likewise accused of having been involved in the plot, met the same fate, at the Convent of the Assumption, under the name of Sister Margaret.

The convent struck Peter as an excellent solution for getting rid of women. His wife had long been a burden to him. After the elegant, sprightly females he had known abroad, Eudoxia seemed dowdy, dull, without spice or mystery. He found her deplorably Russian. She belonged to an anachronistic world that he had sworn to do away with. He had not written her once during his journey. On his return he summoned her to Postmaster Vinius's and advised her coldly to withdraw to a cloister. She indignantly refused. What crime had she committed to deserve such a punishment? Never had her name been pronounced during the investigation of

---

*She was to die five years later, on July 14, 1704, at the age of forty-seven.

the machinations of the *streltsy*. She loved the Czar with all her soul. And she was the mother of the Czarevich. Was it possible that Peter meant to separate her from her son? Patriarch Adrian intervened in support of the legitimate wife. Peter dismissed him angrily and after enduring three weeks of Eudoxia's tears and solemn oaths, had her bundled into a simple two-horse carriage and sent without escort of any kind to the Convent of the Intercession of the Holy Virgin in Suzdal. Her nine-year-old son, Alexis, had been taken from the poor woman and entrusted to the care of her worst enemy, Peter's favorite sister, Natalya. At the age of twenty-six Eudoxia, repudiated and stripped of her titles and privileges, became Sister Helen. She received not one kopeck of allowance and had no one to serve her. In want of everything, she wrote to her brother, Abraham Lopukhin: "I do not need much, but one still has to eat. I do not drink myself, but I would like to be able to offer drink to others. . . . Here there is nothing. Everything is rotten. I know that I am a trouble to you, but what am I to do? While I live, for pity's sake feed me, give me drink, clothe the poor beggar woman!"

Since Eudoxia was henceforth the "bride of Christ," she could no longer be the bride of the Czar. Peter considered himself totally freed from the bonds of marriage. In the eyes of the Church itself he was a kind of widower, free and ready for other adventures. During the great punitive campaign he had performed at table with incredible gusto, as if the sight of blood and tears whetted his appetite for drink. He had gone from scaffold to banquet hall and from banquet hall to scaffold. Actually, torture was common in the world of his time, as one of the obligatory elements of justice. Peter's father, Alexis, "the very peaceable Czar," had had more than seven thousand persons executed after the Moscow revolt of 1663. Why should his son have been more magnanimous? Besides, the methods of torture that he applied were more or less the same as those in other countries. In acting as he did, Peter had no sense that he was betraying his European models. At most the difference was his enthusiasm, his Slavic tendency to excess.

Having cut off heads, he turned again to cutting off beards. He was obsessed with his subjects' hair. More and more he regarded it as an insult to civilization. His associates, the members of his inner circle, were clean shaven, but the others? The English engineer John Perry wrote that the Russians "had a kind of religious respect and veneration for their beards; and so much the more, because they differed herein from strangers [i.e., foreigners]." He noted that it was their custom "like the Patriarchs of old, to wear long beards hanging down upon their bosoms, which they combed out with pride and kept smooth and fine, without one hair to be diminished."[3] Since he could not personally undertake to shear all his people properly, Peter published a ukase forbidding all but members of the clergy to wear beards. Those who, notwithstanding the wishes of the Czar, wanted to keep hair on their chins had to pay a tax determined by their social status. One hundred rubles a year for noblemen and high officials; sixty rubles for courtiers and tradesmen; thirty rubles for lackeys and coachmen; a half-kopeck for peasants on entering and leaving the city. As a receipt each of them was given a bronze medallion with the inscription, "The tax has been collected." The medal was also engraved with the picture of a beard and sometimes the motto, "The beard is a useless burden." Individuals thus taxed were required to carry their medallions with them and to produce them on demand; they were to be renewed every year. Most of the nobles and merchants found the tax too heavy and shaved their faces in the end. But the peasants preferred to pay their dues as they passed through the gates of the city and come home to the village with flowing beards like true males and true Christians. Captain Perry tells the story of how one day in the shipyards of Voronezh he met an old carpenter he knew coming clean-shaven from the barber's and asked him in jest what he had done with his beard. Whereupon, says Perry, "he put his hand in his bosom and pulled it out and showed it to me; further telling me, that when he came home, he would lay it up to have it put in his coffin and buried along with him, that he might be able to give an account of it to St. Nicholas, when he came to the other world; and that all his brothers (meaning his fellow-workmen, who had been shaved that day) had taken the same care."[4]

In short, while the nobility, wealthy merchants, army, and navy had willy-nilly adopted the new fashion, the Russian masses remained hostile to it. Peter was surrounded by a clearing of felled beards, but ten steps away there was still forest. Other, harsher ukases followed: if a bearded man came to an office, his request was to be denied; he would be obliged to pay fifty rubles, and if he was unable to do so he would be sent to Roggervik to work off his fine. Anyone who met a bearded man not dressed according to regulations could take him by force before the police authorities. As a reward, he would receive half the fine on the beard and the recalcitrant's clothes.

But was it conceivable to have beardless, modern European faces above long Byzantine caftans? The dress had to match the face. Having attacked beards, Peter now attacked apparel. In Russia garments had not varied for a century. Stiff and ample, worn one on top of another, they were awkward in cut and superb in ornamentation. A velvet collar stood high framing the jaws. Very wide sleeves were closed at the wrists with buttons made of semiprecious stones. A coat of rich stuff fell to the heels. In winter an enormous fur pelisse was the top layer worn by a boyar, proud of his potbelly girdled with a Persian sash. His fur hat was inordinately tall. For a long time the Czar, who liked simplicity and comfort, had been offended by this unalterable costume. He thought the men bundled up in brocade and satin looked like bulky, lazy, hairy women. Some of them, indeed, like the boyar Plescheyev, had their court robes cut out of their wives' old gowns.[5] A great strapping fellow might wear an earring sparkling between two locks of hair. All of them moved slowly and stiffly. Ridiculing their long, loose sleeves, Peter said: "See, these things are in your way. You are safe nowhere with them. At one moment you upset a glass, then you forgetfully dip them in the sauce."[6] He had no better an opinion of the clothes of the Russian muzhiks. They were made without pockets, so that, according to a traveler,* they were obliged to carry "their papers in their boots and their money in their mouths." During the solemn processions of the Great Embassy abroad, Peter had noticed that the onlookers made fun of the Russian getup. Working in shipyards he had become even more convinced that a young and active people needed clothes that didn't hinder their movements. If Russia was going to stride boldly forward, she couldn't be all tangled up in finery dating from the time of Boris Godunov.

*The Croatian Knijanich.

The Czar's own wardrobe included just one old-style caftan, which he had worn as a joke at the wedding of two of his buffoons. For the rest, he had nothing but military uniforms of wool—gray, black, green, or "carnation."

On January 4, 1700, a ukase decreed that "boyars, courtiers, and officials in Moscow and other cities must dress in the Hungarian fashion, the outer caftan reaching down to the garter and the inner one shorter, of the same sort." On August 20 of the same year the application of the ukase was expanded in the following terms: "For the glory and beautification of the State and the military administration, men of all categories excepting the clergy, servants of the Church, coachmen, and peasant farmers, are to wear Hungarian or German dress. Their wives and daughters likewise are to wear Hungarian or German dress." Poor people, however, were given a delay of five years in which to wear out their old clothes. The following year the new costume was described in further detail: for men, German jacket, pants, boots, shoes, and hats, French or Saxon overcoats; for ladies, German skirts and shoes, hats with turned-up brims.

Models of these garments were displayed at the gates of the city, and those who failed to obey the ukase were fined: forty kopecks for pedestrians and one ruble for those on horseback. In addition, it was not uncommon for the inspectors to slash to pieces garments that did not conform to the rules. The Czar himself had fun cutting off the sleeves of some of his close companions when he found them too long. Soon all the boyars at his receptions were wearing woolen frock coats. Unaccustomed to this curious garb, they looked at each other and laughed as at a masquerade. Peter himself guffawed at the sight of the troop of dressed-up monkeys. He was looking at a caricature of Europe. But he had no doubt that in time all these Russians would come to have the elegance of the English, the Austrians, the French. Of course some of the old dignitaries complained that their legs were cold in the knee-breeches and exposed stockings. They whispered that such garments were not suited to the harsh climate of Russia. The young Czar, they said, didn't show enough respect for ancestral wisdom. However, no one dared protest openly.

Another reform that conflicted with people's habits related to the calendar. According to the Russian calendar, which was faithful to Byzantine tradition, the year began on September 1, the alleged day of the creation of the world in the year 5508 before the birth of Jesus Christ. In other words, according to the Russians Peter had been born in 7180 (1672), and in Moscow the year 1700 was the year 7208. On December 20, 1699, at the turn of the century, Peter issued a ukase ordering that henceforth years were to be counted in the European style, each year beginning on January 1. Still, he did not go so far as to adopt the Gregorian calendar, which, since it was the one used by Rome, could not be suitable for the Orthodox, and settled for the Julian calendar, which was eleven days behind.* On January 1, 1700, he decreed that all people "should decorate their doors with branches of pine and juniper, in accordance with the models displayed in the great market and at the pharmacy in the lower part of town." The entire population was ordered to attend services that day and to exchange new year's wishes as they left the church. Those who owned muskets were invited to shoot them off as a sign of joy. The troops massed in Red Square set the example at noon with artillery and musket salvos. In the evening fireworks lit up the sky. These officially imposed rejoicings did not correspond to any deep feeling of gladness in the hearts of the Muscovites. Some of them muttered: "Could God have created the world in winter?" Others, among the Old Believers, went further: "The Bible announces that the Antichrist will change the time. Peter I is therefore the Antichrist."

In 1699, as an incentive to the nobility, Peter had founded the first Russian order of knighthood: the Order of St. Andrew, patron saint of Russia. Members wore a broad pale-blue cordon across their chests. In 1702 the *terems* were opened, women were given access to social gatherings, and an obligatory six-week engagement period before marriage was instituted, during which time the couple were allowed to see each other freely. A year later the first Russian newspaper appeared in Moscow; it was *The News,* a four-page collection of brief notes on what was going on in Russia and

---

*The discrepancy was twelve days in the nineteenth century and thirteen days by the twentieth. The difference between the old and the new style was abolished on February 1, 1918, by the government of the USSR.

Europe. From time to time a piece of information was provided to enlighten the readers: "Lisbon, the capital of Portugal, is located on the Tagus, in Europe. . . . Versailles: village and place of recreation for the King of France, not far from Paris. . . . A lord is an English boyar."[7] The newly created printing houses used secular Russian characters as opposed to the old Slavonic-Serbian alphabet preserved by the Church. Quinte-Curce's *Life of Alexander* was translated, manuals of arithmetic were prepared and even a dictionary. The French envoy Baluze attended a performance of two comedies, one in Russian, the other in German, and wrote to Louis XIV: "The auditorium is made of wood, but large; the boxes are well arranged and the theater is quite deep."[8]

While the Czar was in the midst of all these efforts to modernize the country, he suffered two bereavements that came like undeserved punishments from heaven. He was in the shipyard of Voronezh when he learned that his friend Lefort had died, on March 2, 1699. At the age of forty-three, Lefort, infantry general, admiral, leader of the Great Embassy, and irreplaceable drinking companion, had succumbed to overwork and excesses. "My friend is no more!" the Czar sobbed. "He was the only one who was faithful to me! Whom can I count on now?" Returning to Moscow in haste, he had the coffin opened, kissed the forehead and hands of the corpse, and insisted on a magnificent funeral. As the cortege moved toward the reformed church, it was led by the Czar in deep mourning. A rider dressed in black and carrying a naked sword with the point down preceded the body. The coffin was borne by twenty-eight colonels. The ambassadors, boyars, high dignitaries, and generals followed with bowed heads. Three regiments participated in the procession. The military band played mournful music. Forty cannon fired salvos of honor. The widow walked with unsteady steps, supported by weeping women. The people of Moscow could not understand why the Czar was so grieved at the death of a foreigner. After the interment in the cemetery of the German Settlement, friends of the deceased gathered at his house for a banquet. Each guest received a gold ring with an emblem of death engraved on the bezel. The Czar drank a great deal, but his companions seemed dispirited. When some of them made as if to withdraw before the end of the funeral festivities, he became angry and shouted: "You seem glad that Lefort has disappeared!"

A few months later the sovereign was saddened by another loss: the death of Patrick Gordon, a capable and devoted general. On the other hand, it was with a secret sense of relief that he learned, in December 1700, of the demise of that adamant opponent of his reforms, Patriarch Adrian. To avoid establishing another rival power by his side, he appointed no successor to the Patriarch but named Stephen Yavorsky, the metropolitan of Ryazan, to the post of "temporary guardian of the Holy Throne of the Patriarch." Stephen Yavorsky was a Little Russian (Ukrainian) with a keen mind who had been educated abroad and who, the Czar thought, would not stand in the way of his intended innovations. Besides, he was given only day-to-day affairs to handle. The management of the monasteries was entrusted to an office presided over by a layman, Count Mussin-Pushkin. This was the first step in bringing the Church to heel.

In reality, the Church had never openly opposed the Czar's initiatives, at least so far as his private life was concerned. Even when Peter repudiated his wife without giving any reason, Patriarch Adrian had confined himself to feeble protestations. Now Peter's romance with Anna Mons was in full flower. The official favorite enjoyed an allowance of seven hundred rubles a year and a fine mansion in the German Settlement, whose richest ornament, according to a witness, was the bedchamber. The common people called her "the Czarina of Kokuy"* or "the tramp." Covered with jewels, she appeared at the Czar's side at banquets of friends and even at official ceremonies. When a Danish diplomat asked Peter to be the godfather of his child, the Czar insisted that she be the godmother. He gave her the estate of Dubino and for a moment even thought about marrying her, all the while blithely allowing himself adventures on the side with serving girls at inns, prostitutes, and even one of Anna's friends, the German Helen Fademrecht. This latter lady referred to the Czar in her letters as "my darling little sun, my adored with black eyes and eyebrows of the same color."[9]

Anna's rise seemed irresistible, when an unexpected event

---

*Kokuy: a district of Moscow known for its brothels, and the Muscovites' nickname for the German Settlement.

brought it to an end. At the beginning of the northern campaign of 1703, the Saxon envoy Königseck drowned while crossing a river. Peter, who was always on the lookout for political information, had the diplomat's pockets searched and found in them not the confidential notes he had been hoping for, but love letters. Everything about them—the handwriting, the style, the signature —pointed to Anna Mons. Moreover, the deceased was wearing on his chest a locket containing a portrait of the fair one and a lock of blond hair with the inscription: "Love and faithfulness." Although Peter was broadminded so far as affairs of the heart were concerned, he considered himself offended. He had the faithless woman thrown into prison, along with some thirty persons suspected of having helped her in her liaison. Although no one knew exactly what they were guilty of, the "accomplices" remained under lock and key indefinitely. Anna Mons, however, was quickly freed. Stripped of almost all her property, she refused to part with a miniature portrait of the sovereign, "because of the diamond frame," people said. But she did not admit defeat. As interested as ever in the diplomatic corps, she soon became the mistress, then the wife of the Prussian envoy Kayserling. One evening, at the end of a copious supper, Kayserling went up to the Czar and, taking advantage of His Majesty's good humor, dared to ask him for an appointment for the ex-favorite's brother. At once Peter's old bitterness was reawakened. In spite of the passage of years, the affront still stuck in his throat. He said roughly: "I raised up the Mons girl for myself, with the intention of marrying her. You seduced her. Keep her. But never speak to me again about her or her family!" And as the Prussian diplomat tactlessly insisted, Menshikov cried: "Your Mons is a whore! I've had her just like you and everybody else! Leave us alone about her!" Choked with indignation, the indiscreet husband wanted to protest, but the Czar and Menshikov beat him with their fists and threw him down the stairs. The next day Kayserling presented his apologies to his illustrious assailants.*

While Peter harbored a grudge, he was not inconsolable.

*Anna was widowed in 1711, became the mistress of a Swedish officer named Miller, and died a few years later.[10]

Menshikov, who now replaced Lefort as his confidant, supplied him with young ladies of easy virtue. The two men liked to exchange mistresses. The court of Natalya, the Czar's younger sister, turned into a harem where the sovereign and his friend would come to seek their partners for a night. More than ever, lovemaking was to them a health measure and a form of recreation.

Peter paid no attention whatever to the opinion of those around him. Still less to the opinion of the people. Yet the police reports he read abounded in examples of incendiary words spoken by preachers at secret meetings. "The Czar shaves beards and consorts with the Germans; faith too has become German," said one of these mystics. "The Czar," said another, "lives as the foreigners do. He eats meat on Wednesday and Friday and he did not observe the fast of St. Philip. He has ordered everyone to wear German dress. He has done away with the Patriarchate so as to reign alone and have no rival. On January 1, 1700, he had the new year celebrated, thus violating the oath of the holy fathers. The years of God have been abolished, the years of Satan are proclaimed."[11] Before, Peter had had only the sectarians, the Old Believers, against him. Now it seemed that the adherents of the new faith had joined those of the old in censuring his reforms. The stubborn resistance that was spreading throughout the masses was no longer just a refusal to accept Nikon's corrections of the holy books. It was also and especially a refusal to accept the abolition of beards, the adoption of "German" dress, the changing of the calendar, the use of tobacco, the emancipation of women. From now on, the people's hostility was directed against those who copied foreign ways; it was no longer purely religious but nationalistic. In the towns, in the countryside, people were repeating more and more insistently that the true Czar had died while traveling abroad and that he who now claimed to rule the country was the Antichrist. For the first time, Russia and its sovereign did not coincide. A rift was widening between the small, Europeanized ruling class and the multitude who were faithful to the traditions of their fathers. The demarcation between those two worlds was symbolized by the shaved chin and the new costume. Sometimes Peter had the feeling that he was struggling alone against fourteen million subjects. The disproportion didn't worry him. He found it a challenge.

8

From Narva to Poltava

It was at Rawa, during his interview with Augustus II of Poland, that Peter had decided to turn away from Turkey and attack Sweden. But it was only logical that before declaring war on Charles XII he should wait for the end of the peace negotiations that his envoy Ukraintsev was carrying on with the representatives of the Ottoman Porte.* And those negotiations were dragging on. In the meantime Johann Reinhold von Patkul, an adviser to Augustus II, had devised a plan for a coalition that would unite Denmark, Poland, and Russia against the Swedes. Each of the partners would be rewarded with a choice piece of territory from the defeated country. Peter dreamed of gaining access to the Baltic and of annexing the former Russian cities of Dorpat (Yuryev) and Narva. He waited impatiently for the news from Constantinople. His allies, who were in even more of a hurry, made the mistake of opening hostilities without him. Charles XII immediately arrived off

*The Sublime Porte (or High Gate—the palace gate at which justice was administered) was the official name of the Ottoman court in Turkey.—TRANS.

Copenhagen with his fleet, landed in force, carried the forward entrenchments, and forced the city to capitulate. After this mortal blow Denmark ignominiously withdrew from the coalition and signed the separate peace of Travendal. Augustus II, for his part, captured Dunamunde but failed to take Riga. Peter was secretly delighted: now Riga would fall into his own pocket.

At last, on August 8, 1700, a courier from Ukraintsev brought him news that an accord had been signed with Turkey for thirty years. On the very day that the population of Moscow was celebrating to the sound of bells the long-awaited return of peace, he ordered his troops to set out on another campaign. However, contrary to the promises he had made to his allies, he marched not north but toward Livonia, a sector that had originally been reserved for Augustus II. As every war requires a pretext, he stated in his manifesto that he was launching his troops against Sweden in order to avenge the disrespectful treatment he had suffered during his stay in Riga—which, however, he had visited incognito. In short, the Czar was defending the carpenter Peter Mikhailov.

He hoped to steal a march on his adversary, who was young and inexperienced. In 1700 Charles XII was eighteen, ten years younger than Peter. When he had ascended the throne at the age of fifteen and a half, the king had surprised his entourage by his daring, forcefulness, insolence, and authority. Tall, thin, with an oblong face, a high, broad forehead and piercing eyes, he often neglected the duties of his office in favor of crude diversions not unlike the Czar's own. He had read all the classics, and his model was Alexander the Great; but he shoved his ministers around, broke furniture for amusement, hunted hares in the hall of the Diet, cut off the heads of sheep and goats with his saber, and rode through the streets of Stockholm at high noon clad only in his shirt. Peter thought he was half mad and no threat to anyone. He was mistaken. When Charles XII saw his country in danger he was suddenly transformed. Overnight the capricious adolescent—the bear hunter, boozer, and womanizer—gave up all his pleasures. The protection of his country became his sole concern, the army his only passion.

On campaign he was a soldier like the others, sleeping on bare boards, eating on the run, and neglecting his appearance. "His shirt and his wrists are ordinarily very dirty," wrote the English envoy Stepney. "His hands are the same color as his wrists, so that one can hardly distinguish them. His hair is light brown, short, and very greasy, and he never combs it but with his fingers. . . . He eats quickly, never stays more than a quarter of an hour at table, and says not a word during the meal. . . . Small beer is his only liquor. . . . He has no sheet or canopy to his bed."[1] When he learned that Russia had gone to war, Charles XII had the Czar's ambassador, Khilkov, arrested along with his associates and servants and all Russian merchants. Peter, on the contrary, had authorized the Swedes to leave Russia. The Dutch and British ambassadors were still trying to persuade him to give up his plan; in response, he drew his sword in their presence and swore not to sheathe it again until after total victory. The forces at his disposal amounted to about forty thousand men. His first objective was Narva, a Swedish city formerly controlled by the Russians. He expected that Charles XII, detained in Denmark, would not be able to intervene in time and that the citadel would fall without the Russians' having to fight in open country. The whole thing looked like a pleasant military excursion. He reached Narva on September 23, but to his surprise the siege went badly from the start. The Russian artillery was inoperative, the gun crews didn't know their business, they were short of powder and shot, the walls of the city resisted, and bad weather was setting in. Nevertheless, Peter hoped that the besieged would grow weary and capitulate. But during the night of November 17–18 he learned from some Swedish prisoners that Charles XII was approaching by forced march.

Peter was thunderstruck at the news. He felt as if a trap were slamming shut on him. In a flash he foresaw the defeat of his army, and immediately decided to leave: flight rather than captivity. But he needed an excuse for this shameful desertion. In Peter's *Journal* there appears the following note, corrected by the Czar's own hand:* "On the eighteenth, His Majesty left for Novgorod in order to hasten the advance of the regiments marching toward the siege

---

*Starting in 1698 Peter caused a journal to be kept of his public affairs. Some of the entries were written by him, in the third person, some by others at his orders and with his editing.—TRANS.

of Narva; but the chief reason for his departure was that he wanted to have an interview with the king of Poland, who had raised the siege of Riga, and to deliberate together about their common plans." Miserable excuses: the plain truth was that Peter was giving way to panic. His advisers begged him to go before it was too late. Demoralized, he left his camp at night, abandoning the command to Prince Charles Eugene of Croy. To be sure, this general whom the Czar had engaged two years earlier had experience and authority, but he knew nothing about the regiments entrusted to him, had no understanding of their mentality, and didn't even speak their language. No sooner had he been rash enough to accept the command than Charles XII appeared before Narva at the head of ten thousand men. The Swedish soldiers were only a quarter as many as the Russians. To reach the citadel they had crossed barren plains, braved the elements, slept on empty stomachs. They were exhausted. Their horses had not eaten for two days.

But sustained by the presence of their young king, their courage was intact. On the very next day Charles XII threw two columns against the Russians. He himself led the attack. His opponents were blinded by a blizzard. Notwithstanding the resistance of the Semeonovsky and Preobrazhensky regiments, the Russian camp was overrun in half an hour. The Muscovites took flight. The cavalry tried to swim across the Narva. A thousand men were drowned in the river. Foot soldiers rushed to two bridges, which collapsed under their weight. Charles XII, fearing a reversal of the situation, had a new bridge built during the night to enable the fleeing soldiers to decamp. They needed no further invitation. The disaster was complete. The Russians had lost ten thousand men. Among those taken prisoner were the Prince of Croy himself, who had been the first to surrender, and Prince Dolgoruky, Generals Weide, Hallart, Langen. . . . The immense booty included sixty flags and standards, the army's coffers, all the artillery pieces. General Hallart declared in disgust that his soldiers had "as much courage as a frog has hair on its stomach!"

Of course it was forbidden in Russia to speak of the defeat in public. Everybody knew what had happened but nobody talked about it. The Russian ambassadors abroad were ordered to present the Narva affair as the result of a betrayal. But in The Hague as in Vienna, in London as at Versailles, no one was deceived.

Everywhere the boastful Czar was ridiculed and mocked in front of his envoys, who had to swallow their gall. A medal circulated that represented him fleeing in tears, without sword or hat, with the following legend taken from the Bible: "And he went out, and wept bitterly."[2]

In Moscow Peter was gloomy and distraught. He doubted himself, he doubted his army. His soldiers were cowards. Faced with a handful of seasoned Swedish troops, they had thrown down their arms, despite their superior numbers. Because of them the Czar would have to renounce his plans for conquest. Russia would not expand to the shores of the Baltic. The Russian flag would not fly over the northern seas. The world would not tremble before the will of Moscow. He could thank his stars that Charles XII was not pursuing his advance into Russia. After a moment's hesitation, the king had decided to settle affairs with Poland first. Peter intended to take advantage of the respite to make peace at any price. In this hope he addressed piteous appeals to all the sovereigns of Europe asking them to mediate. The foreign courts laughed at his efforts. Prince Golitzin, the Russian envoy in Vienna, wrote Peter: "The prime minister, Count Kaunitz, on whom everything depends, will not even talk to me. And it's the same with the others. They only laugh at us. I went to the Opera, at the Palace of the Favorite, with the Polish ambassador. The French ambassador came up to us with the Swedish ambassador. . . . The Frenchman suggested that it would be a good idea for Sweden, Poland, and Russia to sign a treaty. The Swede replied that his king was prepared to sign such a treaty with Poland, but that between him and the Czar there could be neither treaty nor peace. And he began to laugh."

In his humiliation Golitzin also wrote to Golovin: "By all possible means we must try to obtain a victory over the enemy. . . . Otherwise, even if we conclude an eternal peace, how can we wipe out the eternal shame? Our Czar must have a victory, even if only a little one, so that his name may again be honored throughout Europe: afterward, we can sign a peace treaty. Now, everyone is laughing at our army and its command."

Suddenly, Peter got hold of himself, as after his first defeat by the Turks. Having despaired of Russia, he now remembered how vast the country was, how inexhaustible its resources, how limitless the endurance of its people. A nation so strong, so bountiful, he thought, could lose ten, twenty battles, but it would wear the enemy down at last and force him to his knees. He who until now had only played at being a soldier and sailor bowed to reality and drew the lesson from his failure. He who had always been boiling with impatience realized that he must rely on time and labor to achieve his revenge. "I am well aware that the Swedes will keep beating us for a long time, but in the end they will teach us how to beat them," he said. And also: "This whole affair [the first campaign in the North] was only child's play." In the same vein, he had the following comment entered in his *Journal*: "This victory [of the Swedes over the Russians] was regarded as a sign that God was very angry; but on closer examination it can be seen that on the contrary the views of Heaven were favorable to us; for had we won a victory over the Swedes at that time, when we knew so little of the art of war and politics, into what disaster would such good fortune not have drawn us afterward?"

At his orders all of Russia set feverishly to work. Men, women, children, soldiers, and ecclesiastics busied themselves fortifying the cities and monasteries that might stop the enemy offensive. Since the Narva debacle had reduced the regular army to twenty-five thousand men, mass levies were conducted and ten new regiments were formed in the region of the Volga. An iron foundry was created at Neviansk-Kamensky and the Czar ordered one fourth of the bells in the churches and monasteries to be confiscated and melted down to make cannon. Two hundred fifty young men were sent to schools to be trained as officers in the artillery and the corps of engineers. In Liège the diplomat Matveyev bought fifteen thousand muskets, rapid-firing cannon, field glasses and precision instruments. Warm clothing was made for ten thousand new recruits. The shipyards hastily built light galleys on Lake Peipus and Lake Ladoga. Soon, to strengthen his army, Peter would reconstitute the regiments of *streltsy* that he had dissolved. For the time being he had to consolidate his alliances. They were not exactly brilliant, but he had no choice.

In February 1701 he met Augustus II at the Castle of Birze near Dünaburg. To celebrate the joyful reunion they held a contest in cannon firing. The king of Poland hit the target twice, the Czar of Russia not once. But that same evening Peter had his revenge at table. Augustus II got so drunk that it was impossible to wake him up next morning for Mass. Peter, the Orthodox monarch, attended the Catholic service alone with a fresh complexion and a bantering look in his eye. Then, when Augustus II had slept it off, the banqueting began again. It lasted for three days and three nights. Between libations they talked politics. To demonstrate his strength the king of Poland took a silver plate in his hand and rolled it up into a tube. Peter laughingly imitated the feat and suggested that Augustus do the same with the king of Sweden's sword.[3] In the end the two sovereigns signed a new treaty, which provided that after victory Livonia and Estonia would go to Poland and Ingria and Karelia to Russia. Peter also concluded an alliance with Denmark.

The coalition got off to a bad start. The joining of the Russian and Polish armies resulted only in defeat under the walls of Riga. Charles XII captured Mitau, Bausk, and Birze and drove the Russians and Saxons out of Livonia and Kurland. Meanwhile, in the month of June, a gigantic fire had ravaged the Moscow Kremlin. Administrative offices with their files, shops with their food supplies, arsenals with their munitions, palaces and churches with their treasures had burned like torches. The bells had fallen from the tower of Ivan Veliki. The biggest bell, weighing 128 tons, had broken in its fall: a bad omen. But snow brings the Russians good luck. A few months later, in the depths of winter, Sheremetev surprised the Swedes commanded by Schlippenbach with superior forces and beat them at Erestfer. Peter greeted this first Russian victory as the dawn of national resurrection. During the festivities ordered for the occasion, with artillery salutes and fireworks, a few Swedish prisoners were paraded through the streets, after which they were sold in the market for three or four florins apiece. The demand for Swedes was so great that the price quickly rose to thirty florins.[4] "When they have gained the slightest advantage here," observed the Dutch representative Van der Hulst, "they make so much noise about it that one would think they had turned the whole world upside down." The following year, 1702, there were fresh Russian victories at Wolmar and Marienburg, while Charles XII beat the Saxons and the Poles at Klisov and entered Cracow. As autumn drew near, Peter decided to turn his efforts toward the Neva. He had a depot of food and artillery set up on the shores of Lake Ladoga. Boats were prepared there for attacks by river. The initial goal was the Fortress of Nöteborg, which was located on an island at the point where the Neva flowed out of the lake. In the days when Russia had ruled the area this fortress had been called Oreshka.* As Peter put it, he wanted to "crack that little nut between his thumb and forefinger." The assault lasted for thirty-five hours. At last, on October 11, 1702, the garrison of 450 men supported by 142 cannon capitulated. Peter forthwith renamed the fortress, which would henceforth be known as Schlüsselburg, the "key citadel." In the Czar's mind that key was the one that opened the gates of the Neva and the sea. To complete the operation Sheremetev, with 20,000 men, advanced through the forest along the right bank of the river to the fort of Nienschantz at the very mouth of the Neva. Peter himself made his way there with other troops by water, on about sixty small boats. On May 1, 1703, after a short bombardment the fort opened its gates. Then six days later two Swedish men-of-war, not knowing that Nienschantz had fallen, ventured into the delta at the entrance to the Gulf of Finland. On orders from "Captain of Bombardiers" Peter and "Lieutenant" Menshikov, soldiers of the guard immediately sprang into some thirty longboats, rowed out to the two vessels, boarded them, massacred 58 sailors, and captured 19. Peter exploded with childish joy: the first Russian naval victory! He wrote to all his friends to announce it and accepted their overblown congratulations: "We have never had such a capture of ships at sea," Streshnev wrote him. "We would search our treasure chests in vain and find nothing like it. The affair is without precedent." For this brilliant action "Captain of Bombardiers" Peter and "Lieutenant" Menshikov received the insignia of the Order of St. Andrew, of which they had not felt themselves worthy at the time of its creation. Gold medals with gold chains were distributed to the other officers. "The soldiers," Peter wrote in his *Journal*, "also received medals, but smaller and without chains."

The pleasure he took in these flattering decorations and encomiums was as nothing compared to the deep, historic happiness he felt at having reconquered the waterway by which the first Varangians had come to Russia in the ninth century. On May 16,

*Both the Swedish and Russian names derive from "hazelnut," after the shape of the island.—TRANS.

1703, nine days after the capture of the Swedish vessels, he had wooden huts built on one of the little islands nearby for him and his close companions. Did he have any idea at that moment that he was laying the foundations of his future capital? A few months later there appeared at the mouth of the Neva—oh, wondrous to behold!—a Dutch merchantman with a cargo of brandy and salt. Peter went on board at once and had vodka, cheese, and biscuits brought to the crew. Following his instructions, Menshikov gave five hundred florins to the captain and thirty crowns to each of the sailors to thank them for having cast anchor in the roads of "Piterburg."

Meanwhile, having gained access to the Gulf of Finland, Peter was busy consolidating his position. A fortress arose on the island of Kronslot at the entrance to the gulf to defend the delta of the Neva. Shipbuilding was pushed to the fastest pace possible. During this time Sheremetev was attacking Estonia and Livonia. In July 1704 Peter was present at the capture of Dorpat. The next month it was Narva that capitulated after a murderous assault—the commandant himself beat the drum in signal of surrender. Rampaging Russian soldiers did not spare the defeated. "There where God inflicted a painful ordeal on us four years ago," wrote the Czar, "He has now transformed us into joyful victors; I took this celebrated fortress in three-quarters of an hour, sword in hand. We lost but three hundred men."[5] Actually, this success was due mostly to the weakness of the adversary, the chief part of the Swedish troops being engaged in Poland. Flying from one victory to the next, Charles XII forced the Diet of Warsaw to elect King Stanislas Leszczynski. To support Augustus II, who still claimed the throne, Peter marched across the country. Menshikov beat the Swedes at Kalisz, captured about a hundred officers and nearly two thousand men. All Swedish posts in Kurland fell one after another into Russian hands. A slim satisfaction, because in the meantime Augustus II, terrified by the arrival en masse of Swedish troops in Saxony, betrayed the promises he had made to Peter and on September 24, 1706, at Altranstadt signed a peace treaty with Charles XII. The conditions were Draconian: Augustus was to renounce the Polish crown in favor of Stanislas, break the alliance with Russia, and hand over deserters and traitors, including Patkul, whom the Czar had made his ambassador. Viewed by some as a schemer, by others as a hero and martyr, Patkul was broken on the wheel and beheaded.

With Augustus II, Peter had lost his last ally. Now he stood alone against the king of Sweden. Both of them were obstinate madmen. But Peter's enthusiasm was blazing, disordered, violent, and improvisational, while his opponent's was icy, secret, and calculating. Charles XII's victories, his tactical daring, good luck, courage, and austerity were the admiration of Europe. In his camp at Altranstadt he treated with disdain the English and French diplomats who had hastened thither to try to obtain his support, or at least his goodwill, in the affair of the Spanish succession. The German ministers asked deferentially but in vain for his decisions as to the future of the old empire. They all urged him to turn to the West. Always taciturn, Charles XII revealed nothing of his intentions. Nevertheless, when the French envoy, Jean-Victor de Besenval, indicated to him that the Czar would be disposed to negotiate, he replied that he would demand the restitution of all the territory conquered by the Russians, including the banks of the Neva, with that new town of St. Petersburg that had risen from the marshes. When Vienna and London intervened in turn, they ran up against the same determination. Charles XII was adamant. If Peter wanted to keep St. Petersburg and the adjoining coast that were so dear to him, he had to continue the war. Besides, he had never really believed in the possibility of a separate peace.

While waiting for the decisive onslaught Peter accelerated the fitting out of ships, ordered a levy of fresh recruits at the rate of one soldier for every five peasants, and improved the weaponry of the foot soldiers by adopting the bayonet, which Vauban had been advocating in France for several years. He organized the horse-drawn artillery corps, one of the first in Europe. His passion for ballistics made him push the manufacture of cannon. His adviser Vinius, who had traveled through the Urals and Siberia, had found so many different ores there that he said there should be "enough to last until the end of the world."[6] To pay for all this indispensable war matériel the people, who were already groaning under the weight of taxes, would have to bear more.

In Moscow there was general discontent. In 1705 a rebellion broke out in Astrakhan against the rich and the foreigners. Supported once again by the *streltsy,* the revolt was crushed by regular troops. Three hundred leaders were put to death and four thousand insurgents were forced to join the army. In January 1706 Charles XII left Warsaw with twenty-four thousand men and put to flight fifty thousand Russians at Grodno. Another defeat for the Russian and Saxon troops followed, at Franstadt. "For all the money I poured out to the king of Poland, I have received only misfortunes," Peter wrote Golovin. But these "incidents" made no dent in his determination to squeeze the nation. For the final victory some would give their blood, others their sweat, still others their money. More than ninety percent of the resources of the state were devoted to the army. The government monopolized the postal service, the fisheries, the salt works, tobacco, tar, chalk, axle grease, fish oil, pig bristle. Taxes were imposed on inns and mills, and the rents on old state leases were increased. Peter decided to issue "credit currency," in other words, to remint all the existing money, reducing the weight of the coins. Result: a huge and immediate profit.

"This court has become a veritable business firm," wrote the English ambassador, Whitworth. And it was true that so far as the Czar was concerned, any means would do when it came to financing the war. The French envoy Besenval declared: "The campaign against the Russians will be difficult and dangerous, for the Swedes have taught the Muscovites the art of warfare and have made them formidable, while it is impossible to destroy this vast power."[7]

At last Charles XII began to move. "I am wedded to my army, in good times as in bad, for life and for death," he wrote. In June 1708, he crossed the Berezina, took Mogilev, looked covetously toward Smolensk, and could already envision himself in Moscow. The Czar had the capital fortified in haste. As a crowning piece of bad luck, he had to send troops to put down a revolt by Bulavin, the leader of the Cossacks of the Don, and another by the Bashkirs in the region of Kazan and Ufa. These two operations dispersed his manpower. But in any event he had decided to refuse combat and to fall back repeatedly so as to draw the enemy into the heart of Russia, laying waste the country behind him. His allies would be time, space, cold, and hunger. The Cossacks attacked the Swedes by surprise, killed a few, and disappeared. As they advanced

Charles XII's soldiers found only burned villages, empty store-houses, razed fields, a desert. "The king of Sweden pursued the Russians now from one side now from the other," says Peter's *Journal.* "The army retreated continually. But of everything we found in our path, a part we took for our own use and the rest was burned so that the enemy could not have the benefit of it. To the right, the Swedes could still obtain some sustenance. But on the left, where the Russian troops had passed, we left them nothing."

Charles XII hoped that Lewenhaupt's army would join him to swell the ranks of his troops, which, weakened by hunger and sickness, were melting away. But the Czar foiled that plan by barring Lewenhaupt's path, near Lesnaya, on the Sozh. After a bloody battle that even came to hand-to-hand combat with bayonets and swords, the Swedes gave ground. The king, who was expecting reinforcements of eleven thousand troops with seven thousand wagons of food, fodder, and munitions, witnessed instead the arrival of a little more than six thousand fleeing, exhausted men who had spiked their cannon and abandoned the supply train to the enemy. "This victory," wrote the keeper of Peter's *Journal,* "may be regarded as the first that we had won, for we had never gained such an advantage over regular troops, and with a force inferior to the enemy's. In truth it was the cause of all the fortunate successes that the Russian armies had after that time. It was the first test that heartened the soldiers and filled them with confidence."

Charles XII had hardly recovered from this disappointment when bad news reached him from Ingria, where Lybecker had been beaten, losing three thousand soldiers and all his baggage. Then the young king made a desperate decision: abandoning the idea of marching on Smolensk and Moscow, he executed a flanking movement and headed for the Ukraine. In that rich region he hoped to find abundant provisions and to secure the assistance of the neighboring Turks and of the hetman Mazeppa, who had just betrayed the Russian cause. But when he arrived there he was dumbfounded to find that the flourishing countryside had been despoiled by the Russians and that instead of the forty thousand Cossacks Mazeppa had promised him, the traitorous old chief could only round up two thousand. This small force was not even enough to protect Baturin, seat of the hetmans of Little Russia, which Menshikov entered in triumph. Instead of following their turncoat leader, the people elected another hetman, Skoropadsky, and engaged in guerrilla warfare against the Swedish invaders.

The Turks were evasive. And winter was coming on, a winter so harsh that the birds died of cold on the branches. The army of "Carolinians"* was twelve hundred versts from Stockholm, without any possibility of reinforcements and without supplies. Even the proud Life Guards, a band of heroes each of whom had some armed exploit to his credit, bowed their heads in apprehension of the future. The men collapsed from starvation; the horses died; Cossacks appeared out of the mists of snow, massacred stragglers, and intercepted convoys; at the edge of the track in wind-lashed tents, surgeons amputated frozen limbs. "We have three good doctors," said the Swedes: "brandy, garlic, and death." Of the large and glorious army there soon remained only twenty-four thousand men who plodded on with haggard looks, their clothes in rags, led by a fanatical king as ill-provided as the least of his soldiers. At any cost he wanted to bring them to Poltava. The capture of that city was his supreme goal. Once he had driven the Russians out, he thought, he could replenish his supplies there and resume the struggle with some chance of success.

In the month of April 1709 the Swedes reached Poltava, in the center of the Ukraine. The old city, which was poorly fortified, contained a garrison of six thousand men. Charles XII surrounded it but didn't launch an attack. Doubtless he preferred to husband his strength so as to strike one great blow, in the open countryside, against the Russian army that his scouts told him was approaching. Disillusioned, his best generals and Mazeppa himself advised him to raise the siege and fall back. The king was obstinate: "If God sent me one of His angels to invite me to follow your advice, I would not listen to him," he said. General Stenbock wrote: "The king can no longer think of anything but war. He will no longer listen to reason. He talks as though God Himself inspired his decisions. . . . Had he only a thousand soldiers left, he would throw them upon an entire army." Too many easy victories had gone to his head, and he made the mistake of underestimating his oppo-

*The name given in Sweden to the soldiers of Charles XII.

nent. He didn't want to hear about the new Russia that Peter had been able to rally around him. But Peter, for his part, had learned from bitter experience and hesitated to intervene. For the time being the Russians were content to dig trenches, lob shells, and engage in light skirmishes. During a reconnaissance, Charles XII received a bullet wound in his left foot. He stayed on his horse, continued his inspection, returned to camp, and fainted as he dismounted. While the surgeons were working on him he said with a smile: "Go to it, gentlemen, it's only the foot! . . . It's nothing! . . ." But he was so weak that he turned the command over to Marshal Carl Gustav Rehnskjold. Once again he was advised to retreat. And once again he refused to yield. On the contrary, he decided that the battle would be launched on the very next day, June 27, 1709, at dawn.

When Peter learned that Charles XII had been wounded, he saw it as a good omen. He addressed his men: "The hour has come when the destiny of the motherland is to be decided. It is of her that you should think, it is for her that you should fight. . . . As for Peter, know that he does not care about his own life so long as Russia lives in glory and prosperity." And he sent the following orders to Sheremetev: "Marshal, I entrust my army to you. I hope that in exercising your command you will follow exactly the instructions that have been given you and that in unforeseen situations you will act like an able and experienced general. As for me, I reserve the task of watching over your operations as a whole and of being prepared to intervene at any point where danger or need may require it."

Day was breaking when the Swedes went on the attack. Before them lay a small plain, a marsh, entrenchments, redoubts. The center of the Russian army was commanded by Sheremetev, the right wing by Ronne, the left wing by Menshikov, and the artillery by Bruce, the Czar in person taking part in combat at the head of the second battalion of the Novgorod regiment. But in reality he was everywhere at once, racing over the battlefield on his Arab mare, Finette, with a wild look in his eyes and foam on his lips, shouting orders, encouragement, insults. Was this the same man who not long since had fled in time of peril? Today, to set an example, he not only braved danger but sought it. A bullet passed through his hat; another struck him in the chest but was miraculously stopped by a gold cross set with precious stones, which the monks of Mount Athos had given to Czar Feodor; a third buried itself in the wood of his saddle.

Charles XII, meanwhile, still suffering from his wound, was present on the field borne on a stretcher. A cannonball smashed the fragile litter. They made him another one of crossed lances. Then he pulled himself up onto a horse. The seventy-two Russian cannon were gutting the lines of enemy infantry. The weak Swedish artillery was out of ammunition and no longer replied. Now it was hand-to-hand fighting with cold steel. Giving way before the number and fury of the enemy, the "Carolinians" retreated in disorder. In vain did Lewenhaupt shout: "Hold, in the name of Jesus! Hold! Here is the King!" All around him the heroes of yesterday had become only terrified, bloodied shades who threw down their weapons and took to their heels, heading for the Dnieper. After two hours Charles XII himself, swept along by the general rush, left the scene of operations. His horse had been killed under him. They had brought him another. As night fell the remains of the Swedish army, about thirteen thousand men, had their backs to the river, which was impossible to swim. Charles XII turned over the command to Lewenhaupt and crossed the Dnieper in a carriage attached to two boats. He was followed by Mazeppa and a few hundred horsemen. The others were taken prisoner, after Lewenhaupt had signed the surrender. Some threw themselves into the Dnieper in despair or tore off their bandages, preferring death to captivity. The act of capitulation stipulated that Mazeppa's Cossacks, who had served in the Swedish ranks, would be turned over to the Czar and treated as rebels. Charles XII, meanwhile, was fleeing toward Ochakov and Bender in Turkey. Perhaps he hoped to continue the struggle side by side with the Turks, by means of an alliance between the Cross and the Crescent.

Behind him he left chaos. Among the captives were a marshal, ten major generals, fifty-nine staff officers, and eleven hundred other officers, plus Prime Minister Piper, senators, secretaries, and the king's whole household—lackeys, writer, cook, doctor, chaplain, apothecary. . . .

On the very evening of the victory, Peter celebrated the event with a banquet to which he had invited the captured Swedish generals. Turning toward them and raising his cup, he cried: "I drink to the health of those who taught me the art of winning victory." Then, addressing the Swedish marshal Rehnskjold, he offered him his own sword as a token of esteem with, says the *Journal*, "permission to wear it."

The rewards poured down thick and fast: Sheremetev received estates, Menshikov was elevated to the rank of second marshal, Ronne became general-in-chief, Golovkin was made chancellor, the "little Jew" Shafirov vice chancellor. The soldiers were given medals. Peter was not forgotten in the distribution. The officers whom he had recompensed begged him to take the rank of major general on land and of rear admiral at sea. Had he not shown more skill and valor than anyone else in the Poltava affair? "His Majesty accepted," notes the keeper of the *Journal*, "which was followed by the congratulations of the generals, ministers, and officers and the acclamations of the soldiers."

After which they broke camp, for, says the *Journal*, "it was impossible to remain longer near Poltava, both because of the stench given off by the dead bodies and because of the other consequences of the stay of two great armies."

From Turkey, meanwhile, Charles XII sent his sister a report so unrelated to reality that it verged on madness: "Everything went well! It was only at the end, and by a curious chance, that we met with misfortune: the army had a setback, which I hope will soon be remedied. I myself was wounded in the foot a few days before the battle, which prevented me from riding for a time; I hope to mount again soon. . . . It's a little compliment they paid to my foot."

The victorious Russian troops with their host of prisoners turned north again toward Moscow. They had hardly started the journey when Peter ordered two Swedish detachments, one of cavalry the other of infantry, to execute maneuvers in front of him, so that he could see closer up how they operated on campaign. The prisoners obeyed. Peter applauded. He never tired of learning.

Sending Sheremetev to Livonia to besiege Riga and Menshikov to Poland to drive out Stanislas and return the throne to Augustus II, he continued on his way. He expected to rest in Kiev, where there awaited him a woman who for the last seven years had shared his anxieties, his troubles, and his joys. He had met her in July 1702, not long after Sheremetev's siege of Marienburg. The Swedish commandant, who had decided to blow himself up with the citadel and the garrison, had authorized a few civilians to leave, including the Lutheran pastor Glück, with his wife, children, and maidservant. The pastor had been arrested at the outposts and had offered himself as an interpreter. A deal: he would be sent with his family to Moscow. But the servant girl? She was seventeen years old, fresh, blonde, buxom. Sheremetev sized her up at a glance and decided to keep her in camp for the entertainment of his officers. That very evening she found herself at table with companions who were free enough with their hands. The hautboy players struck up a dance tune. There was no lack of partners. They shoved back the benches. Suddenly the music was interrupted by a thundering explosion. The Swedish commandant had kept his word. Marienburg was only a smoking ruin. As soon as she recovered from the first shock, the young girl realized that a new life was beginning for her and that she had only her charms to count on to ensure her future.

The daughter of humble peasants in Swedish Livonia, the Skavronskys, she had been orphaned at an early age and taken in by Pastor Glück. At the time, her name was Martha or Maria, it is not clear. In the household she had a mixed role, part servant, part adopted daughter, and she looked after the younger children. She had a few notions of the catechism but didn't know how to read or write. It was only much later that she would learn to sign her name. She spoke Russian with a strong German accent. On the other hand, she had no equal at cooking, baby tending, sewing, washing, ironing. These domestic virtues were accompanied by a passionate temperament. Fearing that she might seduce all his pupils, some of whom had already succumbed to temptation, the pastor hastened to betroth her, and maybe even to marry her, to a Swedish trumpet player, Kruse. He disappeared after the fall of the town.

At army headquarters in Livonia Martha was first the mistress of a noncommissioned officer who beat her, then of the general-in-chief himself, old Sheremetev, who soon tired of her and yielded her to General Menshikov, a great admirer of ripe beauties. With him she divided her time between serving his bed and his household: he was equally appreciative of the way she made love and the way she ironed his shirts. One day Peter, who had just arrived in his favorite's camp, noticed the young woman among the servants busy around the table. He questioned Menshikov in low tones, turned to Martha, and entered into conversation with her. "He found her clever," wrote Villebois, Peter's aide-de-camp, "and ended his badinage with her by saying that when he went to bed she must bring the torch to his room. This was a decision from which there was no appeal, although it was delivered with a laugh. Menshikov subscribed to it. And the fair one, with the consent of her master, spent the night in the Czar's room."

But Menshikov had not given Martha up when he lent her to the Czar. The monarch and his favorite liked to share women and compare notes afterward. In their traveling gynaeceum were several interchangeable females, including Barbara and Darya Arsenyeva, the former homely and intelligent, the latter pretty and not too bright. Attracted by the plainer one, the Czar said to her one day at a banquet: "No doubt you have never known love. Since I have a fancy for extraordinary things, I don't want you to die without having been loved." And without more ado he undid his buttons and suited action to word. Martha, for her part, was no classical beauty either. Robust and stocky, with a full bosom and thick thighs, she had a short neck and a round face with bovine eyes and a turned-up nose. She coated her face with white and pink to enhance her complexion. Her hair was ash blond, but she was soon to dye it black. Such as she was, this plump little person charmed Peter by her sturdiness, her health, and her cheerful equanimity. She was like a vivandière or some junior officer's wife, born to travel in a wagon, sleep in a tent, and take potluck around the campfire. Exactly what he needed, the Czar thought.

Suddenly he regretted that she was sometimes his, sometimes his favorite's. "I'm taking her away," he told Menshikov. And he ordered his friend to marry the pretty Darya Arsenyeva while he would devote himself to Martha. The young woman was taken to Moscow under escort of a captain of the Guard and given lodgings in a secluded house with "a lady of good family but modest fortune," writes Villebois. Peter went to see her every day in secret, accompanied only by the grenadier who drove his sleigh.

In 1705 she had already had two illegitimate sons by him, who were to die in early childhood. Others would follow.* Soon she converted to Orthodoxy and abandoned the name Martha to become Catherine Alexeyevna. Peter visited the little house more and more frequently and took fewer and fewer pains to hide the affair from the people around him. He got to the point where he would receive his advisers in the presence of his mistress and ask her opinion on the most important matters. "This prince who had a rather poor opinion of women and thought they were only good for making love," says Villebois, "went so far as to consult Catherine when he disagreed with his ministers; he took her advice, gave in to her arguments, and treated her, in a word, as we are told that Numa Pompilius treated the nymph Egeria."

Thus patiently, through lovemaking, domestic services, and friendly conversations, Catherine gained an ascendancy over the Czar that he no longer even tried to resist. In all circumstances she had the power to calm him. When he gave in to one of the crises of ungovernable rage that unhinged his mind and convulsed his face, she would approach him without fear, speak to him gently and firmly, run her fingers through his hair, and draw the sick head down upon her opulent bosom. With his face buried in the warm pillow of flesh, he would grow drowsy, his breathing would become regular. Mother and wife all in one, she would sit motionless for two or three hours without getting weary, the overgrown child collapsed on her breast. When he awoke, refreshed and cheerful, he would scarcely remember his fit of fury. To complete his cure, she would draw him into a merry dance or tell him some good spicy story that made him roar with laughter. . . . Although a stout drinker herself, she saw to it that he didn't endanger his health by boozing too late with his cronies. She didn't hesitate to go fetch him in the midst of a banquet, saying with authority: "It's time to come home, *batiuskha* [little father]!" He laughingly obeyed. She

---

*She gave Peter twelve children in all, of whom two survived him: Anna, the future Duchess of Holstein-Gottorp, and Elizabeth, the future Empress of Russia.

took no pride in her influence over him. Before Peter left Moscow to rejoin his army, which was fighting Charles XII, he wrote the following note: "If, by the will of God, I were to meet with an accident, order to remit the three thousand rubles that are in Menshikov's house to Catherine and her daughter.—Piter."

Three thousand rubles for the woman whom he already considered as his wife! A czar could scarcely be more parsimonious in making out his will. But miserliness and love are not mutually exclusive. When Peter was separated from Catherine he sent her affectionate letters. Curiously, it was not the passionate mistress that he missed (no doubt he found agreeable compensations on campaign), but the friend, the adviser, the housekeeper. "It is dull without you, and my linen is not properly looked after," he wrote her. In her reply she guessed that his hair was wild. He wrote back that she was quite right; but she had only to come, and they would surely find an old comb to smooth the hair tousled by the winds of the battlefield. She did come to Poltava and cheerfully shared camp life beside the Czar, riding horseback, chatting with the soldiers, giving them a bumper of vodka to take the edge off their fatigue, distributing clean clothes and bandages to the wounded. Kindly and courageous, smiling and efficient, she confirmed Peter's feeling that notwithstanding her lowly origins, she was the born mate for him. Shortly before the great confrontation he obliged her to leave. She went to Kiev. The very evening after the battle he wrote her: "Good day, little mother! I inform you that God in His bounty has enabled us to win an unprecedented victory today. In a word, I tell you that all the enemy forces are crushed. I wanted to give you this news myself. As for the congratulations, come here yourself!—In camp, June 27, 1709—Piter."[8]

He joined her in Kiev and in her arms found a silent reward that was worth all the acclamations of his generals. She told him that she was pregnant again. And what if it were a son? he thought. He was so delighted at the prospect of being a father again that he thought about marrying Catherine. She deserved a hundred times over to be proclaimed Czarina before the world. But right now he had something else to do. The festivities were only beginning. Celebrating the victory of Poltava in the Cathedral of St. Sophia in Kiev, Father Feofan Prokopovich declaimed: "When our neighbors hear about what has happened, they will say: it was not into a foreign land that the army and power of Sweden ventured but some deep sea; they plunged in and disappeared like lead in water."

On December 21, 1709, the Russian army made a triumphal entrance into Moscow. Peter and his generals and the two regiments of the Guard marched past, followed by the endless stream of Swedish prisoners, with three hundred flags and thirty-six cannon taken from the enemy. Twenty sleds driven by Lapps, surrounding a so-called king of the Samoyeds, added merriment to the solemn procession. The crowd shouted themselves hoarse for joy. From time to time a boyar or a wealthy merchant would greet the sovereign at the door of his house and offer him a drink. Peter never refused. Despite the alcohol he marched with a firm step. People pointed to the broken stretcher that had carried Charles XII through the battle. Seven arches of triumph were spaced along the route. One of them represented Hercules (Peter I) subduing Juno (Sweden). In front of another, children dressed like Romans held out laurels to the Czar. The mock king Romodanovsky, rigged out like one of the ancient Muscovite princes, dominated the ceremony, seated on a throne and surrounded by his court. It was he whom Peter addressed, saying humbly: "By the grace of God and the good fortune of your Caesarean Majesty, I have fought victoriously with my regiment at Poltava." The astonished Swedish prisoners no longer knew which was the real Czar of Russia, the simple officer dressed in the coarse woolen uniform or the costumed potentate flanked by buffoons. True to the duality of his character, Peter liked to organize his triumph and at the same time make crude fun of it.

The next day a Te Deum was celebrated in the Kremlin. Lost among the crowd of the faithful, the Czar sang hymns in a strong voice, without missing a word. He had donned for the occasion an old wig lifted from the head of one of his valets. The religious service was followed by a gigantic feast. There were so many guests that to supervise the proceedings the master of ceremonies circulated on horseback. Catherine was not present. She kept to her room in Ismailovo, near Moscow, where she was about to give birth.* For each toast, the master of ceremonies stood behind the

---

*Her daughter Elizabeth was born on December 29, 1709.

Czar's chair and fired a pistol shot that was answered by an artillery salute. To eat and drink more at ease, Peter had taken off his cordon of the Order of St. Andrew. His generals did likewise. They caroused elbow to elbow by the light of candelabra, amid an infernal uproar. A display of fireworks brought the feast to a close, with so many crackling explosions and dazzling lights that the Danish ambassador confessed he had never seen the like, "even in London."

His wondering admiration of the great Russian celebration was shared by all the diplomats present. In less than two years Russia, which all Europe had been sneering at after the defeat at Narva, had come to be regarded with respect and anxiety. In the months that followed, ambassadors extraordinary came one after another to convey to Peter the congratulations of their sovereigns. Queen Anne of England even went so far in her message as to call him "emperor." Duke Frederick William of Kurland wed Grand Duchess Anna Ivanovna, the Czar's niece. There was talk of a probable marriage between Charlotte of Brunswick-Wolfenbüttel, the daughter of Duke Louis, and the Czarevich Alexis, Peter's son by his first wife, Eudoxia. In the meantime Peter had pacified Poland and set "his devoted creature" Augustus II back on the throne. He had also renewed his alliance with Denmark, after having taken Vyborg, Riga, and Reval and thus completed the conquest of Karelia and Livonia. Having destroyed the power of Sweden, he had upset the balance of the continent. Now it was he, and no longer Charles XII, who laid down the law in the North. Only France was reluctant to accept this situation, which deprived her of two of her principal allies, Poland and Sweden. But the "Richelieu system" included a third base of support: Turkey. The Czar's enemies, with Charles XII at their head, were maneuvering to draw Sultan Ahmed III into the war. Meanwhile, the Christian peoples of the Balkans and Asia—the Greeks, Serbs, Montenegrins, Walachians, Moldavians, Armenians, Georgians, Copts, Croatians—were begging Peter to liberate them from the Turkish oppressor. He realized that his task was not finished. Would it ever be? He was seized by weariness and doubt. After nine years of armed expeditions, he sincerely longed for peace.

9

St.
Petersburg

When Admiral Golovin looked at the first structures in St. Petersburg—little huts, trenches, temporary fortifications—he saw the place only as a convenient base for the war against the Swedes. Peter certainly shared that view, but he already had in mind another future for the burgeoning town. He was enchanted to be so near the water. The idea of being able to breathe sea air all year round, feel the salt spray in his face night and day, and watch ships through a telescope was so exciting that he forgot the most elementary caution in working out his building plans. Here he felt more at home than anywhere else in Russia, both on land and on water: an amphibious czar in an amphibious landscape. He loved the marshy lowlands, the lonely moors, the dark, gloomy forests haunted by wolves, the floating mists through which Finnish fishermen passed like phantoms. The more desolate and amorphous the region seemed, the more he wanted to set his mark upon it. A great city, he said to himself, could rise out of this murky nothingness. A city that would be entirely his own creation. In vain did his advisers point out to him that the place was ill chosen, that the province of Ingria was very poor and had no means of providing food supplies, that it was far from the capital and near Swedish cannon; he didn't care. Nor did he take any notice of those who warned him against the difficulty of building a solid city on muddy ground. He admired the Dutch and wanted to tame the water as they had. St. Petersburg would be the Russian answer to Amsterdam. A city on piles, crisscrossed by canals, divided into little islands, a port in the midst of masses of spongy land. According to a Finnish legend that sprang up later, the houses of this city were built in the air and set down by a mysterious power at sea level, where they did not sink into the mud but came to rest like aquatic birds. *Neva* in Finnish means "mud." Here everything was sticky, ill defined, unhealthy. But to Peter the place was paradise. No matter that when the west wind prevented the Neva from flowing to the sea the river surged violently back and flooded the houses on its low banks. No matter that the harsh winter blocked the ships in ice for six months of the year. No matter that in spring when the ice broke, roads were impassable and the town was cut off from the rest of the country. In building St. Petersburg he was defying nature—and at the same time Russia's past.

For St. Petersburg was to be the antithesis of Moscow. Peter detested the old residence of the czars, its continental climate, hoary traditions, local superstitions, court intrigues, and oriental spirit, at once backward and rebellious. To him Moscow was the Czarevna Sophia, the *streltsy* and their bloodthirsty arrogance. If he wanted to turn his country toward the future, he had to "open a window" on the sea, on the West.[1] Thus St. Petersburg, a settlement sprung from nothing, conceived arbitrarily and built by command, would not be simply one more city on the map of Russia. It would incarnate his desire to make a fresh start, the desire of a czar who rejected the heritage of his fathers. It would immortalize his name and symbolize his reign. He had a vague sense of this, even though as yet he had no thought of changing his capital.

The construction began without any precise plan and continued by fits and starts, depending on the sovereign's whims. At first he tried to establish the center of the city on one of the two big islands near the right bank of the Neva, but he found himself obliged to place the main buildings on the left bank, which was higher and in less danger of flooding. Then he changed his mind again, and to make the new city more like Amsterdam, chose the lowest site, on Vasilevsky Island to the west. That plan too was abandoned. First, near the right bank of the Neva a wooden fortress was built on a little island, Hare Island, at the place where the river was widest: the future Fortress of St. Peter and St. Paul. Next there rose a church, also made of wood, the Church of the Trinity, and a merchants' hall. Not far off was a log cabin with pine walls and a roof made of shingles in the shape of tiles: Peter's first residence in his city. A vestibule, two rooms with walls and ceilings whitewashed and hung with linen, and a workshop with lathe, axes, planes, hammers, saws—all the tools of a master carpenter. The doors were so low that the Czar had to bend his head to pass through them. But he who was so tall had always liked little, dark rooms. He felt comfortable in this house that was scarcely better than a peasant's hut. He looked confidently from the corner where the map of Europe was pinned to the corner where—glittering with gold, diamonds, and precious stones—there stood a miraculous icon of the Redeemer, which went everywhere with him.*

The following year, to underline the cosmopolitan character of the new city, Peter had a Lutheran church built and also an inn, the "Four Frigates," which for a long time served as the town hall, a place where the state sold tobacco, brandy, wine, beer, and cards. A covered bazaar offered foreign merchandise. The bustling market was thronged with people from all classes of society. Behind these shops patronized by honorable citizens stretched the Tatar flea market and the quarter inhabited chiefly by Kalmuks, Tatars, and Turks. Weber, the Hanoverian ambassador, described the "Tartarian rag-fair" in his memoirs. "The goods are sold there very cheap," he wrote, "either in the open streets or in two rows of shops. They consist in secondhand suits of divers nations, basten shoes,† old iron, pack-thread, old cord, wooden saddles with proper housing to them made of felt, and other such curiosities. Those shops generally have most customers, and the throng there-

---

*To preserve this little house, from which the Czar had overseen the construction of St. Petersburg, Catherine II had the walls covered with a stone facing. It can still be seen today.
†Made from plaited strips of the inner bark of the linden tree.—TRANS.

abouts is such that he who chances to come among them ought well to look to his purse, sword, and even hat and peruke and, for the better security, carry them in his hands."[2] In the Moika quarter the butchers slaughtered animals outdoors and dumped the entrails to the side. The stench was such that buyers hesitated to approach the stalls. It was not long before all the butchers were ordered to wear the same uniform and to display their merchandise in identical shops. Inhabitants were responsible for the cleanliness of the streets: each had to sweep in front of his door. It was forbidden to throw refuse into the canals and streams.

The Czar's associates moved into cabins like his. The project was launched. Nothing would stop it. As always, Peter was stimulated by obstacles. Few sovereigns have had as much contempt for human life as he. Any idea that germinated in his brain seemed to him to justify the sacrifice of the nation. Troops of workers were collected in the neighboring regions and brought by force to the mouth of the Neva. They included both specialists—masons, carpenters, blacksmiths—and unskilled laborers. Some were employed for a few months, others requisitioned for life. In 1704 the different provincial governors received an order to supply forty thousand men a year. Working from sunup to sundown, lodged in filthy huts, underfed, mistreated, they didn't even have the indispensable tools for their task. No pickaxes, no wheelbarrows. To build up the low banks of the river, the wretched workers carried earth in the skirts of their garments or in sacks made from old matting. Often they labored in the middle of marshes, in water up to their waists. The knout was used for the least breach of discipline. If a man was caught attempting to flee, his nostrils were cut to the bone. The ragged throng that swarmed about the scaffoldings was attacked by the elements, by scurvy, by dysentery. Every day corpses piled up in the common grave. Those who were too weak to work were replaced by convicts, but they did not suffice. Peasants were rounded up, to the great annoyance of landowners. Torn from their villages and families, they were sent to construction sites as soon as they arrived, to work under the surveillance of armed soldiers. Between accidents and diseases, the mortality rate rose constantly. To justify his enterprise, Peter told himself that the art of architecture was comparable to the art of war—one couldn't win a battle without losing soldiers, and one couldn't build a city without losing workmen. According to the diplomats, never in the history of warfare had there been a battle with as many casualties as the construction of St. Petersburg: they spoke of 100,000 dead. The Hanoverian Weber put the figure at 200,000. Doubtless this is an exaggeration, but there is no question that St. Petersburg was built on a charnel house. The real piles that supported the city were the bones of the workers who perished so that it might rise in magnificence above the waters.

In February 1704 the Czar summoned the Italian architect Domenico Trezzini to direct the army of workers. Most of Trezzini's associates were foreigners—Dutch, Italians, Swiss, Germans, French. All were appalled by the living conditions imposed on them in this city perpetually "in progress." They were paid irregularly, they shivered in makeshift housing, turned up their noses at the bad food, protested about the petty administrative annoyances, and complained of the lack of skilled labor. At the first opportunity they deserted the hell that Peter insisted on calling his "paradise." Trezzini replaced them and went on with his work as best he could. The production of bricks and tiles was speeded up in all factories. Lime kilns functioned day and night. Whole forests were chopped down around the city to supply the lumber needed for construction. Mechanical sawmills, powered by water or wind, were set up all over. As there was a shortage of glass, even the grandest buildings had windows of mica. But it was stone that posed the greatest problem—there was hardly any to be found in the region, and the architects demanded it. So the Czar prohibited the use of stone throughout the rest of the country. All of it was reserved for St. Petersburg.* Ships were not allowed to dock in the city unless in addition to their normal cargo they carried thirty quarry stones. Every coachman whose carriage entered the gates of the city had to present a load of at least three paving stones. It was a labor of ants, each insect bringing its twig to the anthill.†

The Czar himself supervised the work. He would run from

---

*In 1600 Boris Godunov had already forbidden the use of stone except to build the ramparts of Smolensk.
†This order was not rescinded until 1776.

one construction site to another, holding in his hand his famous cudgel, his Russian *dubina*, which he used to strike the lazy. As much at ease with workmen as with architects, he would criticize the work of a stonecutter, reject a drawing for a palace, shout insults at a foreman, encourage a carpenter giving a virtuoso performance with an ax, and seize a plane himself to smooth a board. As yet the city was nothing but a collection of construction sites separated by vacant land and a maze of canals with banks held up by posts and fascines. The indefatigable Trezzini built the Church of St. Peter and St. Paul, in the fortress of the same name, with its belfry surmounted by a gilded point, the fortifications of Kronstadt, the Monastery of St. Alexander Nevsky, palaces for the ministers, the Senate, and the Synod, drew the plans for the quays, threw wooden bridges over the canals. Other architects took over from him: the Frenchman Alexander Le Blond, the Germans Schaedel and Schluter, Härbel from Basel. . . .

But the wonderful city was still only an empty shell, a trompe l'oeil stage setting, uninhabited, dead, and cold. Life had to be poured into it. In 1706 Peter instructed Admiral Golovin to settle in St. Petersburg, where he would have a new building for the Admiralty, a port, and a shipyard. In 1707 this shipyard employed three thousand men. The Czar, who was proud of his carpenter's diploma, liked to mingle with them and swing an ax or raise a mast. Every launching of a new ship was the occasion for violent festivities in which equal honor was done to Neptune and to Bacchus. In 1708 Peter firmly invited his sister Natalya, his two half sisters, the two dowager Czarinas, the high dignitaries, and a few rich merchants to join him. For most of the courtiers, accustomed as they were to the happy, luxurious life of Moscow, this command invitation was the equivalent of a sentence of exile. "They take great quantities of baggage with them" wrote Ambassador Whitworth, "because it is said that nothing can be obtained on the spot. They go with heavy hearts, but no one is allowed to excuse himself on grounds of age or illness."[3] That was only the beginning. Soon 350 noble families were summoned to settle in St. Petersburg. Then, when a fire ravaged one-third of Moscow, a new ukase was issued forbidding the people to rebuild the houses that had been destroyed and ordering 5,000 families who were victims of the disaster (nobles, merchants, craftsmen) to move to St. Petersburg and start a new life there. This dictatorial transfer of population was completed in the years that followed.

The first inhabitants of St. Petersburg, transplanted to an artificial city without links to the past, were in despair. Not only had they lost their property, but they felt as if they were no longer in Russia. As they walked along the canals, they thought sometimes they were in Holland, sometimes in Italy, sometimes in Germany. If at least they had been left alone to build their houses as they liked, but that too was regulated by ukase. The size and location of each residence depended on the rank of the owner, the number of his serfs, and the amount of taxes he paid. Any habitation built on the principal island or along the Neva had to conform to the plans drawn up by Trezzini. He had decided there would be three categories of façades corresponding to the social levels of the proprietors: one for important personages, another for persons of quality, still another for ordinary people. Thus one had only to look at the ornamentation of a wall or the height of a window to tell the rank of the man hidden behind it. The principle of the uniform carried over into the domain of housing. One decree specified the design of cast-iron balustrades, another commanded that the moss used for stopping up chinks in wooden walls be scalded to prevent the proliferation of cockroaches, a third provided that houses were to be built side by side and joined together by a common wall so as to economize on bricks.

Ancient Moscow, emptied of its high dignitaries and administrative offices, was already bowing its head. In 1713 St. Petersburg was designated as the capital. The following year it had as many as 34,550 inhabitants. The figure grew from one month to the next. Ten years later it would be 70,000. Foreign craftsmen and merchants set up shop in the city, lured by the prospect of money to be made there. But everyone complained in the watery capital, both those who had chosen to settle there and those who had been condemned to do so. They lamented the detestable climate, the snowstorms in winter, the mosquitoes in summer, the floods in autumn. The French ambassador Campredon spent twelve hundred rubles going from Moscow to St. Petersburg, got mired in the sodden roads, drowned eight horses, lost part of his baggage, and took twenty-four days to make the journey. Peter himself, who had gone ahead of the diplomat, was obliged to cover part of the route on horseback, swimming across rivers.

Because communications were so precarious, provisions were in short supply in the new capital and the cost of living very high. The price of food there was three times higher than in Moscow. According to regulations, shopkeepers had to sell their merchandise at prices fixed by the state until noon, after which time they could raise them as much as they pleased. It is true that for some of the residents, especially the young, these disadvantages were compensated for by a complex feeling of national pride and confidence in the future, as if the mere fact of living inside new walls placed them in the vanguard of the battle for progress. The stones around them spoke not of yesterday but of tomorrow. They left it to their fathers to regret the old legends, to worship their roots.

The Czar was not unaware of this. He was betting on the youth. If he had left Moscow, it was in order to escape from the obstinately reactionary spirit that reigned in the Kremlin. There, he knew that his work would be constantly threatened, at the mercy of a palace intrigue or a popular uprising. Here, with the nobility disoriented, uprooted from their natural environment, it would be easier for him to impose his views. His new capital satisfied both his esthetic taste and his political sense. In the beginning it had been only a collection of hamlets dispersed on the islands and riverbanks, with a fortress, boathouses, and barracks. Now there were a few fine stone houses along the Neva. All the great dignitaries—Golovkin, Shafirov, Gagarin, Yaguzhinsky, Chernyshev, Menshikov—had splendid private mansions in the Italian style. Just in front of the Admiralty a broad tree-lined avenue stretched diagonally, the future Nevsky Prospect. Swedish prisoners swept it every Saturday. On either side of this road stood other princely residences. At the far end could be seen the scaffolding of the Monastery of St. Alexander Nevsky. In 1711, on another avenue, parallel to the Neva, Peter had his Winter Palace built. It stood back to back with private houses and was distinguished from them only by a portal with two columns, over which hung the prow of a ship. This modest building contained a great reception hall and a series of little narrow rooms such as Peter liked. Although he was obliged to build fairly high stories so as to preserve harmony with the neighboring houses, in the rooms where he usually stayed he had a second ceiling constructed below the first.

The same desire for simplicity was apparent in the Summer Palace, which was built some distance away on a tributary of the Neva, which would come to be called the Fontanka. In the middle of a park with flower beds, lawns, grottoes, arbors, fountains, statues, and covered galleries, all in the style of Versailles, stood a sort of Dutch country house with a metal roof and pale yellow walls with whitish bas-reliefs. Beyond the Summer Palace was the Arsenal, where two hundred workmen were busy casting cannon. Farther on was the Museum of Curiosities, where Peter kept a natural-history collection and a few specimens of living monsters. All around, upstream, were scattered the little wooden houses of the "Muscovite Quarter," so called because almost all of its inhabitants were of Russian nationality. In this quarter the air was foul with the smells from nearby factories—tanneries, brick kilns, roperies, gunpowder factories, tar works, and so on. But in the center of town one breathed the sea air. Even when Peter was walking the streets with his long, swinging step, he felt as if he were on the deck of a ship.

While here and there the canals were crossed by wooden planks, there was no question of building a bridge across the Neva. Ferrymen took inhabitants by boat from one bank to the other. The price of the trip was one kopeck per person for "people of quality." Soldiers and workers were carried free of charge. Peter, with his passion for ships, insisted that every great family must have its private boat with a liveried crew. Instructions were given on boat maintenance; owners had to attend sailing classes every Sunday. If they were unable to do so, they were required to send their sons instead. In good weather the Neva was dotted with schooners gay with flags and rowboats with their oarsmen dressed in multicolored jackets. For important personages it was a contest to see who cut the most elegant figure on the water under the practiced eye of the Czar, who steered his own yacht. The whole court, in full fig and full sail, would float by between the new palaces, the shipyards, huts, palisades, boathouses, and stretches of waste ground, while cannon thundered in the Fortress of St.

Peter and St. Paul, and musicians, brought on board for the occasion, played lively tunes for the ladies who might be prone to seasickness.

In winter as soon as the Neva iced over, the different pieces of the city were welded together into a single block. No more need for bridges or boats in order to come and go in the capital. But it was forbidden to cross the frozen river until a team had laid out the path from one bank to the other. When the Czar was in residence in St. Petersburg, he himself inaugurated the white track in a sleigh. A cannon shot fired from the Fortress of St. Peter and St. Paul announced the event. Behind His Majesty there would be a rush of people eager to cross the Neva without getting their feet wet. Actually, Peter didn't like the snowy season, the enemy of navigation in the North. Every year when the ice broke up in spring it was a time of celebration for him. On the waters that had been freed at last he could move around his "paradise," which soon extended beyond St. Petersburg along the southern shore of the Gulf. There Peter and his close associates built their country palaces: Strelna, Oranienbaum, Peterhof, etc.* It was at Peterhof that the Czar stayed when he went to the country in summer. A magnificent garden in the French fashion, overlooking the waters of the Gulf. A great two-story palace built according to the plans of Le Blond. Small, elegant rooms; a study furnished with a library. Despite the charm of this residence, the Czar preferred to spend his nights in a simple Dutch-style pavilion at the very edge of the water called Mon Plaisir. From his tiny bedroom decorated with glazed terra-cotta tiles he could see the fortifications of Kronstadt and the men-of-war riding at anchor. He was both in the country and close to St. Petersburg; it was only a few steps to the dock where his launch was waiting for him. He loved St. Petersburg so much that he would have liked to build hundreds of copies of it to replace all the old Russian patriarchal cities.

No sooner had his sister Natalya arrived, in 1708, than she set up a theater in a big frame building. To attract the public Peter decreed that admission would be free and open to all. The troupe

---

*In 1721 he was to begin building Sarskoye, which would later become Czarskoye Selo, the vast Summer Palace of Catherine the Great.

consisted of ten Russian actors and actresses and sixteen musicians. The repertoire included both original plays and translations. Among the original plays were some from the diligent pen of the Czarevna Natalya. In *Peter or the Golden Keys,* for example, she tried to show the necessity of sending young men abroad to complete their education, as the Czar wished. During intermissions the company performed merry "interludes" mocking old-time customs and preaching the reforms desired by His Majesty. These propaganda shows had no great success. Later Mann's German troupe took over from the Russian company.

And there was more evidence of the young city's vitality: the establishment within its walls, in 1711, of a press and the publication of a newspaper, *The St. Petersburg News.* The Czar kept tight control over its contents. The paper, printed in octavo in secular characters and with very narrow margins, gave diplomatic and military bulletins but also information on public works undertaken in the city or the arrival of new "monsters" in the Museum of Curiosities. A bookshop opened its doors and the few intellectuals at court went there to stock up on foreign books.

All these developments augured well. Yet Peter was impatient because his "paradise" had not yet eclipsed other European capitals. He had appointed Menshikov governor-general of the town, with Bruce as his deputy. They were assisted by a Chancery of Municipal Affairs, under whose jurisdiction the architects worked. In spite of the efforts of all these people, St. Petersburg was still only a collection of separate pieces in which handsome stone residences stood next to rickety huts, elegant districts were surrounded by vast muddy spaces, and in winter people living on the outskirts of town trembled to hear the howling of wolves from nearby forests. These wolves ventured to the very houses and attacked isolated sentries. In 1714 two soldiers who were on guard duty outside a cannon foundry were eaten alive. Lighting was almost nonexistent. A few rare hemp-oil lanterns were hung around the Winter Palace and in front of the principal houses.

The police service, which had at first been administered by a voivode, or military chief, was entrusted in 1717 to a chief of police, General Anton Devier. But that energetic man, of Portuguese extraction, had only 10 officers, 20 noncommissioned

officers, 160 soldiers, and 10 scribes to see that the city was kept
clean, make sure chimneys were swept, protect the security of the
citizens, interrogate suspects, check on travelers, arrest thieves,
and punish with the knout any serf caught moving about without
a "letter of authorization" from his masters. At night the streets
were barred at each end and sentries, taken from among residents
of the quarter, mounted guard until dawn. Everyone was called on
to take his turn in performing this service. Even members of the
clergy were under obligation to participate in guard duty, though
one could get out of it by hiring the services of a neighbor. A
replacement cost fifteen kopecks a night. After eleven at night the
amateur sentries let no one pass except important noblemen,
workers going to construction sites, doctors, midwives, and
priests, providing they were carrying lanterns. Highway robbery
was a frequent occurrence. Troops of bandits roamed the neighboring countryside. The ambassador of Saxony wrote his government that the city was threatened by a horde of nine thousand
robbers: thirty-six of them were caught and hanged; the rest
of the band dispersed. But that was not enough to reassure the
inhabitants.

In addition, residents were obsessed with the fear of fires. The
great number of wooden houses made it easy for fire to spread. As
a precaution, it was ordered that public steam baths be heated only
on Saturday. A few watchmen perched in towers would give the
alarm by ringing a bell as soon as they saw the first flames. Drum
rolls would carry the news to every quarter. Inhabitants who had
been designated to act as firemen would rush to the spot armed
with axes, ladders, and buckets. In serious cases, soldiers would
help residents to put out the blaze.* Peter himself often joined in:
ax in hand, he would leap into the midst of the flames, like some
wild-eyed devil with no fear of fire. "I have often seen him the first
to arrive at a fire, with a small pump in his sleigh," wrote the
Danish ambassador Juel. "He takes part in all the rescue operations, and since he has an extraordinarily quick mind he sees at
once what has to be done to extinguish the fire; he climbs up to

---

*Not until 1722 did St. Petersburg have a company of firemen equipped with four
  Dutch pumps.

the roof; he goes to the points where the danger is greatest; he urges the nobles, like the common people, to take part in the struggle, and he does not stop until the fire is out. . . . But when the sovereign is not present, it is another thing entirely; the people look on, indifferent, and do nothing to extinguish the fire. It is no use to remonstrate with them or even to offer them money, they only wait for an opportunity to steal something."

The population of St. Petersburg had another calamity to worry about: floods. Nearly every year in late autumn storms buffeted the city, the wind tore off roofs and knocked down scaffolding, the Neva overflowed its banks, inundating the ground floor of houses. The inhabitants would hastily gather up provisions and take refuge in upper stories; cattle were taken to nearby forests. In 1703 the Austrian ambassador Pleyer spoke of two thousand sick and wounded submerged by rising waters. On September 11, 1706, Peter calmly noted that there were twenty-one inches of water on the floor of his little house. Outside he saw men, women, and children clinging to planks swept along by the river. "It's very amusing," he wrote Menshikov, in a letter dated from "Paradise." In 1717 the fortifications of the Arsenal crumbled, undermined by the waters. In November 1721 the Neva rose so high that the ruined city seemed to be living out its last hours. Boats broke their moorings and drifted in the current amid a jumble of furniture, beams, empty carriages, barrels, and chests. Horses drowned. People stranded on rooftops shouted and waved their arms. "The storm," wrote de La Vie to Cardinal Dubois, "blew with such violence that if it had gone on for two more hours this city would have been utterly destroyed. The damage it has caused is indescribable: not one house remains untouched. The losses are estimated at two or three million rubles. . . . I shall refrain from expressing all my thoughts on this occasion; suffice it to say that the Czar, like another Philip of Spain,* showed the greatness of his soul by remaining calm."

As soon as the Neva returned to its bed, workers set about repairing the damage. They scraped mud from the streets, patched roofs, nailed down floors that had been lifted by the rising waters.

*A reference to Philip II and the wreck of the Spanish Armada in 1588.—TRANS.

No matter how great the catastrophe had been, everyone knew that the Czar would never give up his obsession. Yet many of the common people thought that St. Petersburg, by usurping the traditional place of Moscow, had called down upon itself the wrath of heaven. It was rumored that a celestial figure had appeared in the Church of the Holy Trinity and announced to the faithful: "St. Petersburg will become a wilderness again." The deacon of the church was condemned to three years of forced labor for having repeated this prophecy. But his words made their way among the peasants, the Old Believers, and even among the sovereign's entourage. St. Petersburg, people said, a city rapidly constructed, was destined to perish rapidly. Only the will of the Czar kept the artificial city alive. If he disappeared, the walls would crumble, the canals would fill up with mud, and the inhabitants would disperse, only too happy to return to their old ways. But Peter behaved as if he and his capital were eternal.

10
Journey
to
France

While Peter was building his new capital and strengthening his old alliances, Charles XII, who was still a refugee in Turkey, was trying to persuade Sultan Ahmed III to resume hostilities against Russia. Meantime, Peter Tolstoy, the Czar's ambassador to Constantinople, was demanding that the king of Sweden be turned over to the Russians, or at least arrested. But he had only twenty thousand ducats and a few sable skins with which to buy Ottoman consciences, while Charles XII could pay his hosts large subsidies.

For the man who had been so badly defeated at Poltava was rich. He had saved his war chest; he had negotiated loans from the Cook brothers of the English Levant Company; he had borrowed money from Holstein; last, he had inherited some barrels of gold from Mazeppa after the Cossack, weary of a life of betrayals and failures, had taken poison. The Turks, who appreciated the liberalities of their "distinguished guest" and were worried about Russia's growing power on the Black Sea, were preparing for war. To make them see reason Tolstoy presented an ultimatum. The Sublime Porte replied by formulating unacceptable conditions:

Russia must recognize Stanislas Leszczynski as king of Poland, return Livonia and Ingria to Sweden, and make a commitment never again to enter the Black Sea. On November 20, 1710, at a solemn session of the Divan, war was declared. As was the custom, Tolstoy was immediately imprisoned in the Castle of the Seven Towers.

At nightfall after the religious service on January 1, 1711, the inhabitants of St. Petersburg attended a display of fireworks composed of two designs. The first showed an Ottoman star "as a sign of war against the Turks."[1] The star was accompanied by an inscription: "Lord, show us Thy ways!" The second represented a column surmounted by a key and a sword, with another inscription: "Where justice is, there also is the help of God." These shining billboards informed the good Orthodox folk that the holy crusade was beginning again. Unfortunately a few days later the Duke of Kurland, husband of Grand Duchess Anna, died of an illness. In spite of this loss, the Czar did not postpone his departure for Moscow. There, since military action called him to the front and he foresaw an extended absence, he instituted a Senate of eight members, which would take over the conduct of day-to-day affairs. On February 25 a Te Deum was celebrated in the Cathedral of the Assumption. A manifesto was read out praying God to grant His help "against the breakers of the peace and enemies of the Christian name." Two regiments of the Guard were massed in front of the church. Their usual white flags had been replaced with red ones bearing the words: "For the name of Jesus Christ and Christendom," and "By this sign you shall conquer."

The victory of Poltava had strengthened Peter's confidence in his soldiers and generals: the Turks would meet the fate of the Swedes. Nevertheless, since the campaign was likely to last for several months, he decided to take with him his beloved Catherine. She had shown so much courage, simplicity, and kindheartedness when she was with the armies during the last fighting that he regarded her as a sort of mascot, his walking good-luck charm. In fact, now that she had been his official mistress for so long, shouldn't he marry her? After having beaten about the bush for eight years, he made up his mind in a few minutes. On February 19, 1711, at seven o'clock in the morning, in Prince Menshikov's private chapel, the marriage of Rear Admiral Peter (the Czar of Russia) with the servant of God Catherine Alexeyevna (his mistress) was celebrated in haste, in the presence of a few witnesses. No cabinet minister attended the ceremony. The maids of honor were two little girls aged five and three: Anna and Elizabeth, the couple's illegitimate children. Thus the former Livonian prisoner who had done Peter's laundry and humbly shared his couch officially became Czarina of Russia.

When the ceremony was over, the whole company climbed into sleighs drawn by six horses each and drove to the palace escorted by trumpeters and drummers. There Peter hurried to the banquet hall and hung from the ceiling a six-branched candelabrum of ebony and ivory that he himself had made on a lathe. That evening the gala dinner was followed by a ball and fireworks. The Czar proudly pointed out to the English ambassador that his new union was fruitful, "since it had already produced five children."* He told his sister Natalya and his two half sisters that he was counting on them to respect Catherine, his wife before God, and that if he should disappear they were to accord his widow the rank, privileges, and revenues of a dowager czarina. On March 6 the Muscovites were informed by heralds that "the Czarina Catherine Alexeyevna [was] the true and legitimate spouse of Czar Peter I."

On the same day the Czar left Moscow with his wife to join his army. Toward the end of the month he fell ill of scurvy, at Luck. Racked by doubt and anxiety, he wrote Menshikov that there lay before him a path "of which he had no idea" and to Apraxin that he was "sick and in despair" and didn't know what orders to give him. But he had no sooner recovered than he set out again, still with Catherine, who refused to abandon her convalescing husband. He caused to be written in his *Journal:* "His Majesty had intended to send his wife, with the other ladies, to a safe town in Poland so as to spare them from fatigues unsuitable to members of their sex. But Catherine, who was above these weaknesses, begged him so earnestly to allow her to remain with the army that His Majesty was obliged to consent. From that time on the Czarina followed him on all his military expeditions."

*Three of the five had died in infancy.

171

Having set forth to meet the Turks, Peter was counting on the support of Poland, the Christians of the Orient, and the hospodars of Moldavia and Walachia. Only Cantemir, the hospodar of Moldavia, answered his call, and he brought with him only a paltry five thousand horsemen armed with bows and half-pikes. The enemy army had already crossed the Danube. Some of Peter's generals, including all the foreigners, thought the regiments should take up positions along the Dniester and await the attack of the Turks, for it would be rash to advance to meet them in the desert where there was no possibility of obtaining supplies. The Russian generals, however, supported by Golovkin and Shafirov, shouted that national honor demanded they march forward.

The heat was suffocating, the landscape parched. The Russian soldiers, accustomed to the cold mists of the Baltic, were exhausted before they had fought. Thirst made their noses bleed and their ears buzz. Food and fodder were low. The grass in the fields had been "eaten down to the roots by the grasshoppers."[2] To stay where they were meant possibly losing thousands of men and horses from sickness; better to lose them in battle. Peter decided in favor of action. Crossing the Dniester with his army, he entered an infinity of burning sand shaped into grayish hills and valleys. They camped on the banks of the Pruth, partly to rest, partly to celebrate the anniversary of Poltava. Catherine did justice to the Tokay wine.

Ten days later, on the evening of July 7, 1711, disaster struck. The Russian army, reduced to about 38,000 men, found itself surrounded by a Turkish army five times larger, occupying both banks of the Pruth. Attacked with grapeshot and hand-to-hand weapons, the Russians suffered heavy losses. "We could no longer either retreat or stay where we were, having neither provisions nor forage, so that we had to conquer or perish," says Peter's *Journal*. So far as conquering was concerned, everyone soon realized that that was out of the question. But perishing? Did it make sense to condemn the best troops of Russia to a massacre? And what would happen to Peter and Catherine, who were in the midst of the camp? The *Journal* states that one could not contemplate "exposing Their Majesties, who were present and upon whose preservation the happiness of the whole Russian Empire depended."

While the musket fire raged around him and men were falling on every side, Peter experienced one of the worst moments of terror in his life: the humiliation of defeat, the prospect of slavery in Turkey, anxiety over the fate of his wife. . . . At first he thought to flee, crossing enemy lines with the help of a Cossack guide. But Catherine dissuaded him from that dangerous solution. Amid the general panic she alone kept a cool head. Calmly, she advised the Czar to negotiate with the Turks. To buy off the Grand Vizier she offered all her jewels, all the gold in her money box. Shafirov was chosen to take the gift to the victor. The Turk appraised the diamonds with an expert eye. Sheremetev, meanwhile, who was known for his shrewdness, went to the enemy camp to discuss peace terms. He pointed out that the Russians were still strong enough to inflict a bloody counterblow on the Ottoman army.

The Grand Vizier was aware that the Russian cavalry, commanded by Generals Ronne and Tchirivov, was threatening Braila, which would cut off his retreat. Furthermore, he realized that his janissaries, who had been sorely tried in the fighting, were eager to go home. Catherine's present, joined to these strategic considerations, inclined him to be conciliatory. The treaty of Pruth was signed. Under the terms of this agreement, Russia was to return Azov to Turkey, dismantle some neighboring forts, stop meddling in the affairs of Poland, and promise to let Charles XII return freely to his kingdom. Peter, who had been ready to accept much harder conditions (such as surrendering all conquered places, abandoning Livonia to Sweden, and ceding some Russian cities of the Center), listened to the Grand Vizier's reasonable demands with relief. Once again he was getting off easy. "Divine justice, exercising its rights," says the *Journal*, "truly worked a miracle on this occasion, saving us from the unavoidable peril into which we had ventured only because we sincerely desired the deliverance and advantage of the Christians."

When Charles XII learned that peace had been concluded he was furious. He galloped to the Turkish camp, rushed into the Grand Vizier's tent, and railed at him for not having wiped out the Russian army and captured the Czar when he had the chance. "We have fought the Russians," replied the Grand Vizier. "If you want to come to blows with them too, you can do so with your own men.

As for us, we are not going to break a peace that has been concluded."[3]

While Charles XII was fulminating, the Russian army retreated in good order following the course of the Pruth. At first overwhelmed by the shame of the defeat, Peter, as was his habit, got a grip on himself, denied the obvious facts, and began to swagger. "Although it is not without sorrow that we are deprived of those places [Azov] that have cost us so much labor and expense," he wrote Apraxin, "yet I hope that by this loss we shall be greatly strengthened on the other side [the Baltic], which will be an incomparably greater gain." Count Golovkin likewise wrote to Prince Dolgoruky assuring him that the peace was very advantageous, "since the Czar now has his whole army at his disposal."

These comforting ways of saving face deceived no one. The Czar's prestige abroad, which had risen after Poltava, dropped again in a free fall. His allies smiled behind his back and their friendship, none too reliable to begin with, cooled even further. The Czar, shaken by the ordeal he had been through, went to Carlsbad, where he hoped the waters would restore his health and optimism. But he was soon scowling again. Separated from Catherine, he wrote her bitterly: "This place is so gay you might call it a prison. It is situated between mountains so high that one can hardly see the sun. Worst of all, there is no good beer."[4] And a few days later: "Thank God, I am in good health, but the water I drink has made my stomach swell up, for they water us like horses."[5] After a few days' rest at Carlsbad, he pushed on to Torgau to attend the wedding of his son Alexis, aged twenty-one, and Charlotte of Brunswick-Wolfenbüttel.

Meanwhile, the Russian army—diminished, demoralized, trailing its sick and wounded—was moving north again. It still had work to do. Having temporarily given up on the Black Sea, Peter was turning toward the Baltic. He wanted to finish his business with Sweden. Europe, however, was wary. Berlin feared that if it supported the Czar the world balance of power would be permanently changed to Russia's advantage. The same opinion held sway in London. Lord Strafford, the English ambassador to Holland, wrote Kurakin defining the traditional rule of British diplomacy as follows: "England does not desire that the Swedish crown should be ruined and enfeebled, for she seeks to maintain the balance of all the powers in the North." Moreover, English merchants were afraid that if the Czar seized good seaports, Russia might trade with all countries on her own ships instead of going through the intermediary of the English and Dutch. As for the Austrians, while they were worried about the increased power of Turkey after the Russian defeat on the Pruth, they preferred to use Prussia rather than Russia to counterbalance the influence of Sweden. Abandoned on all sides and no longer sure if the indecisive European powers were his allies or enemies, Peter decided to act alone. In 1713 he undertook the Finnish campaign. He described his intentions candidly and bluntly in a letter to Apraxin: "The purpose of the campaign is not to lay Finland waste but to take possession of it, not because the Czar wishes to keep those territories but for two reasons: the province may serve as an object to be exchanged or to be held in pawn at the time of the peace treaty; in addition, Finland is Sweden's foster mother, providing her with meat, other food products, and wood. If God permitted us to take Abo, the Swedes would not be so stiff-necked."

The newly formed fleet was commanded by Admiral Apraxin with Peter as Rear Admiral. As soon as it went into action, it took Helsingfors (Helsinki), Borga, and Abo. Meanwhile Menshikov forced Tonningen to capitulate. On July 27, 1714, at Hangö the Russians had another naval victory, over the Swedish fleet, former mistress of the Baltic. This time Peter had taken personal command of the operation. Rear Admiral Ehrenskjold had been taken prisoner, ten Swedish ships had fallen into the hands of the Russians, the Aland Islands had been conquered, and the Czar returned to his "paradise" of St. Petersburg in triumph to receive a promotion to vice admiral and a medal with the inscription: "The Russian eagle does not catch flies." On November 24, 1714, the Czarina's name day, the Czar decorated her with the newly founded Order of St. Catherine, in recognition of her steadfastness during the battle of the Pruth, where, says the *Journal*, she had behaved "not like a woman but like a man." A discreet allusion, perhaps, to her having given her jewels to save Peter from disaster.

The memory of that disaster had already been erased by the naval victory. In Russia as abroad, Hangö produced the effect of a second Poltava. The European powers no longer doubted that the Czar had resolved to strike a decisive blow against Sweden. How far would he go afterward? The English and the Danes, his alleged allies, needed a fair amount of persuading to help him in his plans for conquest. A Russian squadron of forty-eight galleys was already concentrated off Copenhagen. King Frederick IV of Denmark, who was worried about this armed presence in his waters, wondered if Peter didn't mean to attack his friends before going after Sweden. While at court brilliant receptions were being held in honor of the Czar, elsewhere in the city fortifications were being hastily repaired, and arms were being distributed to the townspeople to resist a possible Russian assault. The Danes smiled at the Czar and secretly maneuvered to trip him up.

On his ship the *Ingermanland,* Peter reviewed the Russian, Danish, English, and Dutch squadrons gathered in the roads. It was the first time that a British squadron had been placed under the orders of a foreign admiral. Shafirov wrote to Menshikov that "such an honor had never fallen to a monarch since the beginning of the world." Peter wanted to bequeath to posterity the ship on which he had sailed during these maneuvers. But the allied fleet never came to trial with the Swedish fleet, which slipped away, and the expedition was cut short. In spite of the homage paid to "navigator Peter," a persistent rumor circulated that the English wanted to seize him and force him to go home and take his ships and expeditionary corps with him, so as to put an end to Russian expansion in the Baltic. The "Muscovite ogre" was supposed to have the diabolical intention of appropriating Danish Pomerania, Mecklenburg, Hamburg, Lübeck. . . . And indeed, in Pomerania Peter was behaving like a potentate and treating King Augustus like his vassal. As for Mecklenburg, that business too was off to a good start, for one of the Czar's nieces, Catherine,* had just married the duke, Karl Leopold of Mecklenburg.

This match, supplemented by a treaty of alliance, enabled Russia to move into North Germany. Forty thousand Russian soldiers were placed at the disposal of the Duke of Mecklenburg to support him against his nobles, who were in revolt. King

*Eldest daughter of the widow of Ivan V.

*Peter the Great, by Sir Godfrey Kneller, 1698. (London, Kensington Palace.
Photo A.C. Cooper. Copyright reserved to Her Majesty Queen Elizabeth II.)*

above: *Peter the Great. Engraving by Oubraken, after Moore, 1718. (Paris, Bibliothèque Nationale. Photo B. N.)*

right: *Engraving after a wax bust of Peter the Great. (Leningrad, Hermitage Museum. Photo Harlingue-Viollet.)*

opposite: *Peter the Great. Portrait formerly attributed to Aert de Gelder. (Amsterdam, Rijksmuseum. Photo by the museum.)*

above: *Peter the Great. Anonymous drawing from the seventeenth century. (Chantilly, Musée Condé. Photo Giraudon/Art Resource, New York.)*

opposite top: *Military uniform and dress caftan of Peter the Great. (Moscow, Museum of History. Photo Novosty Agency.)*

opposite bottom: *Peter the Great's carriage sled. End of the seventeenth century. (Moscow, Museum of History. Photo Novosty Agency.)*

above left: *The Czarevna Sophia. Anonymous portrait from the end of the seventeenth century. (Photo Novosty Agency.)*

above middle: *Prince Boris Golitzin. (Moscow, Museum of History. Photo Novosty Agency.)*

above right: *The Czarevich Alexis, by G. Danhauer. (Leningrad, Hermitage Museum. Photo Harlingue-Viollet.)*

below right: *A strelets. Drawing from the album of E. Palmqvist, 1674. (Photo Novosty Agency.)*

opposite top left: *The Czarina Eudoxia. (Paris, Bibliothèque Nationale. Photo Flammarion.)*

opposite top right: *The Empress Catherine, wife of Peter the Great, in 1717, by J. M. Nattier. (Leningrad, Hermitage Museum. Photo Harlingue-Viollet.)*

opposite bottom: *The repression after the revolt of the* streltsy. *Engraving from the eighteenth century. (Photo Novosty Agency.)*

above: *Punishment: the ordinary knout and the great knout. Engravings by Tilliard after Jean-Baptiste Le Prince. (Paris, Bibliothèque Nationale. Photos Flammarion.)*

below: *Abolition of the Russian caftan, replaced by the Hungarian coat. Engraving by J. C. Philips, 1742. (Photo Roger Viollet.)*

АщерЬю Его Пруского ВелІчества,
но обаче сіе еще негораздо подлІнно,
ГрафЪ СтарембергЪ Цесарской по-
сланнікЪ, не давно пріѢхалЪ сюды
изЪ Лондона чрезЪ Брабандію.

Печатано   вЪ СанктЪпітербурхѢ
1720, Августа вЪ 31 день.

9Υ

ВѢДОМОСТИ.

ИзЪ КОПЕНГАГЕНА отЪ 3 Августа.

КоролЬ поѢхалЪ третьяго дня
на время вЪ ЛаландЪ, прежде своего
отЪѢзду. Его ВелІчество, подарІлЪ
МІлорду Картерету АнглІнскому
Послу шпагу сЪ алмазами, цѢною
вЪ три тысячи ефІмковЪ; также
Его ВелІчество, пожаловалЪ свои
портретЪ сЪ Алмазами Генералу
МаІору Леувенору, за велікіе и
вѢрные его службы, которые онЪ
52   показалЪ

top: The News. *First Russian
newspaper. (Moscow, Museum of History.
Photo Novosty Agency.)*

left: *A barber cutting a beard at the
orders of Peter the Great. Anonymous
engraving from the eighteenth century.
(Paris, Bibliothèque Nationale.
Photo B. N.)*

above: *Medallion certifying payment of
the tax for Russians who kept their beards.
(Photo X.)*

opposite top left: *François Lefort. Engraving by Dreyer. (Paris, Bibliothèque Nationale, Photo B. N.)*

opposite top right: *Sheremetev. Engraving by Antipyev after a portrait by Argunov. (Photo Novosty Agency.)*

opposite bottom: *Prince Menshikov. (Leningrad, Hermitage Museum. Photo by the museum.)*

above left: *General Gordon. Engraving from the eighteenth century. (Leningrad, Hermitage Museum. Photo Novosty Agency.)*

above right: *Shafirov. Engraving from the eighteenth century. (Moscow, Museum of History. Photo Novosty Agency.)*

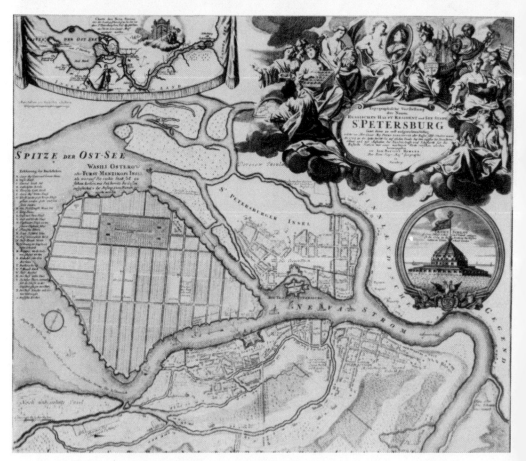

top: *St. Petersburg at the time of Peter the Great. The banks of the Neva, the Admiralty, and the Academy of Sciences. (Paris, Bibliothèque Nationale. Photo B. N.)*

bottom: *Map of St. Petersburg at the time of Peter the Great, drawn by Jean-Baptiste Homann of Nuremberg, 1717–1725. (Paris, Bibliothèque Nationale. Photo B. N.)*

top: *St. Petersburg at the time of Peter the Great. The old Winter Palace and the canal between the Moika and the Neva. (Paris, Bibliothèque Nationale. Photo B. N.)*

bottom: *The battle of Poltava, June 27, 1709, by J. M. Nattier. (Moscow, Pushkin Museum. Photo by the museum.)*

LA ROYALE RECEPTION ET LES HONNEURS RENDUS A PARIS PAR LE ROY AU LOUVRE LE 11 MAY M.DCC.XVII AU TRI

Jardin des Tuilleries

La Place Royale

Mr Le Regent   LE ROY   SA MAJESTE CZARIENNE

Madame de ....   Prince Kurakin

ALMANACH POUR   L'ANNÉE M.DCC.XVIII

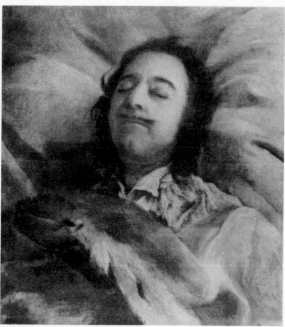

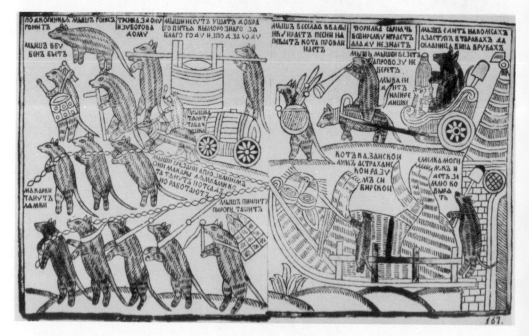

top left: *Peter the Great, on his deathbed, giving the imperial crown to his wife, Catherine I. (Photo Roger Viollet.)*

top right: *Peter the Great on his deathbed, by Ivan Nikitin. (Leningrad, Hermitage Museum. Photo Novosty Agency.)*

bottom: *Burial of the cat by the mice. Satirical engraving that appeared after the death of Peter the Great. (Paris, Bibliothèque Nationale. Photo Flammarion.)*

George I of England asked in vain for Peter to withdraw his troops from the territories they had brazenly occupied. Anonymous pamphlets appeared expressing the complaints of the population about the conduct of the Russians in Mecklenburg, Pomerania, and Holstein. The coalition against Sweden was pulling apart in so many directions that Peter wrote Catherine: "As for what's happening here, I can tell you that we have gone on a pointless excursion, for our joint action is like that of young horses harnessed to a coach; while the one in the middle is trying to advance, the two others aren't even thinking about moving. Because of all that, I think I shall soon be with you." The disagreements among the allies broke out during meetings of the council of war. Action against Sweden was postponed until the following summer. The fleets separated, each returning to its own bases. Peter, exasperated, left Copenhagen for Amsterdam. On the way he met the king of Prussia and consolidated the alliance between their two countries.

This time Holland welcomed not "carpenter Peter" in search of instructors but the leader of the European alliance against Sweden. This haughty guest was a nuisance and he did not find favor in the United Provinces: you never knew what he was up to, his pockets were full of firecrackers. In Amsterdam he had secret contacts with Baron Goertz, plenipotentiary and confidant of Charles XII. That wily gentleman proposed that he sign a peace treaty with Sweden according to which the shores of the Baltic would be ceded to Russia. In exchange, Peter would help Charles XII, his former enemy, to conquer Norway, which at that time was a Danish possession. They would then take advantage of the commotion to overthrow King George I of England and place the pretender, the son of James II, on the throne. News of this imbroglio was brought to the ears of George I, who was outraged. Veselovsky, secretary of the Russian embassy in London, wrote a memorandum protesting "these false insinuations, these shameful calumnies spread by the enemy, the outrageous conspiracy behind this imposture. Never did it enter the Czar's mind to take part in such a detestable plot; he takes all his pride in living with his allies in a frank and upright way. . . . He observes all his alliances and commitments religiously."[6]

These declarations of good faith fell on deaf ears. No matter what Peter's envoys said, his erstwhile friends were suspicious of him. And rightly so. Disappointed by the English and the Danes, the Czar wanted to make overtures to France, wean her away from the system of alliances with Sweden, Holland, and England, and offer her in exchange an alliance with Russia, Poland, and Prussia. To do that he had to go to Paris. He had expressed his intention of making such a visit while Louis XIV had still been alive. But, on grounds of age and ill health, the old king had rejected any plan for them to meet. Since September 1, 1715, the child Louis XV had been on the throne with the regent, Philippe d'Orléans, at his side. Would they once again refuse to receive the master of Russia? Out of the question; nevertheless, France was bound to Sweden by a secret agreement that had not yet expired, and the Abbé Guillaume Dubois, the regent's chief foreign policy adviser, was completely on the side of the English. He wrote the regent: "If you do not remain united to His British Majesty, you will fall from the attic to the cellar." On January 7, 1717, the Marquis de Châteauneuf, French ambassador to The Hague, received orders to act circumspectly, without offending the Czar, but to discourage him insofar as possible. All this equivocation was exasperating to Peter, who could not understand why Paris showed so little eagerness to welcome the victor of Poltava and Hangö.

In the end, overcoming his repugnance for Russian politics and its representatives, the regent gave in. So let him come, this unwelcome guest emerging from the polar ice! The Duc de Saint-Simon noted in his *Mémoires*: "There was nothing for it but to appear very pleased about the visit, although the Regent would gladly have dispensed with it. The expense of entertaining the Czar would be great and the trouble no less great, with a Prince so powerful and perspicacious but full of whims, with some remnants of barbarous manners. . . ." Having gotten his way, Peter chose an escort for the journey. This time, as an exception, he deprived himself of Catherine's company. He had exhibited her at the courts of all the foreign princes without worrying about the impression she might make with her rustic manners and gaudy dresses, but he thought it best not to have her along when he confronted the Parisian court, which was known for its refinement and malicious gossip. He would content himself with writing her from each stage of the journey.

In a day and a half in Antwerp, he and his escort emptied 269 bottles of wine. In Brussels, he went to see a monk who was celebrated for his skill with a lathe, took out a pocket ruler to measure a fragment of the true cross when it was presented to him by the dean of the church of St. Gudule, and after a drinking bout cooled his head in a fountain near the ducal mansion. In Ostend, he wanted to learn all about the operation of the locks. In Nieuport, he received the Duke of Holstein and the Prince de la Tour, who came to pay their respects and to wish him smooth sailing for the rest of his trip.

On April 21, 1717, he landed on the French coast, at Dunkirk. M. de Liboy, a gentleman of the king's household who had been assigned to welcome him, was dismayed by the size of the Russian suite. He had been told that His Majesty the Czar would be traveling incognito with an escort of twenty persons of quality and twenty servants. But he found himself having to make arrangements for fifty-seven persons, with twenty-three more due to arrive in the next few days. How was he going to entertain all these people, when the funds available to him were limited by a decision of the government? Timidly, Liboy offered the visitors a fixed sum of fifteen hundred livres a day for their maintenance. This procedure was standard at the Russian court for foreign diplomatic missions. But Kurakin, the Russian ambassador to France, bellowed in outrage: How could one think of pinching sous when one had the honor to receive the Czar! Liboy obediently transmitted the complaints and waited for orders. To his great relief, Versailles finally agreed to loosen the purse strings. France was too eager to satisfy the distinguished guest to haggle. But the distinguished guest was not easy to satisfy. Half the time he didn't even know what he wanted. Liboy wrote to Versailles: "This little court is very undecided and, from the throne to the stable, very prone to anger. The Czar does have seeds of virtue in him, but they are all wild. . . . He rises very early in the morning, dines around ten o'clock, has a light supper when he has dined well, and retires at nine; but between dinner and supper he consumes a prodigious amount of aniseed cordial, beer, wine, fruits, and all kinds of food. . . . He always has at hand two or three dishes prepared by his cook. He abandons a sumptuously laden table to go eat in his room. He says the beer he is offered is detestable and complains about everything."

Even the means of transportation used in France failed to find favor in Peter's eyes. He peevishly rejected all the coaches Liboy offered him. "No gentleman was ever seen riding in such hearses!" exclaimed Kurakin. Expressing his master's desire, he demanded five two-wheeled post chaises with two seats each. Where were they to be found? All of Dunkirk was searched, all of Calais. When at last Liboy arrived triumphant with the desired conveyances, the Czar had changed his mind. Any vehicle would do, he said, but he wanted special relays to be organized so that he could reach Paris in four days. Once he arrived in Calais he forgot he was in a rush and took his time visiting the fortifications, the port, the harbor installations—no doubt because the person conducting him around the city was the charming young Mme. de Thosse, wife of the king's justice of Calais. No doubt he had notions of luring her into bed, the better to appreciate France. Liboy, who was concerned for the virtue of the judge's lady, had only one thought in mind: to leave as soon as possible. But Peter began to quarrel with him again over the means of transportation, and the affair grew acrimonious.

There were days when Liboy wondered whether the Czar really intended to continue on his way. By May 2 Liboy considered the journey "broken off," but then the distinguished young Marquis de Mailly-Nesle arrived in Calais, sent by the regent to greet His Majesty. The emissary from Versailles was not aware that that day was the Russian Easter. To celebrate the resurrection of the Lord, Peter had gone to drink in a tavern with his suite and his musicians. The suite was dead drunk, and the musicians were in no better condition. Only Peter was still more or less upright, but that didn't mean he was in a mood for the bowing and scraping prescribed by protocol. Mailly would have to wait until the Czar was sober to present his compliments. Irritated by the affectation of his visitor, a dandy who changed his clothes several times a day, Peter growled: "Really, I feel sorry for M. de Mailly-Nesle. He has such a bad tailor that he can't find a coat cut to his liking."

At last, having exhausted all of Calais's attractions, Peter agreed to move on. Refusing coaches and berlins, he invented a conveyance of his own: a discarded phaeton fastened onto shafts, the whole thing carried by horses. It was no use pointing out to him that the teams were not trained for this sort of service; he was not to be dissuaded. For greater security, men on foot had to support the shafts and lead the horses by the bridle. It was feared there would be an accident, but the Czar was delighted with his perilous rig. His escort trailed behind in berlins, litters, chaises. Mailly, exasperated by all the foolishness, wrote: "Men are ordinarily led by reason; but these (if so be that one can apply the word man to those who have nothing human about them) do not understand reason at all. . . . I wish with all my heart that he [the Czar] had arrived in Paris and even that he had departed thence. When His Royal Highness has seen him, and when he has stayed a few days, I am persuaded, if I may venture to say so, that His Royal Highness will not be sorry to be rid of him. The Czar changes his mind every moment. I have nothing positive to tell you about the days he has been traveling."

In Amiens the civil authorities and the bishop had prepared a magnificent reception for the sovereign, but he didn't stop, refused to have anyone presented to him, and insisted on going straight to Beauvais. It was drawn to his attention that no relays were supplied at this time of day. He replied with abusive language and climbed back into his phaeton on shafts. The intendant of Beauvais, who had been alerted in haste, rounded up the sixty horses necessary as best he could, laid on a supper, a concert, an illumination and fireworks, and decorated the palace with the arms of the Czar. The cream of Beauvais society was assembled for the reception. Suddenly they learned that the Czar had raced through town and stopped a quarter of a league beyond, at an ill-famed tavern, where he had dined with his suite, for eighteen francs, and where he intended to spend the night. With him were Ambassador Kurakin, Vice Chancellor Shafirov, Adjutant General Yaguzhinsky, Lieutenant General Dolgoruky, Privy Councillor Tolstoy, officers, chamberlains, pages, and the buffoon, the Prince Pope Zotov, whom Dubois later described as "an old dwarf with long white hair falling to his shoulders, of unbearable ugliness and deformity, and with a voice like a frog's."

At nine o'clock at night on May 7, 1717, the Czar made his

entrance into Paris escorted by three hundred mounted grenadiers. Despite the lateness of the hour, a crowd of curious spectators jostled one another on the Rue Saint-Denis and the Rue Saint-
Honoré, which had been illuminated for the occasion. The regent
had had the Queen Mother's sumptuous apartment in the Louvre
prepared for the "monarch of the snows." Coypel had cleaned and
restored the paint and gilt. Sergent recounts that they had moved
into the apartment "the beautiful bed that Mme. de Maintenon had
caused to be made for the King, which is the richest and most
magnificent thing in the world."[7] Two tables set for sixty persons
each and laden with comestibles waited to satisfy the appetite of
the travelers. The Duc d'Antin, Superintendent of the Royal Buildings, who was charged with housing the chief officers in the sovereign's retinue, could think of no better solution than to requisition
the meeting hall of the Académie Française, which was located in
the Louvre itself. When on May 5 the illustrious company was
notified of this decision, it thanked the duke for his "civilities,"
moved out tables, armchairs, and armoires, and installed itself in
the hall of the Academy of Inscriptions next door. Meanwhile,
Tolstoy, who had come ahead to reconnoiter, suggested that the
Hôtel Lesdiguières be prepared as well, in case Peter preferred
more modest lodgings. The beautiful private mansion on the Rue
de la Cerisaie was hastily refurbished with furniture and tapestries
belonging to the crown. Was it there that Peter would choose to
stay? No, he went straight to the Louvre. There he stood in front
of the two tables set for sixty persons each. He cast a scornful
glance over the culinary display, asked for a piece of bread and
some radishes, tasted six kinds of wine, downed two glasses of
beer, had the candles put out, and left. He had opted for the Hôtel
Lesdiguières.

But once he got there he thought the bedchamber too fine,
too big, and had a camp cot set up for him in a dressing room.
Once settled in, he refused to budge until the king of France had
come to visit him. The morning after his arrival it was the regent
who presented himself. Peter advanced a few steps toward the
visitor, embraced him "with a great air of superiority," writes
Saint-Simon, and turning on his heel entered his study first "without the least courtesy," followed by the regent and Kurakin, who
was to serve as interpreter.

According to Saint-Simon, "the Czar understood French well and, I think, could have spoken it if he had wished, but as a matter of pride he always had an interpreter. Latin and many other languages he spoke very well." Two armchairs stood facing each other. The Czar imperiously chose the upper one. After an hour of pleasant, rambling conversation, he rose and left the room again. The regent followed him. When they parted, the regent made a deep bow that was "indifferently returned." There was every indication that the Czar did not deem it sufficient that he had been paid a visit by the second personage in the kingdom. Two days later, on May 10, the court yielded to his demands and the king of France, preceded by the chamber orchestra and surrounded by a large escort, came to the Hôtel Lesdiguières in a coach drawn by eight horses. Crowds gathered along the Rue Saint-Honoré and the Rue Saint-Antoine to cheer the little boy of seven who, with his long wig, lace jabot, and blue cordon of the Order of the Holy Ghost, embodied the hope of France.

This time Peter went down to the courtyard, received the child at the door of the coach, and, walking beside him on his left, conducted him to his room, where two identical armchairs had been prepared, the one on the right being designated for the king. For a quarter of an hour they exchanged official compliments through the intermediary of Kurakin. Louis recited his lesson, Peter replied in a jovial manner. The audience looked on delighted at this confrontation between the royal child—powdered, painted, and refined—and the wild giant who devoured him with his eyes. At the moment of parting the Czar, forgetting protocol, seized the boy and lifted him up. "Everyone was astonished," wrote Saint-Simon, "to see the Czar take the King under the arms, lift him up to his level, and embrace him thus in the air, and to see the King, young as he was, show no fear, although he could not have been prepared for it. Everyone was struck by his charming manner with the King, his affectionate air, and the politeness that was natural and spontaneous and yet mingled with greatness, equality of rank, and a touch of the superiority of age; because all these things made themselves very distinctly felt." According to Dubois, the Czar is supposed to have said to his small visitor after embracing him: "Sire, that is not a kiss of Judas." He escorted the child back to his coach. Then, delighted with the interview, he wrote to Catherine:

"[L]ast Monday I had a visit from the little King of this place, who is two fingers taller than our Luke [a court dwarf], a child who has a very pleasing face and figure and is quite intelligent for his age." On the next day, Tuesday, May 11, he made his visit to the king, a ceremony regulated down to the smallest detail. This time he walked on the right of the sovereign of France. Another quarter hour of conversation. The two monarchs were even. Peter, having discharged all his obligations, could at last abandon himself to his insatiable passion for discovery. The Parisians saw him racing here, there, and everywhere, preferring hackney carriages to coaches.

"He was a very tall man," writes Saint-Simon, "very well proportioned, rather thin, with a somewhat round face, a high forehead, and well-shaped eyebrows. His nose was rather short, but not excessively so, and broad at the end, his lips rather thick, his complexion a ruddy brown. He had fine black eyes, large, keen, piercing, and wide apart, an expression majestic and gracious when he chose to make it so, at other times stern and fierce, with a tic that did not frequently appear but that distorted his eyes and his whole countenance and was frightful to see. It would last for a moment, giving him a wild and terrible look, then quickly pass away. . . . He wore only a linen collar, a round brown wig that seemed unpowdered and that did not touch his shoulders, a plain brown justaucorps with gold buttons, a waistcoat, knee-breeches, stockings, no gloves or cuffs, the star of his order on his coat and the cordon underneath, his coat being often quite unbuttoned, his hat upon a table and never upon his head even out of doors. For all this simplicity, and however poor his carriage and his escort might be, one could not fail to recognize him by the air of greatness that was natural to him." Others, including Buvat, had seen him dressed somewhat differently: "A gray surtout of rather coarse wool, very dirty, with a waistcoat of a gray woolen stuff with diamond buttons, with no cravat and no cuffs or lace at the wristbands of his shirt." The Russian sovereign's costume soon came to have a certain vogue, being known as the "Czar's coat" or the "wild man's coat." The City Council presented the ill-dressed monarch with twelve dozen boxes of preserved fruits and twelve dozen white wax candles worth two livres apiece, "tied with ribbons in as many packages and placed in three cunningly made white baskets covered with white taffeta." In a sudden fit of concern for his appearance, Peter ordered a new wig from a famous maker, who saw fit to send him one with long curled hair according to the fashion of the court. Dissatisfied, Peter attacked it with a pair of scissors until he had reduced it to the form of the wig he usually wore. And he refused to powder it.

On May 14 he went to the Opera, where the regent received him in the royal box, over the front of which hung a rich carpet. The Czar was bored by the performance and called for beer. It was brought in a large goblet on a salver. Out of deference, the regent stood up, took the salver, and presented it to the Czar himself. Peter accepted it "with a smile and a polite nod," says Saint-Simon, drank, and returned the goblet to the tray, which the regent was still holding. The regent then offered him a napkin, which he likewise accepted and used without rising, to the astonishment of the spectators. At the fourth act he walked out on his companion and went to have supper. He found social functions deadly dull. He preferred taverns, shops, and workshops to drawing rooms. He liked to disappear without telling anyone and go wherever his fancy beckoned. He was annoyed that his tall figure and rough appearance made people stop and stare. The Maréchal de Tessé, whom the regent had given him as a guide, never had a moment's peace, except when His Majesty had taken a purgative and kept to his room. He wrote his master: "I have no idea where the Czar will dine or if he will return to Versailles. He has changed lodgings so often that it would make any man dizzy."

Peter visited the Louvre and the gardens of the Tuileries, where he examined the work on the Pont Tournant, went to the Invalides (then a hospital for disabled veterans), tasted the soldiers' soup, drank their health, and clapped them on the shoulder, calling them "comrades." At Meudon he presented a valet with a "gratuity" in the form of a piece of paper that Buvat states he had just used for an intimate and dirty purpose.[8] At Versailles the gentlemen of his suite had brought "ladies" with them. "They had them sleep," says Saint-Simon, "in Mme. de Maintenon's former apartment, right next to the Czar's. Blouin, the governor of Versailles, was highly scandalized to see the temple of prudery thus profaned; its goddess, and he himself, would have been less shocked in their younger days. It was not the habit of the Czar or his people to restrain themselves." At Marly the Czar admired the machine*; at the Trianon he amused himself splashing his French entourage with the water in the fountains; at the Mint he presided over the striking of a medal commemorating his stay in France; at the Louvre he weighed the Crown jewels in his hand and delivered himself of the opinion that the enormous sum of money they represented could have been put to better use.

But as always, he was attracted by scientific questions. He went to see tooth pullers at work on the Pont Neuf, questioned the geographer Delisle at the Observatory, attended an operation for cataracts performed by the English oculist Woolhouse, learned the secrets of tapestry making at the Gobelins work-shops, and at the Sorbonne kissed the bust of Richelieu and ex-claimed: "I would give half my empire for him to teach me how to govern the other half!" However, when the learned divines of the Sorbonne discussed the possibility of uniting the Catholic and Orthodox churches, he answered modestly that he had no competence in the matter, that his business was to rule Russia and to end the war with Sweden, but that he strongly urged the French theologians to correspond with the most eminent bishops of his country.

On June 11 he went to Saint Cyr, inspected the famous school for daughters of the nobility, reviewed the pupils, and demanded to see Mme. de Maintenon. The widow of Louis XIV, now eighty-two years old, had fled to her room and taken to her bed to escape the traveler's curiosity. But she had reckoned without the Czar's impetuosity and lack of discretion. He pushed open the door, strode into the room, opened the window curtains then the bed curtains, coolly stared at the mortified old woman, and sat down at her side. "He asked me if I were ill," wrote Mme. de Maintenon to her niece, Mme. de Caylus. "I replied that I was. He had his interpreter ask me what was my illness. I replied, 'Great age.' He didn't know what to say to me and his interpreter seemed not to

---

*The "Marly machine" was a huge hydraulic engine that supplied water to the fountains of Versailles. It was considered one of the wonders of the world. —TRANS.

have heard me. His visit was very short. He is still in the house, but I don't know where."

While he had been relatively pleasant with Mme. de Maintenon, he showed perfect disdain for the royal princesses. Though he consented to visit the duchesses de Berry and d'Orléans, he did so with obvious coldness. As for the ladies around the duchesses, "all of them standing and under arms to receive him," says Saint-Simon, he didn't even give them a glance. They were only "sightseers." Other women had more power to charm him. He was aroused by Parisian prostitutes. He slept at Versailles with one he had picked up, sent her away after paying her two crowns, and boasted to the regent about his exploits in bed. The whore, he said, had called him a "splendid male" and a "stingy sovereign." Talk of these orgies in the royal residences reached the ears of Mme. de Maintenon, who wrote indignantly to her niece: "I have just been told that the Czar is taking a low woman about with him, causing a scandal at Versailles, Trianon, and Marly." Notwithstanding these amorous side excursions, the Czar maintained an affectionate correspondence with Catherine. He wrote her that he felt old and was bored away from her. She replied: "I hope to cherish unto death so beloved an old man."

Actually, the disordered life he led did sometimes have an effect on his vigorous constitution. At Fontainebleau after a stag hunt—an exercise not at all to his liking—he gorged himself until his eyes were starting from his head. "What he ate and drank at his two regular meals is inconceivable," notes Saint-Simon, "without counting the beer, lemonade, and other kinds of drinks he consumed between meals . . . a bottle or two of beer, as many and sometimes more of wine, dessert wines afterward, at the end of the meal liqueurs, a pint, and sometimes two. When he rose from table the Czar climbed into his coach, but the jolting soon made his stomach queasy. He soiled the carriage and at Petit-Bourg two village women had to bustle about to clean the cushions. "I remember," wrote Voltaire, "having heard Cardinal Dubois* say that the Czar was nothing but a crazy eccentric born to be a boatswain's mate on a Dutch vessel."[9] When the Duchesse de Rohan

*The Abbé Dubois had been made a cardinal on July 16, 1722.

expressed surprise that a personage of such high station could be so crude, her husband replied: "What ails you, Madam, that you expect civility from that animal?" And Saint-Simon, while he felt the Czar's charm, declared: "He was not free of a strong imprint of his country's barbarous past, which rendered all his manners abrupt, nay precipitate, and his wishes unpredictable, brooking no constraint or opposition."

Peter was completely indifferent to public opinion and quite satisfied when he compared his own uncouth and servile courtiers with the cynical, skeptical fops of the regent's court. On the Russian side of the scales were obedience and weight, on the French side disorder and lack of substance. Decidedly, he preferred his country to all others. Foreign countries had value only insofar as they could help Russia become even greater. For Peter, to travel was to learn. The eternal student, he would pull a notebook out of his pocket and take notes on the run—in the street, in workshops, at Versailles, at the Louvre. Having heard about the Académie Française, he suddenly decided to visit it on June 19. But he neglected to notify the academicians of his intention. When he arrived, the meeting was already over and most of the members had dispersed. He found only two or three, who on behalf of the rest took great pains to show him their meeting room, which was to have been turned into a dormitory for the Russian officers in his retinue. Peter admired a portrait of Louis XIV and another of Cardinal de Richelieu. A notation for that date in the records of the Academy indicates that "He was struck by the beauty of the head and the nobility of its physiognomy." The philologist André Dacier, perpetual secretary to the Academy, thought it appropriate to show the Czar also a portrait of Queen Christina of Sweden, who, like him, had once taken advantage of her journey to France to visit the company. This unexpected association with the ex-sovereign of an enemy country was offensive to Peter, but he gave no sign of his displeasure. He listened distractedly to Dacier's explanations of the work on the *Dictionary*. All these French words buzzed in his ears like flies. To entertain him they took him to the Academy of Painting, where he looked at a few oil paintings and showed "a great liking for that art." He was even more interested in his conversation with members of the Academy of Sciences and enjoyed examining La

Faye's pump, Lémery's "tree of Mars,"* the jack invented by Da-
lesse, and so on.

But the real reason for his journey was political. In difficulty
with his allies and on cold terms with England, he was hoping that
France would break with Sweden and ally herself with Russia by
signing a convention of mutual military and commercial assistance.
But France was loath to betray a country that had long been an
unfailing friend in order to form a partnership with an ambitious,
impatient newcomer. Shafirov, who represented the Russians in
the negotiations, ran up against the reluctance of Maréchal de
Tessé, whom the regent had instructed to "keep the Czar up in the
air and amuse him until his departure, without concluding anything with him."[10] An interview between the Czar and the regent
only served to increase ill feeling. Finally, on August 15, 1717, the
interminable diplomatic talks resulted in the laboriously drafted
Treaty of Amsterdam among the Czar, Louis XV, and Frederick
William I of Prussia. The official purpose of the treaty was to
establish among the three countries "a close union, a friendship,
and a solid and lasting alliance." But contrary to Peter's hopes,
France made no commitment to breaking with England and Sweden. At the most she promised her mediation to promote peace in
the North—a meager result with which Peter had to be content.
London had been kept informed of all these allegedly secret
negotiations by Dubois. It was George I who pulled the strings.
The regent and his advisers were resolutely pro-English. Saint-
Simon, beside himself with rage, accused Dubois of having sold
out to Albion and deplored "the fatal charms of England" and "the
folly we have shown in scorning Russia."

At court, however, Peter heard nothing but congratulations
and promises. Rumor had it that there might be a marriage between the Czar's second daughter, Elizabeth, and King Louis XV,
a rumor quickly denied. But gifts rained down on both sides. While
Peter liked to economize on the gratuities he gave as a private
person, he wanted to show his munificence as a monarch. To
perpetuate the memory of his visit, he gave fifty thousand livres to
the members of the king's household who had furnished his table

*Fanciful name for the branching crystals formed by mixing solutions of iron
silicate and potassium carbonate.—TRANS.

189

in France, thirty thousand livres to the guard who had watched over his person, thirty thousand to the workers in the workshops and factories he had inspected. He gave his portrait set in diamonds to the king, Maréchal de Tessé, and a few high dignitaries and distributed quantities of medals commemorating his outstanding deeds. The king sent him in exchange a sword with a diamond-studded hilt. For reasons of etiquette, Peter declined this gift as being too sumptuous. But he gladly accepted two magnificent Gobelins tapestries. At the regent's invitation, he also agreed to pose for two portraits, by Rigaud and Nattier. But when the paintings were finished he found them rather insipid: they should have portrayed him as more powerful and intimidating. When he left Paris, on June 20, 1717, he declared his attachment to the industrious, welcoming, frivolous country. "He spoke feelingly of France," writes Saint-Simon, "and said it grieved him to see that her great luxury would soon be the ruin of her."

Since the doctors had recommended that he take the waters to repair the ravages of alcohol and lovemaking, he decided to go to Spa. The towns he passed through vied with each other in lavish hospitality. In Rheims, where he stopped for only a few hours, the municipality spent 455 livres for one light meal. In Charleville it cost more than four thousand livres to house the sovereign and his retinue for a single night. The next morning he hurried to the arms factory, invited some of the master craftsmen to come back to Russia with him, and when it was suggested that he visit next a lace-making establishment, replied tartly: "Lace? That's of no interest to me! It would be more in the Czarina's line if she were here!"

A ship dressed with his colors was waiting on the Meuse to take him to Liège. Mountains of food were taken on board: "170 pounds of divers meats at 5 sous the pound, one roe-deer, 35 chickens or hens, 6 big turkey-cocks at 30 sous, 83 pounds of Mayence ham at 10 sous, 200 crayfish, 200 eggs at 30 sous the hundred, one 15-pound salmon at 25 sous the pound, 2 large trout, 3 barrels of beer, one beef tongue and 2 pork tongues, 6 brace of pigeons, 2 pike, 20 pounds of butter. . . ." Doctor Erskine was worried about the overindulgence presaged by the loading of these supplies. He found that His Majesty presented "a relaxation of the fibers of the stomach, with a swelling of the legs and bilious colics." Peter shut him up: no course of treatment until Spa! Quite the contrary, in anticipation of the tiresome diet he was threatened with, he was going to eat twice as much as usual. In Namur he was amused by the fighting on stilts, followed the water tournament with passionate interest, showed himself standing in the middle of a boat with his hand resting on the head of a rower, responded to the cheers of the crowd, ate and drank enough for twelve, danced until a late hour of the night, then refused to sleep in the palace where everything had been made ready to receive him, and went back to his cramped cabin on the boat. Likewise in Liège, frustrating the plans of the organizers, he scorned the sumptuous apartment that awaited him at the palace and insisted on staying at the Hôtel de Lorraine. It was as if he secretly relished throwing his hosts off balance. From the windows of the lodging he had chosen he beheld with satisfaction the display of fireworks in which his personal coat of arms was represented beside that of the Prince Bishop. On the morrow he visited the city, studied the properties of a burning mirror, and even went to visit a coal pit, where he observed with interest the work of the humble laborers, black with coal, who dug in the bowels of the earth.

When he finally reached Spa, with a retinue of forty persons, he drank the water with the same single-minded purposefulness with which he had recently drunk wine. Every morning he would go to the spring of Géronstère, one league from Spa, on horseback, in a berlin, or in a light carriage that he drove himself over bad roads that were deeply rutted and strewn with rocks. For good measure he would down as many as twenty glasses of water one after the other. Then he would stuff himself with six pounds of cherries and a dozen figs. But eventually he found the colorless, tasteless liquid flowing down his gullet depressing. He improved its flavor by adding a stiff dose of alcohol. And to keep the whole mixture from disagreeing with him he went for walks in the countryside. At ease everywhere and in all circumstances, he would go into farmhouses, question the peasants, take their tools in his hand, inspect their barns and cattle sheds. Clearly these singular muzhiks of the region around Spa were not serfs. And on the whole, they looked less wretched than the Russian muzhiks. But, thought Peter, in Russia freedom and well-being would only make them soft. A happy people always had fat bellies and a rebellious spirit. It was only with a nation of slaves that one could carry out great political schemes.

Dinnertime found His Majesty back in Spa, in a tent with a dozen guests around him. He presided at table in a nightcap and without a cravat. When he didn't have enough broth in his bowl, he would dip into his neighbor's. Everyone gesticulated and shouted at once, while the sovereign devoured the meal. A witness to these table manners, the Canon de La Naye, wrote to His Most Serene Highness the Elector: "Almost all the bowls were over-turned on the tablecloth, as were the wine bottles, which were not well corked. When the first course was cleared away, the cloth was soaked with grease and wine. The second course appeared. . . . It consisted of a single dish containing two loins of veal and four chickens. His Majesty, who had noticed one chicken fatter than the others, took it in his hand, rubbed it under his nose, and, having made a sign to me that it was good, did me the favor of throwing it onto my plate. The dish merely slid from one end of the table to the other without hitting anything, since it was the only one and the cloth, which was covered with grease, smoothed the way. Dessert came. It was a plate with three plain Spa cakes on it. At last the company rose from table, and, going over to a casement window, the Czar found a pair of greasy, rusty candle snuffers and used it to clean his nails."[11]

After four weeks of this strange cure that combined taking mineral waters with gorging himself, Peter felt back in top form. He gave a banquet for the authorities of the town, distributed some commemorative medals, and ordered his physician to certify in writing that His Majesty the Czar had recovered his health thanks to the highly salutary waters of Spa. Later, from Amsterdam, he sent to Spa a votive table of black marble with an inscription recalling his happy and beneficial stay at the resort.

When he was reunited with Catherine in Holland, his heart overflowed with manly tenderness. She was the most frequently deceived woman in the world and the most beloved. He had not wanted to show her at Versailles, but he took her with him to Berlin. King Frederick William I and the queen of Prussia gave a gracious welcome at the castle to the illustrious travelers and their large suite: the Czar's escort had now been joined by the Czarina's.

It made quite a crowd, and an exceedingly noisy one. Their hosts' daughter, the spiteful-tongued Margravine of Bayreuth, who was eight years old at the time, wrote in her *Memoirs* that "to prevent the havoc which the Russian gentlemen had wrought in every place where they had stayed, the Queen of Prussia had the whole house stripped and the most fragile objects removed." On greeting the child, the Czar caught her in his arms and scratched her cheeks with violent kisses. She found him "very tall and rather hand-some," but "with a countenance so fierce that it was frightening." As for Catherine, the Margravine considered her tolerably plain, badly dressed, and ill bred. "The Czarina," she wrote, "was short and stocky with a very swarthy complexion, having no distinction or grace. One had only to look at her to tell that she was lowborn. From the way she was gotten up you would have taken her for a German actress. Her gown had been bought at a secondhand shop; it was out of fashion and loaded with silver and dirt. . . . She had a dozen orders and as many portraits of saints and relics sewn all along the facings of her dress, so that when she walked you would have thought you heard a mule jingling."

Baron von Pöllnitz, for his part, admitted that Catherine, with her face covered with red and white paint and her thickset figure encased in a tasteless dress, was scarcely attractive. But, he said, "there was nothing unpleasant about her manners, and one was tempted to think them good, when one recalled the origins of this princess. It is certain that if she had had a reasonable person at her side she would have learned something, for she had a great desire to do the right thing; but nothing was more ridiculous than the ladies of her suite. People said that the Czar, a prince extraordinary in everything, had taken pleasure in choosing them so, in order to mortify the other ladies of his court who were more worthy to be presented." The Margravine of Bayreuth went even further, add-ing venomously: "She [Catherine] had with her a retinue of four hundred so-called ladies. They were, for the most part, German servant girls who performed the functions of ladies, chamber-maids, cooks, and laundresses. Almost every one of these creatures carried a richly dressed child in her arms, and when asked if the child were hers, replied, bowing and scraping after the Russian fashion: 'The Czar did me the honor to give me this child.'"

In Berlin, when Peter went with his escort to see the collection of antique medals and sculptures of which the king was very proud, he went into raptures over a statuette representing "a pagan divinity in a highly indecent posture." In a mood for ribaldry, he insisted that Catherine kiss the obscene figurine in front of everyone. "She tried to get out of it," wrote the Margravine. "He became angry and said to her in bad German: 'Kop ab,' which meant, 'I will have you beheaded if you don't obey me.' The Czarina was so frightened that she did whatever he wanted." Then, with his usual offhand effrontery, Peter asked the king to make him a gift of the rare treasure. Reluctantly, Frederick William yielded to his guest's wish. Thus encouraged, Peter also asked permission to carry off "a cabinet all paneled in amber." Once again the King gave in, although the piece of furniture had cost him dear.

During their brief stay in Berlin Peter and his companions offended their hosts by a total contempt for correct behavior, an open display of intemperance, and the chaos in which they left the lodgings that had been assigned to them. "This barbarous court finally left two days later," the Margravine of Bayreuth wrote in her *Memoirs*. "The Queen repaired to Mon Bijou. There she found the destruction of Jerusalem; I have never seen anything like it; everything was so ruined that the Queen was obliged to have almost the whole house rebuilt."

On October 9, 1717, Peter was back home in St. Petersburg, in his beloved "paradise." He was not sorry for his long absence. In light of what he had seen in other countries, he understood better what he still had to do to transform his capital into a truly European city. It was his dream to wed Western science to the Russian soul. The day when Russia, while keeping her own distinctive character, acquired the technical ability of her neighbors, she would be invincible. But how many obstacles had to be surmounted before she achieved world hegemony! The nation was poisoned by the spirit of reaction. Peter had to combat it even in his own family. And, on the very morrow of his return, his son Alexis, instead of being a help to him, had behaved like such a fool that he had become Peter's greatest source of anxiety.

II

The Czarevich Alexis

Alexis, a sickly child, had spent his early years in the shadow of his mother, the affectionate, pious, superstitious Eudoxia. Terrorized by her husband, she had raised her son amid a murmur of prayers and fables. From her he had learned a blind respect for the Church and a distrust of reforms that tended to upset the old order of things, willed by God. His tutor was the pedantic and ignorant Prince Nikifor Viazemsky. But in 1699, after the trial of the *streltsy,* the Czarevich was suddenly deprived of his mother's protection. For reasons he did not understand, his father had shut his mother up in the Convent of Suzdal. At the age of nine, entrusted to the care of his Aunt Natalya, he had the strange sense of being an orphan, though both his parents were still living. Wishing to instill in the heir to the throne a liking for progress and a love of Europe, Peter thought for a time of sending him abroad, to Dresden, Paris, or Vienna, where, he was assured, the Czarevich would be treated at court "like a son." Then he changed his mind and, keeping Alexis in St. Petersburg, gave him for tutor the German Baron von Huyssen. A cultivated, energetic man, Huyssen took his functions seriously and drew up a program that included, in addition to the reading morning and night of two chapters of the Bible, the accelerated study of French (with a close reading of Fénelon's *Télémaque**), German, mathematics, fortification, equitation, military maneuvers, and so on. Over this omniscient tutor reigned the inevitable Menshikov, the Czar's all-purpose adviser, who became Grand Master of Alexis's court. Unfortunately, Huyssen was soon charged by the Czar with an important diplomatic mission and left the country. Prince Viazemsky reappeared over the child's shoulder. Alexis's education became chaotic. He was transferred to Moscow. Menshikov came to see him only at long intervals, and by way of encouraging the boy to work hard at his studies, pulled his ears or his hair. Monks and mystical priests revolved around the adolescent. He swore to his confessor, the archpriest Jacob Ignatiev, that he would always regard him as "his guardian angel, the judge of all his actions, the bearer of Christ's word." But a man who made an even greater impression on Alexis than the authoritarian ecclesiastic was one of the Czar's former pages, Alexander Kikin, a quick-tempered, scheming, debauched personage, who disturbed him by criticizing all his father's innovations. Under the influence of the people around him, the Czarevich became a curious combination of devoutness and laziness, drunkenness and veneration for the past, filial piety and repugnance for his progenitor. The mere sight of the Czar was enough to make the weak-willed boy's blood freeze in his veins. When his father kissed him, he was repelled by the masculine smell of tobacco, leather, and sweat that clung to the sovereign's clothing. He grew cunning, hypocritical, by turns amiable and surly, brutal and cowardly. Life was frightening to him, and he sought refuge from his fears in the Bible, delighting in the Old Slavonic letters.

To accustom this unnatural offspring to war, Peter made him serve in the army, as a simple bombardier, at the age of fourteen. In 1703 Alexis was present, shielded from all danger, at the cap-

---

*Telemachus is a pedagogical novel (1699) composed for the edification of Fénelon's pupil, the Duc de Bourgogne (Louis XIV's grandson). Fénelon, a prelate and a quietist, recommends to his charge the ideal of a benevolent and peaceable monarch who lives simply and devotes himself to the welfare of his people. —TRANS.

ture of Niennschantz. The following year, after the victory at Narva, the Czar told him solemnly in the presence of a large number of officers: "If I took you with me on this campaign it was so you should see that I am not afraid of either work or danger. But as a mortal man, I may be destined to disappear tomorrow, and you must know that you will have small satisfaction in life if you do not follow my example. At your age you should love everything that serves the interest and honor of the country. . . . Devote yourself to working for the public good. . . . If my words of advice are blown away by the wind, if you refuse to act in accordance with my will, I shall no longer recognize you as my son and I shall pray God to punish you in this world and the next." The poor Czarevich, transfixed by a steely gaze, fell to his knees, kissed his father's hand distractedly, burst into tears, and cried: "Beloved sovereign and father, I am still too young and I do what I can. But I assure you, as an obedient son, that I will try to emulate you in all things."[1]

Actually, this stammering submission concealed a sullen rebellion, a profound antipathy. By his very nature Alexis was the opposite of Peter. Everything about him set him apart from his father. In his veins flowed the blood of the weak, pious Eudoxia, not that of the despot who wanted to mold him in his own image. Peter took pride in his herculean strength, while Alexis was a feeble young man subject to hallucinations. The father loved war, the son detested it; the one defied the Church, the other found peace only in the company of priests; the one devoured scientific books, the other saw the world through the sacred texts; the one wanted to rouse Russia from her age-old sleep, the other respected the old Muscovite customs; the one was ready to sacrifice everything to go forward, the other obstinately looked back. To be sure, both of them had a marked penchant for debauchery, but that was not enough to give them common interests. Besides, Alexis could never forgive his father for having deprived him as a child of the affection of a vulnerable and charming mother. At the beginning of the year 1707 he went secretly to visit the recluse in the Convent of Suzdal. Peter, informed of this breach of discipline, suspected a conspiracy, summoned his son, deafened him with threats and abuse. As usual, Alexis gave in obsequiously, mumbled excuses, promised never to do it again. But each explosion alienated him a little more from the father whom he admired and detested at the same time.

Soon the Czarevich's house in Moscow became a magnet for all who were dissatisfied with the regime. Those who yearned for the old days gathered there among themselves, whispered against the folly of a sovereign who wanted to cut all roots, predicted the disappearance of St. Petersburg, which would sink into the marshes. In 1708, in an attempt to involve his son in affairs of state, Peter appointed him, at the age of eighteen, governor of Moscow, with responsibility for supervising the fortifications of the Kremlin, the recruitment of soldiers, the provision of food supplies, and the collection of taxes. The young man found these administrative tasks a bore. He would sweep the registers, account books, and manuals of pyrotechnics and artillery off his table and plunge into the lives of the saints and the works of Thomas à Kempis. Peter heard about it and was angry. Faced with his father's wrath, Alexis wrote to the new favorite who had taken his mother's place and whom he politely called Catherine Alexeyevna, to implore her support: "If you please, try to find out why my father, the sovereign, is angry with me: he writes that I neglect my occupations, that I loaf about in idleness; I am very perplexed and grieved over it." No doubt Catherine quickly intervened in his favor, for a week later he wrote her to express his gratitude: "Catherine Alexeyevna, I thank you with all my heart for this demonstration of your affection and I beg you not to abandon me in future in similar cases. I place my hope in your benevolence."

In the following year, 1709, while leading up reinforcements demanded by the Czar, Alexis caught cold and was unable to be present at his father's right hand at the triumph of Poltava. Peter was annoyed to have an heir of such a frail constitution. Since the boy isn't strong, he thought, let's make him clever. He decided to send him to Germany, to Dresden, to complete his education. "I order you," he wrote him curtly, "during your stay there [in Dresden], to conduct yourself honorably and to apply yourself seriously to your studies, especially to the foreign languages of which you have already acquired a few notions [German and French]. Also learn about geometry and fortification, as well as political affairs.

When you have finished with geometry and fortification, you will write me. This being said, may God keep you on your journey."

Alexis, however, delayed his departure. He was happy only in Moscow, the holy city, where there were so many churches that every house, it seemed to him, was the antechamber of a sanctuary. Finally, in March 1710, he set out. He was apprehensive about the journey but it had one advantage: it placed a great distance between him and his father. When he reached Dresden he was disturbed to find himself among heretics without a spiritual guide at his side and wrote to Jacob Ignatiev asking him to send him secretly, for the salvation of his soul, a priest, who was to shave his beard and disguise himself as a lackey. He also corresponded with his mother, his grandfather, and his friends in Moscow, but in secret, by roundabout routes, "because of the many spies," he said. Unlike his father, he was not drawn to the arsenals, shipyards, and factories he found abroad but to religious books. He commissioned Professor Heineccius to draft an Orthodox catechism and took pleasure in annotating the *Annales ecclesiastici* of Baronius. The extracts he made from this work bear witness both to his spirit of tolerance and to his reverence for religion's most antiquated forms: "Valentinian and Theodosius freed the prisoners at Easter time. . . ." "Theodosius had ordered that there be no executions during Lent. . . ." "In France, men wore long robes. Charlemagne forbade the wearing of short coats. . . ." "King Chilpéric of France was slain because he had appropriated the wealth of the churches. . . ."

Reading sacred books and performing his daily devotions did not prevent Alexis from running after women and drinking himself into a stupor. For companions during his stay abroad he had been given the sons of two great families: Ivan Golovkin and Yuri Trubetzkoy. It was not long before he drew them into a life of the lowest dissipation. Excessive drinking was so customary and so well thought of in Russian society at the time that he boasted of it to his confessor, Jacob Ignatiev: "We send word to Your Holiness that we have celebrated the commemoration of the holy martyr Eustachius with spiritual exercises, vespers, compline, matins, liturgy. After which, we have rejoiced, both in body and in soul, by drinking your health; and we have poured wine on this letter so that when you receive it, it shall be given unto you to live long and to drink heartily, remembering us. May God reunite us as soon as possible! This missive is signed by all the Orthodox Christians who are here with us. Alexis the sinner and the priest Ivan Slonsky have witnessed these signatures with glasses and certify them with jugs, and we have celebrated your health not in German style but in Russian. We all empty our glasses to your health! Forgive us if you have trouble reading this, but the truth is, we were drunk when we wrote it."[2]

All good things come to an end. Suddenly Peter took it into his head to marry off his son. The fiancée chosen for him was Charlotte Christina of Brunswick-Wolfenbüttel, whose older sister had married the future Holy Roman Emperor Charles VI. Alexis received this news with consternation. The princess, sixteen years old, was very tall, skinny, and had a pockmarked face. True, he was no beauty himself with his narrow face, pointed chin, and shifty eyes. But such as he was, he had possessed many easy, appetizing women. He found it discouraging just to look at this Germanic beanpole. Further, she was a Lutheran. How could he, a fierce defender of the Orthodox faith, reconcile himself to a heretic? Even if she converted, she would still bear the original taint. By touching her he would damn himself. Too weak to oppose his father's will, he played for time and asked to see other princesses. Old Duke Anthony Ulrich wrote in August 1710: "The wife of the Russian ambassador to Dresden, Mme. Matveyev, says that the Czarevich will never agree to marry a German princess. I have no doubt as to the Czar's intentions. But can he force his son into such a marriage, and what is in store for the Princess if the Czarevich takes her against his will? Everyone feels sorry for her."

In February 1711 the Czar himself married, ahead of his son, to regularize his union with Catherine. To him this was such a minor formality that he neglected to inform the Czarevich of it. Strangers undertook to bring him the news. Anxious to win his stepmother's friendship, Alexis wrote to her on May 7, 1711: "Madam, I have learned that the sovereign my father has condescended to recognize Your Grace as his spouse. For this reason I congratulate you and beg you, having always been honored with your benevolence, to continue to show it to me as I hope. I dare not congratulate the sovereign my father, having as yet received no news from him in writing."

After the disastrous battle of the Pruth, in the course of which the Czar and Czarina were nearly taken prisoner, Peter went to Carlsbad to take the waters. On October 14, 1711, in Torgau on the Elbe, he attended his son's nuptials. The ceremony took place in the castle of the queen of Poland, electress of Saxony, and godmother of the bride. In the great hall an altar had been raised under a red velvet canopy. The floor was covered with a green carpet. The flames of candelabra flickered on the walls. All the windows were closed. The orchestra played a solemn air as the Czar stepped forward escorting the Czarevich; behind him came the bride on her father's arm. According to the agreement that had been concluded a few months before, Charlotte was to keep the Lutheran religion, but the couple's children would be baptized Orthodox. The pope read prayers in Russian and from time to time addressed the bride in Latin. Peter surreptitiously watched the young woman who would be his daughter-in-law and would perhaps give him heirs. Plain, flat-chested, but with a soft light in her eyes that gave her charm, she was weeping, while Chancellor Golovkin held the heavy ritual crown over her head. A sacrificial victim beside that idiot Alexis, who didn't seem to be enjoying himself much either. At this wedding only the two fathers seemed satisfied, as if they had made a good deal at the expense of their children. What a pity the Prince Pope wasn't there, thought Peter. And that very day, as soon as the wedding ceremony was over, he wrote to Catherine: "I ask you to inform the very comical Prince Pope of the event and to order him to put on his ceremonial robes and pronounce the blessing for the young couple."[3]

After the supper and ball he accompanied the newlyweds to their apartment and put them to bed. The next morning at dawn he went to visit them in their room and breakfasted there unceremoniously with his ministers. Knife in hand, this connoisseur of country matters studied the expressions of the two "lovebirds" just risen from bed. Then, as if to deprive the union of its last chance of success, he sent the Czarevich to Thorn, where he was to organize the procurement of military supplies.

In the months that followed, Alexis, obeying his father's orders, would be almost constantly on the road. Charlotte, in his absence, dragged out a miserable existence in Thorn, Elbing, Marienburg, towns half destroyed by war. When her husband came back, his only thought was to get drunk and mock her anxieties and tenderness. "There is no doubt that this world is full of sadness and that fate has greater sorrows in store for me in future," she wrote her parents. "I am terrified when I consider what awaits me and my grief comes from a person too dear for me to have the right to complain."

Since the allowance the Czar had promised the young couple was paid very irregularly, they sometimes found themselves in straitened circumstances. As early as 1712 Charlotte, at the end of her resources, appealed to Menshikov, who advanced her five thousand rubles from the funds earmarked for outfitting a regiment. The same year she wrote her mother: "I am married to a man who has never loved me, who loves me less than ever. . . . My situation is terrible. . . ." Then she changed her mind; the Czarevich had just been nice to her for a change. "He loves me passionately," she decided, "and I love him to distraction." But the fair weather didn't last long. A little later, in another letter, she admitted that she had tried to cast a veil over her husband's character, "but the mask has fallen off now." In desperation she fled to her parents' home in Wolfenbüttel, where she spent the winter months. In the spring of 1713 Peter came in person to rout her out, gently but firmly, and sent her to St. Petersburg. There she was very well received by Catherine, but Alexis couldn't have cared less about her. All she was good for was to serve his friends during riotous, interminable banquets.

The number of Alexis's partisans was growing from day to day. For now it really was a question of partisans. Everyone knew that the Czarevich was hostile to Peter's reforms, that he had been married to a Lutheran against his will, that he had a deep-seated attachment to the practices of the Orthodox Church. Without doing it deliberately, without even noticing it, he grouped around him those who opposed the regime. The clergy were sympathetic to him; representatives of the old aristocratic families, like the Dolgorukys and the Golitzins, were betting on him; even the common people venerated him as a righter of wrongs who was inspired by the sacred texts. When he was drunk he said things in public that worried his wife. One day he cried out in a thick voice: "When what is to happen happens, the friends of my father and step-mother will become acquainted with the pale.* . . . The fleet will be burned and St. Petersburg will sink into the marshes."

All the same, he was careful not to defy the Czar openly. Quite the contrary, when Peter asked Alexis to draw some plans in front of him so that he could see what progress the Czarevich had made abroad, he was so afraid of his father's judgment that he hid in his room and fired a pistol into his right hand. The bullet missed, but the powder flash burned his palm, and he was excused from the examination. His father threw him a searching, mistrustful look; he went faint with shame and sorrow under the mute interrogation. After such terrors, nothing was better than a good binge. "The Czarevich," wrote Pleyer, the emperor's resident, "has brought back from Germany neither German customs nor the German spirit. He spends most of his time with Muscovite popes and dis-reputable persons; above all, he likes to get drunk."

The inveterate souse was not even excited when he learned that his wife was expecting a child. A few weeks before she was to give birth he left to take a cure at Carlsbad. Peter and Catherine were then in Finland. By order of the Czar, Charlotte's German entourage was kept away from her room. Three Russian matrons watched over her night and day, to make sure that no infant was fraudulently substituted for the rightful heir. She was insulted and wrote to her father-in-law: "I think that my conduct can have given no cause for malicious gossip. . . . God is my only hope in a foreign land. And as I am abandoned by all, He will hear my sighs and cut short my suffering. . . . The midwife whom I brought with me has my complete trust, she should accomplish her task. However, since I am entirely dependent upon Your Majesty, I cannot object to having another midwife look after me. But then my eyes will fill with tears and my heart will bleed." And to her mother: "I am a poor victim of our House, without its gaining the least advantage from that. And as for me, I am dying a slow death from sorrow."

On July 12, 1714, Charlotte gave birth to a daughter, Nata-

*The stake used for impalement.—TRANS.

lya.* Alexis saw no reason to return to Russia for so trifling an
event. He didn't reappear in St. Petersburg until the end of December. Quite unmoved by this woman who had just borne his
child, he insulted her by installing under the conjugal roof his new
mistress, Euphrosyne, a serf who had belonged to his former tutor,
Nikifor Viazemsky. According to contemporaries, she was a short,
homely, plump redhead with thick lips and the manners of a scul-
lery maid. Illiterate and a toper, she made a pleasant change from
Alexis's legitimate wife. With Euphrosyne he could have a good
time, say anything that was on his mind, satisfy a coarse sexual
appetite; with Charlotte he felt constantly at fault. Charlotte,
scorned and made ridiculous, courageously endured the presence
in her house of so arrogant a rival. "Only the walls see her tears,"
wrote the envoy from Hanover. She didn't even dare to resist her
husband when by chance he had the impulse to come at her again.
Now she was pregnant for the second time. Shortly before her
confinement she fell on the stairs and complained of violent pains
in her side. Some said she had been beaten by Alexis. Specifically,
that he had kicked her in the stomach. A doctor bled her. She said
she felt better. On October 12, 1715, she gave birth to a son: Peter.

Immediately afterward she was seized with agonizing pains
that only grew worse as time passed. The six physicians who had
hastened to her bedside sadly shook their heads: no hope! Charlotte knew the end was near and prepared for death as for a deliverance. In a sublime burst of selflessness she worried about the
consequences her death might have for the relations between her
family and her husband's. Not for anything did she want to be a
pretext for discord. Taking advantage of a momentary remission,
she dictated a letter to her mother and sister: "During my lifetime
slanderous rumors were spread about me. There are people who,
after my death, will say that my illness was caused more by sorrow
than by the dangerous deterioration of my organism. To give the
lie to this spiteful talk, tell my family from me that I have always
been satisfied with my lot and proud of the affection of Their
Majesties. Not only has the Czar fulfilled all the stipulations of my
contract, but he has been full of kindness for me and I here express

*Natalya died in 1728.

my gratitude to him. . . ." When she had reread the letter Charlotte said: "Now I have nothing more in my heart. I leave this world of tumult and all my thoughts turn to God." The Czar, who had been suffering from violent attacks of colic, left his room to visit his daughter-in-law for the last time. She implored him to let her friend, the princess of East Friesland, bring up the two orphans. Then she bade farewell to those around her and gave her pardon to all. The person most in despair was the one who had caused her the most pain: her husband. Whether it was playacting or sincere remorse, he sobbed, wrung his hands, and fainted three times beside the bed of the dying woman. She breathed her last during the night of October 22, 1715, at the age of twenty-one.*

The next day, October 23, Peter ordered an autopsy of his daughter-in-law. Always interested in the opening and examination of cadavers, he attended the operation in person. The sight of the viscera laid bare satisfied both his elementary scientific curiosity and his excessive taste for the macabre. On the very same day that he studied the anatomy of the dead woman, he took part in the baptism of the child she had carried. Little Peter received the first sacrament of his life a few steps from the dissected body of his mother. The juxtaposition did not bother the Czar. The funeral ceremony, which took place on October 27, was on a grand scale. Peter and Alexis were chief mourners; Catherine did not appear in the procession. Nine months pregnant, she was herself about to give birth.

When Alexis went home after the funeral, he received a letter from his father dated October 11, 1715, the eve of little Peter's birth. It was clear that this long missive had been written much later and that the day of the month had been changed to suit the writer's purpose. Recalling the reverses, then the successes of the war against Sweden, the Czar lamented the fact that his son paid no attention to the art of warfare. Not knowing how to command, the Czarevich would surely sink to the lowest level: "You will do nothing, nor judge of anything, but by the eyes and help of others,

---

*It was rumored at the time that Charlotte had not died in St. Petersburg but had fled to Louisiana, where she had married a French officer, and that she had finally passed away in Brussels in old age after a rewarding married life. Unfortunately, that is only a legend belied by all documents.

like a young bird that holds up his bill to be fed. You say that the weak state of your health will not permit you to undergo the fatigues of war. This is an excuse that is no better than the rest. I desire no fatigues but only inclination, which even sickness itself cannot hinder. . . . For instance, the late king of France [Louis XIV] did not always take the field in person, but it is known to what degree he loved war and what glorious exploits he performed in it. . . . Remember your obstinacy and ill-nature, how often I reproached you with it and even chastised you for it, and for how many years I almost have not spoken to you. But all this has availed nothing, has effected nothing. It was but losing my time, it was striking the air. You do not make the least endeavors, and all your pleasure seems to consist in staying idle and lazy at home. Things of which you ought to be ashamed (for as much as they make you miserable) seem to make up your dearest delight, nor do you foresee the dangerous consequences of it for yourself and for the whole State. . . . After having considered all those great inconveniences and reflected upon them, and seeing I cannot bring you to good by any inducement, I have thought fit to give you in writing this act of my last will with this resolution, however, to wait still a little longer before I put it in execution to see if you will mend. If not, I will have you to know that I will deprive you of the succession, as one may cut off a useless member. Do not fancy that, because I have no other child but you, I only write this to terrify you. I will certainly put it in execution if it please God; for whereas I do not spare my own life for my country and the welfare of my people, why should I spare you who do not render yourself worthy of either? I would rather choose to transmit them to a worthy stranger than to my own unworthy son."[4]

First he had lost his wife, now he was disinherited. In panic, Alexis turned to his usual advisers: Kikin, Viazemsky, Basil Dolgoruky. They all thought he should renounce the crown on the pretext of poor health. They were confirmed in their opinion by an important event. On October 29, two days after Charlotte's funeral, Catherine gave birth to a boy. By decision of His Majesty, he would be called Peter, like Alexis's son. It was now clear that in the order of succession the Czar would give his preference to the son of Catherine, the official Czarina. Better, then, thought

Alexis, to make his move first and withdraw his claim. On October 31 he wrote to his father: "Most clement Lord and Father: I have read the paper Your Majesty gave me on the twenty-seventh of October 1715 after the funeral of my late wife. I have nothing to reply to it but that if Your Majesty will deprive me of the succession to the crown of Russia by reason of my incapacity, your will be done. I even most instantly beg it of you because I do not think myself fit for government. My memory is very much weakened and yet it is necessary in affairs. The strength of my mind and of my body is much decayed by the sicknesses which I have undergone and which have rendered me incapable of governing so many nations; this requires a more vigorous man than I am. Therefore I do not aspire after you (whom God preserve many years) to the succession of the Russian crown, even if I had no brother as I have one at present, whom I pray God preserve. Neither will I pretend for the future to that succession, of which I take God to witness and swear it upon my soul, in testimony whereof I write and sign this present with my own hand. I put my children into your hands, and as for myself, I desire nothing of you but a bare maintenance during my life, leaving the whole to your consideration and to your will. Your most humble servant and son—Alexis."[5]

Drunk with pride at the idea of having, at the age of forty-three, a second son who would surely console him for the first, Peter celebrated the birth with artillery salutes, banquets, and illuminations. But as always, he mixed the splendor with farce. During the banquet that followed the baptism, servants placed on the men's table an enormous pie: the top crust rose and a female dwarf, entirely naked, sprang out amid shouts of laughter. She recited a compliment, drank the health of the company, and ran off. A similar pie appeared on the ladies' table. This time, it was a male dwarf, likewise stark naked, who offered himself to the view of the guests.[6]

Peter was delighted with this witty invention but apparently had eaten and drunk too much at the feast. He was taken ill and had to go to bed. As his condition grew worse, on December 2 he asked to receive the sacraments. Worried ministers and senators slept in the room next to his bedchamber. Alexis ventured to his father's bedside only once. When he returned from his visit he was perplexed. Was this really the end? Was there reason to hope so? And what would happen to him when the Czar died? His friend Kikin undeceived him: "Your father is not so sick. He is confessing and taking communion on purpose to make the people around him think he is very ill. But it's only playacting."[7]

Peter did recover. On Christmas Day he appeared before his courtiers with keen eye and confident step. On January 19, 1716, he answered his son with a "last admonition." In this bombastic epistle he rebuked Alexis for not having tried to defend himself against the accusations of laziness and incompetence; he applied to him the words of King David: "All men are liars," and said in conclusion: "Do you assist [your father] in his cares and pains since you have attained the years of maturity? Certainly in nothing; all the world knows it. Quite contrary, you blame and abhor all the good I do at the hazard and expense of my own health for the sake of my people and for their welfare, and I have all the reasons in the world to believe you will be the destroyer of it, if you outlive me. And so I cannot resolve to let you live on according to your own will, like an amphibious creature, neither fish nor flesh. Change therefore your conduct and either strive to render yourself worthy of the succession or turn monk. I cannot be easy on your account, especially now that my health begins to decay. On sight therefore of this letter, answer me upon it, either in writing or by word of mouth. If you fail to do it, I will use you as a malefactor."[8]

The cold darkness of the cloister, a slow death in obscurity and neglect, the inevitable separation from Euphrosyne! It gave Alexis gooseflesh to think of it. As was his habit, he consulted the people close to him. Kikin comforted him: "They do not nail the cowl to one's head," he said.[9] The monastery was not a tomb. How many men had come back from it! So let him agree to being shut up in some monastery. There he would bide his time. And his reputation would be enhanced in the popular imagination. Alexis was convinced and scribbled a short note: "Most clement Lord and Father, I received this morning your letter of the nineteenth instant. My indisposition hinders me from writing to you more at large [i.e., at length]. I will embrace the monastical state and desire your gracious consent for it. Your servant and unworthy son— Alexis."[10] In order to be able to say afterward that he had not been thrown into a monastery to expiate some crime, he sought out

Father Gregory, archpriest of St. Petersburg, and told him that he was taking monastic vows under compulsion and against his will. The priest reassured him: "I will tell it when it shall be time," he said.[11] Similarly, Alexis took the precaution of giving his mistress, Euphrosyne, a note for Kikin and another for Father Ignatiev informing them that he was being *forced* to become a monk.

Peter, who was about to leave for Holland, entered his son's room—the Czarevich was feigning illness—asked him if he still intended to take the habit, and, as Alexis declared that it was his dearest wish, said with a sigh: "It is not easy for a young man. Think it over and take your time. Then write me what you have determined. . . . I will give you another six months."

Accustomed to judging others by himself, Peter refused to believe that a man—his own son—could be so spineless. He would give him a last chance to redeem himself. Alexis was overjoyed at this unlooked-for reprieve, and in the absence of his father returned to the enjoyment of his mistress and his bottle, uninterrupted by the reading of exhortations to self-improvement. The dead young wife was soon forgotten. Euphrosyne had replaced Charlotte in the house. With her, the Czarevich had seven solid months of joyous abandon, a holiday free from care. As if the Czar were never coming back from his travels. Suddenly, a letter from Peter dated August 26, 1716, from Copenhagen sobered Alexis like a bucket of cold water: "I have expected [your decision] this seven months past, and you send me no word at all about it to this very instant. You have [had] time enough to think upon it; therefore upon the receipt of my letter choose one or the other. In case you determine for the first, which is to apply yourself in order to be capable of the succession, do not delay above a week to repair hither, where you may arrive [in] time to be present at the operations of the campaign. But if you resolve on the other side, let me know where, what time, and even what day you will execute your resolution, that my mind may be at rest and that I may know what I am to expect from you. Send your answer back to me by the same courier who is to deliver you my letter. . . . I repeat it to you that I absolutely will have you resolve on something, for otherwise I must judge that you seek only to gain time to pass it in your usual idleness."[12]

Once again Alexis asked the advice of his entourage. Some of them had reason to believe that the Czar had already chosen the monastery where his son would be confined, in Tver, and that he had had made ready there a cell worse than those reserved for the greatest criminals in the state prisons. At their urging, the Czarevich hurried to Menshikov and announced that he was going to join his father. He would take Euphrosyne with him. But he needed money for the journey. Menshikov gave him a thousand ducats and the Senate, to which he made the same statement, advanced him two thousand rubles. He left St. Petersburg on September 26, 1716, with his mistress, her brother Ivan Fedorov, and three servants. Before leaving he confided his secret intentions to his major-domo, Afanasiev: he was not going to join his father in Copenhagen but to take refuge in Vienna with his brother-in-law, who had become the Emperor Charles VI, or perhaps in Rome, with the Pope. Kikin had gone abroad a few months earlier to test the ground. The news he had sent from Vienna was reassuring: everything was ready to receive the Czarevich.

In Riga Alexis borrowed another five thousand ducats from a military procurement officer. On the road to Libau he met his aunt, the Czarevna Maria Alexeyevna, who was returning from Carlsbad. She asked him: "Where are you going?" "I'm going to see my father," he replied. "That's good," she said, "one must always obey one's father. That is pleasing to God. What did you have to gain by becoming a monk?" "I don't know anymore," he groaned, "I'm so miserable I'm going out of my mind. I'd be happy if I could go hide somewhere!" "Where could you hide from your father?" she exclaimed. "No matter where you went he would find you!" Alexis burst into sobs and confessed that he placed great hope in Catherine's kindheartedness. "Why do you praise her so?" said the Czarevna Maria Alexeyevna. "She is not your mother. She has no reason to wish you well."

Alexis was perturbed by this encounter and wondered whether it wouldn't be better to abandon his plan to flee. But in Libau he found Kikin, who soon cheered him up. "Go to Vienna, to the emperor," he said. "They will not deliver you up there. . . . According to Vice Chancellor Schönborn, the Emperor has said that he would welcome you like a son. No doubt he will give you some three thousand guldens a month." The Czarevich's spirits were revived and he set out again with Euphrosyne.

Meanwhile, when his son failed to arrive, Peter soon suspected a trick. Furious, he sent his best bloodhounds out in pursuit: Veselovsky, his resident in Vienna, Rumiantsov, and Peter Tolstoy. His emissaries crossed borders, pounded the roads, checked the registers at inns. They were optimistic. "We are on the trail," they wrote. "We will catch up with the quarry." But their prey eluded them.

On October 29, 1716, the Czarevich reached Frankfurt and signed the official register as Lieutenant Colonel Kokhanovsky, traveling with wife and servants. The proprietor of the inn noted that his guest had "the beginnings of a black mustache in the French fashion," and that his wife was "of short stature." A brief rest, and they harnessed up again. In Breslau, in Neisse, in Prague, the hunters tracking the fugitives arrived too late to run them to earth. Veselovsky had been in the saddle so long that he was suffering from hemorrhoids. But he refused to give up the chase and set off again, shivering with fever. In the meantime, Alexis had reached Vienna. At the inn of the Black Eagle he posed as a Polish gentleman named Kremenetsky. The first thing he did was to buy a "coffee-colored" suit of men's clothes for Euphrosyne. She immediately disguised herself as a man to allay suspicion.

The following day, November 10, 1716, around ten o'clock at night, Vice Chancellor Schönborn was getting ready for bed when an officer on duty announced to him that a visitor who spoke poor German insisted on seeing him at once. After some hesitation, Schönborn slipped on his dressing gown and consented to open the door. It was Euphrosyne's brother, Ivan Fedorov, who presented himself. "My Lord," he cried, "the Czarevich is downstairs in the square and wants to see you!" The astonished Schönborn thought at first it was a bad joke, then, calculating the risk, ordered that the heir to the Russian throne be admitted. There appeared before him a disheveled man with jerky movements and a mad look in his eyes. Pacing up and down the room, Alexis poured out his terror, his hope, stammered, wept, asked for drink, downed a glass of Moselle in one draught and went on, hiccuping. "The emperor," he said, "must save my life and guarantee my rights and the rights of my children to the throne. My father wants to deprive me of existence and of the crown. Yet I am not guilty of anything with regard to him, I have done nothing against him. I know I am weak. But that is the fault of Menshikov, who raised me so. They purposely undermined my health, pushing me into drunkenness. Now my father says I'm not capable either of making war or of governing. But I have enough intelligence to reign. . . . They mean to tonsure me and lock me up in a monastery. . . . I don't want to be a monk. . . . Everything was spoiled for me the moment the new Czarina too gave birth to a son. She and Menshikov have done everything they could to set my father against me. . . . My father is surrounded by malicious men. He himself is cruel and bloodthirsty. He thinks he is like God and has the power of life and death over men. He has spilled much innocent blood. Sometimes he has even executed poor wretches with his own hands. He is quick to anger and vengeful. He spares no one. If the emperor turned me over to him it would be as if he took my life. Besides, even if my father spared me, my stepmother and Menshikov would not rest until they had driven me to drink myself to death or given me poison!"[13]

With great difficulty, after two hours of discussion, Schönborn persuaded the Czarevich to go back to his inn and wait until the emperor had made a decision, in all friendship, as to his fate. Charles VI, who was informed of the matter the next day, found himself in a very awkward position. He decided to try to reconcile father and son and to hide the Czarevich in expectation of a peaceful solution. Alexis, his servants, and Euphrosyne, now disguised as a page, were secretly taken to Weierburg, not far from the capital, then to the Fortress of Ehrenberg, a veritable eagle's nest at the top of a great rock in the Tyrol. The commandant of the fortress had been ordered by the emperor to consider the newcomers important prisoners, to give them comfortable cells, "with strong doors and bars on the windows," to provide them with a good cook and supply them with books and paper, but not to seek to know their names. In this old castle keep at the end of the world, Alexis at last felt safe. He did not know that his father's hounds had already tracked him to Vienna.

On December 20, 1716, Peter wrote to Charles VI that he had ordered his representative Veselovsky to find the Czarevich and bring him back: "Consequently, if he [Alexis] should be on your territory, I beg Your Majesty to send him back to us under the guard of a few officers for security during the journey, so that we may chastise him paternally for his own good." When he had read the letter that Veselovsky handed him, Charles VI told the Russian coolly that he had not been informed of the presence of the Czarevich in any corner whatever of his empire. Now in the meantime, Veselovsky had learned, by bribing a clerk of the Imperial Chancery, that Alexis was being hidden in the Tyrol. He immediately dispatched Captain Rumiantsov to sniff out the various possible trails. In a few days Rumiantsov picked up the scent and came prowling around the fortress. Rumor had it that he was under orders to seize the Czarevich by force. It was said that the province was infested with Russian spies. To avoid a scandal, the emperor chose to transfer the fugitive to Naples, a city that had been recently ceded to the imperial house.

The Austrian secretary Kühl went to Ehrenberg, informed Alexis of the decision, and showed him Peter's letter to the emperor. The Czarevich read, burst into sobs, fell on his knees in the middle of the cell, and raising his arms to the ceiling cried: "I beseech the emperor, in the name of God and of all the saints, to save my life and not to abandon me, the most wretched of men! I am ready to go wherever he wants and to live however he sees fit, if only he does not deliver me up to a father who is unjustly angry with me!" They made hurried preparations. This time, according to the emperor's instructions, Alexis could take with him only Euphrosyne (still dressed as a page) and a single servant. Kühl acted as their escort. From Mantua he sent a terse report to Vienna: "As far as Trent we had suspicious-looking persons at our heels. Nevertheless, all goes well. I have done what I could to prevent our little company from sinking into frequent and excessive bouts of drunkenness; but in vain."

At last, on May 6, they reached Naples; on the ninth Alexis, Euphrosyne, and their servant moved into the Fortress of St. Elmo, which stood on a mountain overlooking the bay. A splendid view, Vesuvius, the blue expanse of the sea. What peace after the nightmare of the journey! Kühl, his mission accomplished, heaved a sigh of relief and wrote in French to Prince Eugene of Savoy: "Our little page has at last admitted to being a female, but without benefit of Hymen, and apparently also without hymen, because declared to be a mistress and necessary for health. The Tyrol was crawling with persons from the nation in question, furnished with passports from their master of recent date and made out in false names of Polish officers. The departure was well planned, prompt, and secret, as was the delivery at the time and place you know."

On this point Kühl was flattering himself. In fact, at every stage of the journey to Naples he had been shadowed by the indefatigable Captain Rumiantsov. The Czar was very soon informed of Alexis's new hiding place. On July 10, 1717, he wrote directly to the emperor expressing surprise that a friendly sovereign should have left him in ignorance of his son's movements: "Your Imperial Majesty can readily imagine how painful it is to us, as a father, to note that our eldest son, having shown such disobedience to us and having left without our consent, is presently either under the protection of someone else or under arrest. Finding this situation inadmissible, we beg Your Imperial Majesty to enlighten us on the subject. We are therefore sending you our Privy Councillor Peter Tolstoy, with orders to discuss all these things with you during a private audience. He is to see our son, communicate our paternal will to him orally and in writing, and ask you to send him back to us at once. To assist the aforementioned Privy Councillor, we have sent Captain of the Guard Rumiantsov, who has witnessed our son's departure from the fortress in the Tyrol and his transfer to Naples. We cannot allow Your Imperial Majesty to oppose our demands, for such a refusal would be based neither on law nor on any possible reason. Indeed, natural laws, especially in our country, and even among private persons, forbid any third party from judging between a father and his son; all the more so when that father is a sovereign and independent monarch. . . . Awaiting your final decision, which will determine the measures we will have to take on our side, we remain Your Imperial Majesty's good brother—Peter."

On July 29, 1717, Tolstoy and Rumiantsov were received by the emperor. They handed him the Czar's letter and gave him to understand that their master was prepared to take extreme measures to obtain satisfaction. Charles VI glanced over the message, said it was not very clear, and promised to reply after he had studied it further. Immediately afterward he summoned his ministers for a secret conference. They were all of the opinion that the Czarevich was an embarrassing guest. Nevertheless, the emperor would lose face before Europe if he handed over to a father's justice a poor unfortunate who implored his protection and who, moreover, was his brother-in-law. On the other hand, it was to be feared that if Peter were angered by a refusal he would send his troops in Poland against Silesia and Bohemia, where he would be welcomed by the local Slavic population.

After interminable discussions with Tolstoy and Rumiantsov, it was decided that the two confederates would be allowed to visit the Czarevich, deliver to him a letter from the Czar, and exhort him to return to the fold. On August 21 the emperor wrote to Count Daun, viceroy of Naples, instructing him to prepare the fugitive for this crucial interview: "It would be useful to know the Czarevich's intentions before he has discussed them with that woman dressed up as a man, for she might dissuade him from the right decision. You should be present in person at his meeting with Tolstoy or have some qualified person represent you, as you prefer. As the conversation will certainly take place in Russian, I am sending you a courier who is perfectly acquainted with that language and very capable. He will take note of all Tolstoy's proposals and the Czarevich's replies. . . . The meeting will be organized in such a way that neither of the Muscovites (rogues who will stop at nothing) seizes the Czarevich or raises a hand against him. . . ." Before the departure of the said rogues, Charles VI again recommended that Alexis be gently dealt with: "I would be very happy to learn that the Czarevich had at last received his father's forgiveness," he told them.

On October 5, after five weeks of travel over sodden roads, Tolstoy and Rumiantsov arrived in Naples. The first meeting with the Czarevich took place in the viceroy's palace. Alexis was terror-stricken at the sight of his father's two envoys. He could scarcely read the letter they handed him: "My son, your disobedience and the contempt you have shown for my orders are known to all the world. Neither my words nor my corrections have been able to bring you to follow my instructions, and last of all, having deceived me when I bade you farewell and in defiance of the oaths you made, you have carried your disobedience to the highest pitch by your flight and by putting yourself like a traitor under a foreign protection. This is a thing unheard-of hitherto, not only in our family, but among our subjects of any consideration! What wrong and what grief have you thereby occasioned to your father, and what shame have you drawn upon your own country! I write to you for the last time to tell you that you are to do what Messrs. Tolstoy and Rumiantsov will tell you and propose to be my will. If you fear me, I assure you by this present and I promise to God and His Judgment that I will not punish you, and if you submit to my will by obeying me and if you return, I will love you better than ever. But if you do not do it, I as a father, by virtue of the power I have received from God, [will] give you my everlasting malediction for the contempt and offenses committed against your father; and as your Sovereign, I [will] declare you traitor and I assure you I will find means to use you as such, in which I hope God will assist me and take my just cause into His hands. As for what remains, remember I constrained you in nothing. What need had I to give you a free choice what side to take? If I was willing to force you, was it not in my power to do it? I had but to command and I had been obeyed."[14]

Alexis's mind was in turmoil and he didn't know how to answer. Should he believe his father's promise of forgiveness? Was this a way out of his difficulties or a trap? Seeing their quarry at bay, Rumiantsov and Tolstoy split up the roles. Rumiantsov scowled at him, barked, threatened. Tolstoy, all honey, appealed to his sentiments, preached reconciliation, dangled before his eyes the prospect of happy days in store. "I cannot give any answer yet," stammered Alexis. "I must reflect upon it." They separated, promising to meet again two days later.

In the interim Alexis must have consulted his dear Euphrosyne, and at the second interview he seemed firmer: "It would be dangerous for me to return to my father," he said. "I will explain the reasons for my refusal, in writing, to His Imperial Majesty who is protecting me." Tolstoy promptly changed tactics and grew angry. "I have orders not to come away until I have you in my custody!" he cried. "If they move you somewhere else I will follow you!" He added that the Czar meant to recover his son "dead or alive." Alexis wept but once again refused to leave. A third meeting between him and the plenipotentiaries was postponed because he complained of headaches.

Tolstoy took advantage of the delay to prepare a new plan of attack. First, for 160 ducats he bought the complicity of Weingarten, the viceroy's secretary. This man, who had won Alexis's confidence, dropped a word in his ear to the effect that the emperor had decided to abandon him, so as not to risk a war with Russia. Tolstoy himself, during a fourth meeting with the Czarevich, told him that the Czar was ready to take up arms, if necessary, to regain possession of his son and that in any event he would probably come to St. Elmo in person to fetch him. "Who can forbid him to see you?" he asked. "You know yourself that your father has long wanted to visit Italy. This gives him a reason to come at the earliest moment." Then Count Daun joined in the scheme, telling the fugitive that if he wanted to remain at St. Elmo he would have to part with his mistress. Euphrosyne, bribed by Tolstoy, pretended to believe this lie and begged Alexis to yield.

Assaulted from all sides, fearing both that his father would arrive and that he would lose his beloved, he was compelled to surrender. The next day he announced to Tolstoy and Rumiantsov that he would go back with them to Russia on condition that his father authorized him to marry Euphrosyne; further, he earnestly requested that the wedding be celebrated before they reached St. Petersburg, for the lady was pregnant. Tolstoy, not a man inclined to be indulgent, noted nonetheless: "It is hard to imagine the love and consideration he has for this girl." His real feelings he expressed in a letter to Vice Chancellor Shafirov: "I am of the opinion that he should be granted what he asks: first, because he will thus show the world that he fled only on account of his mistress; second, because by so doing he will anger Emperor Charles VI, who will no longer have the least trust in him. I would like the Czar to write me his intentions on this matter, among other instructions, so that I can show the letter to the Czarevich without leaving it with him. If the Czar should oppose this plan, he would have only to write me that the marriage is to take place in St. Petersburg. The Czarevich, filled with hope, will not insist further. As for me, I think that allowing him to marry this whore will show the whole country what sort of man he is."

Urged on by Euphrosyne, who was playing a double game, Alexis soon regained confidence, and on October 4, 1717, he wrote the Czar: "Most clement Lord and Father, I received Your Majesty's most gracious letter by the sieurs Tolstoy and Rumiantsov, by which, as also by them by word of mouth, you most graciously assure me of a pardon for my going away without leave, in case I do return. I give you thanks for it with tears in my eyes, I own myself unworthy of all mercy, throwing myself at your feet. I implore your clemency to forgive me my crimes, though I have deserved all sorts of punishment. But I rely on your gracious assurances, and giving myself up to your will, I am setting out without delay from Naples, to repair to Your Majesty, to St. Petersburg, with those whom Your Majesty has sent. Most humble unworthy servant, undeserving to call himself son—Alexis."[15]

When Peter received this letter in St. Petersburg, he had only just returned with Catherine from his long journey through Europe. After the frills and refinements of France, he had come back to rough, primitive Russia. At the same moment his cares had settled down again upon his shoulders like a heavy mantle. The Czarevich had made him ridiculous in the eyes of the other sovereigns. As he saw it, the affair was a more serious blow to his prestige than another defeat by the Turks or the Swedes. He would not forgive his son for this public insult. But the most important thing was to bring him back. By lies and trickery if necessary. Anything was permissible to a monarch fighting for his reputation. Besides, he was not displeased that the Czarevich had become infatuated with this Euphrosyne. The father had married a former laundress, the son wanted to marry a floor washer—it was the natural order of things! On November 20, 1717, he sent Alexis a short note: "My son, I have received your letter of October 4. I am answering it. You ask for pardon. Tolstoy and Rumiantsov have promised it to you in my name, orally and in writing. *Once again I confirm it to you. Be well assured of it, therefore.* [emphasis in original] As for certain of your wishes which Tolstoy has communicated to me, they will be satisfied. He will talk to you about that." The same day he wrote Tolstoy: "You write me that my son wants to marry that girl he has with him and live on his estates. I will authorize him to do so when he is here. The thing can be done in town or in the country, after his arrival."

Later, in another letter addressed to Tolstoy and Rumiantsov jointly, he clarified his position: "The fact that my son, believing in the sincerity of my pardon, has set out to join me, gives me the greatest satisfaction. You tell me that he wants to marry the girl who is living with him. Let him do so if he wishes, when he is in Russia; even in Riga or in Kurland, at my niece's. But to be wedded in a foreign country would be shameful. If he imagines that I will oppose it in any way, let him reflect for a moment: after having pardoned him so great a fault, how could I hesitate to grant him so small a favor?"

To make sure that his son was securely hooked, that he wouldn't struggle anymore, that he wouldn't change his mind en route, he reiterated his promises and commands in writing. Alexis was so badly in need of reassurance that after having doubted everyone, he no longer wanted to suspect anyone. Reinvigorated, he contemplated his future with a cheerfulness that surprised even his two guardians. Their carriages jolted along from Naples to Rome, from Rome to Bologna, over roads so rough that the Czarevich feared for the health of his beloved. In view of her pregnancy, he decided to leave her in Bologna with her brother. She would join him in St. Petersburg, traveling by easy stages. He had hardly parted from her when he began to worry about her. At each relay he wrote her loving letters: "Dear soul, have the medicine well prepared in Venice according to the doctor's prescription, and take the prescription back afterward. . . ." "Do not be sad, my soul. Set out on your way and may God keep you. Take good care of yourself. . . . Rest as much as you can. . . . Don't worry about the expense. Your health is dearer to me than anything in the world. . . ." "All goes well, I feel that I am to be forgiven for everything and that I will be able to live with you where God wills, in the country, and that we will no longer have to worry about anything." He also wrote to Euphrosyne's brother: "Ivan Fedorovich, greetings! I beg you, for the love of God, to watch over your sister and my wife (although she is not yet so officially, but I have received instructions for her to be); do what is necessary to keep her free from care, for nothing must stand in the way of the fulfillment of her pregnancy, which, with God's help, will come to a happy end." The letter ended with a coarse postscript addressed to one of the beloved's servants: "Peter Mikhailovich, son of a bitch and son of a whore, amuse Euphrosyne as much as you can so that she isn't sad, because all goes well; it's only on account of her belly that we can't make things go faster."

Alexis was so concerned about the belly that from Danzig he sent a midwife to Berlin to accompany his mistress on the journey. Euphrosyne responded to all this solicitude with vapid, banal notes dictated to some secretary. She talked about her health, about the purchases she had made en route: thirteen ells of cloth of gold, a cross, some earrings, a ruby ring. But above all she was obsessed with food. Perhaps it was her condition that gave her such an appetite. She was always asking the Czarevich for things to eat: "Send me in Berlin some pressed caviar, fresh caviar, black and red, salted salmon and smoked salmon, fish of all sorts and some more kasha." He did as she asked. Nothing was too good for his Euphrosyne.

When he crossed the Russian border, he was struck by the affection shown him by humble people in the provinces. Some of them prostrated themselves as he passed and begged his blessing. As if by defying the Czar he had become the champion of all who suffered in Russia. He was both delighted with this popularity and worried by it. Wouldn't his father take offense? But no, he had promised "to God and His Judgment" that henceforth he would treat his son with sincere affection. The Czar could not betray an oath that committed him before the Almighty.

Since the court was in Moscow, it was there that the Czarevich went to meet his father. He arrived on January 31, 1718, late in the evening. The Czar did not receive him but summoned his Privy Council of prelates, ministers, and dignitaries to a meeting on February 3. The brilliant assembly, which had not been advised of the purpose of the meeting, gathered in the great hall of the Kremlin. The white wigs of the senators alternated with the tall black hats of the priests. Three battalions from the regiments of the Guard were posted around the palace carrying loaded muskets. Having taken his seat on the throne, Peter commanded that his son be brought in. Two strong guards with naked swords in hand entered with the Czarevich between them. Pale, without a wig, without a weapon, dressed in a modest black coat, he seemed even thinner and feebler than when he had left Russia. When the Czar saw him he burst into imprecations. He denounced Alexis for everything at once—his scant education, his laziness, his desertion from the army, his base attempts to turn foreign princes against his father. Terrified, the Czarevich fell to his knees and between sobs stammered out excuses, implored the sovereign to give him back his love. In a curt tone the Czar ordered him to state exactly what he was asking for. "My life and pardon!" groaned Alexis, striking his forehead on the floor. Peter told him to get up and promised to pardon him on two conditions: the Czarevich, guilty and unworthy, must solemnly renounce the crown, and he must name the persons who had helped him to flee. He was given paper, ink, a pen. Hoping to get off cheap, he wrote with a trembling hand: "Most clement Lord and Father, after having confessed my transgression before you, my Father and my Lord, I bring here the paper of confession of my crimes, which I sent you from Naples. I confess once more at present, that I have swerved from the duties of a child and of a subject, in evading [i.e., running away from Russia] and putting myself under the Emperor's protection, and by applying to him for support. I implore your gracious pardon and your clemency. The most humble and incapable servant, unworthy to call himself son—Alexis."[16]

Having read the text, Peter led his son into an adjoining room where they were alone and in a dramatic confrontation demanded that he divulge the names of all his accomplices, even those who had only given him friendly encouragement. Let him search his memory well! Let him forget no one! A single omission and he would lose the benefit of his return to favor! Under the black, cold, searching look Alexis finally gave way. Sweating with fear, he denounced Kikin, Viazemsky, the majordomo Afanasiev, Prince Dolgoruky, others too. At each name Peter growled with anger. At last he returned to the audience chamber with the Czarevich, who, although he had spilled everything, still didn't dare to believe he was pardoned. Before the attentive Council, Vice Chancellor Shafirov read aloud the text of an oath that was to be submitted to Alexis for his signature: "I, the undersigned, acknowledge before the Holy Gospels that by reason of my crimes against my father and sovereign, described in my letter and in my confession, I have forfeited all right of succession to the throne of Russia. Therefore, because of my crime and my unworthiness, I promise and I swear by Almighty God, glorified in the Trinity, and by His Judgment, to submit entirely to the paternal will and never at any time to seek, nor desire, nor accept that inheritance. I recognize as legitimate successor my brother the Czarevich Peter Petrovich.* Whereunto I kiss the holy cross and sign with my own hand."

Then the entire assembly moved in a great wave toward the Cathedral of the Assumption. In the rood loft before the open sacred doors stood the new Archbishop of Pskov, Feofan Prokopovich, in ceremonial robes, the cross in his hand. Beside him, the Czar. Before the Gospels Alexis took the sheet of paper handed him by Shafirov and in his turn read aloud in a feeble voice the act of renunciation of the throne. At the same time in Red Square an interminable manifesto relating the vices and crimes of the Czarevich was being read aloud to the assembled crowd. Everything was included: idleness, drunkenness, friendships with unsavory individuals, licentious ways, ingratitude toward a benevolent father, shameful conduct toward an admirable spouse. "Even while his wife was alive, he took up with an idle creature of base extraction and lived with her unlawfully, forsaking his legitimate consort, who later died, from an illness, of course, but also from the sorrow caused her by her husband's dissolute life," said the manifesto. And further on: "In spite of the shame inflicted upon us before the world, as a father and as a sovereign, by our son's flight and the calumnies he has spread about us, for all of which deeds he would have deserved death, we have pity on him in our paternal heart, we pardon him for his misdeeds, and we exempt him from all punishment. But in consideration of his unworthiness and of the crimes mentioned above, we cannot in conscience allow him to inherit the throne of Russia. . . . That is why, for the good of the state, we deprive him, our son Alexis, of that succession and name and proclaim as heir to the said throne our other son, Peter, although he is still very young. . . . If anyone were to oppose the present decision and consider our son Alexis as our heir or dare to lend him any assistance, that person would be declared a traitor to us and to the country."

*The son of the Czar and Catherine.

Thus the people learned with amazement that the Czar had changed the order of succession, preferring a child of twenty-seven months to a man of twenty-eight years. It was true that the first was the son of Catherine and the second the son of Eudoxia, that the first represented innocence and the second debauchery, that the first might one day continue Peter's work while the second already thought only of undoing it.

On the following day, February 4, the Czarevich was invited to reply in writing to a seven-point questionnaire, so as to confirm and expand upon the denunciations he had made orally the day before. A preamble written in the Czar's hand reminded him that if he concealed anything he would be punished with death. An unnecessary precaution: for a long time the Czarevich had been ready to do anything to save his skin. After four days of reflection, he drew up a reply in which he implicated not only Kikin, Dolgoruky, Viazemsky, and Afanasiev "who had had ideas," but also the Czarevna Maria Alexeyevna and, consequently, his mother, the ex-Czarina Eudoxia. Fearing that he might not have named enough names, he added still others who had played minor roles. Some fifty in all. Would that be enough to appease the Czar's wrath?

As soon as they were designated by Alexis, the "guilty" were brought to Moscow. Among them was the Bishop of Rostov, Dositheus. He admitted that he had prophesied to the ex-Czarina that Peter would soon die and Alexis come to the throne. Summoned before his peers, the prelates, who were charged with pronouncing his divestiture, he cried: "Am I then the only one who is guilty in this affair? Look into the depths of your hearts, all of you! What do you find there? Harken to the people. What is on their lips? A name I will not pronounce!" Stripped of his titles and insignia and dubbed "Diomedes the unfrocked," he was put to torture. With his limbs broken, he confessed that he had harbored a black hostility to the reforming Czar and denounced an uncle of Alexis, Abraham Lopukhin. Under similar interrogation Lopukhin, brother of the former Czarina Eudoxia, blurted out that he had indeed corresponded with her.

Immediately Captain Skornyakov-Pisarev was sent to the Convent of Suzdal to investigate the machinations of Peter's first wife, who was living there under the name of Sister Helen. He was stunned by what he discovered. After eighteen years of privations and disgrace, the ex-Czarina had found consolation in the person of Captain Stepan Glebov. Glebov, who had come to the region of Suzdal for purposes of recruitment, had been touched by the fate of the unfortunate woman and as she complained of the cold in her cell had had furs brought to her. She had thanked him by letter, then received him, and from visit to visit their relations had become increasingly intimate. Having become Glebov's mistress, Eudoxia, who was past forty, had abandoned herself to a rapturous love while he—young, ambitious, and calculating—had been interested in her chiefly because if there were a change of reign she might assure him a brilliant future. They soon gave up any attempt to conceal their affair, exchanging kisses in public and sending the nuns away so that they could make love. She had wanted him to leave the service so she could see him more often, had saved out of her meager income to help him with expenses, suffered because he was married and their sin was all the greater. At each separation they had written each other passionate letters. The investigator discovered them during a search. Not one was in Eudoxia's hand; she had dictated them to the nun Kaptelina, her confidante. But on each of them the imprudent Glebov had written: "Letter from the Czarina."

Skornyakov-Pisarev rubbed his hands. A good haul. Nine love letters to place before the Czar. Peter read with a mixture of indignation, disgust, and retrospective jealousy: "Where your thoughts are, my *batko* [more affectionate form of *batiushka*, little father], there are mine also; your words express what is in my mind; I have no will but yours. . . ." "Do not forget the love borne you by a poor woman so unhappy that she hardly has a soul left. . . ." "Oh my light, how could I remain on earth separated from you? At least, oh my heart, wear the ring that I gave you and love me a little, a little. I have had one like it made for me. . . . Oh my whole world, my adored, my *lapushka* [little paw], answer me. . . . Come to see me tomorrow, don't let me die of sorrow. I have sent you a cravat, wear it, oh my soul! You don't wear anything that comes to you from me. Is that a sign that I am no longer pleasing to you? . . . For me to forget your love would be impossible!" "Who has stolen my treasure? . . . Why do you abandon me? . . . How can you not have pity on me? . . ." "Send me, oh my heart, send me the waistcoat that you like to wear. . . . Send me a piece of bread from which you have taken a bite. . . ." Peter noted with irritation that in this amorous litany reeled off by Eudoxia she dared to call her lover by the pet name *lapushka* that she had given him twenty years before. He considered that even after having been repudiated, she owed him fidelity—one never ceased being the Czar's wife. In any case, there was nothing political in this sentimental nonsense from an aging woman. Nevertheless, she and her lover deserved to be punished as an example. He issued an order to bring the couple to Moscow.

En route Eudoxia wrote the Czar: "Very merciful sovereign, in the past (when, exactly, I no longer remember) I had my hair shorn in the Convent of Suzdal and I took the name of Helen; after which for half a year I wore a nun's habit. But not wishing to be a nun, I gave up religious dress and lived secretly in the convent as a lay person. . . . Today I place my hope in the generous humanity of Your Majesty. I fall at your feet to implore your grace and pardon for my crime, that I may not die an unworthy death. I promise to become a nun again and to remain one until my death. . . . Your former wife—Eudoxia."

Questioned by the investigating commission, she confessed in writing: "I admit that I have lived in sin with Stepan Glebov and am therefore guilty. Written by my hand—Helen." But she denied having had any evil thoughts about the Czar. Glebov did likewise. As he remained obstinately silent on the most important charges against him, they knouted him, burned him, broke his ribs, tore out pieces of his flesh with pincers, and locked him in a dungeon bristling with sharp wooden spikes that tore his bare feet at every step. Notwithstanding these torments he refused to acknowledge that he had been implicated in a plot and denounced no one. To learn more the investigators had some fifty nuns flogged, some of whom died under the blows. The Czar was present at all these tortures and lent an eager ear to the death rattles and babblings of the victims. But from the testimony of the various witnesses it emerged that while the Czarevich enjoyed great popularity among the people, who were being crushed under the burden of taxes, the clergy, who had been despoiled, and the old nobility, who had been humiliated, he was by no means at the head of an organization, much less a faction. The investigators were dealing with friends of Alexis, not with conspirators.

No matter, the trial must take its course. In view of the extent of the judicial machinery that had been set in motion, the sentences could only be very heavy. On March 14 and 16 the court, composed of ministers of the Czar, condemned Kikin, Glebov, and Dositheus to "cruel death"; Pustynnik, the chief administrator of the Convent of Suzdal, and the cantor Zhuravsky to "simple death"; Prince Shcherbatov to having his tongue cut out and his nostrils torn off; others were destined for the knout, forced labor, exile; some, like Viazemsky and Dolgoruky, got off with the confiscation of their property. Dositheus, the defrocked bishop, was broken on the wheel but found the strength before he died to cry out to the Czar: "If you put your son to death, his blood will be on your hands and the hands of your line from father to son unto the last czar! Have mercy on your son! Have mercy on Russia!"

After the torture, Dositheus was decapitated, his body burned, and his head planted on a stake. As for Kikin, the executioner broke his arms and legs. "His torture was slow," wrote the Austrian envoy Pleyer, "with intervals, so that he might have plenty of time to suffer." The next day Peter came to see the bloody body bound to the wheel and still breathing. According to certain witnesses, the Czar asked the dying man: "How could you get mixed up in an affair like this, you who are an intelligent man?" Kikin is supposed to have replied: "Intelligence loves the open air, and you stifle it."[17] In conclusion, his head was struck off. The executioner picked it up and presented it, fixed on a stake, to the silent crowd. The third man condemned to "cruel death" was the ex-Czarina's lover, Glebov. For him—and for him alone—the Czar had chosen the pale. As it was very cold, which might cut short the culprit's suffering, he was dressed in a pelisse, fur hat, and warm boots before the stake was driven up his rectum. Impaled at three o'clock in the afternoon, he lingered in fearful agony until 7:30 in the evening of the following day. Eudoxia, on the other hand, had her life spared. But she was sent to a more isolated convent on the shores of Lake Ladoga. Before being shut up there she was whipped by two monks in front of all the inmates.[18] The Czarevna

Maria Alexeyevna was incarcerated in the Fortress of Schlüssel-burg. Of the minor figures, one Princess Troyekurovna, some nuns, and a few gentlemen were knouted; Princess Anastasia Golit-zina, who had been informed of the relations between Eudoxia and Glebov but had not denounced them to the authorities, was laid on the ground in the middle of a circle of soldiers and beaten with rods. Then she was returned to her husband, who sent her back to her father. Peter made his son witness the most spectacular punishments and took a fierce joy in seeing how shaken he was. The iron stakes on which the heads of the *streltsy* had been planted twenty years before had been cleaned up to receive fresh heads. "In the city," wrote Pleyer, "in the great square in front of the palace [of the Kremlin] where the executions took place, stood a four-cornered scaffold of white stone, about six cubits high, sur-rounded with iron stakes on which the heads were fixed. At the top of the scaffold was a square stone one cubit high. On this stone the bodies of the executed were piled in a circle, with Glebov's seated, as it were, in the center."

On the evening of the last execution Peter called a meeting of the "Synod of Fools and Jesters" and along with his cronies, who were dressed up in clerical costume, got drunk at a merry banquet. A new Prince Pope, Peter Buturlin, had just been elected to replace Nikita Zotov, now deceased. In the course of the feast the mock chasuble and miter were turned over to him. During the bloody days of the investigation the Czar had found time to plan all the details of the blasphemous ceremony. Under a velvet canopy stood a throne built of kegs and decorated with lamps made out of empty bottles. Each guest in turn bowed before "the Holy Father of drunkards," who held in his hand a cross made of pipestems. An icon of Bacchus shone above his head. He blessed the company with a pig's bladder dipped in vodka and gave them communion holding out an enormous ladle full of peppered brandy. The priests of the chapel sang obscene hymns in chorus. Then they sat down to a boisterous banquet. Elbow to elbow they guzzled, gorged, belched, and farted only a stone's throw from the platform where the corpses of Alexis's friends were lying. Venerable digni-taries soaked in alcohol argued, exchanged slaps, seized each other by the hair, then were suddenly reconciled and embraced each other with tears. When one old boyar refused to drink, his neighbor poured vodka down his throat with a funnel. High on his throne, the Prince Pope vomited on the wigs of the other guests seated below him.

The next day, March 18, 1718, the Czar left for St. Petersburg. Alexis followed, together with other accused persons whose fate had not yet been decided. But the Czarevich was not worried: the broken limbs, the cut-off heads, he thought, must have appeased the hunger of the Moloch of Russia. He himself felt no pity for the victims who had been immolated in his name. Adversity had hardened him. He had gotten out of a tight spot—that was all that mattered. As soon as Euphrosyne arrived in St. Petersburg they would get married. Her pregnancy was still keeping her in Berlin. He wrote her that his father had invited him to dinner, that all was well, that he was relieved not to be the official heir to the throne anymore: "As you know, we never dreamed of anything but to live quietly in Roschestvienka. To be with you and at peace until I die is my only wish." In the meantime, he drank more than ever, perhaps in order to forget the blood spilled because of him. The Czar had assigned him a house near the Winter Palace where he could keep an eye on him. On Easter Sunday, April 13, 1718, he exchanged the triple kiss of peace with Catherine, threw himself at her feet, and begged her to intercede with the Czar so that he could marry Euphrosyne. She gave no definite answer, but her attitude was very affectionate, her eyes moist. The Czar also kissed Alexis like a Christian, three times according to custom. Was this the reconciliation? The Czarevich desperately hoped so, as he felt the rough, shaven cheeks, the stiff little mustache. The familiar odor of his father enveloped him.

Two days later Euphrosyne arrived. While Alexis was looking forward to the joy of their reunion, he learned that his mistress had been taken directly to the Fortress of St. Peter and St. Paul. They began by questioning the young woman's servants. Then, as soon as she had given birth, she was taken out of prison and transported in a closed rowboat to Peterhof, Peter's summer residence.* There the Czar spoke with her personally,

---

*Nothing is known about Euphrosyne's child. No doubt it was done away with at birth.

looking her in the eye, insisting, hoping to learn new facts. She had only one thought: to save her head. Guessing that her questioner expected a further indictment from her, she accused Alexis, reported the least gestures, the slightest words that could incriminate her lover. Peter noted with pleasure a few details that had been missing, but on the whole he was disappointed by Euphrosyne's confession, for she made no important revelations. At his request the young woman confirmed her deposition in writing: "Alexis often sent letters to the emperor complaining about his father. . . . When he heard news of a mutiny of the troops in Mecklenburg he rejoiced, for he still wanted to inherit the throne; that is why he had left. . . . When he learned that the Czar's youngest son was ill, he said to me: 'You see, my father does what he wants and God does what He wants. . . .' He said: 'When I am Czar I'll live in Moscow, and St. Petersburg will become an ordinary town; I won't maintain the ships, I will have no more fleet, I will only keep enough troops to defend the country, I will not make war on anyone, the old empire will be enough for me. . . . Maybe my father will die, or there will be a rebellion. I don't know why my father does not love me and wants to make my brother his heir, when he is still but a little boy. He thinks his wife, my stepmother, is clever, and when he dies we will have a female reigning. That is not good. The people will rise up. Some of them will be on my brother's side, some of them on mine.' "

In Naples Alexis had given Euphrosyne the draft of a letter to two bishops and the Senate, so that she should burn it. But she had not destroyed the document, secretly hoping to use it someday if necessary as a bargaining chip. The Czar would be grateful to her for her foresight and loyalty. Now she held out the paper to him. He read: "The continual ill-usage and the disorders have obliged me to quit my dear native country. They designed to shut me up in a convent in the beginning of the year 1716, though I had committed nothing that had deserved it. None of you can be ignorant of it." The end of the letter was even more insolent: "I desire you not to forsake me then, and as for the present, to give no credit to the news that may be spread of my death, or otherwise, out of the desire they have to blot me out of the memory of mankind, for

God keeps me in His guard and my benefactors will not forsake me. . . ."[19]

This letter had been stopped by the cabinet of Vienna and had never reached its destination. Peter read it with savage jubilation. Euphrosyne, exhausted and happy, had nothing more to say. Having squeezed her like a lemon, the Czar had her taken back to the fortress by boat. Shortly afterward he ordered that his son be confined there too. Alexis still had not seen his mistress.

One day he was taken out of his dungeon and brought to Peterhof. After the sweating walls of the damp cell, he now found himself in Mon Plaisir, the charming pavilion at the water's edge, where his father received him. Alexis hardly looked at him. All his attention was focused on a familiar figure: Euphrosyne, standing beside the Czar. She was no longer big with child. Even her face had changed—pale and hard, with a stubborn expression, and above the hostile mask, the red hair like the flames of hell. He wanted to rush to her. The guards prevented him. As soon as he heard her first words, he understood that she had betrayed him. Every time he tried to vindicate himself, she coldly contradicted him. Abandoned by the one in whom he had placed all his hope, he collapsed. If he had wanted to go on living it had only been out of love for Euphrosyne. What was the point in struggling now? Let them do what they wanted with him. Besides, maybe by accusing himself of all crimes, true or false, he would disarm his father, and the Czar's anger, encountering no further obstacles, would dissipate like smoke in the air. Filled with disgust, weary and disillusioned, Alexis acquiesced to everything held against him. He confirmed his statements, point by point, in writing. On May 26, under pressure from Tolstoy and Buturlin, he went so far as to write the most compromising of notes to his father: "As I have owned in my last confession . . . if the rebels had called me at any time, even during your life, I would have joined them."[20]

Peter immediately published a supplementary manifesto to reveal his son's turpitudes and accuse him of having tried to make a mockery of justice by hiding part of the truth. During further examinations Alexis, his strength exhausted, denounced a few more of his friends, including his confessor Ignatiev. They were given the knout, the strappado, and finally confessed that they had wished for the Czar's death. They were decapitated. Peter would have liked to see inside the heads of all his subjects to track down subversive ideas. He felt as if all Russia were peopled with traitors. The most candid smiles seemed suspicious to him. The deadly proceedings he had launched drew him ever deeper into horror. Caught in the machinery of interrogatories and tortures, he no longer knew how to put a period to the bloody series. Where should he stop? Whom should he set at the top of the pyramid of corpses?

Weber, the Hanoverian representative, wrote in a coded report: "In this state, everything will one day end in a horrible catastrophe. Millions of souls cry out to heaven against the Czar. The general hatred that is smoldering needs only a gust of wind to burst into flame. People are only waiting for a leader to appear." Was not the Czarevich that leader? Yes, yes, thought the Czar, Alexis was the cause of Russia's sickness. The rotten root must be torn out. The monastery? Death? Peter hesitated.

On June 13, 1718, he addressed a letter to the metropolitans, archbishops, and bishops asking their advice on the punishment that the Czarevich deserved: "Though our son has violated his promise, in concealing the most important things touching his rebellious designs against us his Lord and father, yet . . . we are desirous to get all sorts of light in this affair. Reflecting on that passage of the Word of God where He exhorts to ask on the like occasions the opinion of churchmen, to know what God ordains about it, pursuant to what is written in Deuteronomy, chapter 17, we desire of you archbishops and the whole ecclesiastical state, as doctors of the word of God, not that you should pronounce judgment on this affair but that you do examine it and give us thereupon, according to His Holy Scriptures, a true instruction, to know what punishment so horrid a crime of our son, like that of Absalom, has deserved . . . which you are to give us in writing, signed with everyone's own hand, to the end that being sufficiently instructed in this affair, we may not in any thing charge our conscience. And so we place our confidence in you, as guardians of the divine law, according to your dignity, as faithful pastors of the Christian flock, and as well intentioned for your country, and we conjure you by the judgments of God and your own consecration to proceed herein without any dissimulation and fear."[21]

The assembly of prelates responded prudently, citing nine

examples from the Old Testament that authorized a father to punish his son with the greatest severity, and seven examples from the New Testament that urged tolerance. The conclusion was a genuflection to power: "[T]his affair is not of the competency of our jurisdiction: who would establish us judges over those that command us? How can the members [i.e., limbs] govern the head? . . . Besides, our jurisdiction being spiritual, it ought to be according to the spirit, and not according to flesh and blood. The power of the iron sword was not given to the Church, but the power of the spiritual sword, which is the word of God. . . . We submit all this to the exalted imperial consideration, with a due obedience. May the lord do what is agreeable in his eyes. If he will punish him who is fallen, according to his actions and the measure of his crimes, he has before him the examples we have drawn from the Old Testament. If he will show mercy, he has the example of Jesus Christ himself, who receives the son that was lost, when he returned to repentance; who leaves the woman at liberty that was taken in adultery and had deserved death according to the law; who prefers mercy to sacrifices. . . . After having briefly set forth all this, the Czar's heart is in the hands of God: may he choose the side to which the hand of God shall turn him."[22]

On reading this document Peter had a strange feeling of treading on empty space, as if a support had suddenly slipped from under him. Having taken all authority away from the Church, he could no longer count on its help. He was alone in the midst of a nation that was fearful and evasive. Yet he refused—perhaps from fear of God—to take personal responsibility for a death sentence that would be an example to all. It was not he but a High Court that would condemn his son. He chose its members from among the ministers, senators, functionaries, dignitaries, generals, and subordinate officers—127 persons in all. The special court sat in the audience chamber of the Senate, in the Czar's presence. The approaches to the palace were barred with bristling chevaux-de-frise and guarded by troops. The Czarevich, meanwhile, had been transferred to a cell in the Trubetzkoy Bastion of the Fortress of St. Peter and St. Paul. For the sake of convenience, the adjoining room had been fully equipped as a torture chamber. On June 17, 1718, the prisoner appeared for the first time before his judges, who, after examining him, decided that his responses were insufficient and that he should be put to torture. Two days later he was taken next door and hoisted on the strappado so that his feet were off the floor and he hung with all his weight on his outstretched arms twisted behind his back. Thus racked, he was subjected to twenty-five blows of the knout. He screamed in pain as the flesh was torn off his back and gasped out a confirmation of his confessions. Peter witnessed the session—at each blow of the lash he hoped for a revelation that would justify his hatred. The smell of blood and sweat intoxicated him. When the executioner threw him a questioning look, he said: "Go on!" But on the advice of the doctor they had to stop. Alexis was only a panting rag with drooling lips and chattering teeth. They took him away, dressed his wounds, and let him rest for three days.

On June 22 Tolstoy, who was serving as examining magistrate, came to see Alexis in his cell and suggested that to mollify his father he should make, in all humility, a more complete and sincere confession of his misdeeds than he had yet done. The Czarevich took the proffered pen in his aching right hand: "[My disobedience to my father] proceeded from my living, when a child, with a governess and young women, of whom I learned nothing but amusements and to play in my chamber, and to act the bigot,* to which I was naturally inclined. . . . My father, taking care of my education and being desirous that I should apply myself to what might render me worthy of being the Czar's son, ordered me to learn the High Dutch tongue [German] and other sciences, to which I had a great deal of aversion. I applied myself to them but with great carelessness, only to pass away the time, nor had I ever any inclination for them. And as my father, who then was often in the army, was far from me . . . the said Naryshkins and Viazemsky, seeing that my inclinations run solely upon bigotry, idleness, frequenting priests and monks and drinking with them, not only did not dissuade me from it, but even took delight in doing as I did . . . and they more and more alienated me from my father by

---

*In eighteenth-century English (as still in modern French), a "bigot" was not necessarily an intolerant person but one whose profession of religion was hypocritical, or whose excessive piety was based on superstition and formalism. —TRANS.

diverting me with such sort of pleasures, and by degrees I came to abhor not only my father's military affairs and his other actions, but even his very person. . . . As to my having desired the succession by other means than that of obedience, all the world may easily guess the reason of it; for being once stepped out of the good road, unwilling to imitate my father in anything, I endeavored to obtain the succession by any other method whatsoever than what was fair. I was for having it by a foreign assistance, and if I had obtained it, and that the Emperor had put in execution what he had promised to me, *viz.*, to procure the Crown of Russia to me even by armed force, I would have stuck at nothing to lay hold of the succession. For instance, if the Emperor had demanded Russian troops against any of his enemies whomsoever, or large sums of money in return for his service, I would have done whatever he had desired, and I would also have made great presents to his ministers and generals. I would have maintained at my own expense the auxiliary forces he should have given me to put me in possession of the Crown of Russia, and in short nothing would have been too dear for me to satisfy my own will."[23] When he had signed, Alexis wondered in terror if by deliberately blackening his conduct to satisfy the Czar, he had not fallen into a trap. He wanted to retract. Too late. Tolstoy had taken possession of the document and carried it off.

On June 24, came another session in the torture chamber, in the presence of the Czar. Fifteen blows of the knout on a back still striped from the first beating. The result: nothing, or almost nothing. Not knowing what to say anymore, Alexis groaned that he had written to the metropolitan of Kiev to incite a rebellion. Then he fell silent. He could no longer speak. The doctor feared he might succumb. He was taken down from the strappado. On the same day the High Court met. The 127 judges knew what sentence the Czar expected of them. Not one dreamed of displeasing him by granting the accused extenuating circumstances. The decision was unanimous. The verdict was signed by, among others, Menshikov, Admiral Apraxin, Chancellor Golovkin, Vice Chancellor Shafirov, Peter Tolstoy, Buturlin—all the great names of the country. If there were a few signatures missing at the bottom of the document, it was only because several of the ad hoc magistrates didn't know how to write:

"June 24, 1718. . . . The underwritten ministers, senators,

states military and civil, after having been several times assembled in the Chamber of the Regency of the Senate at St. Petersburg . . . after mature reflection and in Christian conscience, without fear or flattery and without regard to the person, having nothing before their eyes but the divine laws suiting with the present case, both of the Old Testament and the New, the holy writings of the Gospel and of the Apostles, as also the canons and rules of the Councils, the authority of the holy fathers and doctors of the Church . . . and conforming themselves to the laws of all Russia, especially the constitutions of this empire, to the military laws and statutes, which are conformable to the laws of many other governments, and chiefly to those of the ancient Roman and Grecian Emperors, and of other Christian Princes . . . did unanimously, without contradiction, agree and pronounce that the Czarevich Alexis Petrovich deserves death for his crimes aforesaid, and for his capital transgressions against his Sovereign and his father, being his Czarish Majesty's son and subject. . . ."[24]

Now it was up to Peter: should he commute the sentence or let the executioner finish his work? Catherine suggested that he wipe the slate clean. "Be content to make him a monk," she said. "His death would be on your head and the heads of your descendants." His other advisers remained silent, careful not to cross him in anything. All Russia was holding its breath. Suddenly a thunderbolt: a rumor spread that Alexis had died, on June 26, in his cell. The following day Peter published a report on the Czarevich's end, drafted by Shafirov, Tolstoy, and Menshikov:

"When the court's sentence against our son was announced, we, his father, were torn between natural compassion on the one hand and, on the other, the concern to ensure peace in our empire. We were unable to make a decision in this affair, which was so painful and so serious. But almighty God in His mercy was pleased to deliver us from our doubts and to save our house and our country from danger and shame. Yesterday, June 26, he cut short the days of the Czarevich Alexis. The latter succumbed to a serious illness with which he had been stricken on reading the death sentence and the list of his crimes against us and the State. In the beginning, the illness was a kind of apoplexy. Later he regained consciousness completely, made confession, received the last sacraments like a Christian, and asked us to come to see him, which we did, forgetting all his misdeeds, accompanied by all our ministers and senators. He sincerely acknowledged his crimes against us, wept abundantly, and received the pardon that we owed him as his father and sovereign. It was thus that on June 26, toward six o'clock in the afternoon, he departed this life in Christian fashion."

The story of the death from apoplexy deceived no one. The most varied rumors circulated among the people, at court, and especially in diplomatic circles. The emperor's resident, Pleyer, wrote that the Czarevich had been beheaded in prison with a sword or ax; the Dutch resident, Jacob De Bie, reported to the States General that his veins had been opened by a lancet and he had bled to death. A young woman by the name of Anna Kramer, who was Catherine's maid, claimed that the Czarevich's head had been cut off at his father's orders and that she had sewn it back onto the trunk of the corpse and hidden the stitching with a long cravat. Peter Henry Bruce believed Alexis had been poisoned. Others, including Rumiantsov, held that he had been strangled or suffocated under pillows. Later Jean Lefort,* an adviser in the Saxon legation, and Count Rabutin, Pleyer's replacement, recounted that on June 26, after the sentence had been passed, Alexis had been beaten with the knout, no doubt by his father himself, and had expired in agony. The journal of the St. Petersburg garrison corroborates that statement, since it mentions an additional torture session on June 26: "It took place in the presence of the Czar, from eight to eleven o'clock in the morning. The same day, at six o'clock in the evening, the Czarevich died." So it was after this final torture, which took place *after* the verdict, that the exhausted Czarevich, weakened, perhaps by a timely bloodletting, had expired. Had his father personally raised his hand against him? It is possible: after the cudgel, the knout. The Czar had never disdained the executioner's trade. Looking at the dead body of Alexis he had no doubt thought of Ivan the Terrible, who, in 1581 in a fit of rage, had likewise killed his eldest son, striking him with the steel point of his staff. In an attempt to redeem his crime, Ivan the Terrible had sunk into prayers and mortifications. That was not the case with Peter.

*Jean Lefort, the nephew of Peter's close associate François Lefort, was the representative of the elector of Saxony at the Russian court.

The day after Alexis's death he celebrated in St. Petersburg the ninth anniversary of the victory of Poltava. A yellow banner bearing the black two-headed eagle was raised over the fortress, a Te Deum was celebrated in the Church of the Trinity, cannon thundered, bells pealed joyfully, a feast was served at night in the open gallery of the Summer Garden, at the foot of the statue of Venus the orchestra played light melodies, and sprays of fireworks exploded in the sky. Questioned by members of the diplomatic corps as to whether or not they should wear mourning, Chancellor Golovkin replied in the negative, "the prince having died a criminal." During the banquet, while Catherine seemed distracted, the Czar, according to Pleyer, was full of good spirits. And one of Menshikov's secretaries confirmed: "After dinner the company went down to His Majesty's garden and were very merry."

While this was going on, in the fortress they were washing the corpse, dressing it, laying it in a coffin. On the morning of June 28 it was transported to the Church of the Trinity. The people, dumb with astonishment, filed in front of the body. On Sunday, June 29, for St. Peter's Day, the Czar's name day, there were more festivities: mass, artillery salutes, resounding carillons, dinner with music, and in the evening the launching of a frigate in front of the Admiralty. Afterward, on board the ship there was the usual drinking party with shouts of laughter, toasts, cheers. The keeper of the garrison log noted: "There was great merrymaking."

On Monday, June 30, Alexis's funeral was held in the presence of the Czar, the Czarina, ministers, senators, and all the military and civilian dignitaries. A large crowd of people who had been unable to get in surrounded the little church. The coffin, hung with black velvet, was placed on a high catafalque under a canopy of white brocade, surrounded by an honor guard with drawn swords. Were they not the same soldiers who had stood on either side of Alexis when he had come as a prisoner before his judges? The prelates did their office gravely. Most of the faithful, in their brilliant uniforms, had not yet recovered from the libations of the night before. In their foggy brains the hymns collided with snatches of drinking songs. At the end of the divine service the Czar climbed the steps of the catafalque, bent over the coffin, and kissed his son's cold lips. Witnesses assure us that when he straightened up he showed a human countenance and eyes wet with tears.

Yet he did not regret his decision. This time he was sure he had rooted out the evil. He wanted to show his gratitude to those who had helped him in the necessary, thankless task: The two-faced scoundrel Tolstoy became a count; Rumiantsov was promoted to major and received two thousand serfs; Euphrosyne, as the price of her betrayal, was allotted certain effects that had belonged to the Czarevich. Freed from the fortress, she was favored with Their Majesties' indulgence and ended up marrying an officer of the St. Petersburg garrison, with whom she lived another thirty years in peace and abundance. At the end of the year 1718 Peter was so convinced that he had chosen the only reasonable solution to this affair that he had a medal struck representing a crown lit by a triumphal sun whose rays pierced the clouds. Around it was the inscription: "The horizon has cleared."

That was not the view of foreign diplomats. Weber, the chargé d'affaires from Hanover, analyzed the situation shrewdly: "However much the monarch may love his subjects, he acts alone. . . . Everything that he has changed during his glorious reign has been changed in spite of the reluctance of the Russians and has been accomplished solely by obedience. The sleepless nights they spend thinking about the future of their country make most of them hope that His Majesty's days are numbered and that the empire will return to its old forms. . . . St. Petersburg, the ships, the sea, the German fashions, and the beard shavers, all the foreign customs and languages are, for the majority, a nightmare. All those who have had to settle in St. Petersburg yearn for their homeland as for Paradise and desire nothing so much as to return to their old Russia sunk in the mire. . . . As the Czar is very much aware of this resistance, and as he saw that the Czarevich was not following in his footsteps but in the footsteps of his ancestors, there is nothing surprising in the fact that he had recourse to extremely harsh means, which seemed unjust in the eyes of the world and contrary to the law of nations, but which were already justified in the minds of those who still had sound judgment on these questions."

As if he had read those lines, a few months after the trial Peter justified himself, saying to the nobles: "You have seen me punish the crimes of a son who was ungrateful, hypocritical, and malicious beyond all imagination. . . . By so doing I hope to have ensured the endurance of my great work, which is to make the Russian nation forever powerful and formidable and all my states flourish-ing—a work that has cost me so much labor, and my subjects so much blood and so much money, and that in the first year follow-ing my death would have been undone if I had not set things in order as I did."*

Among the people, however, Alexis was remembered as a martyr personifying Holy Russia. There was no doubt that if he had reigned after his father he would have returned power to the popes and the long beards, would have ceased making war, would have turned away from impious Europe. Was he really dead? Some people whispered that he was not. Soon, false Alexises appeared here and there in the country: there were five of them in five years. But Peter didn't care. By one spectacular deed he had bowed the reactionaries under a terror greater than that which had followed the execution of the *streltsy*. The opposition was decapitated. The Czar could go back to his true mission: to make Russia greater by pushing back its borders and educating its subjects. The sword abroad, the cudgel at home. If today there were some who suffered from that policy, tomorrow, Peter thought, posterity would do him justice.

*Voltaire's comment was: "When we consider this catastrophe, the tender-hearted shudder and the stern approve."[25]

12
Emperor and Empress

*F*or the Czar, the year 1718 was marked by two important deaths: that of his oldest son, Alexis, and that of his hereditary enemy, Charles XII. On November 30 the king of Sweden was killed by a musket ball while besieging the Fortress of Frederikshald. His sister, Ulrica Eleonora, who succeeded him in March 1719, ordered the execution of Goertz, who was accused of being in league with the Russians, and let it be known through her plenipotentiaries that Sweden was no longer disposed to grant concessions on the Baltic but in Germany. Peter's response was immediate. In July 1719, while negotiations in the Aland Islands were bogged down, a sizable Russian fleet—30 big ships, 130 galleys, and 100 smaller vessels—landed an armed force on the Swedish coast. Hundreds of villages, mills, storehouses, and factories were burned by Cossacks and Russian sailors. A party of Cossacks even advanced to within a league and a half of the capital.

In spite of their losses, the Swedes refused to be disheartened. In September the Aland Congress was broken off. Ulrica Eleonora had in the meantime obtained the support of England and of the court of Vienna, which had been on bad terms with the Czar ever since the affair of the Czarevich Alexis. Through crafty maneuvering London was able to isolate Russia diplomatically. But while the great powers spoke out against the Czar, they did not have the means to carry out their threats. In May 1720 an English squadron under the command of Admiral Norris joined with a Swedish squadron and tried to intimidate the enemy by bombarding his positions. The result was laughable: one log hut and one bathhouse went up in flames. Meanwhile, Baron von Mengden carried out a second landing in Sweden, burning the homes of 1,026 peasant families. Menshikov wrote facetiously to Peter: "The loss which Your Majesty has sustained on the Island of Nargö through the action of the two united fleets is a grievous one. But all things considered, we can accept the sacrifice, abandoning the log hut to the Swedish fleet and the bathhouse to the English fleet."

After this sham battle Admiral Norris left the Baltic Sea. The Swedes realized that despite all their friendship, not the king of England or the regent of France or the emperor of Germany was going to risk supporting them in an unequal struggle. Peter, meanwhile, had accepted the skillful mediation of Campredon, Louis XV's envoy, to bring about a rapprochement between the two parties. Campredon threw himself into his work, made personal contact with this one and that, conferred with Ulrica Eleonora's husband, Frederick, who had become king of Sweden, corresponded with Peter, and at last, in April 1721, arranged another meeting of Russian and Swedish negotiators in Nystad. After long discussions Sweden agreed to abandon certain territories but insisted that the Czar must not support the Duke of Holstein, Charles XII's nephew, in his claim to the Swedish crown. Early in summer, however, the Duke of Holstein was received in St. Petersburg in the most flattering manner. There was talk of a forthcoming engagement between him and Peter's daughter, the Czarevna Anna. Frederick was worried and decided to agree to all the Czar's wishes so as not to run the risk of a dynastic war.

The peace of Nystad was signed on August 30, 1721. In exchange for an indemnity of two million thalers, payable over a period of four years, Russia received in perpetuity Livonia, Estonia, Ingria, part of Karelia with Vyborg and the islands of

Osel and Dagö; she restored to Sweden the rest of Finland and promised not to intervene in her internal affairs. Inhabitants of the provinces that had been ceded to Russia would retain the rights they enjoyed under the Swedish regime as well as freedom of religion and education; landowners could keep their possessions on condition that they became Russian subjects. Poland and England were parties to the treaty. There was no mention of the Duke of Holstein.

On September 3, 1721, a courier arrived in Vyborg bringing the Czar word that the peace was signed. Peter, who had achieved his ends after twenty-one years of war, was exultant. By gaining access to a long coastline on the Baltic he had changed the political map of Europe. Henceforth Russia could breathe freely. The sufferings and privations the people had endured would not have been in vain. The Czar's intransigence toward his subjects was, in a way, justified by success. He wrote to Basil Dolgoruky: "The course of instruction for students normally lasts seven years. Our schooling has lasted three times that long, but it has ended so well that we could not have wished for anything better."

He returned at once to St. Petersburg, sailing up the Neva on his yacht. Throughout the trip trumpets sounded, drums beat victoriously, the three cannon on board fired salutes. In the capital the crowd rushed to the wharf on Trinity Square and saw in the distance the Czar standing in the prow of the ship waving a handkerchief and shouting at the top of his lungs: *"Mir! Mir!* (Peace! Peace!)" He sprang lightly onto the dock, despite his forty-nine years, and hurried to the Church of the Trinity. A Te Deum was celebrated there, while on the square in front of the church a wooden platform was quickly erected and barrels of beer and brandy were brought. When he came out after the service, Peter climbed nimbly onto the stage and, looking out over the sea of heads moving beneath him, cried out: "Good day, my children! Orthodox people, give thanks to Almighty God, who grants us a beneficial and eternal peace with Sweden after so long and hard a war. I drink to the health of all of you, who have thus brought glory to your motherland!" Then, seizing a glass of brandy, he downed it at a draft amid roars of enthusiasm. That was the signal for the libations to commence. Until late in the night heralds in helmets, wearing white scarves over their shoulders and carrying white flags decorated with laurel branches, ran through the streets blowing trumpets and announcing the advent of a new era of peace. The people wept for joy, blessed the sovereign, danced, drank, and sang in the illuminated streets.

The entire week following was taken up with a masquerade in which, at the Czar's orders, a thousand people participated. High dignitaries and their wives, dressed up in the most varied costumes, formed a procession and for hours paraded slowly around Trinity Square. There were shepherds, nymphs, Spaniards, Turks, Indians, Harlequins, Scaramouches. The Czarina was dressed as a Dutch peasant, the Czar as a Dutch sailor. He walked at the head of the procession and beat the drum tirelessly. No one dared stop or leave his place in line until he had given the signal for them to disperse. The centerpiece of the celebration was the marriage of the new Prince Pope Buturlin and his predecessor Zotov's widow, who was some sixty years old. The Czar had decided upon this match despite the entreaties of the two interested parties. For the wedding feast the Prince Pope was seated under a canopy beside the Czar; his wife, under another canopy beside the Czarina. Men and women drank heartily at Peter's summons. Everyone was drunk, so that the dancing that followed the banquet consisted largely of swaying interspersed with falls and laughter. After they had had a little exercise the Czar and Czarina conducted the bride and groom to the nuptial chamber, which had been installed on the ground floor of the great wooden pyramid of the "Four Frigates" facing the Senate. Casks of wine and brandy surrounded the bed, and when the couple had gotten in it they drank again before Their Majesties. Then Peter and Catherine withdrew, closing the doors behind them. But holes had been drilled in the walls of the pyramid so that people on the outside could watch the pathetic newlyweds in their intimate moments. Czar, Czarina, and entourage, turned voyeurs, laughed at the antics of the old Prince Pope and his wife, who thought they were unobserved.[1]

The next day the Czar, who was decidedly in good spirits, devised another farce. An enormous open cask of beer was placed on a raft; on its surface floated a vat; and in the vat crouched the Prince Pope, tin tiara on his head, Venus-decorated crook in hand.

He looked around in panic while a boat with twelve oarsmen towed the raft onto the Neva. His "cardinals" followed, sitting astride barrels, their red robes tucked up around their waists. A sailor dressed as Neptune used a trident to turn him around in his tub. The Prince Pope screamed and clung to the rim. The tub capsized and the Prince Pope found himself splashing about in the beer. Spectators massed along the shore applauded. Then everyone gathered in the great hall at the headquarters of the postal service for a gigantic blowout. On the following days the masquerade continued, increasingly merry and absurd. On pain of a hundred-ruble fine, notables were forbidden to go out into the street unless they were in fancy dress.

After a week of folly the court returned to serious matters. On October 22, 1721, as soon as the text of the treaty with Sweden had been received, another Te Deum was celebrated in the Church of the Trinity. The archbishop of Pskov extolled the sovereign's wisdom, and Chancellor Golovkin, on behalf of the Senate, made an emotional address to Peter:

"Thanks to the celebrated deeds of Your Majesty, to the greatness of your courage both in politics and in war, and to your indefatigable labors, we have left the darkness and ignorance in which we were plunged and stepped onto the world stage of honor, so that one may say that by incorporating us into the society of civilized peoples, Your Majesty has made something out of nothing. . . . The Senate takes the liberty of begging Your Majesty, with the most profound submission, to receive the title of Peter the Great, father of his country, Emperor of all the Russias. . . . Long live Peter the Great, father of his country, Emperor of all the Russias!"

Peter pretended to be surprised and embarrassed but in the end accepted and made a brief speech calling upon his subjects not to abandon their warlike virtues. Thereupon frenzied cheering rose from the crowd, trumpets sounded, and the artillery of the Admiralty Fortress fired salutes that were answered shot for shot by the cannon of 150 galleys. Then in the audience chamber of the Senate the highest personages in the empire gathered to congratulate their sovereign, who was seated on a throne of gilded, sculpted wood surmounted by the two-headed eagle. On his right, Catherine in a gown of red velvet embroidered with silver; on his left, the Princesses Anna and Elizabeth in white gowns trimmed with gold braid. Each of the visitors in turn climbed the steps of the dais and kissed the new Emperor's hand. Then they all assembled for a great banquet, men in one room, women in another. Toast followed toast, each emphasized by the roll of kettledrums and artillery fire. Having eaten and drunk his fill, Peter walked out on his companions, forbidding them to budge, and, as was his habit, went to lie down on his yacht. Sentries posted in front of the doors prevented the guests from leaving the room, even to relieve themselves. Nailed to the spot, some of the oldest fell asleep in their chairs with their heads on the table.

At last Peter returned, refreshed and cheerful after his nap, and gave the signal for the dancing to begin. Polonaises and minuets roused the company, who reluctantly tripped about to the music to amuse the monarch. At nine o'clock in the evening the dances ended and the fireworks began: unfortunately the master pyrotechnist proved to be dead drunk and could not be counted on for this dangerous work. No matter, the new Emperor was also an expert in the art. He ran out, rolled up his sleeves, and proceeded himself to light the displays exalting his glory. The doors of a temple of Janus opened slowly, sparkling inscriptions proclaimed Peter I Emperor of Russia, the figures of a Russian warrior and a Swedish warrior held out their hands to each other under the sign *"Pax."* Symbolic representations of Justice, Prudence, and Victory appeared in the background, a thousand rockets burst into multicolored flowers against the night sky, the galleys anchored in front of the Senate fired blanks, and at each salvo the walls trembled as if they were about to collapse. Massed in front of the windows, the guests exclaimed in admiration. At street corners whole oxen roasted on spits, fountains of vodka and wine flowed without ceasing. The people jostled one another to tear off a piece of meat and drink a gulp of alcohol. The guards had a hard time keeping order. The common people wondered what changes were in store now that Peter had become Emperor. Would they be happier or unhappier? Would they pay more taxes or less?

Peter had wanted to limit the scope of his prestigious new title. He had agreed to be Emperor of all the Russias, not Emperor of the East, as certain persons had suggested. But even though he had restricted his claims to Russian territories only, his new status did not coincide with the political notions of other European powers. The heads of the diplomatic missions made it plain that they would have trouble persuading their respective governments to recognize him as Emperor. And indeed, while Prussia, Holland, and Sweden hastened to give him his new title, Austria, England, Turkey, France, Spain, and Poland still refused to do so.

In any case, Peter himself felt no transformation since rising to imperial rank. Neither his ideas nor his way of life had changed. Fierce, indefatigable, ruthless, he astonished everyone who came near him. Portraits, accounts, and memoirs of the time all represent him as a broad-shouldered giant with a swarthy complexion, full cheeks, a sensual mouth under a small mustache, a dominating eye, and short, curly brown hair. He had a wart on his right cheek. He walked with a quick step and a long stride, back bent, arms swinging—a sailor who had just left the deck of his ship. From time to time his head would be shaken by a nervous tic and his face would become twisted, his eyes would take on an expression of demented rage; it would pass like lightning. Already the Czar's features would have returned to their former harmony, but his interlocutors would remain as frightened as if they had seen the muzzle of a beast appear from behind a human face. He used curious medicines to combat these convulsions, such as a certain powder made from the stomach and wings of a magpie. He didn't like to sleep alone for fear he would have an attack. When no woman shared his bed, he would instruct an aide-de-camp or a servant to lie down beside him and would grip his shoulders in an iron fist. Woe to the other if he moved or even snored—he would be punished with the cudgel. On campaigns, when taking a nap, Peter often used a servant's abdomen for a pillow—if the man's stomach growled, the Czar would become angry and strike him. In 1717, when he was at table with the queen of Prussia, he was seized with a spasm so violent that she was frightened and started up from her chair. To reassure her he grabbed her arm, gripping it with such force that she cried out. He shrugged his shoulders and said: "My Catherine doesn't have such delicate bones."[2] Peter was so powerful that for amusement he would bend a horseshoe in his hands or roll a silver plate up into a tube.

His dress was always deliberately simple and even slovenly. A hat without braid, a threadbare coat of coarse wool, a dirty vest, patched socks, down-at-heel shoes. Sometimes, too, he would put on the green uniform with red facings of the Preobrazhensky regiment, with a black sword knot at his side. In his hand, his famous cudgel, the *dubina,* a stout rattan cane with an ivory head, which he used to make his orders penetrate recalcitrant noggins. But on holidays he consented to put on a red tunic embroidered with silver, with wide lapels in the French fashion and a little Swedish collar. His brown, unpowdered wig was so short that his real hair, which he didn't bother to have cut, showed beneath it. Often when he was irritated he would stuff the wig in his pocket. Or else he would forget to put it on, and, feeling cold, would snatch a wig from a lackey or from the man next to him and clap it onto his own head. When it snowed he wore a sheepskin hat, soft deerskin boots with the hair side out, and a fur-lined caftan. Persons who visited him in the morning, even ambassadors or princes, found him wearing an old dressing gown that was too short and left his hairy legs uncovered. On his head would be a cotton nightcap with green ribbons, lined with linen to absorb the sweat from his forehead and temples; he perspired a great deal.

With visitors he would go straight to the point. Pressed with questions, they always felt as if they were taking an examination in front of a schoolmaster who knew their business better than they themselves. When he had found out everything he needed to know he would send them away, dress quickly, drink a glass of vodka, eat a hard biscuit, and run off to the shipyards. If the weather was fine he would go on foot; if not, in a little red one-horse carriage. In winter the carriage was replaced by an ordinary sleigh. Thus inhabitants of St. Petersburg would see their Czar going about the city like a private person, unescorted, wearing any old clothes. Sometimes he would drop into a house, ask for a drink, have a bite to eat. He forbade people to fall on their knees in front of him in the street. He never rode in a coach, except when there was a grand reception—and in that case he would borrow one of Menshikov's, which were famous throughout the city for their princely splendor.

When he got back to the palace he would toss off a glass of brandy and work on his files until it was time for dinner. But sometimes, too, he would interrupt his reading of reports to go to his workshop. For years he had been working at his lathe to make a great ivory chandelier for twenty-four candles to be hung in the Cathedral of St. Petersburg. Nothing was so relaxing for him as manual labor. Even when he gave entertainments for the court, he liked to be physically involved, lighting the fireworks, playing the drum, leading the dance. In 1722, at the wedding of a daughter of Romodanovsky, he played the role of majordomo, gravely carrying the baton that was the symbol of his office, supervising the service, and insisting on eating with the servants, after everyone else. When the company complained of the heat, he had a locksmith's tools brought and with his own hands opened a window that had been sealed off.

He needed only a few hours' sleep to restore his energy. His associates panted to keep up with his breathless pace as best they could. Late at night, glass in hand, he would still be discussing matters with his exhausted table companions, bewildering them with questions, orders, advice, startling them with bursts of merriment or anger that were equally disturbing. And at four o'clock in the morning he would be on his feet again, pacing up and down in his dressing gown while waiting for the first audience.

His legendary simplicity manifested itself not only in a marked preference for small, low-ceilinged rooms, hard, narrow beds, and plain, sturdy furniture but also in his indifference to the way his household was run. It cost him barely fifty thousand rubles a year to maintain his court, and his entire domestic staff consisted of a dozen young men, nobles or commoners, who performed the functions of valets, messengers, and secretaries. One of them, Nartov, helped him in his work at the lathe on wood and ivory. They all feared him and revered him. He treated them with cheerful brutality. It was whispered that he had an ambiguous affection for some of them. In any event, his demonstrations of friendship were as surprising as his demonstrations of anger. In a burst of enthusiasm, he might plant a rough kiss on a man's mouth. Berkholz notes that one day the Czar took the Duke of Holstein's head in his hands, pulled off his wig, and kissed him on the forehead, the neck, and even gave him "a deep kiss on the mouth." For a time there was a young black man among his pages, one Abraham Petrovich Hannibal. Purchased in Constantinople by Ambassador Tolstoy and baptized at the age of eleven with Peter for his godfather and the queen of Poland for his godmother, he entered the Czar's service and charmed him at once by his intelligence and sweet disposition. He slept in the sovereign's woodworking shop and followed him on all his campaigns. Peter was so solicitous of him that one day he personally removed a tapeworm for him, without hesitating to dirty his fingers. Pushkin, who reports the incident, notes laconically: "The anecdote is rather dirty, but it gives a good picture of Peter's habits."[3] When Abraham reached the age of twenty-two he was sent to finish his education in Paris. He enlisted in the French army, earned the rank of lieutenant during the campaign of 1720 against Spain, was wounded in the head, returned to Paris, entered the School of Engineering, came out with the rank of captain, and finally went back to Russia. There he served as a lieutenant in the company of bombardiers commanded by Peter. The Czar appreciated his dark-skinned associate's devotion and sense of responsibility. After many vicissitudes, Abraham died in old age; he was the maternal great-grandfather of Pushkin.

During his stay at court "the Negro of Peter the Great,"* like other members of his master's household, made the acquaintance of the *dubina,* or cudgel. They were not the only ones to do so. Often the Czar would summon to his room some distinguished official who had given him cause for complaint and there, without witnesses, would strike him with his stick. To take a thrashing from His Majesty was no disgrace—since the punishment took place in secret, it was almost a mark of favor. When he left the room the victim would draw himself up again and pretend to have had a confidential conversation of the highest importance. Sometimes Peter assigned one of his favorites to wield the cudgel on his behalf. "Tomorrow you will dine at so-and-so's house," he said to Captain Senyavin, "pick a quarrel with him during dinner and give him, in my presence, a good fifty blows with your cane."[4] One night during the Persian campaign Peter ventured out of his tent, fell upon his trusty adviser Artemius Volynsky, whom in the darkness he had mistaken for someone else, finally realized his mistake, burst out laughing, and said: "That's all right, sooner or later

---

*Title of a story by Pushkin about his ancestor.

you'll deserve what you got today; then you'll only have to remind me that it's already paid."

These acts of violence were attributable, of course, to Peter's irascible nature, but they also corresponded to his conception of the way to govern Russia. One day he noticed a ship's captain trying to hide a book he was reading. Peter glanced at the page and read: "A Russian is like a cod; if you don't beat him often, you will never make anything good out of him." And while the terrified captain already envisioned himself on the strappado, he smiled and declared: "You read instructive books. You will be promoted." In his mind the *dubina* was reserved for people whom he was fond of; he chastised them for their own good. Others were doomed to harsher treatment. It was not unusual for him to beat one of his close associates black and blue and that same day invite him to dinner: his way of pouring balm on the wound.

His tastes in dining were as rustic as his tastes in lodging and dress. When he ate alone with Catherine they were served by a single page. When they were joined by a few guests, the cook, Velten, presented the dishes himself with the help of two orderlies. On gala occasions they dined at the home of Menshikov, who unlike the Czar had tableware of gold and porcelain, several chefs, and a host of servants.

Peter's table manners were primitive. He ate with his fingers, dripped sauce on himself, wiped his mouth with the back of his hand. The Polish minister Manteuffel, who had supped with him in Berlin at the prince royal's, praised the Czar, who, he said, had outdone himself because "he neither belched nor farted nor picked his teeth—at least, I neither saw nor heard him do so." Peter always carried his own utensils—a wooden spoon trimmed with ivory and a knife and fork with handles of green bone—but he didn't use them much. He was so much more comfortable using his fingers! He had no interest in culinary refinements. He liked stews, kasha, cabbage soup, suckling-pig jelly, salted cucumbers and lemons, Limburg ham, raw onions with black bread. Never any fish or sweet dishes; they disagreed with him, he said.

He was a big eater and an insatiable drinker. Vodka, ale, Cahors wine, Tokay, Médoc, anything would do. "He never passes a day without getting tipsy," declares Baron von Pöllnitz. The least cause for celebration—a saint's day, the anniversary of a victory, a promotion, the launching of a ship—was an excuse for interminable drinking. Some of the banquets lasted for several days and nights. Since he held his liquor well, Peter demanded the same capacity of his guests: if you had the honor of sitting at the sovereign's table, you had to thank him by bending your elbow as often as he did. Diplomats were terrified by this obligation, and they weren't alone. Most guests were filled with anxiety to see the team of six grenadiers come in carrying huge buckets of cheap vodka on a stretcher. The smell of this drink was so strong that the whole table reeked of it. Each guest had to ingurgitate a volume determined by the Czar. Those who tried to evade their obligation were forced to down an additional amount, "the cup of the Great Eagle." If they protested that they had already had enough, a major of the Guard would ask them to blow in his nose so he could check whether their breath smelled sufficiently of alcohol.[5] Even women were subject to the rule. When the daughter of Vice Chancellor Shafirov, who was a converted Jew, refused to drink a large cup of vodka, Peter shouted at her: "Wicked seed of the Hebrews, I'll teach you to obey!" And in front of the whole company he gave her two hard slaps.[6] Sentries prevented the participants from leaving the hall before the Czar had adjourned the session. He himself, although steady on his feet, sometimes felt fatigued after he had "sacrificed to Bacchus." But he knew his limit and never made an important decision when inebriated.

Accustomed from earliest childhood to doing exactly what he pleased, Peter tolerated no obstacle to his will. Few men have been so incapable of putting themselves in another's place. His most extravagant whims seemed justified to him simply by virtue of the fact that they had occurred to him. Terrorizing his subjects, he took pity on no one. To amuse spectators he forced eighty-year-olds to dance to the point of exhaustion, imitating the sprightly movements of the young, while the young had to dance slowly and heavily like old people. When Catherine interceded for Marshal Olsufiev's wife, requesting that she be excused from a drinking party because she was pregnant, he was indignant that the lady should ask for a special privilege, insisted that she attend the banquet, and showed no remorse on learning that she had thereafter suffered a stillbirth. The minister Feodor Golovin refused to take salad at dinner because he couldn't stand vinegar. The Czar was furious, had the ungracious guest seized and pinioned, and poured vinegar into his mouth until he was half choked and spitting blood.[7] Another Golovin, Matthew, an old member of an illustrious family, was ordered to appear in a masquerade in a devil's costume. When he objected on the grounds of age and rank, Peter had him undressed, had a hat with horns placed on his head, and made him sit naked on the ice on the Neva, where he was kept, exposed to the wind, for an hour. When he got home he went to bed, seized with a "hot fever," and died. Peter did not hold himself in any way responsible.

In 1721 at the wedding feast of Prince I. I. Trubetzkoy—a man well on in years who had just married a young thing of twenty—a fruit jelly, the new groom's favorite delicacy, was served. Peter immediately forced the prince's mouth open and stuffed him with the sweet, sticking his fingers down his throat to push it farther in. Meanwhile, on order of the empress, other guests were tickling the bride's brother, who writhed and bellowed, says Berkholz, "like a calf having its throat cut." In Copenhagen Peter saw a magnificent mummy and wanted it for himself. It was a unique treasure, however, and the king of Denmark politely refused his guest's demand. The Czar went back to the museum, tore off the mummy's nose, and after a few other mutilations told the horrified curator: "Now you can keep it." On June 30, 1705, emerging from a nocturnal orgy at dawn, he visited the monastery of the Ruthenian Basilian Fathers in Polotsk, planted himself in front of the statue of the blessed Jehoshaphat, who was represented with an ax driven into his skull, and demanded in a thick voice: "Who put this holy man in such a sad state?" "It was the schismatics," replied Father Kozikovsky, the superior of the order. On hearing the word "schismatics" applied to Orthodox soldiers by a servant of the Pope, the Czar flew into a rage. He ran his sword through Father Kozikovsky and killed him; officers of his suite struck down three other monks, mortally wounding two of them, and slashed the breasts of some pious women who protested the carnage. The same evening Alexis Makarov, the Czar's secretary, wrote in His Majesty's *Journal*: "Entered the Uniat church of Polotsk and killed five Uniats for having called our generals heretics." The affair made a scandal that reached as far as Rome. But Peter was perfectly indifferent to the fact that far away a few Catholic priests were getting all worked up over nothing.[8] Five years later in Moscow, during a celebration of the victory of Poltava, he went up to a soldier who was carrying the Swedish flag and, with his face contorted in fury, struck him with the flat of his sword, although no one could tell what the man had done wrong. In 1721 at Riga, seeing another soldier carrying off a fragment of copper that had fallen from the roof of the Church of St. Peter when it was struck by lightning, he killed him with his cudgel. Once when he was in one of his fits of anger and Romodanovsky and Zotov were trying to calm him, he drew his sword, whirled the blade in the air, half cut off the fingers of one and wounded the other in the head. Not long after, noticing in the middle of a ball that Menshikov was dancing with his sword at his side, he slapped him so hard that the favorite's nose began to bleed.

On the other hand, some of Peter's excesses were inspired only by the desire to laugh and make others laugh. Thus on April 30, 1723, he had the alarm bells rung at night so that the inhabitants of St. Petersburg awoke with a start and, thinking there was a conflagration, rushed to the presumed site of the disaster. All they found was an ordinary brazier that had been lit at the Czar's orders. The soldiers who were fanning the flames laughed and told them it was only His Majesty's joke.[9] Another time, he set fire to the old wooden house he had had built for himself in Moscow in 1690, attached Roman candles to the rafters as they began to burn, and beat the drum while the roof collapsed, setting off a superb display of fireworks. Finding one of his clowns asleep, he glued the man's beard to his chest with tar and roared with laughter at the man's contortions when he woke up.[10]

The function of these clowns—he had as many as sixty in his entourage—was not only to amuse him with broad jokes. At table they would loudly recount, with guffaws of laughter, the peculations, extortions, and blunders of various officials, while the Czar kept a sharp eye on the reactions of those in question. The most famous fool was the Portuguese d'Acosta. Peter had put him in charge of organizing the various grotesque ceremonies and directing the performers. Another fool, Balakirev, was the favorite butt of the Czar, who considered him the deceived husband *par excellence* and never missed an opportunity to make fun of him in public.

In addition to the clowns were the dwarfs. Peter was mad about them. To make more of an occasion out of the wedding of two of his favorite dwarfs, he had seventy-two of them come from the farthest provinces in the empire. In the church, he himself held the ritual crown over the head of the bride, who came up to his waist. Later all the guests assembled at Menshikov's palace for an enormous feast. "Normal people" were seated at big tables, the "monsters" at smaller tables, where they ate from miniature dishes. Soon the entire company of Lilliputians was dead drunk. A contemporary described the ball that followed the dinner: "It is easy to imagine how much the Czar and the rest of the company were delighted at the comical capers, strange grimaces, and odd postures of that medley of pygmies, most of whom were of a size the mere sight of which was enough to provoke laughter. One had a high hunch on his back and very short legs, another was remarkable by a monstrous big belly; a third came waddling along on a little pair of crooked legs like a badger; a fourth had a head of a prodigious size; some had wry mouths and long ears, little pig eyes and chub-cheeks, and many such other comical figures more. When these diversions were ended, the new married couple were carried to the Czar's house and bedded in his own bedchamber."[11]

A few years later the burial of the same dwarf gave Peter the opportunity to stage another ceremony that he was very proud of. At the head of the funeral procession walked a priest chosen for his short stature. All the choristers were children. The little coffin, placed on a little hearse, was drawn by little horses with black trappings. Behind came all the dwarfs wearing mourning capes. Their deformity and limping gait amused the onlookers and even the Czar. To accentuate the contrast, he had the procession flanked by fifty tall grenadiers, each carrying a lantern. After the funeral the dwarfs were received at the palace by Their Majesties. A few days later the death of a chef inspired Peter to arrange another masquerade: all participants in the procession were dressed as cooks, with white aprons and hats.

Peter was attracted to giants as well as dwarfs. He had brought back from his trip to France a fat, flabby seven-foot-six colossus by the name of Nicolas Bourgeois and married him to a Finnish woman of the same height in hopes that they would produce giant children for him. Disappointed in this entirely scientific expectation, he nevertheless continued to pay the couple an annual salary of six hundred rubles and to include Bourgeois in his grotesque ceremonies, dressed up like a baby and held in leading strings by dwarfs.*

Early on, Peter's morbid tastes led him to establish the Museum of Curiosities, where he assembled everything that represented a freak of nature: a man without genital organs, a child with two heads, a sheep with five feet, a deformed fetus. He loved to walk among the jars of abnormal specimens pickled in alcohol. A ukase instructed the provincial governors to seek out and send to St. Petersburg any phenomenon, human or animal, living or dead, to be found in their territory. A schedule of rewards was established for persons who discovered monsters: so much for a living monster, so much for a dead one, so much for a human being, so much for an animal. The caretaker of the museum, who kept it heated, was a dwarf who had only two fingers on each hand and two toes on each foot. He knew that when he died he would be stuffed and put on display in the gallery where he tended the stoves.

By a natural progression, this fascination with the horrible led Peter to attend the interrogation of suspects in torture chambers and to look on with interest as the executioner wielded pincers or knout. If need be, he lent him a hand, even when the victim was his own son. According to Semevsky, "he pursued the condemned prisoners to the very scaffold with reproaches and invectives, mocking the dying and the dead."

Peter had no sense of the mysterious majesty of death, regarding the human body merely as an interesting mechanism. He enjoyed exploring it, scalpel in hand. Ever since his stay in Holland he had kept his kit of instruments by him. The doctors at the St.

---

*When Bourgeois died he was stuffed and enshrined in Peter's Museum of Curiosities. He was still there in 1800. His heart, stomach, liver, and kidneys were preserved in alcohol.

Petersburg hospitals were under orders to inform him as soon as they had a good patient to operate on. Generally he would attend the operation and have the surgeons explain it to him as it progressed. Often he himself would use the lancet; none of the physicians present would dare criticize what he did. In this way he removed twenty pounds of water from the wife of the merchant Borst, who was suffering from dropsy. He was bursting with pride over this result; but four days later the patient died. As furious as if she had disobeyed him, he ordered an autopsy to be carried out in his presence so as to vindicate himself before the medical profession. Naturally, no one ventured to blame him. As a supreme honor, he attended the deceased's funeral, for which the widowed Borst thanked him with tears in his eyes. In a similar case, according to Dolgoruky, Peter personally opened the body of the Czarina Martha Apraxina, widow of Feodor III, who had died of indigestion, in order to find out if she had still been a virgin at age fifty-two, as people at court maintained.

Less dramatic were his operations on the jaws of those around him. His passion for dentistry had only increased with time. He never missed an opportunity to examine the aching teeth of his servants and courtiers. The sight of a swollen cheek filled him with joy. He hurled thunderbolts at those who refused to have a molar extracted. His famous bag of teeth swelled from year to year like a miser's purse.*

A talented jack-of-all-trades, Peter wanted to embrace all branches of human knowledge, although he had neither the time nor the patience to go deeply into any of them. He was fascinated by details and neglected general concepts. Abstract ideas confused him. In a kind of intellectual myopia, he constantly concerned himself with the infinitely small. Everything he did was based on sudden inspiration, mood, whim. Yet out of this multitude of disparate impulses there emerged a direction. The building of St. Petersburg, which had been chaotically begun, came to beautiful completion; a war that had been undertaken rashly ended in considerable territorial gains. His ability to interest himself simultaneously in the most dissimilar questions, those most unequal in ur-

*It is still preciously preserved in Leningrad.

gency and importance, can be seen in every one of his writings. His head seethed with so many thoughts that he hardly had time to make note of them. He always carried writing tablets; he would take them out of his pocket and cover them with hieroglyphics. When he ran out of space on the tablets he would seize the first document that came to hand and write on that. In the margins of a report on the plan to establish an academy in St. Petersburg, he scribbled these few lines: "We must send Rumiantsov in the Ukraine orders to exchange the oxen he can get from his province for lambs and sheep and to send someone abroad to learn how to look after that sort of animal, how to shear them, and how to dress the wool."[12] In a letter of September 1706 to Apraxin, he gave simultaneous instructions for the military campaign in progress, the translation of certain Latin books, and the training of a couple of young dogs, which absolutely had to be taught to jump over a stick, to take off their master's hat, to sit at heel, go fetch, and so on. His elastic mind bounced from one subject to another: the reorganization of the army and the prohibition of oak coffins, the building of a fleet and a recipe for tripe jelly, whale fishing and the appearance of sunspots, negotiations over ceding Schleswig back to the Duke of Holstein and the search for a girl with the snout of a pig for the Museum of Curiosities. He was in such a hurry that most of his letters were short, barely legible notes. Words are left unfinished; thus, to Menshikov: *"Mei her Brude un Kamara,"* for *"Mein Herr Bruder und Kamerad."* Even his signature was abbreviated.

The Czar's curiosity was equaled only by his capacity for work. Fourteen hours a day, said his close associates. "He applies himself tirelessly to affairs of state," observed Campredon. "He penetrates them and understands them better than any of his ministers; he is present at all their deliberations." He never engaged in pure meditation. His brain refused to work to no purpose, for the mere pleasure of intellectual exercise. Every thought should find expression in an action. But this man, who was nothing if not decisive, this thoroughgoing materialist who mocked the superstitions of his subjects, did believe in dreams. He noted them down as scrupulously as if they had been physical phenomena. He dreamed he was climbing a rope up a huge tower with the two-headed Russian eagle hanging over it, or that he was capturing the Grand Vizier, who surrendered his saber to him, or that he was fighting tigers until they were dispersed by four white-robed figures. This last dream strengthened his inclination to go to war.[13] He also had certain phobias that are surprising in so coarse-grained a man. For example, he would faint at the sight of a cockroach. Thinking to please him one day, an officer showed him one he had just crushed. Peter turned pale, fell upon the unfortunate man with his cudgel, and fled.[14]

So far as religion was concerned, Peter was a jumble of contradictions. The traditional piety implanted by his mother Natalya remained solidly rooted in his soul notwithstanding his wild conduct. He believed in God the creator of the universe, considered himself the chosen representative of the Almighty in Russia, thought that any lack of respect for the Czar was a crime against the Christian faith, and invoked the aid of the holy cross against "the Moslem devils." All his victories were celebrated with Te Deums that lasted five hours. He never set out on campaign without an image of the Savior to guarantee his safety. He was fond of saying: "He who forgets God and does not keep His commandments accumulates nothing by his labor and will never obtain the blessings of heaven." And: "God is over all." Following the example of his fathers, he took part in the principal divine services. In church he sang in the choir with the assurance of a deacon. He took communion, discussed theology with priests, imposed fines on those who talked or dozed during Mass.

But a few hours after having prayed, he would throw himself into orgies where he gave free rein to his basest instincts. He promulgated harsh penalties for anyone who insulted the Church but devised blasphemous ceremonies around the Prince Pope and amused himself ridiculing the symbolic objects of the faith. He forced the Orthodox to go to confession at least once a year on pain of being brought before territorial judges, but he himself never showed the least remorse. He behaved as if there were a special agreement between God and him that left him completely free on earth and exempted him from any responsibility toward heaven. No matter what he did, he felt his position as Czar justified him. He would have been astonished if anyone had told him he was not a sincere Christian. He said: "I would have wanted the people not just to concern themselves with fasts, genuflections, candles, and incense, but to trust in God and to understand what faith, hope, and love are."[15] But love, precisely, was a notion beyond his ken. He loved his country; he did not love his neighbor.

Peter was very openminded with regard to other religions. He liked to surround himself with Calvinists and Lutherans and listened with interest to their talk, although it smacked of heresy. He even liked to go to Protestant churches. By an ordinance of 1702 he guaranteed freedom of religion to foreigners. But he distrusted Roman Catholics, feeling the Pope had too much power. First he welcomed the Jesuits, then expelled them, saying: "I know that they are very learned, but I also know that they use their religion only through method and their schools only for their secret practices in favor of the Pope, so as to gain a measure of authority over sovereigns."[16] It was the Capuchins who replaced the Jesuits in Russia. Then the Czar became suspicious of them too and entrusted the administration of Catholic churches to the Franciscans. He was even more wary of Jews and forbade them to immigrate: "This is not the time to open the empire to those people!" he said. But his Vice Chancellor Shafirov was a converted Jew, and His Majesty's entourage included a Meyer and a Lups, both Jewish, who assisted him in his financial operations.

Above all, Peter was a practical man. What mattered to him was not an individual's ancestry but his ability to serve the Czar. In general, he distrusted principles. After meeting Leibniz several times during his travels, he called him his "intimate adviser," but he failed to carry out any of Leibniz's broad plans. The philosopher seemed to be soaring in the clouds, while Peter wanted to feel the earth under his feet at all times. "We have a common point of departure, Sire!" Leibniz had told him. "Both of us are Slavs, belonging to that race whose destinies no man can yet foresee, and both of us are pioneers of the centuries to come."[17] Peter was annoyed by the man's conceit. Incapable of appreciating the subtleties of this far-reaching intelligence, he regarded the father of differential calculus as nothing more than a schemer greedy for honors and sinecures. And Peter thought himself no mean judge of men. To penetrate the innermost thoughts of a member of his entourage, he would seize him by the hair, pull his head back, and plunge an inquisitorial look deep into his eyes.

He was equally boorish in his relations with women, interested in them only insofar as they could satisfy his momentary desire. His love for Catherine did not prevent him from having numerous mistresses. In 1717 he was in Magdeburg receiving delegates from the king of Prussia, including Baron von Pöllnitz. The Baron described the audience as follows: "As the King had ordered that the Czar be given every honor imaginable, the different colleges of the State came in a body to pay their respects, the president of each being its spokesman. When M. de Cocceji, brother of the Grand Chancellor and head of the College of the Regency came to greet the Czar, he found him leaning on two Russian ladies and letting his hands wander over their breasts, which he continued to do while his visitor made his speech."[18] Pöllnitz also recounted the meeting between Peter and his niece, the Duchess of Mecklenburg: "The Czar ran to meet the princess, kissed her tenderly, and led her into a room where, having stretched her out on a sofa, without closing the door and without any consideration for those who had remained in the antechamber, or even for the Duke of Mecklenburg, he acted in such a way as to suggest that nothing could contain his passions." He passed easily from a court lady to a servant girl and from a servant girl to a court lady. According to Pöllnitz, one of the latter, Princess Golitzina, served as his *dura* or fool. "As she often ate with the Czar," he wrote, "that Prince would throw the leftovers on his plate at her head. He would make her stand up and give her flicks of the finger on the nose."

Among the Czar's mistresses was a certain Eudoxia, the wife of Captain Tchernichov. Peter called her *boi-baba*, "the virago." She gave birth to seven children, of whom it was impossible to tell which were by her husband and which by her lover. From his relations with her Peter contracted a venereal disease, which he transmitted to Catherine. To punish the faithless one for having contaminated him, he had her whipped by her husband. The adventure of Maria Matveyevna was similar. Peter gave the young lady in marriage to Major Rumiantsov, who had performed so efficiently in the tracking and capture of the Czarevich Alexis. It was both a reward for services rendered and an invitation to close his eyes to what had happened afterward. Maria, who became one of the Czarina's maids of honor, belonged more to the Czar than to her husband. She gave birth to a son, who was named Peter.*

Catherine's court was a convenient hunting ground for the sovereign. There he had handy an abundance of beauties of easy virtue. Catherine let him do as he pleased; she was indulgent and sometimes even abetted him. And husbands were only too happy when their wives caught the monarch's fancy. He sowed the imperial seed generously. As the father of many bastards, he felt that in that way too he was working for Russia. One of his "conquests," Mary Hamilton, another maid of honor, was descended from a great Scottish family that had long been established in Russia. Pretty and accessible, she too was favored with the Czar's repeated attentions. When he tired of her she consoled herself with his aides-de-camp, became pregnant several times, and systematically did away with her children. One of her lovers, the young Orlov, deceived her, maltreated her, and demanded money from her so insistently that in order to hold him she stole money and jewels from the Czarina. She was immediately suspected. Questioned by the Czar, she confessed the affair, the theft, and the infanticides all together. The investigation revealed further that in front of witnesses she had made fun of the Czarina's ruddy complexion. Catherine generously intervened in favor of the guilty woman, as did the Czarina Prascovia, widow of Ivan V. In vain: Peter wanted to make an example of her. The woman had deceived him, had killed children, one of whom might have been his, had laid hands on his wife's money box. The verdict was death.

Mary Hamilton walked to the scaffold on March 14, 1719, before a great gathering of people. The Emperor insisted that she wear for the occasion a white silk gown trimmed with black ribbons. He himself attended the execution, as was his custom, tenderly kissed the condemned woman at the foot of the ladder, and said: "I cannot save you without breaking laws both human and divine. Accept your punishment in the hope that God will pardon you if you repent." Then, having helped her up to the platform, he again exhorted her to pray and left her to the executioner. The

---

*He grew up to become one of Catherine II's marshals; contemporaries were struck by his resemblance to the late Emperor.

ax fell with a dull sound. Peter calmly picked up the bloody head, which had rolled on the floor, lifted it by the hair, examined it and, turning to the crowd of courtiers, changed into a professor of anatomy. In a steady voice he pointed out how clean a cut the ax had made and named the organs that were visible in cross section: the carotid artery, the trachea, the vertebral column, the nerves, muscles, and so on. When he had finished his lecture he placed a kiss on the dead lips that had so often pressed his own and murmured words of love, dropped the head back in the mud, crossed himself, and walked away.

No woman was irreplaceable, he thought. Except, perhaps, Catherine. She had grown even stouter over the years. Her bosom overflowed. Her arms were as big as her thighs. Her complexion was blotchy. She wore heavy makeup and put perfume on her clothes, which were overloaded with embroidery. But she was always cheerful, available, and devoted, and at table she could hold her own with the best of them. She was not one to be frightened by a bucket of vodka or to jib at downing "the cup of the Great Eagle" that Peter made his dinner companions drink as a fine. She was so strong that she could lift the Czar's scepter holding it by one end with her arm out straight. None of His Majesty's young aides-de-camp could match that feat, although perhaps they were only pretending weakness to flatter the Czarina.

During a display of fireworks the names Peter and Catherine appeared inside a heart, and it was Peter himself who set off this emblem of love. Having reached the summit, the former Livonian servant was suddenly reminded of her humble origins. On the road from St. Petersburg to Riga, a postilion who was being beaten by a traveler protested, asserting that he was a close relative of His Majesty. The impudent postilion, one Feodor Skavronsky, was arrested. The Czar ordered an investigation and discovered that the man really was Catherine's older brother. Another of the Czarina's brothers was an agricultural laborer. One of her sisters was a serf, another the wife of a shoemaker, a third worked as a prostitute in Reval. Peter generously allotted a small pension to these none-too-distinguished in-laws and kept them away from court. All the same, he felt the life the prostitute was leading was too compromising and had her locked up.

Nothing, it seemed, could shake his confidence in his legitimate wife. And now that the Czarevich Alexis was dead, she was the mother of the heir to the throne, little Peter Petrovich. The Czar adored the four-year-old child, who was strong and handsome and whom he already saw as a soldier, a sailor, the one who would carry on his great enterprise of renovation and conquest. Then on April 16, 1719, little Peter, the dear Petrushka, died suddenly of an illness. The Czar was in the deepest despair. Wounded in his own flesh, he screamed with pain. Perhaps he felt that this bereavement was a punishment for the violence he had inflicted on his other son, Alexis, less than ten months earlier. God was striking him as he himself had struck. All the sons that Catherine had given him had disappeared one after the other. Of his six daughters, only three were still living: Anna, Elizabeth, and Natalya. Wasn't there a curse upon his second marriage?* Wouldn't he be forced to leave the crown of Russia to the other Peter, the son of that abominable Alexis who had dared to defy him, the grandson of that miserable Eudoxia whom he had thrown into a convent?

After a moment's panic he got hold of himself. God, who had always been on his side, could not betray him at the last minute. At his age he still felt capable of begetting a child. He had to have another son. Whom should he ask it of? Fat Catherine? No. For some time he had had a new mistress, the very young, very pretty Maria Cantemir. She was the daughter of Prince Dmitri Cantemir, who, having lost his sovereignty over Moldavia in the treaty of Pruth, had taken refuge with his family in St. Petersburg. If she gave birth to a boy, the future of the dynasty would be assured. If necessary, Peter would repudiate Catherine so as to wed Maria, whom he prized more and more for her freshness. Catherine guessed as much, but true to her line of conduct, feigned indulgence and said not a word. Peter entered into a period in which the purposes of love and politics were tightly interwoven. He could no longer think of himself without calling to mind the interests of

*The twelve children of Peter and Catherine were Paul (1704–1707); Peter (1705–1707); Catherine (1707–1708); Anna (1708–1728), who in 1725 married Karl Frederick of Holstein-Gottorp and had a son by him, the future Peter III; Elizabeth (1709–1761), who was Empress of Russia from 1741 until her death; Natalya (1713–1715); Margaret (1714–1715); Peter (1715–1719); Paul (1717), who died the day after he was born; Natalya (1718–1725); Peter (born and died in 1723); and Paul (born around 1725, died in the same year).

the state, or take pleasure in bed without considering the problems of the succession.

And now it looked as if war was flaring up again—not on the Swedish side this time but on the eastern border. Volynsky, charged with a diplomatic mission in Ispahan, reported to his sovereign that Persia was disturbed by riots and slipping into anarchy and that she would be an easy conquest. If Russia didn't hurry, he said, Turkey, which was quite ready to restore order in neighboring countries, would get there first. Peter was easily convinced. In 1720 he appointed Volynsky governor of Astrakhan and instructed him to prepare a military expedition for the following year. In 1721 indigenous tribes destroyed the shops and warehouses of Russian merchants in Persia; the Afghans penetrated as far as Ispahan. Here was the pretext the Czar was looking for. He left St. Petersburg to join his armies. Catherine of course went with him, but so did Maria Cantemir. The wife's coach and the mistress's rolled along together. When they made camp the two rivals met before the Czar, and both smiled at him, but when night came it was not Catherine whom he received in his tent.

In Astrakhan Maria Cantemir was obliged to stop, for she was pregnant and the Czar wished to spare her the hardships of a long journey in a country that was none too secure. She could wait here and present him with a male child when he returned. Catherine pretended to share his hopes, although she knew what the birth would mean for her. Courageous as always, she decided to follow the Czar, who in Astrakhan on July 18, 1722, took ship with 23,000 foot soldiers for Derbent on the Caspian. More than 100,000 men —Cossacks, Kalmuks, Tatars—were to join them there by the overland route. On August 23, after a few minor skirmishes, Peter made a triumphal entry into Derbent, where the senators sent him a statement of congratulations urging him to "march on in the footsteps of Alexander." The new Alexander, however, soon found that he had ventured into the region without sufficient preparation. As in Moldavia eleven years before, his soldiers were suffering from heat, thirst, and hunger. The boats bringing provisions sank in the Caspian, thousands of horses died for lack of fodder. The sun was so hot that Catherine cut her hair and put on a grenadier's hat. She reviewed the troops, smiled at the men, joked with the officers. Watching her, Peter couldn't help admiring her stamina and good humor.

At the beginning of the campaign he had hoped to reach Baku, where the Khan, it was said, was taking from the ground a heavy oil, naphtha, which had the property of burning. Baku, however, represented another thirty days' march in the dust under a torrid sky, without drinking water. The Russian army was too exhausted to launch into such an adventure. Peter retreated to Astrakhan, leaving General Matiushkin in Derbent with sufficient forces to resume the campaign when the time came.

In Astrakhan there was a disappointment in store for him. During his absence Maria Cantemir had had a miscarriage. He suspected that maidservants bought by Catherine had given her some sort of drink to induce the accident, but he had no evidence against anyone. The doctors blamed only nature. Catherine commiserated but was secretly triumphant. Maria Cantemir, unable to meet her sovereign's expectations, was repudiated.

Peter was furious that he had no power of command over a woman's womb. Once again consolation came to him from the army. A detachment under General Matiushkin had taken Baku, a strategic position of the first importance. The news reached St. Petersburg on September 3, 1723, while Peter, dressed up as a Catholic cardinal, was attending a costume party at Menshikov's palace. He withdrew with the prince to examine the documents that had been delivered to him by a courier come straight from Persia, then took off his crimson robe, donned his usual uniform of an officer in the Preobrazhensky regiment—dark green with red lapels—and reappeared with head high, radiating strength and pride, to hear Menshikov proclaim the Russian victory to his guests. Shouts of joy burst upon his ears. Catherine, in the costume of a great Venetian lady, offered him the full cup of the victor. Everyone around him drank to the glory of the armed forces. At ten o'clock in the evening there were one thousand empty bottles.[19] Even the sentries were drunk.

Finally, at the request of the Czarina, the Czar beat the drum to mark the end of the festivities. But when he had climbed into his carriage he couldn't bear to go home and instead went back to Menshikov's gardens, where the party resumed with more bumpers of alcohol, more cheering, and more dancing.

Nine days later, on September 12, a peace treaty was concluded in St. Petersburg between the shah of Persia and the Czar. Turkey protested. Was a new war in prospect? The French ambassador in Constantinople, the Marquis de Bonnac, intervened to good purpose. What Turkey actually wanted was a piece of the Persian pie; it was granted. In June 1724, a treaty of partition was signed in Constantinople giving Russia the cities of Baku and Derbent and the three provinces of Ghilan, Mazanderan, and Astrabad, while the Porte appropriated Tauris, Erivan, and a few other places. Peter immediately set about developing his new acquisitions. He gave orders to build roads and fortifications, to send out Christian colonists, to eliminate as many Muslims as possible, and to dispatch the local products to St. Petersburg: sugar, dried fruits, lemons, and above all the famous oil, whose properties he wanted to study. "This ore," he said, "will be very useful, to our descendants at any rate."

Rumiantsov, who had been sent to Constantinople for the exchange of ratifications, met on the way an Armenian delegation that was going to St. Petersburg to entreat the Orthodox Czar to help them combat Muslim oppression. Peter received the deputies sympathetically, for he already had in mind that the protection of the Christian populations, the Armenians and Georgians, could serve as a pretext for fresh territorial conquests at the expense of Turkey and Persia. If only his heirs would not abandon the work he had begun but patiently continue their drive toward the East, toward the Indies!

Meanwhile Peter had made a decision that was to have far-reaching consequences. As he no longer hoped for a son, he wanted to give his old partner, who had so generously supported him in love, politics, and war, the supreme consecration of a coronation in Moscow. On February 5, 1722, he had already published a manifesto arrogating to himself the right to dispose of the throne as he saw fit, "so that that may be an incentive for the children of princes, as well as for those of the people, to be virtuous and not to stray from the right path as did our son, whose example should still be before our eyes." On November 15, 1723, he signed the following ukase:

"It is well known that it has been the unvarying custom among Christian potentates, from the time of the Orthodox emperors such as Basil, Justinian, Heraclius et al., to have their spouses crowned. And no one is unaware of the long hardships and dangers of every kind to which we have been exposed, at the risk of our life, during twenty-one years of wars. These wars have just been ended by a peace as favorable as it is glorious. As our beloved consort, the Empress Catherine, has been of great help to us, accompanying us everywhere, being present at all our military operations gladly and of her own free will, without showing the ordinary weaknesses of her sex . . . in gratitude for all that, we have decided, by virtue of the sovereign power that we exercise, to crown our spouse, which will be done formally, God willing, this winter in Moscow."

The court was astonished: only one woman in the history of Russia had ever been crowned. That was Marina Mniszek in 1606, during the time of troubles. But her husband, the false Dmitri, had been assassinated a week later and she herself had fled. Not much of a precedent. No matter, Peter's will was sacred. And for once, he who was so tightfisted didn't spare the expense. Costumes and equipages were ordered in Paris. The crown, executed by a Russian jeweler in St. Petersburg, was richer than any that had ever been used. Set with diamonds and pearls, with an enormous ruby on top, it cost a million and a half rubles. When Catherine spread out before Peter the superb outfit which he himself was to wear at the ceremony, he was almost ashamed of its magnificence. She had worked on the embroidery with her own hands. The coat was of sky-blue silk taffeta from Tours edged with silver, the belt was silver and the flame-red stockings were ornamented with silver clocks. When the Emperor tried on this unaccustomed finery, some silver sequins became detached from the fabric and fell on the floor. "Look, Katinka," he said with a sigh. "They're going to sweep that away, and it's almost the pay of one of my grenadiers."

At the end of March the whole court moved from St. Petersburg to Moscow. On May 7, 1724, Catherine rode to the Cathedral of the Archangel in the center of the Kremlin in a gilded coach surmounted by the imperial crown. The Emperor in person commanded the newly created "Company of Knights of the Empress" that led the cortege. Bells pealed over the city, cannon thundered as the procession passed, and there were moments when the shrill tones of the trumpets and the deep boom of the kettledrums drowned out the acclamations of the crowd. The Empress was followed by twelve pages wearing brocade shirts, green velvet waistcoats, blond wigs, and hats with white plumes. When she stepped down from the coach four high dignitaries held up her diamond-clasped mantle. Her purple gown embroidered with gold was in the Spanish style and had a train. The nave was filled with delegations from all the provinces. Two thrones had been set up in the cathedral under a canopy of crimson velvet. The archbishop of Novgorod officiated. Peter took the heavy crown and placed it on the head of his wife, who was kneeling before him. She wept and tried to embrace her husband's knees. He raised her up and gave her the globe, emblem of sovereignty. But he kept for himself the scepter, symbol of power.

13
The Last Reforms

Notwithstanding the weight of years, Peter was as impatient as ever. When he looked back over his life he had to admit that he had spent half his time on maneuvers, wars, travels. . . . Despite all the vicissitudes and all the racing here and there, he had pursued his work of reform. But his decisions, which were destined to transform Russia, had been taken without any overall plan, in response to the immediate pressure of circumstances—the military situation, an economic crisis, difficulties with the Church, popular movements, the hostility of the ruling class, and so on. Each time he had firmly righted the helm. But it was especially after the peace of Nystad that he had shown the world his genius for administrative reorganization. Once he was relieved of the heavy burden of the conflict with Sweden, he had been able to devote himself to his task at home. He told his close associates: "The reform has been carried out in three stages of seven years each: 1700–1707, gathering strength; 1707–1714, increasing the glory of Russia; 1714–1721, establishing proper order."

Peter's conception of "proper order" was that of an autocrat. "The Emperor," he said, "is an absolute monarch. God commands that he be obeyed, for he is answerable only to God for the people that have been entrusted to him. The persons around him can only advise him and carry out his sovereign will, which alone determines his decisions." To assist him he created a Private Chancery, replaced the old Duma of boyars with a small Council of Ministers, added a Chamber of Justice, and instituted a Senate having legislative, judicial, and executive authority. Nine colleges, or ministries, were substituted for the old *prikazy*: Foreign Affairs, Financial Control, State Revenue, State Expenditure, War, Admiralty, Justice, Commerce, and Mines and Manufactures. Three more were soon added. Each of them was headed by a council of eleven members. Their organization was copied from the Swedish model. The Senate spelled out in due form the Czar's briefly worded proposals, countersigned the ukases, and appointed the *oberfiscal*.

According to the ukase of March 5, 1711, this *oberfiscal*, a new high functionary, was to be "a good and intelligent man, whatever his birth, whose duty [would] be to maintain secret surveillance over all individuals, not excepting the most highly placed personages." He had under him some five hundred spies, the *fiscals*, who made ceaseless investigations at every level to ferret out corrupt judges, tax evaders, officials who misappropriated public funds—in short, all those who robbed the state. To stimulate their zeal informers were offered a substantial reward; any fines they helped to impose were split between them and the Treasury. This official encouragement of denunciation resulted in abominable abuses of power. The *fiscals* acted like inquisitors and blackmailed their victims with the threat of terrible revelations. Even the innocent were afraid of being accused. The *oberfiscal* Nesterov managed to have Prince Gagarin, the governor of Siberia, convicted of cheating the government of revenue and sent to the gallows. But he was soon justly requited by being himself accused of peculation and lying. The white-haired man, the terror of so many Russian households, was first broken on the wheel, slowly and methodically. Then the executioner dragged him to the block and beheaded him. A few *fiscals* of lesser importance met the same fate. After which Peter abolished the institution of the *oberfiscal* and appointed a procurator-general of the Senate, who was responsible only to the sovereign.

The Senate itself was entirely subservient to the Czar. As the senators spent most of their time in pointless discussion and squabbling, in 1720 Peter laid down a rule limiting the debate on any current affair to half an hour. When the hourglass showed that that time had elapsed, paper and ink were brought into the room and each senator had to give his opinion in writing. "If any senator fails to do so," said the document, "stop everything and come at once to the Czar, wherever he may be." So the threat of a thrashing or a fine constantly hung over the heads of the august assembly. Even that wasn't enough to overcome their inertia. The files awaiting action piled up in the secretariat (according to the Prussian ambassador, Mardefeld, there were more than sixteen thousand of them in 1722). No deal was completed without the greasing of palms, and the high dignitaries grew rich. Prince Menshikov, who of course had a seat in the Senate, shamelessly fleeced all who sought his protection. Peter knew it and from time to time would get angry and honor his favorite with a blow of his cudgel. After the storm had passed, the old habits of corruption would take over again.

The Senate had under its authority the governors, who were at the head of the eight provinces created by the Czar: Archangel, Ingria (St. Petersburg), Moscow, Smolensk, Kiev, Azov, Kazan, and Siberia. These vast territories were soon divided into counties. Governors were of course responsible for police, roads, and the administration of justice, but their chief function was to levy taxes. Each was a kind of tax farmer, a revenue collector who had complete latitude to procure the necessary funds and was then required to make an enormous contribution to the state war chest. These potentates pocketed considerable sums along the way, as did their subordinates on a smaller scale. In order to keep closer tabs on the money that was collected, Peter placed these functionaries under the direct orders of the Senate. This produced conflicts of competence and made the accounting so complicated that it was little short of chaos.

In an attempt to introduce a little order into the diverse population of his empire, Peter divided the inhabitants of the towns into three "guilds." The first was composed of bankers, prosperous merchants, doctors, and master craftsmen; the second included lesser craftsmen and small-businessmen; the third was made up of common people—the ordinary workers and unskilled laborers of the free population. The guilds elected burgomasters for one year. The first guild and the burgomasters appointed "magistrates," or town councillors, who were to administer the town and who had life tenure. Their primary responsibility was the police force—a police force constantly overwhelmed by the banditry that reigned throughout the country. Roads were not safe and bands of robbers ventured to the very outskirts of the big cities. When brigands were captured, the most important were hanged on the spot, while the others were knouted and then had their noses cut off. These exemplary punishments did nothing to discourage malefactors, and their number increased from year to year.

But Peter was not primarily concerned with internal security. Most of his attention was devoted to the army. His wars cost him dear in manpower, and he had to dip deep into the national reserves. After some experimentation, he instituted a system of obligatory service for the different classes of society. At the age of fifteen all noblemen were enrolled as privates in a regiment. The sons of wealthy and illustrious families were usually assigned to the regiments of the Guard, those of the petty nobility to regiments of the line. In St. Petersburg it was not unusual to see a young prince doing sentry duty in front of the entrance to his barracks. Housed, fed, and paid like a simple soldier, he would perform all the chores of a private before rising through the ranks by degrees. Thus the Guard became a kind of school for the training of the country's military and civilian elite. Peter himself had worked his way up in the same hard fashion, starting as drummer, then over the years becoming bombardier, sergeant, ensign, captain, colonel, and lieutenant general. He drew his pay regularly, gave a receipt for it, and noted the sum in his account book: "In 1707, colonel's pay received in Grodno: 150 rubles." He considered himself to be the first servant of the state and expected all his subjects to follow his example and sacrifice their personal lives to the common cause. Thus there was practically no limit to the length of time a nobleman had to serve in the armed forces. He could take retirement only because he was wounded, disabled, seriously ill, or too old. But even in retirement he was used until his mental and physical capacities were totally exhausted: he would be sent to a garrison town or placed in the civil administration. The nobleman was necessary everywhere and at any age. To discourage deception and evasion, the Czar ordered that the property of anyone who shirked his military obligation was to be confiscated and half given to the man who had denounced him, even if it were a serf. Guilty persons were, moreover, punished with "political death." This meant that having been placed outside the law, they no longer enjoyed any protection and could be robbed or murdered without its being considered a crime.

The same concern for efficiency, for making the most of available resources, led Peter to open the ranks of the nobility to men of common extraction. According to a ukase of January 16, 1724, a soldier of the humblest origin could become an officer and, as such, receive hereditary nobility. If a nobleman was an officer by virtue of his lineage, an officer was a nobleman by virtue of his service. Merit could substitute for genealogy. The boundaries of the old aristocracy cracked under the influx of commoners. To the list of great names in Russian history were added a multitude of new names that smacked of the farm or shop.

But it was not enough to have capable officers. Peter also had to have plenty of men. After the disaster of Narva the losses were so high that he forcibly drafted soldiers at random among the lowest classes of the Russian population. To fill up his regiments he even violated the landlords' right to own serfs, permitting serfs to become soldiers without the consent of their master. In 1705 a first general recruitment, at the rate of one man for every twenty taxable households, secured thirty thousand conscripts. The draft applied to all the inhabitants of town and country, including servants, workers, the sons of churchmen, and even clerks of the administration. It was based on a new principle: equality of all classes of society with respect to the obligation of military service. To discourage desertion, in 1712 the Czar ordered that all the recruits be "marked." The sign adopted was a cross tattooed on the left hand. When the design was pricked out on the skin it was covered with gunpowder, which was then lit. A soldier, like a convict, was marked for life.

On November 26, 1718, Peter jotted down some notes for a new ukase: "Require statements from everyone; grant one year's delay; find out the truth about the number of male inhabitants in each village, stating that if anyone tries to hide, all his property will be given to the one who denounces him; establish the number of souls responsible for maintaining one soldier; establish an average tax rate." The purpose behind these confused measures was to settle the army in permanent barracks throughout the entire territory, the population of each region being responsible for the maintenance of the regiments stationed on its soil. To ensure a fair division of the cost, a census was taken of the male serfs and other peasants employed in agriculture. Soon male servants were also included. The individuals counted were officially called "census souls." All census souls were subject to the same tax and the landlord was held responsible for the payment of the sums fixed by the administration. Thus he became a kind of treasury agent, a tax collector for the people who lived on his estates. His power over them was accordingly increased. Consequently, whether peasants or serfs, they were all subject to the same law, the law of slavery. By replacing the household tax with a poll tax, Peter substituted for the old system, whereby the peasant was attached to the soil, a new system, whereby he was attached to the person of the landowner. The latter, who was going to be taxed according to the number of his human livestock, often arranged not to report all the souls he possessed. In the beginning of 1721 it was discovered that in spite of the direct threats, two million souls had been concealed. The governors made the rounds to carry out on-site verification. At last, after arrests, confiscations, and torture sessions, the authorities received a preliminary estimate of five and a half million souls.

In 1724, on the basis of total military expenses for the year, the tax rate was fixed at seventy-four kopecks per soul. In addition, landowners were invited to provide lodging for the army. Most of them refused to build housing for the troops and merely placed at the disposal of the command the existing houses in the village. Without the least compensation, peasants hastily had to arrange quarters for the soldiers who were arriving en masse. Forced to abandon their work in the fields so as to prepare billeting and exasperated by the fresh taxes imposed on them, many took flight. Others bowed once again to necessity. Henceforth they were all serfs for life, hereditarily: servitude was inscribed on their genes. A man who was a slave could only father slaves. Because all were equally subject to the poll tax, farmers and servants now formed only a single class, the class of census souls, part of their master's inheritance and a testimony to his wealth. Henceforth to evaluate a nobleman's fortune, people said: "He possesses five hundred souls, two thousand souls, etc."

To be sure, Peter deplored the selling of serfs like cattle at so much a head, "which," he said, "does not exist anywhere in the world." In 1721 he sent the Senate a draft ukase designed "to put an end to this trade in people and, if it is impossible to root out the habit completely, let them at least be sold by families and not separately." But this measure never got beyond the expression of a wish, which Peter forgot as soon as he had formulated it. He was not interested in the human or judicial aspect of serfdom but in the fiscal aspect. And he knew perfectly well that by basing a tax on a head count of serfs and tying them permanently to the landowner he was assuring the treasury of regular and verifiable income. The development of slavery might offend some bleeding hearts, but one could not fail to recognize the benefits of such a measure for the levying of taxes and the recruitment of soldiers.

At the end of his reign, in addition to the two regiments of his Guard, Peter had at his disposal 50 regiments of infantry, 30 regiments of dragoons, several units of hussars, 60 regiments in garrison, and 6 regiments of militia. All together, the regular forces included more than 200,000 men; in addition there were 100,000 irregulars, Cossacks, and Kalmuks. The combat worthiness of the Russian troops had been brilliantly demonstrated in action. In 1710 Pleyer wrote: "It is astonishing to see the degree of perfection that, thanks to the tireless efforts of the Czar, the soldiers have attained in their drills, the discipline with which they execute the orders of their officers, the courage with which they conduct themselves in combat." In 1714 C. H. Manstein declared that "nowhere in Europe" was there "an artillery to equal that of the Russians, much less to surpass them." He spoke of 13,000 cannon. And the foundries were constantly manufacturing more. Cloth for uniforms was woven by Russian factories, soft iron for the barrels of muskets came from Siberia, hard iron for shells and grenades was supplied by Olonets and Tula, sulfur and saltpeter were mined in the Ukraine. There was not a corner of Russia that didn't pay its tribute to the war in one way or another.

The Army Regulations of 1716 laid down the rights and duties of the soldier. Peter himself had drafted the most important passages. He said that he wanted to "win battles at the cost of the least effort and without too much bloodshed" and that "every man is obligated to help his comrade when facing the enemy and to defend to the uttermost his flag, which should be as precious to him as his life and honor." A special supplement forbade the troops, on pain of inexorable punishment, to molest "mothers, pregnant women, old men, priests, church attendants, children," and so on.

There were many foreign officers on the general staff, fourteen generals out of thirty-one in 1721. But the high command was Russian—Sheremetev, Menshikov, Golitzin, Repnin—Russian also the Commissary-General of the army—Prince Jacob Dolgoruky, "the Incorruptible." In any case, Russian or not, these officers received the same salary, which was paid very irregularly, and were liable to the same punishment in case of misconduct. Some foreign officers complained about their lot, wanted to go home, and were angry that the Czar wouldn't let them, but in his presence all felt a kind of fascination in which admiration was mingled with fear.

If he had reorganized the army from top to bottom, he had done even more for the navy, which had hitherto been practically nonexistent. At the time of his accession Russia had possessed not a single warship, and no one outside of a few fishermen in the Archangel region had had any interest in sailing. In 1725 the Russian fleet consisted of forty-eight ships of the line and 787 galleys. The sailors numbered 28,000, and almost all came from the northern seacoasts or from villages along the rivers. To command them Peter had at first had recourse to foreign captains. But at the same time he sent young Russians abroad to learn seamanship. They soon came to form a corps of experienced officers that grew every year, augmented by the graduates of the Naval Academy.

In the beginning the shipwrights too were Dutch, French, or English. "The Czar flatters them and makes much of them," wrote the diplomat Jefferies. "Their wages are paid punctually; they often dine with the sovereign; they are invited to his table at the largest gatherings." These honored guests taught the Russians who were to replace them. Obsessed with his dream of maritime hegemony, Peter spent enormous sums to dig ports and open shipyards. His efforts in this field often met with failure. For instance, after he had moved the Olonets shipyards to St. Petersburg, he found that the water there was not deep enough for the launching of big ships. And when he thought he had found the ideal location in Roggervik, near Reval, the installation was destroyed by storms. In Voronezh the wood used was of such poor quality that the boats became unusable after a year's service. In these hurried, titanic labors thousands of underfed, ill-housed workers perished. Every project that Peter undertook resulted in a gigantic sacrifice of human lives. But thanks to this young fleet that had cost the nation so much, he could finally impose his will on Sweden.

To maintain his army on a war footing, to expand his fleet, build cities and ports, and make Russia's diplomatic presence felt in Europe, the Czar constantly had to create new sources of funds. The state revenues, which amounted to 1.5 million rubles in 1680, exceeded 9 million in 1725. To the old monopolies on resin, potash, rhubarb, and glue were added monopolies on salt, tobacco, chalk, tar, fish oil, and so on. The most oppressive taxes were applied to persons of every class and condition. Special taxes were imposed on Old Believers, on chimneys, inns, mills, arable land, chess sets, playing cards, horse collars, hats, boots, public carriages (one tenth of the fare), sheepskins, bathhouses, mirrors, cellars, watering troughs, the mooring and unmooring of ships, firewood, watermelons, cucumbers, nuts, beards, beehives, coffins, and wedding headbands. The poll tax on each male census soul alone brought in about 2 million rubles. From year to year the population grew more afraid of the revenue agents and at the same time more determined to deceive them. Landowners and peasants alike often risked their lives to avoid being stripped bare by the tax collectors. In matters of finance Peter's motto was: "Ask the impossible so as to receive as much as possible." At one time he thought of consulting the celebrated banker Law, whom he had met and been impressed by in Paris, so that the financial wizard might help solve the problems of his treasury. But his invitation came at the wrong time: Law had just fled France, after a bankruptcy that had rocked the entire country.

Obsessed with the necessity of finding money at all costs, Peter tried to reconcile the need for a war economy with the need for national prosperity. He wanted to create both new sources of taxes and new sources of production, to increase exports and at the same time reduce imports by developing national industry, to crush the people under taxes and simultaneously stimulate their initiative. Miraculously, he succeeded. He concluded a trade treaty with Persia, encouraged commerce with central Asia and China, facilitated exchanges with the West, instructed bold merchants and consuls to push the sale of Russian merchandise abroad—hemp, flax, rope, wax. Soon Russian commercial agents were opening offices in Paris, Toulon, Bordeaux, Antwerp, Liège, Vienna, Cádiz, and China. Domestically, the Czar protected forests, source of the timber indispensable for his shipbuilding, developed animal husbandry, introduced new breeds of cattle, brought Merino sheep into the provinces of Kharkov, Poltava, and Ekaterinoslav, established the first stud farms, tried to acclimatize the grape to the country of the Don Cossacks and had Hungarian and Persian vines planted near Derbent, taught peasants to cut wheat with a scythe instead of a billhook, concerned himself with the type of seed to be sown and the manuring of fields. But above all, thanks to him, Russian industry expanded with incredible rapidity. "Russia is more favored than many another state with reserves of metals and ores that no one has yet sought to exploit," he wrote. And from the beginning of his reign he determined to take the best advantage of this great "gift of God." Enthusiastically, he launched expeditions right and left, had the ground of his vast empire prospected, and organized the systematic mining of iron, copper, silver, and coal. The owners of metal-bearing land had only the right to exploit it first—if they were slow to take advantage of that right they forfeited it. And if they concealed the existence of a deposit they were liable to the death penalty. Many metal works sprang up in Tula, Olonets, St. Petersburg. Vinius, General Hennings, and the armorer Demidov collaborated with Peter in developing mining in the Urals, where in 1720 production reached more than 100,000 tons. On Peter's initiative the industrial center that would be called Petrozavodsk arose.

In 1725 Russia had eighty-six metal and gun factories, fifteen factories for the production of cloth, fourteen for leather, fifteen for wool, nine for silk, six for cotton; and sawmills, powder mills, paper mills, glass factories. . . . Peter even created a workshop for the manufacture of fine tapestries, employing French weavers from the Gobelins works. But while Western countries were interested in Russia's raw materials, they were not impressed by her manufactured goods. Even in Russia the public favored foreign merchandise, which was cheaper and of better quality. To encourage the growth of Russian industry the Czar established high customs tariffs. Similarly, wishing to stimulate the interest of private persons in trade and industry (the Demidovs' foundries in the Urals, Apraxin's cloth mills), he exempted the founders of manufacturing enterprises and their relatives from state service and from taxes. He freed them from taxes on the purchase of raw materials and the sale of manufactured products, gave them interest-free loans, and in 1721 granted them the privilege of buying serfs from noble landowners to use as workers. Freemen made up only a small part of the labor force. Vagabonds, runaway serfs, convicts, prostitutes, all the riffraff of the country were sent to the factories. The people who worked in them did so not of their own free will but under compulsion. And the masters of these "cattle" formed a new aristocracy that derived its rights not from birth but from invested capital and the spirit of initiative.

Nevertheless, the expansion of trade and industry was dependent on the means of transportation, and in Russia the roads were tracks that were barely negotiable when there was snow or mud. Peter tried in vain to connect St. Petersburg to Moscow by a coach road. The project was too expensive, there was no time to pay attention to it, and the road was abandoned after some hundred versts. Foreign diplomats traveling from the old capital to the new all spoke with horror about the five-week trip across forests, marshes, and sodden moors, with here and there a rickety bridge that was liable to collapse under the weight of the carriages. To guide travelers the Czar had signposts planted along the major routes and had a few "stage houses" built. Nor did he neglect the caravan trade dear to his ancestors. Thus in Hungary he bought standing crops of Tokay grapes and had the product brought to Moscow on hundreds of wagons.

But mainly he counted on the waterways for the transport of goods. He connected the Volga to the Neva by digging the little canal of Vyshny-Volochok. Then, recognizing how difficult it was to sail the stormy waters of Lake Ladoga, he ordered that a hundred-verst canal be built to go around it. Accompanied by a few engineers, he himself sounded the marshy terrain. This gigantic enterprise, which got off to a bad start under Menshikov's orders, advanced slowly: the locks soon silted up, and the workers died by the hundreds, as during the building of St. Petersburg. In 1723 Campredon wrote: "Thirty thousand men have already perished in the building of the Ladoga Canal." This hecatomb did not dissuade Peter from the project.

Yet when it came to the administration of justice, he was sometimes enlightened by ideas of impartiality. He gave orders that in every courtroom, from the highest to the lowest, there be placed on the table behind which the judges were seated a curious little three-sided structure of gilded wood surmounted by the double-headed eagle. To each of the three sides was attached one of three ordinances drawn up by the Czar. The first recommended that magistrates have strict knowledge of the texts that it was their business to apply; the second defined their duties during the session; the third forbade them to violate the laws. As always, these injunctions were accompanied by threats—fines, confiscation of property, or death for the recalcitrant. Procedure was based on torture, both to obtain confessions and to punish the guilty. The greatest crimes were those that harmed the interests of the state. In these cases, even a pregnant woman could be put to torture. Wives who had murdered their husbands were buried alive. Molten metal was poured down the throats of counterfeiters. There were no jurors to assess the guilt of the accused, no lawyer to defend him. The judge decided as he pleased. And the judge was completely dependent on the executive power: the voivode presided over the provincial court, the governor over the central court. As for the *landesrichter*—Swedish-style justices of the peace who acted as surrogates for the governors—they were primarily tax collectors and more interested in extorting money from the litigants than in judging their disputes.

To improve the functioning of the courts Peter had the idea of replacing the old code of Czar Alexis, the *Ulozhenie* of 1649, with the Swedish code, eliminating the provisions inapplicable to Russia. Commissions of experts, including some foreign jurists, met on several occasions and finally concluded in 1722 that it was absolutely impossible to accommodate a foreign body of law to the requirements of the nation. Peter didn't make the task of the codifiers any easier by constantly issuing contradictory ukases. He was always making and unmaking the system of ordinances that governed the lives of his subjects. What was permitted yesterday was forbidden tomorrow; justice changed with the monarch's mood. When he made laws he was concerned not with fairness but with efficiency. Thus a man condemned for murder might, if he were a skilled craftsman, find himself free again at the head of a group of workmen to whom he was teaching his trade. Wasn't he more useful to the country in that job than rowing a galley? Peter's thinking reflected the two simultaneous tendencies of despotism and pragmatism.

Both tendencies were manifested in his relations with the Church. When Patriarch Adrian died in 1700, Peter appointed no successor but named the metropolitan of Ryazan, Stephen Yavorsky, exarch of the "Holy Throne of the Patriarch." The new exarch was responsible only for current affairs; major decisions were taken by the boyar Mussin-Pushkin at the head of the College of Monasteries. This was only a first stage. Feofan Prokopovich, rector of the Academy of Kiev, spent years drawing up a Church Statute in three hundred articles, inspired by the Czar and reviewed by him point by point. In 1721 Peter officially abolished the patriarchate and promulgated the new constitution of the Church. According to this act, the patriarchate was replaced by a college of spiritual affairs, the Very Holy Synod, composed of several archbishops appointed by the sovereign and charged with directing all affairs of the Church. A chief procurator, likewise appointed by the sovereign, would attend the deliberations of this assembly and would have veto power. In no case was the chief procurator to be an ecclesiastic. In this capacity the Czar wanted to have a "good and vigorous" army officer. The first incumbent was one Boltin, a simple colonel of dragoons. The meaning of the reform was set forth in the preamble to the statute: "The common people do not understand the difference between spiritual power and temporal power. Dazzled by the shining virtue and splendor of the supreme pastor of the Church, they imagine that he is another sovereign, equal to the autocrat in power and even greater than he. If such is the opinion of the people, what would happen were an ambitious clergy to fan the flames? On the contrary, if the people see that the Church administration is established by decree of the monarch and decision of the Senate, they will quietly submit and lose the hope that the clergy will support them in their revolts." The lesson was clear: the Church's calling was entirely spiritual; it was inadmissible for it to interfere in politics; there was only one master in Russia, the Czar; even the clergy owed him obedience.

While Peter did not attack the authority of the Church in matters of dogma, by this statute he deprived it of all independence. Members of the Holy Synod, being chosen by him and controlled by a lay chief procurator who kept an eye on them and reported their words to the monarch, were only functionaries like the others. They formed an institution comparable to the Senate and, like senators, had to swear allegiance to His Majesty: "I swear to be a faithful and obedient servant, subject to my natural and true sovereign and to the august successors whom it shall please him to appoint by virtue of his unquestionable power. I recognize that he is the supreme judge of this spiritual college." The religious hierarchy was to be so subservient to the interests of the state that Peter even released the clergy from the secrecy of the confessional in the case of a political crime or plot against his person. Any priest who hid from the authorities a confession of this sort, made in a spirit of repentance, would make himself an accomplice of the guilty person. The statute also prohibited any layman from installing a chapel in his house with a priest to officiate there regularly.

Instead he should attend the parish church. The right to preach would be granted only to priests who had studied in the academies, and the themes of pastoral addresses would be taken always and exclusively from the Scriptures and the Fathers. Surplice fees would be reduced and henceforth provided only through free offerings. Men were prohibited from entering a monastery before the age of thirty, nuns prohibited from taking definitive vows before the age of fifty. Monks were forbidden to write or copy books, "for nothing is more disturbing to their tranquillity than their nonsensical or useless writings."

As an enemy of pomp and idleness, Peter had no patience with high prelates who lived in opulence. He enjoined them to cut back their elaborate households and to make annual tours of their dioceses. Monasteries, with their population of lazy good-for-nothings, were an obsession with him. He closed a great many of them, forbade the others to buy more land, secularized their revenues. "We must avoid," he said, "the fate of Byzantium, where there were more than three hundred abbeys but only six thousand men to defend the city against the Turks." On January 31, 1724, he ordained that monks and nuns should raise orphans and care for the sick and wounded. Ideally, he would have liked to convert all monasteries and convents into hospitals or schools.

In a spirit of tolerance he put a stop to the persecution of schismatics and merely insisted that they wear on their garments a red square with a yellow border. The Old Believers were not in the least grateful for his benevolence. They continued to regard him as the Antichrist, one who frequented foreigners, made men cut their beards, and dabbled in all sorts of accursed sciences. The official Church meanwhile, though it bowed to the monarch's will, was nonetheless hostile to the reforms he envisaged. Pious souls on both sides hated him: some (the Old Believers) because they loved the ancestral traditions, others (the priests and monks) because they were attached to the privileges of their caste. Peter, a friend of the Protestants, sometimes felt like one of them, lost in the throng of the Orthodox. At no time did he ever deny the faith of his fathers. Only, he would have liked to have it oriented not toward the mysteries of the hereafter but toward the misery of the here and now, less mystical and more practical. In his view religion, like other national institutions, should contribute to the welfare and greatness of Russia.

For the state to function properly, each subject must have his designated place in it and not leave that place under any pretext —like chessmen on their squares, with the master of the game leaning over the board. It was from this point of view that on January 24, 1722, Peter established the famous "Table of Ranks." This table substituted for the old register of genealogies a hierarchy of merit divided into three parallel categories: the civil, the military, and the court. Each of these categories contained fourteen classes, corresponding in quality to the classes in the other categories. At the bottom of the scale in the civil service was the registrar of a college; in the military the simple ensign, at court the *Tafeldecker* (the table-setter). At the top of their respective categories glittered the Chancellor of the Empire, the Field Marshal, and the Grand Chamberlain. Between these two extremes stretched a subtle gradation of human values, each with its label and number. Henceforth it was the rank, the *chin,* that would define a man's place in society, in the bureaucracy, the army, the palace. Thus, after a few years of diligent work in the administration, a young commoner could become the equal of a captain without ever having served under the flag. Access to honors was open to all: courageous soldiers of humble birth, smart young clerks, clever foreigners, capable adventurers.

In a supreme audacity, the table made civil and military functionaries of the first eight ranks (down to the grades of college assessor and major in the army), Russian or foreign, equivalent to "the best and ancient nobility"—even if they had been born into the lowest strata of society. Formerly the rule of *mestnichestvo,* the right of precedence, had forbidden a man to serve under the orders of anyone who had previously served under the orders of one of his ancestors. By overturning this tradition Peter was inviting all comers to join the circle of petty and great aristocrats who made up the new ruling caste of the country. To encourage them in the race for fortune, ambitious young commoners had before their eyes the example of a Menshikov, the former pastry cook's assistant who had become the most powerful personage in the empire, a Shafirov, the onetime draper's clerk and present vice chancellor, a Yaguzhinsky, the son of an organist in the Lutheran church of Moscow who had been promoted to procurator-general of the Senate, or a Devier, the Portuguese Jew who had once served as cabin boy on board a merchant ship and had now been catapulted into the post of prefect of police of St. Petersburg. The introduction of this new elite of the *chin* was accompanied by a reduction in the privileges of the nobility. The highest dignitaries could be subjected to the same corporal punishments as commoners. The knout fell upon the prince as well as upon the muzhik, and no title was enough to protect a guilty man's head. Prince Alexis Bariatinsky, for example, was publicly flogged for having hidden men from the army recruiters. To imitate Europe, Peter abandoned the old appellation of boyar and named counts and barons by the dozen among his entourage. At his accession there had been some two thousand noble families. Before long there were nine thousand.

Another reform made a significant change in the condition of aristocratic families. By a ukase of March 23, 1714, Peter established a system of entailment of landed estates. According to this decree, every landowner had to draw up a will designating one of his sons—or failing a son, one of his daughters—to inherit the property. If he neglected to do so, the eldest son—or eldest daughter, as the case might be—would receive all the land and the serfs attached to it. The other children would divide up the movable property. This institution of the single successor for the land, buildings, and muzhiks represented the transposition of the autocratic principle into private life. Of course it avoided the breaking up of estates into small holdings, but it also forced the disinherited sons to "seek their bread" through service, study, industry, or trade. In short, it was a call to work sent out to all the nobility, many of whom were no longer assured of a future as country gentlemen.

At the time of Peter's accession the rural population of Russia included, in addition to landed proprietors, two groups of muzhiks: free farmers and serfs. The first worked the lands of the state or monasteries, the second belonged to private landlords. By issuing the ukase that established the poll tax the Czar had extended slavery to include all categories of peasants. From that time forward, the normal condition of the farmer from one end of Russia to the other was serfdom. At the mercy of an all-powerful master who had the right to punish with the knout but not to kill, to sell but only by families, the serfs also suffered from the demands of the state. They had to endure the quartering of troops who requisitioned their food supplies, burned up their stock of wood, overran the huts, mistreated the inhabitants. The government imposed heavy corvées on them (transport of provisions, fortification works, road construction, digging of canals), which there was no way of escaping and which greatly hampered agricultural work. Tax collectors were after them, the threat of military service hung over them, they couldn't move without a "letter of permission" from their master and lived in fear of both lord and functionaries.

Ivan Pososhkov, the son of an ordinary craftsman and the first economist of his time, stated that no one in the villages knew how to read and that an officer had only to exhibit an alleged "imperial decree" for the muzhiks to turn over to him everything they possessed. Ignorance was further aggravated by laziness; they cut down young trees and fished out streams without considering the consequences of their acts. Their log huts were dark, windowless hovels in which the whole family huddled together in foul-smelling warmth. Men, women, and children slept jumbled together on the stove or on benches lined up around it. "And upon my asking them whether they lay easy and had room enough to sleep, they answered me, they rested perfectly well in such a warm place and wanted no beds," wrote Weber in 1716. "They use no candles but long shivers of wood, which every one of the family carries in his hand, or across his mouth, and so they run about the house and do their work. . . . About their neck they wear . . . their purse, though they commonly keep the small money, if it be not much, a good while in their mouth, for as soon as they receive any, either as a present or as their due, they put it into their mouths and keep it under their tongue."[1]

Their owners treated them like beasts of burden and considered them like any other piece of property. Certain members of the provincial gentry specialized in the trade in girls, whom they bought cheap as small children, raised, debauched, and sold again at high prices to those who fancied fresh young bodies. These girls were often destined for prostitution. In St. Petersburg there was a slave market where whole families appeared with the price of each member indicated on a label stuck on his or her forehead.[2] A good serf was worth up to six hundred rubles; a good horse cost more. Most of the servants in the great houses were serfs. They performed the most varied functions, as valets, cooks, coachmen, seamstresses, embroiderers, clowns, musicians, wet nurses. There were certain servant girls whose chief responsibility was to sit in an armchair and warm the seat before the mistress took her place there. Serf children were sometimes used as postilions and in winter would sit freezing on horseback, strapped in place. Coachmen too would be freezing on their seats. Sometimes country houses, closed for the winter, would be overrun with fleas; when the weather warmed up servants would be sent there first to attract the pests to themselves before the lord and his family moved into the purified apartments. As soon as an epidemic broke out in a town the gentry would emigrate with all their menials. When the danger seemed past, they would send a few serfs back to the contaminated area as scouts. If none died, the whole tribe would return home. Servants slept in garrets, closets, and corridors and only took their clothes off once a week to go to the baths. They were beaten for the most trifling offense. A popular Russian proverb went: "The soul belongs to God, the head to the Czar, the back to the lord."

If serfs had the misfortune to be purchased along with the land to become factory workers, their lives became even harder. When they were paid, which was rare, they earned one copper kopeck a day. When the Scottish engineer Perry tried to obtain wages for the workers in the Voronezh shipyards, Apraxin replied: "There is no precedent for the imperial treasury's spending money to pay people to work: there are enough sticks in Russia to beat everyone who might refuse." The work day varied from thirteen to fifteen hours, according to the season. The lazy were punished by foremen with canes or by the knout. Half starved and dressed in rags, crowded together by the dozens in vermin-infested huts, the poor wretches were veritable convicts whose only crime had been to be counted in the census as serfs.

Between this huge, amorphous, disinherited, illiterate mass

and the small caste of noblemen old and new, there was little room for the nascent bourgeoisie of the towns. And in this class too the creation of the guilds consecrated the predominance of one social stratum. The magistrates elected for life by the guilds could be ennobled for service to the state. Thus the upward mobility that Peter desired made itself felt throughout the empire.

Another of the Czar's concerns was the education of his subjects. He wanted to make it obligatory, but not for everyone. In his view, only the children of noblemen, officials, and popes should have instruction. They would learn "figures"—that is, arithmetic—and a little geometry. But where? Russian schools had to be opened without delay. In 1705 Peter summoned to Moscow the Scot Farquharson, who set up the first School of Mathematics and Navigation there. In 1715 the school was transferred to St. Petersburg and became the Naval Academy. But could one teach navigation to pupils who had never had any elementary education? Unfortunately, it was important to begin by teaching them to read and to count. For that purpose Peter turned to the former Pastor Glück of Marienburg, the same Pastor Glück in whose house had once lived a Livonian servant girl who was now Catherine, Empress of Russia. Glück's "gymnasium" was intended, according to its founder, to teach "geography, strategy, politics, Latin rhetoric, Cartesian philosophy, the French, German, Latin, Greek, Hebrew, Syriac, and Chaldean languages, the art of dancing, the rules of French and German etiquette, knightly equitation and dressage." In the beginning this ambitious program attracted only some forty pupils. A special ukase invited "persons of quality" to bring their children to the gymnasium "without any constraint." No result. The gymnasium vegetated, with few pupils and whatever teachers happened to come along. Then Peter turned his attention to the creation of professional schools. Without worrying about establishments of primary and secondary education, he passed directly to higher education: engineering, navigation, higher mathematics. Beside the Naval Academy there arose schools of artillery, civil engineering, surgery, mines. Instruction was provided by German and English professors, but the benches in front of them were nearly empty. Most of the students were ignorant and had no inclination for study, and their only thought was to escape from the tiresome classes. At the Naval Academy retired old soldiers stood at the door of each room, riding crop in hand, to punish troublemakers and prevent them from leaving. The students in this establishment who passed the examinations were sent to the provinces to teach in turn. It was the first serious attempt in Russia to create secondary schools. In 1716 there were twelve of them. Thirty more would follow. But in 1723, of forty-seven teachers sent in this way to the different provinces, eighteen came back, having found no employment. Among the pupils desertion was frequent. Often, as in Ryazan in 1725, half the class melted away amid general indifference. In 1721 an ecclesiastical regulation urged the bishops to set up diocesan schools in their bishoprics, and in the years that followed forty-six were created. But they were hardly more successful than the lay schools. In 1713, noting that the School of Engineers had only twenty-three students, Peter sent seventy-seven young men, all the sons of palace servants, to join them. Their learned professors started by teaching them the alphabet.

With his usual impatience Peter neglected the base in favor of the summit. Late in his reign he decided to create an Academy of Sciences. This plan had been in the back of his mind ever since his visit to Paris. In the meantime he had been elected an honorary member ("outside any rank") of the French Academy.* To fill the seats in the Russian Academy of Sciences he engaged some fifteen scientists from Germany. The Academy was flanked by a gymnasium and a university. When the illustrious visitors took up their functions they observed that there were no students to hear them. No problem—students would be brought from abroad. And to fill out the sparse audience professors could attend one another's lectures.[3]

In this disorganized struggle against his people's ignorance, Peter realized the inadequacy of the means at his disposal. One could not create a whole educational system from scratch in a few years. The flowers of learning still blossomed beyond his borders. Even as he tried to increase the number of schools in Russia, he continued to send young men abroad. They left by groups of 150

*Session of Wednesday, December 22, 1717.

every year as soon as the good weather returned. Some went to the shipyards and workshops of Holland and England, others were sent to Berlin to learn German, others traveled as far as Asia and Africa to study Arabic. Italy and France welcomed future sailors and architects. A Prince Lvov was placed in charge of Russian students in the Low Countries. Everywhere people remarked upon how badly the intruders behaved. They were short of money, complained they were starving, were always quarreling. In 1717 Prince Repnin begged the sovereign to allow his two sons to return from Germany, where they weren't learning anything and were only running up debts. In London the students knocked down some townspeople. In Venice they hung out in gambling dens and started brawls. In Toulon young Russians who had been allowed to enroll in the Marine Guards made Maréchal d'Estrées furious by their "shameful conduct." The local authorities declared: "They fight among themselves and hurl vulgar insults at each other, like the lowest of the low. That never happens among ourselves: we also fight, but like gentlemen, in a duel, face to face."[4]

Still, these "lowest of the low" came back to their country with enough intellectual baggage to serve the Czar's purposes. Thanks to them he could fill the ranks of his military, scientific, artistic, and industrial cadres. He was still dependent on foreign countries, but he was sure that one day soon Russia would need only her own sons to shine before the world.

In 1721 thirty cartographers set to work to draw up maps of the various regions of Russia. Peter's instructions were concise: "In each town you will determine the latitude by means of the sextant, and then you will walk in a straight line in the various directions of the compass to the borders of each district." Special explorers were sent to the Caspian, Siberia, Persia. With the data thus collected the secretary of the Senate, Ivan Kirilov, would put together a general atlas.

On December 12, 1723, the Czar sent out two frigates under the command of Admiral Wilster with orders to sail to Madagascar and explain to the supposed king of that island how advantageous it would be for him to accept a Russian protectorate. When his troops had occupied the entire territory, Wilster was to continue his way east to the fabulous country ruled by the Great Mogul. But the two frigates had hardly left port when they were damaged by a squall and had to put in at Reval. As the ships were obviously too fragile for so long a voyage, Peter thought of covering the submerged part of their hulls with felt mattresses. Then, in view of the difficulties involved, he gave up. But he immediately turned to another project. He charged the Danish captain Vitus Bering with a scientific mission on the seas beyond Kamchatka.*

To accelerate the dissemination of ideas Peter gave orders for the translation of a thousand works on scientific, technical, and historical subjects. In this connection he wrote to Zotov: "The translator should not be satisfied with a word-for-word version, but after having thoroughly understood the text he should translate it into his own language in such a way that it is as intelligible as possible." He established the first military hospital in Moscow and soon added a school of surgery, an anatomy laboratory, and a botanical garden. He opened pharmacies in all the big cities, starting with St. Petersburg. He introduced the telescope to Russia. He gave orders for all historical documents, which until then had been housed in various monasteries, to be gathered together in one place. The first Russian newspaper and the first Russian theater were founded during his reign. On the stage professional actors rubbed elbows with young persons of the best society who were acting for amusement. Berkholz noted, on November 15, 1722, that on the preceding day one of these professional actors, who had been playing the role of a king, had been given two hundred blows of the cane for insolence. After which, with his back still aching, the mountebank had appeared before the footlights with a crown on his head and an authentic princess for his consort in the play. During the performance Berkholz had laughed so hard at the amusing situation that he had failed to notice when his snuffbox was stolen.

The truth was that in Russia literature, like the art of the theater, was still only in its infancy. Opposite Racine, Molière, Corneille, Pascal, La Bruyère, La Fontaine, La Rochefoucauld, Saint-Simon, and so many others who were the glory of France, Peter could range only the historian and geographer Tatishchev,

*After Peter's death he was to discover the strait that bears his name.

the economist Pososhkov, and the poet Antiochus Cantemir, son of the hospodar of Moldavia. In any event the sovereign, who was of a scientific turn of mind, had nothing but contempt for the pointless games of scribblers, and his courtiers took their cue from him. In Russia it was a time for figures, not for dreams. Peter did buy some libraries, paintings, statues, but not by inclination; he only wanted to do as other European monarchs did. When he looked at a newly acquired work of art, his first thought was of his own greatness.

After he had made men shave their beards and imposed Western clothes on both sexes, the desire to reform Russian customs further inspired him to institute "assemblies." In 1718 he explained the meaning of these periodic gatherings in a letter to the prefect of police: "Assembly is a French term which cannot be rendered in a single Russian word: it signifies a number of persons meeting together, either for diversion or to talk about their own affairs. Friends may see each other on that occasion, to confer together on business or other subjects, to inquire after domestic and foreign news, and so to pass their time."[5] A rigid rule stipulated that these "assemblies" were to be held in the great private residences three times a week from four in the afternoon to ten at night. A sign hung on the door of the house would be the signal for the gathering. People would be free to come and go as they pleased. "Persons of rank, as for instance noblemen, and superior officers, likewise merchants of note, and headmasters [by which are chiefly understood shipbuilders], persons employed in the Chancery, and their wives and children shall have the liberty of frequenting the assemblies."[6] The master of the house would not be obliged to go to greet those who presented themselves at the door, nor to see them out, nor to keep them company. All he would have to do would be to provide seats, lights, cards, chess sets, and drinks. Everyone would be free to do as he liked. "There will be," said the document, "a ballroom, a game room, a third room for smoking and conversation, a fourth where the ladies will play blindman's buff and other innocent parlor games."[7] When the premises were too small, everyone crowded into the same room, where clouds of smoke rose from the pipes and made the women cough. Leather pouches of tobacco and twigs to light it with lay about on all the tables. The chatter and laughter of the guests disturbed the chess players sunk in meditation—there were already many of them in Russia, Peter among the most enthusiastic. But in the program for these soirées, first place was reserved for dancing. As European dance figures were still little known in the country, in this area too the Czar showed his subjects the way. He executed the steps at the head of the gentlemen, who all deferentially imitated his pirouettes and capers. Obedience was the rule even when it came to graceful gestures.

In the beginning the Russian women, only recently liberated from the solitude of the *terem,* were loath to mingle with the men at these animated, noisy gatherings. When an assembly was convoked by special decree to celebrate the peace of Nystad, "all ladies *over the age of ten*" were required to appear "under threat of terrible punishment." The Czar managed to assemble only seventy. They didn't like having their waists squeezed into corsets, and the voluminous panniered gowns prescribed by fashion hampered their movements. Some of them still greeted their interlocutors with a deep bow from the waist, became frightened and blushed, refused to touch the Western dishes, and only came to life a little when they were back in the circle of other Russian ladies. When they were not dancing they remained seated along the wall, silent, absent, perhaps regretting their cloistered life of the past. A row of dolls gotten up in unaccustomed costumes, wearing too much makeup, aping against their will the elegant women of Paris and Vienna. In any event, they chose their dancing partners only among their compatriots, which was a great disappointment to the naïve Berkholz.

But as the months passed the atmosphere warmed up. The women became accustomed to their finery and began to enjoy these free encounters. Prince Cherkassy's daughter soon struck Berkholz as "so good tempered and agreeable for her age that one would think she had received the best of educations in France." One of the Czar's daughters, Elizabeth, had for governess a Mme. de La Tour de Launoy, who taught her French and good manners.* Peter had a Russian translation made of the German handbook of etiquette *The Young Person's Looking-Glass,* which recom-

---

*This lady was later expelled from Russia by the same Elizabeth, who had become Empress, on the accusation of shameless conduct.

mended that one should not clean one's nose with one's fingers or pick one's teeth with a knife or spit in the middle of the room but rather to the side. But he himself hardly followed these precepts of good breeding. Nor did they make much headway with the public. While a few Russian women acquired a true refinement of manners, most only copied German and French fashions superficially. Little by little the dances at the "assemblies" gained in enthusiasm what they lost in elegance. Figures were devised that obliged the ladies to let their partners kiss them on the mouth. Tipsy with vodka-laced wine drunk in large quantities, the ladies would scream with laughter and tear the wigs from their escorts' heads. Any pretext would do to make a guest down "the cup of the Great Eagle." Anyway, the one condemned to the "supreme bumper" was usually delighted with the sentence. Intoxication did not prevent the dances from continuing. The English round, with deep bows, was followed by the minuet, after which the couples would launch into a polonaise that ended in a wild farandole. Peter would watch with satisfaction as different classes of society mixed together in the general excitement. Nobles of yesterday and today, merchants, craftsmen, officers, princesses, and wives of foreign representatives, all in their different styles of dress, were swept up in the same whirl.

Yet it was not at the assemblies that guests felt freest to let go. The rich banquets given by the Czar in Menshikov's palace or the postal-service building were the occasion for far rowdier scenes. On November 24, 1724, when Their Majesties were dining at the Senate with a large company, a drunken senator climbed on the table and walked all the way down it, putting his feet in the dishes. Every ship launching was an excuse for a bash. When the event was announced the population would rush to the banks of the Neva in front of the Admiralty basin. The Czar himself saw to the preparations and struck the first blow of the ax on one of the lashings holding the boat. A hundred more ax blows struck by the carpenters cut the other ropes. The great hull slipped slowly on the greased grooves and splashed heavily into the water. The cannon of the fortress boomed, trumpets blared, the crowd shouted for joy.

The court and diplomatic corps would join in a feast on board the new addition to the Russian fleet. The men lined up in one big cabinet, the women in another. As usual, sentries stationed at the doors prevented guests from going and coming. To the sound of artillery salutes, a first toast would be drunk "to the family of Ivan Mikhailovich"—in other words, to the glory of the Russian navy, of which Ivan Golovin had been the first admiral. One glass followed another as faces grew flushed amid raucous shouts and loud laughter, while the diplomats, in dismay, tried vainly to keep up. "There was prodigious drinking," wrote Campredon in 1721; "the room was so filled with tobacco smoke and a confusion of voices that one could neither hear nor breathe. The *papa* [the Prince Pope] and the cardinals sang, and since the guards let no one leave, I have never in my life been exposed to so terrible an ordeal." Four months later another ship was launched. This time it was Berkholz who attended the binge and was amazed to see the drunken guests making fools of themselves. Old Admiral Apraxin burst into tears; Menshikov rolled under the table; other dignitaries embraced or insulted one another; the German general von Steenpflicht slapped his compatriot von Herlau and tore off his wig.

In fine weather receptions and banquets were held at the Summer Palace, in the gardens on the banks of the Neva. At first glance, the gathering of courtiers dressed in European style and moving amid the shrubbery, ornamental ponds, classical statues, and flower-edged lawns would have made a foreign observer think he was entering another Versailles. The wigs and conversations, the smiles and play of fans conformed to Western models. The only unexpected note was the group of bearded bishops in their tall black hats sitting around a table loaded with bottles of liquor and an avalanche of food. But now the six grenadiers made their fateful appearance carrying on a stretcher the bucket of cheap vodka. The Czar, gigantic and jovial, insisted that each guest down his quota. Above the comic songs of the Prince Pope and his cardinals could be heard the shrill cries of the women who were being forced to drink and laughingly protested. Suddenly Versailles was a long way off. Something crude and primitive showed through beneath the French refinements, something bearing the stamp of old Russia.

In the summer residences around St. Petersburg and Moscow the sovereign and his entourage showed even less restraint than in the capital. The Hanoverian representative Weber, who had been invited to a reception at Peterhof along with the rest of the diplomatic corps, wrote in his *New Memoirs*: "At dinner we were so plied with Tokay wine, though his Czarish Majesty himself forbore drinking too much, that at our breaking up we were hardly able to stand. Nevertheless we were obliged to empty each a bowl holding a full quart, which we received from the Czarina's own hand, whereupon we quite lost our senses and were in that pickle carried off to sleep, some in the garden, others in the wood, and the rest here and there on the ground. At four in the afternoon we were waked and brought again to the pleasure-house, where the Czar gave each of us an hatchet, with orders to follow him. He led us into a wood of young trees, where he marked a walk of about an hundred paces in length to the seashore, to be cut out among the trees. He fell to work foremost, and though we (being seven in number besides His Majesty) found so unusual a drudgery very hard for people who had not half recovered their senses, yet we followed courageously, cutting down after him, so that in three hours we got through, by which time the fumes of wine were pretty well evaporated, nor did we receive any harm, except a certain minister who hacked at the trees with such fury that by the fall of one he was hit and somewhat bruised. The Czar having thanked us for our pains by word of mouth, the actual reward followed at supper, when we received such another dose of liquor as sent us senseless to bed. But having scarcely slept an hour and [a] half, a certain favorite of the Czar's was sent about midnight to rouse us and carry us, willing or unwilling, to the Prince of Circassia, who was already a-bed with his consort, where we were again by their bedside pestered with wine and brandy till four in the morning, that next day none of us remembered how we got home. About eight we were invited to court to breakfast, but instead of coffee and tea, as we expected, we were welcomed with large cups of brandy, after which we were sent to take the air on a high hill near the palace, at the foot of which we found a boor [i.e., peasant] attending with eight poor tits [i.e., nags] without saddles or stirrups, which altogether were not worth four crown pieces. Thus comically equipped we passed the review before their Czarish Majesties, who leaned out at the window."8

The truth was that Peter was only superimposing one set of corrupt manners on another. What he was offering his people was still only a parody of civilization. The new barbarism of St. Petersburg was replacing the old barbarism of Moscow.

In spite of the roughness and inconveniences of life in Russia, foreigners poured in. They were received with open arms in all the houses of the nobility. The imperial palace set the example. The Czar's interest in the German princes had already been demonstrated by the marriage of his niece, Grand Duchess Anna, to the Duke of Kurland. A few days after the wedding the young bridegroom had died on the way to St. Petersburg, in consequence, it was believed, of overindulgence in alcohol. Back in the capital his widow had surrounded herself with a little court of Kurlandish gentlemen, among whom was her future favorite Biron. Not long after, Anna's sister, the fat and frivolous Catherine, married another German prince, the Duke of Mecklenburg. And in 1721 there arrived in St. Petersburg Karl Frederick of Holstein, who had his eye on both the crown of Sweden and the hand of one of the Czar's daughters, Anna or Elizabeth. Two young princes of Hesse-Homburg also presented themselves as possible fiancés. All these wealthy personages were surrounded by greedy, scheming compatriots. The court of the Duke of Holstein attracted many Swedish officers, former prisoners who had married Russian women whom the Czar had forbidden them to take home.

Of course the upper-class foreign colony of St. Petersburg also included the diplomatic corps. Russia had come to play such an important role on the international scene that all European governments wanted to have a permanent representative there. From the Frenchman Campredon to the Austrian Kinski, from the Prussian Mardefeld to the Englishman Whitworth, the ambassadors all complained about the high cost of living in the capital, the petty frustrations caused by the Russian administration, and the excessive eating and drinking required by etiquette. It was impossible to obtain a regular audience with His Majesty; in order to talk to the Czar about political affairs the foreign ministers had to follow him onto his ship in the midst of a storm, or try to capture his attention during a banquet while he amused himself trying to make them drunk. At a feast on board ship the Dane Juel, who feared vodka like vitriol, tried to escape his dose by fleeing into the rigging. The Czar followed him up, glass in hand, and obliged him to fulfill his obligation then and there on his perilous perch.

Around these high and mighty personages revolved more modest foreigners—shipwrights from England or Holland, architects, craftsmen, merchants. A few learned Germans were included among His Majesty's close associates: his personal physician Blumentrost, for instance, who was to become the first president of the Academy of Sciences; Schumacher, the director of the imperial library; and Messerschmitt, who would carry out the first scientific explorations in Siberia. The French colony was not so brilliant. Yet it included M. de Villebois, the Czar's aide-de-camp, M. de Saint-Hilaire, director of the Naval Academy, the architect Le Blond, the painter Caravaque, the sculptor Nicolas Pineau. But most of the French in Russia were humble workers or small-time adventurers. The consular representative M. de La Vie was criticized by Campredon for his ill conduct. "I dare say," wrote the ambassador, "that it would be better for the king to have no one in this country than to leave the sieur La Vie here in his present sorry state." And indeed, La Vie went from bad to worse, selling secret information to foreign countries and turning his house, which was located opposite the Czarina's, into "a public place of debauchery."[9]

At the summit of this little cosmopolitan world, Peter enjoyed the satisfaction of having extended throughout his whole empire the spirit of the German Settlement dear to his youth. But in spite of the attraction he felt for Europe he remained fundamentally Russian. It didn't matter that he declared himself the disciple of the Dutch, the English, the German, the French, even the Swedes: his mad pleasures, his intemperance, his endurance, stubbornness, and vitality, his disdain for comfort, his courage, his quick changes of mood, his enthusiasms and despondencies, rages and joys were typical traits of a Slavic character inclined to extremes. Sovereign of a country of immoderate size and rough climate, he himself was rough and immoderate in all things. And although strongly in favor of foreign customs, he scrupulously observed the great national holidays.

Every winter on Epiphany he attended the ceremony of the blessing of the waters. A square hole was cut in the ice on the Neva. The clergy surrounded this opening, carrying icons and banners; all the priests were bareheaded. The choir sang hymns. The archbishop plunged a silver cross into the water three times, then blessed the flags of the different regiments. The Czar shouted an order and artillery salutes boomed out in the air swirling with snowflakes. After the priests left, naked children would jump into the icy water and climb out again laughing, their skin blotched by the cold, teeth chattering.

For Easter, after the religious service, the Czar received all the dignitaries who had come to congratulate him. Lined up on a long table would be the tall brioches known as *kulich* and the ritual delicacy *pashka,* made of cottage cheese and candied fruits. Each courtier in turn would approach the throne, present a painted egg, receive another from him, and exchange the Easter greeting with him: "Christ is risen!" "Verily, He is risen." A triple kiss between monarch and subject punctuated the joyous affirmation. On that day no one had the right to refuse the Christian embrace. The humblest soldier might claim a kiss from His Majesty. By the time the ceremony was over, Peter had bent his tall figure so many times to respond to the congratulations of his visitors that his back ached.

In summer he liked to organize "aquatic assemblies" on the Neva. A cannon shot would give the signal for the festivities. Flags would be raised in the various quarters of St. Petersburg. Everyone who owned a boat was required to participate in the excursion, on pain of a fine. At the head of the procession sailed Admiral Apraxin's ship, which commanded the movements of the flotilla, and which it was forbidden to pass. Even the Czar, standing at the helm of his own galliot, obeyed the admiral's orders. The richly decorated boats were manned by rowers in white shirts. Most of the great lords had brought an orchestra on board. The sounds of the trumpets and hautboys mingled with the lapping of water under the oars. The long serpent made up of all kinds of craft undulated slowly between the low banks. The flotilla sailed down to the mouth of the river, entered a small canal and stopped at Ekaterinenhof, the Czarina's suburban palace. Tables set up in a meadow in front of the house presented the hungry merrymakers with a whole assortment of cold dishes. They ate standing up, to the sounds of gay music. Tame elks, some with great twelve-pronged antlers, would come fearlessly up to the noisy gathering and let themselves be petted. As always, there was a great deal of drinking. Hungarian wine and vodka did their work. At dusk the drunken company returned to St. Petersburg. The oarsmen were so tired they could hardly speak, notes Berkholz. Sometimes the sky would darken and a cloudburst would descend on the river. In the open boats the women, soaked to the skin, would shiver and try to protect their gowns. The men's wigs would hang down limp and uncurled. The musicians, lashed by the downpour, would put their instruments away. When they finally reached the wharf the guests would scatter in a mad dash for shelter.

It was on the Neva too that in 1724 was celebrated the solemn arrival of the remains of St. Alexander Nevsky, sent from Vladimir on the Klyazma to be interred in the Monastery of St. Alexander Nevsky. A host of boats was dancing on the waves in front of the monastery when the flagship bearing the silver coffin under a canopy drew alongside the quay. Clergy in ceremonial robes surrounded the hallowed remains and escorted them inside the church. The Emperor, the Empress, the two princesses, and all the dignitaries walked in the cortege with heads bowed. When the coffin had been placed in the sanctuary, artillery salutes burst forth, bells rang, and Peter raised his head. In receiving the relics of the man who in this very place in 1240 had beaten the Swedes, he, the new conqueror, was reestablishing a connection with the long national tradition of Russia. He was not only the reformer but also the continuer. The next day he boarded the "grandfather of the Russian navy," the dilapidated little boat on which years ago in the waters near Moscow he had made his first attempts at navigation, and sailed to the Fortress of St. Peter and St. Paul. He was followed by one hundred flag-decked boats. Men-of-war riding at anchor saluted him with cannon salvos. He was proud to pass in this walnut shell before the great vessels of his fleet. What a long way he had come since the days when under the regency of his sister, the Czarevna Sophia, he had begun to learn about sailing on Lake Pereyaslavl! Stepping onto land, he received a cup of vodka from Catherine. A feast was served under tents set up in

Menshikov's gardens. Until late at night Peter and his guests drank to the prosperity of Russia. As it was very cold, notes Berkholz, the Czar looked around for a wig to cover his head, grabbed one at random, and put it on, even though it happened to be blond. Everyone laughed and applauded.

14
The
Giant
Felled

On one of the arches of triumph built in Moscow to celebrate the treaty of peace with Sweden, Peter had had his likeness placed next to that of Ivan the Terrible. If he wished the two images to be associated, it was because he openly asserted a historical connection between the two reigns. He wanted every subject to sense the Czar looking over his shoulder at all times, to be unable to eat, drink, sleep, love, breathe without thinking of him. The days of Peter's despotic government were marked by as many torture sessions as celebrations. The inquisition he promoted was nourished by daily denunciations. An accused person put to torture would name a few accomplices at random, but his revelations being insufficient, he would be paraded through the streets and called upon to point out other guilty persons among the passersby. Wherever he appeared the cry would go up: "The tongue! The tongue!" and people would take to their heels at the sight of a man who to save his own skin would not hesitate to accuse the innocent.

As an incentive to informers Peter promised rewards, usually in the amount of ten rubles. But in serious cases the rate automatically went up. In 1722 in Moscow, for instance, the Czar had ten bags containing one hundred rubles each suspended from a pole. A notice posted below announced that this large sum of money would go to whoever revealed the author of a pamphlet against His Majesty, a copy of which had been found in a church in the Kremlin. The informer would also be given lands and an official post. One had only to go to the police and pronounce the standard phrase *slovo i delo* (word and deed) to be listened to with the greatest interest. A mere suspicion was enough to start a criminal investigation. A peasant was tortured for not having known that the Czar now bore the title of Emperor; a priest who had talked about an alleged illness of the sovereign was sent to Siberia; a student got drunk and made unseemly remarks: thirty strokes of the knout, nostrils torn off, and hard labor for life.[1] . . . "In St. Petersburg," wrote La Vie, "it's an epidemic. There you can only be either accuser or accused." In the end the Russian people, accustomed to living in fear, came to think of injustice as one more natural catastrophe against which it was pointless to rebel. You kept your head low, pitied the comrade who had been struck down, and hoped to be spared again by the next cyclone. This submission to fate was so habitual that there was no general disapproval of the informer. How could he be blamed for accusing his neighbor, when the Czar himself had ordered him to do so? It was as respectable to denounce someone as to be denounced. Especially since the victims were sometimes members of the Czar's immediate entourage.

Not even Menshikov the Magnificent escaped suspicion. Having started from nothing, in the course of a few years he had become the Czar's favorite, his confidant, his accomplice, his shadow. Titles rained on his head: Most Serene Prince, Duke of Izhora, Count of Dubrovna, Gorki, and Potchep, hereditary sovereign of Oranienbaum and Baturin, general, admiral, governor-general of St. Petersburg, lieutenant colonel of the three regiments of the bodyguards, senator, knight of all the great orders of the empire. . . . Violent, grasping, corrupt, stubborn, and barely literate, he had a passion for opulence. In his palace, the finest in St. Petersburg, he maintained a veritable court with chamberlains, gentlemen, and pages. His state dinners were prepared by French chefs and served on gold plates. When he went to the Czar's he rode in a fan-shaped coach with his coat of arms on the doors and a gold crown on the roof. It was drawn by a team of six horses caparisoned in velvet of garnet and gold. Liveried footmen and musicians led the procession.

All this display was expensive. Menshikov's wealth, which was considerable—there is mention of tens of millions of rubles—did not suffice. He sought every opportunity to fill his pockets. His words of recommendation were never given free. Wherever he went he stole, speculated, swindled, squeezed. In the Ukraine he seized fifteen thousand souls in the lands that had once been Mazeppa's. In Poland he forced noblemen to sell him vast estates for trifling sums. He embezzled money earmarked for food for his troops, sold his influence to the highest bidder, requisitioned grain harvests to sell on his own account. It was often said of him that he could go from Riga in Livonia to Derbent on the Persian border and sleep every night on one of his own estates. In a village, a post bearing his arms was the equivalent of a title to the property. And in case anyone should dispute it, a gallows stood next to the post. His cruelty was legendary. Once when he had been attacked while passing through a hamlet, he returned with soldiers and ordered that all the inhabitants be hanged: men, women, children, even the pope. . . .

Peter was both annoyed and amused by this low caricature of himself. As there were more and more denunciations of his favorite, he decided to crack down, ordered investigations, struck the culprit with his *dubina,* and finally pardoned him. The extortions, frauds, misappropriations of funds immediately began again. In the course of one stormy session with the Czar Menshikov exclaimed: "All right, yes, I have stolen! I myself don't know how much. . . . But remember what Yaguzhinsky answered when you talked about having all corrupt officials hanged: 'So you wish to remain alone, Sire, without any subjects?'" Another day Peter, in a paroxysm of rage, threatened to return the arrogant scoundrel to his former condition. That evening the favorite came in wearing a pastry cook's apron with a basket on his head and crying: "Baked *pirozhki** for sale!" The Czar, disarmed, burst out laughing. Once again Menshikov had turned the tables. In his tempestuous rela-

*Little meat pies.

tions with the sovereign he could count on Catherine for support. She had been his mistress and remembered their liaison with complex feelings of affection. Peter himself, while he criticized his old friend's insatiable greed, recognized that in time of trouble the man was resilient, resourceful, and courageous. A necessary rascal. Nevertheless, in the long run the Czar grew weary of inflicting reproaches and fines on this strange personage blazing with gold and jewels, who every time he was knocked over righted himself again like a child's weighted toy. In 1723, when Catherine was defending the favorite in front of him, he cried: "Menshikov came into this world the way he lives; his mother gave birth to him in sin, and he will die in knavery; if he doesn't mend his ways he'll have his head cut off!" The charm was broken. By order of His Majesty Menshikov was removed from the presidency of the War College, the fifteen thousand souls he had stolen from the Cossacks were taken away from him, and he was stripped of most of his estates. But he remained in the palace, at once punished and absolved, eliminated and present, waiting for a problematical return to favor.

That same year of 1723 witnessed another spectacular downfall. Throughout Peter's reign "the little Jew" Shafirov had likewise grown wealthier and consolidated his position. Vice Chancellor of the Empire, a newly created baron, knight of the Order of St. Andrew, powerful, envied, and feared, he lived in his palace on a grand scale, married his five daughters to the greatest nobles in the country—Princes Dolgoruky, Golovin, Gagarin, Khovansky, and Soltykov—and, like his rival Menshikov, helped himself freely from the state coffers. He thought himself invulnerable; then the Czar's wrath struck like a bolt from the blue. The case was judged by a high tribunal in Moscow, where the whole court was gathered. Shafirov was convicted of embezzlement and condemned to death, on February 12, 1723. Three days later the fat man was taken to the scaffold in the presence of the diplomatic corps, dignitaries, and the people. After the sentence was read the executioner's assistants took off the condemned man's wig and his pelisse and led him to the center of the platform. He crossed himself, knelt down, and laid his head on the block, but in an awkward position, so that the assistants had to pull him by the feet until his belly touched the floor. The executioner raised his ax and brought it down heavily on the wood, beside the head. While Shafirov was waiting for a second, better-aimed blow, Makarov, the Czar's secretary, stepped forward and read the letter of imperial pardon, commuting capital punishment to permanent exile. The culprit's property, however, would be confiscated.

"Still trembling and with death in his eyes," says a witness, Shafirov went to the Senate for the ratification of the act. There the same senators who had unanimously condemned him rushed to embrace him and congratulate him on having gotten off with a fright. He was so shaken by the macabre scene he had been through that the surgeon Kovi was obliged to bleed him. In the end he even escaped Siberia and was sent to imprisonment in Novgorod. But his wife interceded with the Czar and he was lodged not in prison but at the home of one of his sons-in-law. Taking advantage of His Majesty's benevolent mood, the widow of Abraham Lopukhin likewise implored his clemency. She humbly asked that her husband's head be removed from the stake on which it had been planted for more than six years. This ball of shriveled, desiccated flesh still offered its hollow sockets and prominent teeth to the view of passersby. It was supposed to remind them of the crimes of one of Alexis's supporters. But perhaps the Muscovites had become so accustomed to the scarecrow that it no longer impressed them. Peter granted the request.

Two days after Shafirov's mock execution, the whole court took part in a masquerade on sleds. Open vehicles filled with dignitaries in fancy dress glided over the snow in a slow procession. Families called to one another. Women shivered in their costumes of shepherdess, dancing girl, Columbine. Peter had had his great sleigh done up as a ship, with masts, sails, and a crew of sailors on board.

There were moments when he felt surprised not to be at war with anyone. His chief concern now was to get his daughters settled. They were not lacking in charm or wit. In 1724 Mardefeld wrote of Anna, the eldest (fifteen): "I do not think there is in Europe today a princess who can rival her in majestic beauty. She is taller than all the ladies of the court, but her figure is so slender, so graceful . . . her features are so perfect that the sculptors of antiquity could have wished for nothing better. . . . Her countenance is without affectation, equable and serene. Her favorite pastime is reading works of history and morality." As for the second, Elizabeth (fourteen), Campredon described her as follows: "There is nothing about the person of the princess that is not pleasing. So far as her figure, complexion, eyes, and hands are concerned, she is a beauty. The faults, if there are any, will be with regard to upbringing and manners." The Duke of Liria was even more enthusiastic: "She is a beauty such as I have never seen, with an astonishing complexion, brilliant black eyes, a perfect mouth, and neck and shoulders of a rare whiteness. She is tall in stature and of a very lively temperament. One senses in her much intelligence and affability, but also a certain ambition." The youngest, Natalya (eleven), was not yet of any interest to the diplomats.

Campredon strongly urged a marriage between Grand Duchess Elizabeth and the Duc de Chartres, who would be promised the throne of Poland. Peter seemed delighted at the prospect of a family alliance with France. But Cardinal Dubois, the prime minister, turned a deaf ear to the proposal. Before giving his agreement he wanted to wait for Frederick Augustus II to die and the Polish succession to open up, which he expected would happen shortly. But it was he who died first. The regent succeeded him as prime minister and, like him, adopted a wait-and-see policy toward Russia. He felt it would be risky, to say the least, to push his son, the Duc de Chartres, into a matrimonial adventure with this girl from the North, of the Orthodox religion, whose mother was a former Livonian maidservant. The Czar received no official reply to his overtures and a few months later learned that the Duc de Chartres was to marry a German princess. Campredon was very upset. "The Russians are not pleased about that," he wrote.

Peter himself was not overly disappointed. His daughters were young, lovely, and would have handsome dowries. There was no lack of suitors. The most enterprising among them was the young Duke of Holstein. However, watching the maneuvers of the ambitious, pedantic, frivolous princeling, Peter could not bring himself to look upon him as a son-in-law after his own heart. Even after he had ordered that Catherine be crowned Empress in the Cathedral of the Archangel in the Kremlin, he did not consider that the problem of the succession had been resolved. Of course, there was no Salic law in Russia excluding women from the line of succession. But the coronation ceremony had been a solemn homage to the woman who was the Czar's partner in life, nothing more. In no way did it give her the right to reign if the throne should become vacant. Peter meant to designate his heir in his will. And maybe it would indeed be his wife that he would choose. His daughters, both Anna and Elizabeth, were too inexperienced for him to entrust them with the fate of a vast empire. And would the men who married them be of sufficient stature to assist them? With Catherine, Peter's mind was at ease. She was in good health, she had a head on her shoulders, and she was accustomed to court intrigues. She had a thorough understanding of his political thinking. And then, she had given proof of her devotion so many times. Yes, decidedly, it was of her he thought to succeed him rather than of his daughters. At banquets he never failed to show his esteem for her with meaningful toasts. In the fireworks her name was lit up with the inscription: *"Vivat Caterina, Imperatrix russorum."* She asked him to have laces made abroad "in which your given name and mine are entwined."[2] When he returned to St. Petersburg while she was staying at Peterhof in the country, he wrote to her at once: "When I go into our apartments I want to flee: it is all empty without you."[3]

Nevertheless, he learned from indiscreet remarks that his wife, who had formerly been so disinterested and upright, had little by little let herself be caught up in the corruption that reigned all around her. Following the example of a Menshikov or a Shafirov, she sold her influence, took commissions for intervening with the Senate, and invested money abroad. Could the Czar tolerate in her what he had punished in others? But how could he punish her without punishing himself, now that he had raised her so high in the people's esteem?

He was in this state of anger and indecision when an anonymous letter revealed to him that Catherine was deceiving him with his chamberlain, William Mons. Everyone at court had known it for a long time. Diplomats mentioned it incidentally in their dispatches. Only the Czar, blinded by his trust, was ignorant of the affair. Curiously enough, this William Mons was the brother of the charming Anna Mons whom Peter had loved so passionately in his youth. The young gallant was handsome, merry, courtly, a poet in his spare time. He was highly superstitious and wore four rings as talismans: gold, lead, iron, and copper, the gold ring being the symbol of love. The police made short work of finding the informer, one of Mons's subordinates. Put to torture in the Czar's presence in a dungeon in the Fortress of St. Peter and St. Paul, the man spilled everything he knew about the affair. It was another sister of Mons, Matriona, the wife of General Balk and Catherine's lady-in-waiting and confidante, who arranged the rendezvous. Indeed, all of Catherine's ladies-in-waiting were involved in the intrigue. The love letters that Mons wrote the Empress were signed with a woman's name and addressed to a lady by the name of Soltykova. Peter's wrath went up another notch with each detail, but he concealed it.

Back in the palace, he supped with the Empress and a few friends as usual and chatted cordially with Mons. Then suddenly he said he was tired and asked what time it was. Catherine consulted her watch and replied: "Nine o'clock." Peter, his eyes flashing, seized the watch, opened the case, pushed the big hand forward three turns, and said sharply: "You are mistaken; it is midnight and everyone should go to bed!" The little company broke up with many bows. A few moments later, Mons was arrested in his room. Taken to the Winter Palace, he was subjected to a close examination by the Czar himself. Without torture being applied, he admitted all the peculation and bribe-taking of which he was accused. But by tacit agreement, no one in the tribunal alluded to the intimate relations between the accused and Catherine. The Empress's reputation being sacred, Mons would be condemned for having stolen the state's money, not for having stolen the Czar's wife. Matriona Balk was also implicated. At first she denied the facts, but at the first blow of the knout she began to confess.

For two days running, November 13 and 14, 1724, criers walked the streets of St. Petersburg and announced to the sound of drums that the chamberlain Mons, his sister, the wife of General Balk, and several minor figures had been declared guilty of serious crimes and that all those who had paid them bribes should come forward and so state on pain of severe punishment. On November 15 the same criers called upon the people to gather at ten o'clock the next morning in front of the palace of the Senate to see the death penalty inflicted upon Mons and lesser penalties on the others. The whole court was in a commotion. Everyone knew the real reasons for the imperial sentence and pretended to believe that it was not the lover that Peter was punishing but the corrupt official. Catherine, unmasked and humiliated, affected a serenity she was far from feeling. In the rooms of the Winter Palace the atmosphere was heavy with suspicion and terror. Courtiers accosted each other with anxious looks. Peter's face was swept with the convulsions that came over him on bad days.

On November 16 the handsome William Mons resolutely mounted the steps of the scaffold. The Lutheran pastor Nazius went with him and spoke in his ear. The crowd in the square was even bigger than that for the execution of the *oberfiscal* Nesterov. The secretary of justice read out the sentence. His hoarse voice resounded in the icy air. William Mons thanked him, bowed to the audience with great dignity, took off his pelisse and jacket, placed his head on the block, and asked the headsman to be quick. The ax fell, not on the wood this time as for the lucky Shafirov, but on the neck. A red stream gushed forth. Justice was done. The Czar no longer had a rival. The executioner picked up the bloody head, planted it on a stake, and tied the decapitated body to a wheel. Immediately afterward Matriona Balk received eleven strokes of the knout on the bare back. Her screams were followed by those of her accomplices, who were likewise beaten with the knout or with rods. As a further punishment she would be exiled to Siberia. Her two sons, one a chamberlain, the other a page, would be sent as simple soldiers to the army in Persia. A placard nailed up near the scaffold gave the shameful list of those who had bought the services of the condemned man and his sister. It included the names of a great many dignitaries, starting with Chancellor Golovkin. The Czarina Prascovia Fedorovna, Prince Menshikov, and the Duke of Holstein also appeared on the list. The entire court was besmirched.

In the midst of these ordeals Catherine showed a breathtaking equanimity. On the day of the execution she summoned the young princesses and their dancing master and blithely studied the minuet with them. Campredon noted in his report: "Although the

Empress hides her grief as much as possible, it is painted on her face, so that everyone is wondering what may happen to her." The next day she learned that the Czar had issued a ukase to all his ministers instructing them henceforth to obey no order or suggestion from the Empress. More, he placed under seal the office that managed the fortune of the faithless one. Catherine immediately found herself so short of money that she had to borrow from the ladies of her entourage. Where would Peter's vengeance stop? Would he deliver Catherine to the torture chamber, as he had his son Alexis? Would he throw her into a convent, as he had his first wife, Eudoxia? Sometimes he mastered his feelings, sometimes he exploded. Seizing a Venetian mirror one day he smashed it in front of Catherine and shouted: "Thus will I do to you and yours!" Undaunted, she replied: "You have just destroyed one of the most beautiful ornaments of your house. Does that give it any more charm?" He took her in a sleigh to the place of execution where Mons's head and body were still on display. As they passed, the Empress's gown brushed against the corpse hanging on the wheel with dangling legs. She looked at the headless puppet without flinching. Some witnesses even claim that she smiled charmingly. The Czar, exasperated by her composure, ordered the coachman to drive on. That evening when Catherine returned to her room she discovered on a table in a jar of alcohol her lover's head, with staring eyes and twisted mouth. Without showing the least surprise, she went about her business under the glassy stare. After leaving her for several days and nights in this macabre company, Peter realized that nothing could shake his wife's steel nerves and had the head removed. But that didn't mean she was pardoned.

"They almost never talk to each other," noted Jean Lefort in a dispatch to the elector of Saxony, "they no longer eat together, they no longer sleep together." The general opinion was that Catherine was done for. According to Villebois, the Czar talked of "nothing less than dealing with his wife as King Henry VIII of England dealt with Anne Boleyn." What held him back was his wish to provide first for his daughters' future. The eldest, Anna, was soon to marry the Duke of Holstein, and for Elizabeth Peter was still dreaming of a French prince, maybe even the king of France himself. Since the regent, who had been opposed to the match, had died on December 3, 1723, the affair was again under discussion. Tolstoy and Andrew Ostermann, who were in negotiation with Campredon, assured their sovereign that to condemn the mother of the grand duchesses for a shameful crime would be enough to ruin so ambitious a matrimonial project. Peter was convinced. On November 23, 1724, the Duke of Holstein gave a serenade with his orchestra under the windows of his future mother-in-law at the Winter Palace. It was very cold. Servants holding torches gave light to the musicians, who were freezing where they stood and could scarcely blow into their instruments. The next day the official engagement of the young duke with the Czar's eldest daughter was celebrated. The imperial couple, come together for the occasion, crossed the Neva on the ice and went to perform their devotions in the old Church of the Trinity. At four o'clock in the afternoon, in the presence of the whole court and the entire diplomatic corps, the Czar slipped onto the fingers of the betrothed couple the rings blessed by the archbishop. The ceremony was followed by a supper, a ball, and fireworks. In the light of the candelabra Catherine, superbly dressed, showed the countenance of a serene wife and happy mother. But no one was deceived by her apparent felicity.

As the days passed, Peter's intransigence gave way to weariness. Jean Lefort wrote: "The Czarina has made a long and deep genuflection before the Czar for the remission of her sins; the conversation lasted three hours; they supped together, then went their separate ways." It was not a tender reconciliation but the bitter acceptance of reality. Peter, withdrawn into himself, felt more alone than ever. When he looked around he saw no one whom he could trust. His closest friends, the chief dignitaries of his empire, highly placed officials had betrayed him for money. The women he had chosen had each in turn proved unfaithful. He had been made a fool of by Anna Mons in the old days, then mocked by Eudoxia, who had dared to deceive him in the very convent where he had shut her up, and now he had to admit that his "Katerinushka," his "little sweetheart," as he had used to call her only yesterday, was no better than the others. Yet he had believed that this one loved him sincerely and for as long as she should live. Even when he had abandoned her for some chance mistress, he had kept his regard for her.

Now he mistrusted her like a stranger. He was at the end of

his rope, mentally and physically. The domestic tragedy had crushed him. Besides, he was suffering from a disease of the urinary tract. He had pains in his back; suppurating tumors appeared on his thighs. Nevertheless, he refused to slow down or to moderate his drinking. One day when he was out walking and heard noise coming from the house of a German baker near the Winter Palace, he entered the tradesman's house, found himself in the midst of a wedding feast, and to the stupefaction of his hosts, sat down at table and drank his fill. Too restless to stay in one place, he went in the middle of winter to inspect the work going forward on the Ladoga Canal; then he went to visit the factories of Staraya-Russa and the ironworks of Olonets. There he planted himself in front of an anvil, hammered out more than six hundred pounds of iron, demanded to be paid like an ordinary workman, pocketed the money, and declared that he would use it to buy a pair of shoes. In spite of the stormy weather, he left Olonets on horseback. In Lakhta, a fishing village near St. Petersburg, he saw a boat that had been driven aground on a shoal not far from shore and was in danger of capsizing. On board a group of soldiers returning from Kronstadt were in panic. Without hesitating, the Czar jumped into the icy waves to take part in the rescue. He shouted orders, flung himself into the struggle. Up to his chest in water, he felt proud that he was still capable of a superhuman effort. He who on so many occasions had sacrificed thousands of lives to the interests of the state cheerfully risked his own life to save a few poor wretches. They all got back to land, safe and sound. The Czar was beaming. At fifty-two, he had acted as he would have at twenty. But this exploit was one more shock to his system. He returned to St. Petersburg with a high fever. He treated the disorder with disdain, as usual. "Every day he goes to the principal houses followed by two hundred persons, musicians and others, who sing and amuse themselves drinking and eating at the expense of the people they are visiting," noted Campredon.

Christmas Eve was the occasion for more carousing. With his head burning, the Czar ate and drank without restraint, notwithstanding the entreaties of his physicians. Not long after, he had to take to his bed. Even there he continued to work. Remembering the voyage of exploration on which he had sent the Danish captain

Vitus Bering, he wrote him: "My poor health has forced me to keep my room. I have therefore had time to reflect and I have remembered several projects that I have not been able to carry out. As the motherland has no more enemies to fear, I must think of covering her with glory through art and science." His condition rapidly deteriorated. Doctors Paulson and Blumentrost diagnosed kidney stones, complicated by a relapse of the old venereal disease. In the night of January 20–21, 1725, Peter complained of violent pain due to an inability to pass urine. On the recommendation of the Italian doctor Lazarotti, the English surgeon Horn carried out a perforation of the bladder. "They drew nearly four pounds of urine from him," wrote Campredon. "It was horribly infected, mixed with pieces of flesh and putrid membranes." The Czar, temporarily relieved, swallowed a few spoonfuls of oatmeal gruel. He made confession and received communion, three times in three days. "I believe, I hope," he murmured. He wanted to meet his end like a devout son of the Orthodox Church, perhaps so that his old offenses against the clergy would be forgotten. Very soon he was again seized with pains. The doctors had no doubt but that gangrene had set in in the cervix of the bladder. Overwhelmed with suffering, Peter groaned softly: "I can't take any more. It seems as if I had a house on my chest."

Catherine never left his bedside day or night. She wept noisily and sometimes even fainted, although the approaching death was clearly a good solution for her. In the rooms of the Winter Palace the members of the Senate and the Holy Synod, the courtiers, the officers of the Guard and of the navy waited in silence for the least word from the sickroom. In the churches people were praying. But what exactly were they hoping for? Recovery or death? To be sure, Peter had served the nation by pushing back the frontiers of his empire and exploiting its natural resources. But the humble people were less concerned with Russia's renown than with the price they had had to pay for it. They would gladly have returned Livonia to Sweden in exchange for a reduction of taxes. The Ladoga Canal didn't make them forget the thousands of men who had perished in the building of it. The façades of the palaces along the Neva were pleasing to look at but didn't fill their stomachs. For them, Peter the Great meant high-priced bread, denunciations, torture, religion oppressed, serfdom expanded. If God recalled him to His side, maybe Russia would be able to breathe freely.

A different question confronted the high dignitaries who were waiting in the antechamber and weighing the consequences of the Czar's death. By the ukase of February 5, 1722, he had arrogated to himself the right to designate his successor. But he had not yet clearly indicated his choice. It was time for him to make it plain, now or never. If he persisted in silence, it was little Peter, aged ten, the son of the "martyr" Alexis, who as sole legitimate heir would ascend the throne. Is that what he secretly wanted? Catherine was more worried than anyone else. Still half in disgrace, she was afraid to provoke the dying man by questioning him on this delicate point. She therefore contented herself with sobbing to show how dear he was to her and how right he would be to proclaim her the one to carry on his work. Then, when he dozed off, she hurried into the next room to confer with Menshikov, Buturlin, and Tolstoy.

On January 26 the Czar summoned his strength and dictated a few orders. But they did not relate to the transmission of the crown. After having signed a decree concerning the sale of fish glue, he ordered that all convicts with the exception of murderers be freed and that amnesty be granted to a number of men who were guilty of infractions of the Army Regulation. The next day at two o'clock in the afternoon, he emerged from a heavy torpor, asked for his writing desk and with great difficulty traced some words on the paper. Anxiously Catherine read: "Give everything to . . ." The pen slipped from the Czar's fingers. His head fell back on the pillow. He could not finish his sentence. Of whom had he been thinking when he began the message: of little Peter, of Catherine? After a moment he regained consciousness and called his daughter Anna. She hurried to his side. By gestures he made her understand that he wanted to dictate the rest. She bent over the bed. Behind her, Catherine, her heart frozen with dread, awaited the verdict. A gurgle escaped Peter's lips. Impossible to understand what he was saying. He was again seized by convulsions that threw him from his couch. They held him down. He panted, writhed, drooled. Then, having received extreme unction, he grew calm and fell asleep. He who had wished to prove his omnipotence by naming the one who would govern Russia after him no longer had the strength or will to do so. He had let pass the moment when he might have settled the problem with a clear mind. Now earthly disputes no longer interested him. Nothing was left but weakness, abdication, and dread in the face of the mystery of the hereafter.

As he lay breathing hoarsely with his mouth contorted, Catherine, Menshikov, Tolstoy, and Buturlin met again to work out a plan of action. The court was divided into two factions. On one side were those who wanted to see Grand Duke Peter, the Emperor's grandson, accede to the throne. They were few and of no great influence—the representatives of the old Russian aristocracy, whom the dying Czar had wanted to remove from power in favor of the newcomers. On the other side, gathered around Catherine, were the formidable clan of all those who had served Peter best—energetic, experienced, resourceful men like Menshikov, Tolstoy, Apraxin, Buturlin. They knew that if the crown fell to Catherine they were assured a future of wealth and honors. Doubtless they would even govern in her stead. The Holy Synod was with them. And, what was more important, the Guard. Were not Menshikov and Buturlin colonels in the Preobrazhensky and Semeonovsky regiments?

During the night of January 27–28 emissaries sent by Catherine's supporters visited the barracks, alerted the officers, prepared their minds for the elevation of a woman to the throne of Russia. In the palace no one was sleeping. Peter was having increasing difficulty breathing. Under his white nightcap with the green ribbons his face twisted in a pitiful grimace. He hardly recognized those closest to him. Everyone around him was frozen in expectation. Impatient, almost, seeing him struggle so long to cling to life. What endurance he had, this man of fifty-three worn out by excesses! At last, on January 28, 1725, at six in the morning he breathed his last sigh. Catherine fell to her knees and cried: "Open, paradise, to receive this angel's soul!" But in her heart of hearts she thanked God for having liberated her in such timely fashion from a husband so quick to anger and so vengeful. His face waxen, his mouth pinched under the curled-up mustache, his closed eyelids bluish and bulging, the giant lay in his canopied bed. The big, hardworking hands had been crossed once for all. Enormous candles were burning around his couch. The priests were

327

there. Heavy censers swung back and forth giving out their sweet perfume. One hundred and one cannon shots were fired in the fortress. The bells of all the churches tolled the knell. Big flakes of snow were falling on the city, which was just emerging from darkness.

Catherine lost no time but went straight to the Council chamber, "shedding torrents of tears," and questioned the senators about the fate they had in store for her. She already knew that most of them were devoted to her cause. The session was purely pro forma. Peter's private secretary, Makarov, was sent for and confirmed on oath that the deceased had not entrusted him with a will.* Menshikov explained that by ordering the coronation of his consort the year before, the late Emperor had meant to indicate that he considered her the heir to his power. This was a flagrant imposture, for in no monarchy in the world did the coronation of a sovereign's wife confer upon her a right of succession. But many senators pretended to believe this interpretation of the imperial will. Apraxin immediately read out a manifesto declaring Catherine I legitimate Empress of all the Russias. A few dignitaries of the aristocratic party, including princes Repnin, Golitzin, and Dolgoruky, tried to protest. But the discussion was suddenly interrupted by the officers of the Guard, all warm supporters of Catherine, who invaded the hall in the Winter Palace where the meeting was being held, acclaimed their new sovereign, and swore to serve her at the risk of their lives. Already in front of the palace the drums and fifes of the loyal regiments were resounding. Vodka had been distributed to them at the opportune time. The members of the opposition bowed their heads. Catherine triumphed.

The embalmed corpse of the Czar was transported to the great hall of the palace and laid out on a ceremonial bed. A mute throng filed in front of the catafalque. Everyone wanted to see him lying still and silent: the man who had chased so far, struck so many

---

*It is true that Peter left no will. The alleged will that appeared at the beginning of the nineteenth century has no historical value. It contains no provisions regarding the inheritance of the throne but a program for Russia's conquest of Europe with thrusts into Constantinople, India, and Persia. No one has ever seen the original of this document. It is obviously an apochryphal text composed by Parisian publicists in 1811 to justify Napoleon's invasion of Russia.

blows, shouted so much in his attempt to awaken Russia from her centuries of somnolence. He was there, stretched full length, gigantic in his scarlet coat with the blue cordon of the Order of St. Andrew across his chest, a wig on his head, boots on his feet, spurs at his heels. Officers of the regiments of the Guard stood motionless, keeping a vigil over the Czar's remains. For a long time Catherine refused to let the coffin be closed. Morning and evening she spent half an hour at the side of her now harmless husband. She would talk to him, kiss his hands, and sob. Her capacity for tears astonished the experts. "One could not conceive," wrote Villebois, that there could be such a great reservoir of water in a woman's brain. . . . Many people flocked to the palace solely to see her weep and sigh. I knew, among others, two Englishmen who let not one of the forty days pass without going there; and I admit that I myself, although I knew what to think of the sincerity of those tears, was as moved by them as if I had attended a performance of *Andromaque.* "*

Despite all the precautions taken, the corpse began to turn black and lose its shape. On March 4, five weeks after the Czar's death, his youngest daughter, Natalya, died of measles. In deep sorrow over this second bereavement, the Empress decided to bury father and child on the same day. Public criers announced that the double funeral would take place on March 10 in the Cathedral of St. Peter and St. Paul. Orders were given that all dignitaries and foreign ambassadors should hang the windows of their houses with black draperies. There was an instantaneous rise in the market price of such fabrics. Diplomats complained of being obliged to make an unexpected expenditure that was beyond their means. They had to go from one shop to another to chase down the smallest scrap of black cloth.

On the appointed day the funeral cortege started out amid gusts of snow and hail. The Emperor's coffin was borne by twelve colonels. Eight major generals held the gold tassels of the canopy made of green velvet and cloth of gold. Natalya's little coffin was surmounted by a canopy embroidered in gold, with red and white

---

*Racine's play (1667) based on the story of Hector's widow Andromache after the fall of Troy.—TRANS.

plumes. Innumerable churchmen were grouped around holy banners. The Empress, in deep mourning, was supported by Menshikov and Apraxin. Her daughters Anna and Elizabeth followed her. High dignitaries, generals, admirals, courtiers, diplomats walked bareheaded in the swirling snow. Detachments of the army and navy marched to the mournful sound of trumpets and drums amid a forest of flags. One hundred forty-four pieces of artillery fired salutes, periodically drowning out the music. The procession had to cross the frozen river to reach the fortress. Campredon estimated the distance at "a good half a French league."* As they started across the ice the storm grew worse. The wind ruffled wigs, turned up black cloaks. The procession lasted two hours. Not everyone could enter the cathedral, vast as it was. During the service women sobbed. After mass Feofan Prokopovich, archbishop of Pskov, pronounced the funeral oration: "What has happened to us, oh men of Russia? What do we see? What are we doing? It is Peter the Great whom we are committing to the earth. . . ." He was interrupted by cries of grief. He was so moved that he wept himself. At last, steadying his voice, he continued: "He has departed, but he has not left us in misery and destitution. . . . The vast wealth of strength and glory that is the result of his labors remains with us. . . . Russia will live on such as he molded her. He made her beloved of the righteous, who will continue to cherish her. He made her fearful to her enemies, to whom she will remain formidable. Before the whole world he covered her with immortal glory. . . ."

One last time the cannon of the fortress fired a salute through the falling snow. Censers were swung over the coffin, it was closed, covered with the imperial purple, and the throng of the living turned toward the new reign.

Abroad, the news of Peter's death was greeted with relief. The Comte de Rabutin, envoy to the court of Vienna, even said that "there was general rejoicing." In Russia, it was not only Old Believers and conservative aristocrats who congratulated themselves on the Czar's demise. The humble people, who had suffered so much under the master's fist, felt as if they were coming out of a

*About two kilometers, or more than a mile.

nightmare. A satirical engraving circulated among the public enti-
tled "Burial of the cat by the mice." It showed a procession of little
mice conducting to his final abode the huge cat who had terrified
them while he was alive. Naïvely, the common people imagined
that their fate would change with this Catherine I, said to be magnanimous.

From the first days of her reign Catherine declared that she
intended to "successfully complete, with God's help, everything
that Peter began." But that was merely the correct thing to say.
Actually, she was not very concerned about the fate of Russia. After
having lived for more than twenty years in the shadow of a despot,
she felt a sudden release of her instincts, a thirst for freedom,
abandon, amusement. This woman of forty-three, this tub of lard
with the overflowing bosom, thick chin, and gluttonous eye, organized great dinners for the officers of the Guard, drank like a hole
in the ground, ate like a python, and took to her bedroom a different favorite every night: Loewenwalde, Devier, Count Jean
Sapieha. . . . On April 1, 1725, scarcely three weeks after Peter's
funeral, the inhabitants of St. Petersburg were awakened at dawn
by alarm bells and rushed into the street, thinking there was a fire
or a flood. Laughing guards undeceived them: it was the Empress
who had wanted to play an April Fool's joke on her subjects. The
Russians, who had never heard of this Western custom, were not
amused by their sovereign's humor. Perhaps she had acted in
memory of the crude farces of former days. A posthumous homage
to her husband's love of pranks. Even Berkholz said in his *Journal*
that he was offended by the incident.

Then on May 21 came the wedding of Grand Duchess Anna
and Duke Karl Frederick of Holstein. The ceremony was conducted in Slavonic by Feofan Prokopovich, but an interpreter repeated the important passages in Latin so that the groom could
understand. During the wedding feast cannon thundered and the
orchestra played lively tunes. They drank as heartily at the ladies'
table as at the gentlemen's. As in Peter's time, a male dwarf and
a female dwarf popped out of two enormous pies. But this time
they were dressed, one as a messenger, the other as a shepherdess.

The new Empress did not forget the family she had come
from. She summoned from the provinces her brothers and sisters,

whom Peter had given pensions but kept at a distance. The Livonian peasants appeared in St. Petersburg gorgeously dressed, under prestigious names and titles: Count Simon Hendrikov, Count Michael Yefimovsky, and so on.

Courtiers disgraced under the preceding reign were called back from exile. More than two hundred of them. Shafirov, the man who had been saved by a miracle, reappeared fat and smiling, ready for new machinations. One fete followed another at an increasing pace, with artillery salvos, fireworks, and all sorts of crackles and bangs. To Berkholz, who expressed surprise at this waste of explosives, persons close to the Empress explained that powder was cheaper to manufacture in Russia than anywhere else.

There was, however, one disappointment for Catherine I: in August 1725, six and a half months after Peter's death, her daughter Elizabeth, who had been proposed as a financée for Louis XV, found that preference had been given—the Lord only knew why—to the very modest daughter of the deposed king of Poland, Marie Leszczynska. The cabinet of Versailles, which was decidedly incorrigible, continued to ignore the power of Russia. They would regret it, the outraged mother swore. And rejoining the camp of France's enemies, on August 6, 1726, she signed a defensive and offensive alliance with Austria.

To govern the country Catherine, who doubted her own competence in political affairs, turned to her former lover, Menshikov. After having incurred the wrath of the deceased Czar, the favorite suddenly found himself possessed of increased wealth and influence. As the adviser to a woman who was on the decline and solely preoccupied with her pleasures, he was the real master of Russia. At his instigation she appointed a Supreme Privy Council of six members, of which he was the head and which included Apraxin, Golovkin, Tolstoy, Golitzin, and Ostermann. Eclipsing the Senate, this new body managed the affairs of the state. It enacted some prudent laws, eased the lot of the Old Believers, and officially created the Academy of Sciences that Peter had wanted to establish.

This lax, disorganized reign under Menshikov's direction was already making some people miss the firmness of the preceding one. With the passage of time the wounds that Peter had inflicted on his people healed over and the essential lines of his policy appeared in the light of eternity. People forgot his crimes and remembered only his conquests. The very ones who had opposed him while he was alive realized what an irreparable loss they had suffered at his death. "He was as regretted in the tomb as he was feared on the throne," declared Campredon. And: "This great prince worked wonders, and while his subjects have not changed on the inside, at least one observes on the outside so great a metamorphosis that those who knew Russia thirty years ago and who see what is practiced there today must confess that it took a monarch as courageous, enlightened, and hardworking as he to produce so fortunate and so general a revolution."

The truth was that with fierce obstinacy Peter had always sacrificed the happiness of the Russians to the glory of Russia. By transforming his country he had wanted to catch up with, and even pass, Europe on the road of progress. His model had not been refined, rebellious, Catholic France, but the Protestant Germanic countries—active, rough-mannered, and sober-minded. Yet in spite of his infatuation with them, he had remained fundamentally Russian. And it was that fact that his contemporaries realized not long after his death. They felt that for more than thirty years they had been living under the orders of an exceptional man endowed with supernatural intelligence and power, a man whose virtues were as much beyond the ordinary as were his faults. A barbarian thirsting for culture, a boon companion capable of murderous rages, a dissolute boozer in love with work, a military leader interested in civil administration, an executioner who wielded the cudgel and the pen by turns, a sovereign who had arches of triumph built in his honor and who also mocked himself, a sincere believer in the Orthodox religion and the inventer of blasphemous ceremonies—he contained within himself every contradiction and allowed himself to be carried away to every excess with equal unconcern. Could one judge by ordinary moral standards this giant boiling with primitive instincts? Would he have succeeded in dragging Russia out of her torpor if he had not swept down upon her like a tornado?

Thoughtful men feared that now he was gone the country would sink back into anarchy. Henceforth the affairs of the empire were abandoned to the whims of the great princes and the Guard. The palace was a ship in distress on which everyone gave commands except the captain. The chief concern of the Supreme Privy Council was—already!—Catherine's successor. And indeed, after a few months of wild living the Empress was suffering from such frequent spells of heart trouble that she herself foresaw the end. She wanted to draw up a will proclaiming her daughter Elizabeth Czarina. Public opinion, however, was in favor of the accession of the deceased Emperor's grandson, the Czarevich Peter. Ostermann, a shrewd man, suggested that the opposing views be reconciled by marrying the twelve-year-old lad to his aunt Elizabeth, who was just seventeen. Young Elizabeth was not displeased with this solution, but in the end she was pushed aside by Menshikov, who imposed Peter as sole heir. The intention of the Most Serene Prince was to have the boy marry his own daughter, Maria, and thus to become, as the Czar's father-in-law, more powerful than he had ever been. He got around Catherine and when she was no longer in full possession of her faculties, persuaded her to yield. On May 6, 1727, after enjoying herself for two years in her role as sovereign, she died of a fever.

During her reign she had had Peter the Great's first wife, Eudoxia, removed from the convent and transferred to a rat-infested cell in the Fortress of Schlüsselburg. The prisoner, who was ill, had only an old dwarf woman to care for her and wash her clothes. She was waiting for death in this filthy hole when suddenly the bolts creaked, the door opened, magnificently dressed personages bowed before her and invited her to follow them. Speechless with astonishment, she learned that the Empress Catherine I was dead and that the new Emperor, who bore the name of Peter II, was her own grandson. Without transition, she passed from the darkness of the prison to the brilliant lights of palaces. Treated with the utmost consideration, taking precedence over other princesses, she went to Moscow to attend the coronation of the young sovereign, the son of Alexis the martyr. But her revenge on fate had come too late. The pomp and ceremony of the court wearied her. Of her own accord she returned to the cloister to end her days there amid silence, prayers, and memories.*

*She died in 1731.

Meanwhile, Menshikov, after the coronation of Peter II, was completely carried away by his own power. With the most high-handed arrogance he dominated the Supreme Privy Council, distributed praise and blame as he pleased, officially announced the betrothal of his daughter to the sovereign, and had himself awarded the title of generalissimo. Little by little, his insufferable pride alienated even his strongest supporters. In the very bosom of the Supreme Privy Council, Alexis Dolgoruky was working behind the scenes to prepare the ambitious man's downfall. Having won the friendship of the young Czar Peter II, he stirred him up against the overweening prince who presumed to govern the country in his place. Soon Menshikov was arrested, judged, deprived of his titles, stripped of his incalculable riches, and exiled to Siberia along with his wife, his son, and his two daughters, including Maria, the sovereign's fiancée. He died two years later in abject poverty, sunk in drunkenness and abandoned by all.

Dolgoruky, who had in turn become Peter II's trusted adviser, followed the example of his predecessor and offered the Czar his thirteen-year-old daughter Catherine as a fiancée. The conservative faction triumphed. Encouraged by the members of the old aristocracy, the young Czar dreamed of reconciling all his subjects, those who wanted reforms and those who held with tradition. Moscow could become the capital of the empire again, St. Petersburg remaining a commercial port. Did Peter II consciously wish to take the opposite course from his formidable grandfather? Was his admiration for Peter the Great less powerful than his hatred for the man who had tortured his father to death and shut his grandmother up in a convent? Was he another Alexis, bearer of the hopes of old Russia? Some people thought so. But he was so young! Under the influence of Dolgoruky, he quickly lost interest in government and demonstrated a taste only for the pleasures of the hunt and the table. On May 15, 1728, he lost his aunt Anna, eldest of the daughters of Peter the Great, who had married Duke Karl Frederick of Holstein. In the meantime the court had moved to Moscow. Catherine Dolgoruky was finally declared "betrothed sovereign." Alas, shortly afterward Peter II contracted smallpox. He died on January 19, 1730, at the age of fourteen, on the very day that had been fixed for his wedding.

And to whom would the crown go now? Once again the Supreme Privy Council was in a fever of activity. The male line of the terrible reformer had died out. It would be necessary to wait another thirty-two years—after the reigns of Anna Ivanovna, of little Ivan VI with his mother Anna Leopoldovna as regent, of Elizabeth Petrovna and of the deplorable Peter III—for there to arise in Russia, under the name of Catherine II, an obscure German princess who would grandly carry on the lifework of Peter the Great.

Chronology

EVENTS IN RUSSIA AND IN THE LIFE OF PETER	PRINCIPAL EVENTS IN OTHER COUNTRIES
1672 *May 30:* Birth of Peter.	Louis XIV takes up residence at Versailles.
1673	Russian embassy visits Versailles. John III Sobieski of Poland defeats the Turks at Khotin, succeeds to the throne after death of Michael Wisniowecki, king of Poland. Jacques Marquette, French missionary, and Louis Joliet, French explorer, travel down the Mississippi River as far as the Arkansas River.

1674
End of the French *jacqueries* (revolt of the French peasantry). Holy Roman Empire declares war on France. Dutch William III of Orange marries Mary, daughter of James II of England. Death of English poet John Milton.

1675
Frederick William of Brandenburg, an ally of the Holy Roman Empire, defeats Charles XI of Sweden at the Battle of Fehrbellin. Leibniz lays the groundwork for the development of modern calculus. Newton publishes *An Hypothesis Explaining the Properties of Light.*

1676 Death of Czar Alexis I; accession of Feodor III, son of Alexis and Maria Miloslavskaya. Czarina Natalya and Peter are sent to Preobrazhenskoye, a village near Moscow. Artamon Matveyev, minister and tutor of Czarina Natalya, accused by the Miloslavsky clan of having provoked the death of Alexis I, is exiled to Siberia.

In England, "Whig" Party draws up a constitution to limit royal authority. John III Sobieski defeats the Turks at Zurano. Poland and the Ottoman Empire conclude the Treaty of Zurano, by which the Turks acquire the Polish Ukraine and Podolia, thus coming into contact with Russia.

| 1677 | | French and Dutch compete to arrive first in Senegal. Death of Spinoza. |

| 1678 | | False "Popish Plot" to murder King Charles II and establish Roman Catholicism in England results in wave of Catholic persecution. |

| 1679 | | Habeas Corpus Act in England establishes protection against unlawful imprisonment. |

| 1680 | Feodor III marries Agatha Gruschevskaya. | |

| 1681 | Death of Czarina Agatha Gruschevskaya. | Turks give up much of Turkish Ukraine to Russia. First government of Frontenac in Canada. Sieur de la Salle, French explorer, claims entire region from Quebec to Gulf of France, and names Louisiana after King Louis XIV. |

1682   Peter is ten years old.
April 27: Death of Feodor
III; accession of Peter I.
Natalya Naryshkina, his
mother, secures the
regency. *May 15–16:*
Revolt of the *streltsy,*
fomented by the
Miloslavskys, Czarevna
Sophia as its head. *May
23:* Thanks to Sophia's
impetus, Ivan Alexeyevich
is named Czar at the side
of Peter. *May 25:* Ivan's
right of precedence over
Peter established. *May 29:*
Sophia secures the
regency. *June 25:*
Coronation of the two
Czars Ivan and Peter in
the Cathedral of the
Assumption. *September 2:*
Suspecting a plot, Sophia
and the two Czars leave
Moscow; confronted by
the *streltsy,* Sophia remains
firm. *November 6:* Both
Czars and the regent
return to Moscow.
December 30: Sophia has
exiled twelve regiments of
streltsy.

Ottoman Empire begins
war with Austria, which is
allied to Poland. Newton
discovers Universal Law
of Gravitation.

1683		John III Sobieski supports Leopold I of the Holy Roman Empire against the Turks; they raise the Turkish siege of Vienna and defeat the larger Turkish army.
1684		The Holy Roman Empire, Poland, and Venice join with the Pope to form Holy League against the Turks. Rebellion in Massachusetts, revoking original charter of Massachusetts Bay Colony.
1685		James II succeeds Charles II as king of England, Scotland, and Ireland. Revocation of the Edict of Nantes, which gave religious freedom to French Huguenots; Edict of Potsdam to protect French refugees. The Albasin Russians surrender to the Chinese.
1686	*April 21:* Treaty of Moscow between Russia and Poland. Russians intervene on the side of Poland against Turkey in return for territorial advantages.	Austrians capture Budapest from the Turks. Russia declares war on Ottoman Empire.

1687	Turks and Tatars defeat Russian troops led by Basil Golitzin, favorite of Sophia.	Louis XIV splits with the Vatican. James II issues Declaration of Liberty of Conscience and dissolves Parliament. Hungarian diet fixes the succession to the throne in the male line of the Hapsburgs. Holy Roman troops defeat the Turks at the Battle of Mohács. Newton publishes *Philosophiae Naturalis Principia Mathematica*.
1688	Second Russian campaign against Turkey.	Louis IX invades Palatinate and seizes Heidelberg; war of the League of Augsburg against France begins. "Glorious Revolution" in England. James II flees.
1689	Peter I marries Eudoxia Lopukhina. *Spring:* Retreat of the Russian army. *August 6–7:* Sophia's coup against Peter fails when the *streltsy* refuse to support her; Peter I has Basil Golitzin exiled and agitators executed. *October 6:* Peter returns to Moscow; Sophia sent to the Novodevichy Convent.	Accession of William III of Orange and Mary II in England. Russo-Chinese Treaty of Nerchinsk. Another rebellion in Massachusetts. Second Frontenac government in Canada.

1690   Peter turns eighteen. Anna Mons becomes Peter's favorite. *February 19:* Birth of Czarevich Alexis, son of Peter I and Eudoxia. Peter devotes himself to fireworks and military exercises. *March 27:* Death of Patriarch Joachim, replaced by the metropolitan Adrian. *June 2:* Peter burns his face during a drill.

Turks recapture Belgrade.

1691

Austrians defeat the Turks at Salankemen; Turks continue to ravage the country.

1692   Peter turns twenty, participates in the construction of ships. Twelve thousand Tatars pillage Nemirov and take thousands of prisoners.

Reinstallation of land tax in England. Kang Xi legalizes Christianity in China.

1693   Peter sails to the White Sea in the Arctic Circle.

1694   *January 25:* Death of Natalya Naryshkina, mother of Peter I. *May 8:* Peter sails to the North to welcome the warship ordered in Amsterdam. *May 17:* Peter's flotilla enters Archangel. *July 21:* Arrival of the frigate *Holy Prophet. October:* Peter organizes a sham battle, the "Kozhukov campaign."

Death of Mary II in England. Bank of England founded.

1695   *January 20:* Peter decrees a mobilization against Turkey. *Autumn:* Construction of a Russian fleet.

Versailles is completed. Mustafa II succeeds Ahmed II in Turkey.

1696   *January 29:* Death of Czar Ivan Alexeyevich, Peter's half brother. *July–September:* Peter launches his fleet against Azov. *July 17–19:* Siege and surrender of Azov. *September 30:* Peter's triumphant entry into Moscow. *December 6:* Peter announces to the Duma the creation of the "Great Embassy."

Peace of Paris. Death of John III Sobieski.

1697   *February 23:* Discovery of a *streltsy* conspiracy against Peter. *March 4:* Torture and execution of conspirators. *March 10:* Departure of the Great Embassy for Europe. *August 7:* Peter's arrival in Amsterdam.

France signs Treaty of Ryswick with England, Spain, and the Netherlands, ending the War of the Grand Alliance. Charles XII succeeds Charles XI in Sweden. Charles Perrault publishes "Tales of Mother Goose."

1698   *January 7:* Peter departs for England. *End of March:* New revolt of the *streltsy,* suppressed by the army. *End of April:* Peter returns to Amsterdam. *August 25:* Peter and the Great Embassy return to Moscow. *September 1698–February 1699:* Peter has *streltsy* conspirators tortured and executed.

New East India Company is founded. African trade is opened to all English subjects.

1699   Peter has Czarina Eudoxia locked away in the Convent of Suzdal. Edict forbidding the wearing of beards, except for members of the clergy. *March 2:* Death of Lefort. *November 29:* Death of Gordon. *December 20:* Peter issues ukase ordering the adoption of the European calendar.

The principality of Liechtenstein founded. Death of Christian V of Denmark.

1700 *January 1:* Czar's edict to celebrate the New Year. Ukase creating eight pharmacies in Moscow. *January 4:* Ukase simplifying dress of members of court and officials. *August 8:* Russo-Turkish Agreement. *August 20:* Ukase extending the wearing of German clothes for almost all social ranks. *September 23–November 19:* Siege of Narva, Sweden; Russian defeat. *December:* Death of Patriarch Adrian, who is without successor. Peter names Stephen Yavorsky "temporary guardian of the Holy Throne of the Patriarch."

Death of Charles II of Spain, succeeded by Philip V (grandson of Louis XIV). Great Northern War begins; Russia, Poland, and Denmark fight Sweden to break Swedish supremacy in the Baltic area.

1701 Ordinance forbidding kneeling at the Czar's passing. *February:* Russo-Polish Treaty. *June:* Fire in the Moscow Kremlin. *Winter:* Russian victory over the Swedes at Erestfer.

Accession of Frederick I of Prussia. Death of James II of England.

1702	Peter turns thirty. Opening of the *terems*, emancipation of women. Institution of obligatory betrothals. *July:* Beginning of Peter's liaison with Martha, who quickly assumes the name Catherine Alexeyevna. Ordinance authorizing Protestantism. *October 11:* Capitulation to the Russians of the Fortress of Nöteborg.	Death of William III of England, accession of Queen Anne. War of the Spanish Succession begins.
1703	Peter has his mistress Anna Mons thrown in prison after discovering her liaison with Saxon envoy Königseck. *January:* Publication of the first Russian newspaper in Moscow, *The News. May 1:* Russian victory at Nienschantz. *May 7:* Capture of two Swedish ships at the mouth of the Gulf of Finland. *May 16:* Founding of St. Petersburg.	Death of Mustafa II of Turkey, succeeded by Ahmed III.
1704	*February:* Italian architect Domenico Trezzini directs construction, St. Petersburg. *July:* Russians sieze Dorpat. *July 14:* Death of Czarevna Sophia Miloslavsky. *August:* Russian victory at Narva.	Stanislas I Leszczynski crowned king of Poland.

1705   Catherine Alexeyevna's
       two sons by Peter die at a
       young age. Rebellion in
       Astrakhan, supported by
       the *streltsy*, crushed by the
       regular army. School of
       Mathematics and
       Navigation founded in
       Moscow.

Death of Leopold I;
accession of Joseph I as
Holy Roman Emperor.

1706   *January:* Russians defeated
       at Grodno by the Swedes;
       defeated again at
       Franstadt. Admiral
       Golovin opens a shipyard
       at St. Petersburg. *September
       11:* Flood in St.
       Petersburg. *September 24:*
       Peace treaty between
       Sweden and Poland.

Act of Union unifies
England and Scotland
into Great Britain.

1707   Three thousand workers
       already employed at the
       St. Petersburg shipyard.
       Russians invade Poland.

Death of Emperor
Aurangzeb of India. End
of Mogul Empire.

1708   Peter appoints Czarevich
        Alexis (eighteen years
        old) governor of Moscow.
        Peter's family and high
        dignitaries ordered to
        leave Moscow for St.
        Petersburg. Rebellion of
        Don Cossacks and
        Bashkirs in the region of
        Kazan subdued by regular
        army; Swedish troops
        cross the Berezina, seize
        Mogilev, and head toward
        Smolensk. Birth of Anna,
        daughter of Peter and
        Catherine Alexeyevna and
        future mother of Peter III
        (who will marry Catherine
        II, known as Catherine
        the Great).

1709   Ukase forbidding the
        reconstruction of homes
        that were destroyed in the
        Moscow fire; transfer of
        the population to St.
        Petersburg. *April:* Swedes
        reach Poltava, in the
        central Ukraine. *June 27:*
        Russian victory over
        Swedes at Poltava.
        December 21: Russian
        army's triumphant entry
        into Moscow. *December 29:*
        Birth of Elizabeth,
        daughter of Peter and
        Catherine Alexeyevna.

1710 Peter sends Czarevich Alexis to Dresden to complete his education. Marriage of Grand Duchess Anna, Peter's niece, and Duke of Kurland. *November 20:* Declaration of war between Russia and Turkey.

Birth of the Duke of Anjou, the future Louis XV. Victory of the Duc de Vendôme at Villaviciosa; Philip V remains king of Spain.

1711 *January 1:* Announcement at St. Petersburg of war against the Turks. *February 19:* Peter marries Catherine Alexeyevna. *February 25:* Departure of Russian army to fight Turkey; Catherine accompanies Peter. *Late March:* Peter contracts scurvy in Luck. *July 7:* Russians defeated by Turks on the Pruth. *July 12:* Russo-Turkish Treaty of Pruth; Russians defeated at Azov. *October 14:* Marriage of Czarevich Alexis and Charlotte of Brunswick-Wolfenbüttel. Construction of Winter Palace at St. Petersburg. Publication of newspaper, *The St. Petersburg News.*

Death of the Grand Dauphin of France. Death of Joseph I, succession of Charles VI as Holy Roman Emperor.

1712   Peter turns forty.

End of the War of the Spanish Succession. Birth of the Infanta of Spain. Philip V renounces throne of Spain. Birth of Prince Frederick of Prussia (the future Frederick the Great). End of religious war in Switzerland.

1713   St. Petersburg designated the capital. Beginning of Finnish campaign.

Charles VI issues Pragmatic Sanction in favor of his daughter, Maria-Theresa. Treaty of Utrecht ends political domination of France. England monopolizes African trade.

1714   St. Petersburg has 34,550 inhabitants. *March 23:* Ukase instituting a single inheritor of estates. Finnish campaign; Russian victories at Helsingfors, Borga, Abo, Tonningen. *July 12:* Birth of Natalya, Peter's granddaughter. *July 27:* New Russian victory at Hangö. *November 24:* Czarina decorated with Order of St. Catherine.

Death of Queen Anne, accession of George I, elector of Hanover, as king of England. Treaty of Rastatt between Louis XIV of France and Holy Roman Emperor Charles VI.

1715 *October:* Peter has Alexis choose between a political life and a monastic one. *October 12:* Birth of Peter, grandson of Peter I. *October 22:* Death of Charlotte of Brunswick-Wolfenbüttel, wife of Alexis. *October 29:* Birth of Peter, son of Peter I and Catherine Alexeyevna. *December 2:* Peter I, seriously ill, receives the Last Sacraments. *December 25:* Peter recovers, begins work on the European alliance against Sweden.

Death of Louis XIV of France, succession of Louis XV. Jacobite uprising in Scotland: James Stuart flees.

1716 *September 26:* In the face of paternal obstinacy, Czarevich Alexis flees St. Petersburg and finds refuge with Charles VI in Vienna. *December 20:* Peter demands that Charles VI return the Czarevich.

1717   The St. Petersburg police
service is turned over to a
chief of police in order to
combat pillaging. St.
Petersburg arsenal
fortifications are
destroyed by floods. *May
6:* Alexis's arrival in
Naples. *April 21:* Peter
disembarks at Dunkirk.
May 7–June 20: Peter I in
Paris. *May 10–11:*
Meeting between Peter
and young Louis XV.
July–October: Demanding
the return of Alexis, Peter
threatens Charles VI.
August 15: Treaty of
Amsterdam allying Russia,
France, and Prussia.
October: Alexis departs for
Russia. *October 9:* Peter
returns to St. Petersburg.

Triple Alliance of the
Holy Roman Empire
against Philip V of Spain.

1718 *January 31:* Alexis's return to Moscow. *February 3:* Alexis officially renounces the throne; Peter I names his young son Peter as his successor. *March:* Torture and execution of "accomplices" in Alexis's flight. *June 17:* Czarevich Alexis appears before a special tribunal. *June 24:* Alexis condemned to death. *June 26:* Mysterious death of Czarevich Alexis. *November 26:* Ukase replacing the household tax with a poll tax.

Death of Charles XII of Sweden. Quadruple Alliance of London. Founding of New Orleans, Louisiana.

1719 *April 16:* Death of young Peter Petrovich, son of Peter I.

Maria Cantemir is Peter's new favorite. *July:* Russian fleet and army in Sweden.

1720 *May:* Ineffective British intervention on behalf of Sweden against Russia.

Philip V of Spain adheres to Quadruple Alliance. Spanish arrive in Texas. Founding of British colony in Honduras.

1721 Official suppression of the patriarchate, replaced by the college of spiritual affairs, the Very Holy Synod. Flood of the Neva in St. Petersburg. Peter seeks an easy conquest of Persia, which is rocked by riots. *August 30:* Peace of Nystad between Sweden and Russia. *October 22:* Peter I receives title of "Peter the Great, father of his country, Emperor of all the Russias."

Sir Robert Walpole becomes Chancellor of the Exchequer in England. Founding of the first Masonic lodge.

1722 Peter turns fifty. *January 24:* Establishment of the "Table of Ranks," instituting a hierarchy of merit. *February 5:* Peter I claims the right to designate his successor. *July 18:* As head of the army, Peter embarks at Astrakhan for Persia. *August 23:* Triumphant entry into Derbent; Baku falls into the hands of the Russians. *September 12:* Peace treaty signed at St. Petersburg between the shah of Persia and Peter I.

1723 Louis XV comes of age.

1724 *January 16:* Ukase granting soldiers of humble origin the opportunity of promotion and access to the class of hereditary nobility. *January 31:* Monasteries and convents receive orders to care for orphans, the injured, and the ill. *May 7:* Coronation of Czarina Catherine Alexeyevna. *June:* Treaty of Constantinople. Peter learns that Catherine has a lover, Peter Mons. *November 16:* William Mons is decapitated. Ukase forbidding obedience to the Czarina.

Abdication of Philip V of Spain, accession of Don Louis. When he dies, Philip V restored to the throne.

1725 Founding of the Academy of Sciences in St. Petersburg. *January 20–21:* Peter ill. *January 23:* Operation. *January 28:* Death of Peter the Great and accession of Catherine I. *March 4:* Death of Natalya, daughter of Peter I. *March 10:* Peter the Great's funeral.

Louis XV of France marries Marie Loszczynska. Philip V disrupts Quadruple Alliance.

Notes

1. VIOLENCE IN THE KREMLIN

1. *Mémoires* of Prince Peter Dolgorouki (Geneva, 1867).
2. La Neuville, *Relation curieuse et nouvelle de la Moscovie.*
3. Report of the Danish representative in Moscow, Rosenbuch.
4. V. Klutchevski, *Pierre le Grand et son oeuvre.*

2. THE REGENCY

1. Constantin de Grunwald, *La Russie de Pierre le Grand.*
2. N. G. Ustryalov, *History of the Reign of Peter the Great.*
3. Ibid.
4. R. P. Philippe Avril, *Voyage en divers etats d'Europe et d'Asie.*

3. PETER OR SOPHIA?

1. Constantin de Grunwald, *La Russie de Pierre le Grand.*
2. Letter of July 13, 1688.

4. THE GERMAN SETTLEMENT

1. Henry Vallotton, *Pierre le Grand.*
2. Letter from Captain Sénébier, dated from Moscow, September 22, 1693, quoted by Vallotton, *Pierre le Grand.*
3. Kasimierz Waliszewski, *Pierre le Grand.*
4. Letter quoted by Vallotton, *Pierre le Grand.*
5. Waliszewski, *Pierre le Grand.*

6. Villebois, *Mémoires secrets pour servir à l'histoire de la cour de Russie.*
7. Constantin de Grunwald, *La Russie de Pierre le Grand.*
8. Villebois, *Mémoires secrets.*

6. THE GREAT EMBASSY

1. Henry Vallotton, *Pierre le Grand.*
2. Ibid.
3. Kasimierz Waliszewski, *Pierre le Grand.* Details of the meeting are taken from the *Correspondance des deux princesses avec Fuchs.*
4. Quoted by Waliszewski, *Pierre le Grand.*
5. Letter from Jacques Lefort, quoted by Vallotton, *Pierre le Grand.*
6. Nartov. Quoted by Waliszewski, *Pierre le Grand.*
7. Gilbert Burnet, *History of His Own Time* (Oxford: Clarendon Press, 1823), pp. 396–98. Quoted in *Peter the Great,* ed. L. Jay Oliva (Englewood Cliffs, N.J.: Prentice-Hall, 1970), pp. 105–106.—TRANS.

7. THE REVOLT OF THE STRELTSY

1. Constantin de Grunwald, *La Russie de Pierre le Grand.*
2. Letter from Pierre Lefort, quoted by Henry Vallotton, *Pierre le Grand.*
3. Extracts from John Perry's "The State of Russia Under the Present Czar" (London: Benjamin Toole, 1716), in Peter Putnam, *Seven Britons in Imperial Russia 1698–1812* (Princeton: Princeton University Press, 1952), pp. 38–39.—TRANS.
4. Ibid., p. 39.—TRANS.
5. N. G. Ustryalov: *History of the Reign of Peter the Great.*
6. Johann-Georg Korb, *Diary of an Austrian Secretary of Legation at the Court of Tsar Peter the Great,* vol. 1, p. 257.—TRANS.
7. Vallotton, *Pierre le Grand.*
8. Ibid.
9. Kasimierz Waliszewski, *Pierre le Grand.*

10. Ibid.
11. Milioukov, Seignobos, and Eisenmann, *Histoire de Russie.*

8. FROM NARVA TO POLTAVA

1. Dispatch of August 19, 1699.
2. Henry Vallotton, *Pierre le Grand.*
3. Kasimierz Waliszewski, *Pierre le Grand.*
4. Ibid.
5. N. G. Ustryalov, *History of the Reign of Peter the Great.*
6. Constantin de Grunwald, *Pierre le Grand.*
7. Vallotton, *Pierre le Grand.*
8. Ibid.

9. ST. PETERSBURG

1. Henry Vallotton, *Pierre le Grand.* Pushkin borrowed this image from Count Francesco Algarotti's letters on Russia (1769).
2. Weber, Friedrich Christian, *The Present State of Russia,* vol. 1, p. 318.—TRANS.
3. Constantin de Grunwald, *La Russie de Pierre le Grand.*

10. JOURNEY TO FRANCE

1. *Journal de Pierre le Grand.*
2. Ibid.
3. Ibid.
4. Letter of September 14, 1711.
5. Letter of September 19, 1711.
6. Henry Vallotton, *Pierre le Grand.*
7. Kasimierz Waliszewski, *Pierre le Grand.*
8. Ibid.
9. Letter to Chauvelin of October 3, 1760, quoted in ibid.
10. Maréchal de Tessé, *Mémoires.*
11. Vallotton, *Pierre le Grand.*

11. THE CZAREVICH ALEXIS

1. According to Huyssen's *Notes,* quoted by Ustryalov, *History of the Reign of Peter the Great.*
2. Henry Vallotton, *Pierre le Grand.*
3. Letter of October 14, 1711.
4. "Manifesto of the Criminal Process of the Czarewitz Alexei Petrowitz," anonymous translation from the French, in Friedrich Christian Weber, *The Present State of Russia,* vol. 2, pp. 99–102.—TRANS.
5. Ibid., pp. 102–103.—TRANS.
6. Goltsev, *Les moeurs au XVIIIe siècle.*
7. Statement made by the Czarevich to the investigating commission on February 8, 1718.
8. "Manifesto," p. 105.—TRANS.
9. Ibid., p. 116.—TRANS.
10. Ibid., pp. 105–106.—TRANS.
11. Ibid., p. 117.—TRANS.
12. Ibid., pp. 107–108.—TRANS.
13. Notes taken by Vice Chancellor Schönborn, published in Ustryalov's documents on the reign of Peter the Great.
14. "Manifesto," pp. 108–109.—TRANS.
15. Ibid., p. 110.—TRANS.
16. Ibid.
17. Vallotton, *Pierre le Grand.*
18. Kasimierz Waliszewski, *Pierre le Grand.*
19. "Manifesto," p. 137.—TRANS.
20. Ibid., p. 155.—TRANS.
21. Ibid., pp. 163–64.—TRANS.
22. Ibid., pp. 185–86.—TRANS.
23. Ibid., pp. 190–93.—TRANS.
24. Ibid. pp. 194–95.—TRANS.
25. Vallotton, *Pierre le Grand.*

12. EMPEROR AND EMPRESS

1. Berkholz, *Journal.*
2. Margravine of Bayreuth, *Mémoires.*

3. Pushkin, *Table Talk*.

4. Prince Golitzine, *La Russie au XVIIIe siècle*.

5. Berkholz, *Journal*.

6. Friedrich Christian Weber, *Correspondence*.

7. Johann-Georg Korb, *Journal du voyage en Moscovie*.

8. Kasimierz Waliszewski, *Pierre le Grand*.

9. Berkholz, *Journal*.

10. Golitzine, *La Russie au XVIIIe siècle*.

11. Weber, *The Present State of Russia*, vol. 1, pp. 288–89.—TRANS.

12. Waliszewski, *Pierre le Grand*.

13. Dispatch from Whitworth dated March 25, 1712.

14. Waliszewski, *Pierre le Grand*.

15. Henry Vallotton, *Pierre le Grand*.

16. Ibid.

17. Waliszewski, *Pierre le Grand*.

18. Pöllnitz, *Memoirs*.

19. Berkholz, *Journal*.

13. THE LAST REFORMS

1. Friedrich Christian Weber, *The Present State of Russia*, vol. 1, pp. 118–20.—TRANS.

2. A. Yatsevich, *The St. Petersburg of Serfdom*.

3. Constantin de Grunwald, *La Russie de Pierre le Grand*.

4. Ibid. and Kasimierz Waliszewski, *Pierre le Grand*.

5. Weber, *The Present State of Russia*, vol. 1, pp. 186–88.—TRANS.

6. Ibid.

7. Ibid.

8. Ibid., pp. 93–94.—TRANS.

9. Report of March 10, 1721.

14. THE GIANT FELLED

1. Semevsky, *Slovo i delo*.

2. Letter from Catherine, April 19, 1717.

3. Letter from Peter, June 26, 1724.

Bibliography

Peter was a man of great complexity. Since his death, opinion about him has been divided, both in Russia and abroad. First the French Encyclopedists showered praise on him because he had opened his people's minds to the light of progress and carried on an effective struggle against the domination of the Church. "Peter I made Russia," wrote Voltaire. "Before him, she did not exist." But Jean-Jacques Rousseau accused him of having betrayed the soul of the Russian nation by trying to bend it to European ways. Joseph de Maistre was even more disparaging of the monarch and considered him "the assassin of his nation." In France, in England, in Germany, Peter the Great soon came to be called a monster who had "done violence to human nature."

In Russia, for more than a century it was fashionable to consider Peter the Great as a genius without failings. "He is your God, he was your God, Russia!" cried the poet and scientist Lomonosov. But at the beginning of the nineteenth century there was an awakening of nationalistic sentiment in the country, and many intellectuals blamed the reformer for not having understood how deep the old Muscovite customs ran. In a sharp ideological conflict, the Slavophiles, who upheld the Russian tradition, were ranged against the Westernists, who praised the sovereign for having shaken his subjects out of their apathy. In 1860 Aksakov wrote: "He failed to understand Russia and her past, and that is why his work is accursed." The great historian Karamzin, for his part, declared: "We have become citizens of the world, but in certain respects we have ceased to be Russian citizens. That is the fault of Peter I." Then there was another reversal of opinion under the influence of the liberals. Belinsky exalted the genius of the creator of St. Petersburg and proposed that altars should be raised to him at every crossroads in the empire. Chaadayev claimed that without Peter's reforms, "Russia would have become a Swedish province," and even Alexander Herzen, from the depths of exile, saluted Peter as "a revolutionary with a crown, a true representative of the revolutionary principle that lives in the soul of the Russian people."

In the Soviet Union, official opinion is more circumspect. Marx and Engels in their time recognized Peter's ability as a head of state. Lenin and Stalin praised his "progressive" action, while at the same time accusing him of a certain contempt for the laboring masses. Following them, the Soviet historians of today pay tribute to his political achievements but criticize him for having reinforced serfdom. To them, as to his contemporaries, Peter I still deserves the title of Great.

Countless works have been written about Peter the Great. Following is a list of the most important ones among those I have consulted.

PRIMARY SOURCES

Archives du ministère des affaires étrangères à Paris. Correspondance politique de Russie. Vols. 1–18 c. and Supplements 1–3.

AVRIL, R. P. PHILIPPE. *Voyage en divers etats d'Europe et d'Asie.* Paris: Barbin, 1692.

BERKHOLZ. *Journal* (in Russian). 4 vols.

BOGOSLOVSKY, M. *Peter the Great* (in Russian). 5 vols. Moscow, 1946.

Correspondance secrète de Louis XV. 2 vols. Paris: Plon, 1866.

Diplomatic Correspondence of Foreign Representatives at the Court of Peter the Great. Collection of the Imperial Russian Historical Society.

GOLITZINE, PRINCE AUGUSTIN. *La Russie au XVIIIe siècle, Mémoires inédits.* Paris, 1863.

GORDON, PATRICK. *Journal* (in Russian). St. Petersburg: Brückner, 1878.

JUEL, JUEST. *Journal, 1709–1711* (in Russian). Moscow, 1899.

KORB, JOHANN-GEORG. *Journal du voyage en Moscovie.* Paris, 1859.

———. *Récit de la sanglante révolte des Strélitz en Moscovie.* Paris, 1859. [English translation of both works: *Diary of an Austrian Secretary of Legation at the Court of Tsar Peter the Great.* Translated from the original Latin and edited by Count MacDonnell. London: Bradbury & Evans, 1863; reprinted London: Frank Cass & Co., 1968. (Two vols. in one.)—TRANS.]

KURAKIN, PRINCE. *Archives* (in Russian). Vol. 1. St. Petersburg, 1890.

LAMBERTY. *Mémoires pour servir à l'histoire du XVIIIe siècle.* 14 vols.

LA NEUVILLE, DE. *Relation curieuse et nouvelle de Moscovie.* The Hague, 1699.

LEIBNIZ. *Collection of Letters and Memoirs.* St. Petersburg, 1873.

MANSTEIN, C. H. *Mémoires historiques, politiques et militaires sur la Russie.* Lyons, 1772.

MARGRAVINE OF BAYREUTH, FRÉDÉRIQUE SOPHIE WILHELMINE. *Mémoires.* Paris: Mercure de France, 1967.

MATVEYEV, KREKSHIN, ZHELYABUZHSKY. *Memoirs* (in Russian). St. Petersburg, 1841.

MOREAU DE BRASEY, JEAN-NICOLE. *Mémoires politiques . . . d'un brigadier des armées de Sa Majesté czarienne.* 3 vols. Paris, 1735.

NARTOV. *Accounts of Peter the Great* (in Russian). St. Petersburg, 1891.

NASHCHOKIN. *Memoirs, 1707–1759* (in Russian). St. Petersburg, 1893.

PERRY, CAPTAIN JOHN. *Etat présent de la Grande Russie.* The Hague, 1717. [English original: *The State of Russia Under the Present Tsar.* London: Benjamin Tooke, 1716.—TRANS.]

PETER THE GREAT. *Journal de Pierre le Grand, depuis l'année 1698 jusqu'à la paix de Nystad.* 2 vols. London, 1773.

PETER THE GREAT. *Letters and Papers of Emperor Peter the Great* (in Russian). 5 vols. St. Petersburg, 1887.

PETER THE GREAT and CATHERINE I. *Correspondence of Peter I and Catherine* (in Russian). Moscow, 1861.

PLEYER, OTHON. *Le gouvernement de la Moscovie en 1710.*

Recueil des instructions données aux ambassadeurs et ministres de France. Vol. 8, Russia (introduction by Rambaud). F. Alcan, 1890.

Reports and Decrees of the Senate during the Reign of Peter the Great (in Russian). 6 vols.

SAINT-SIMON, DUC DE. *Mémoires.* Edited by Gonzague Truc. Vol. 5. Paris: Gallimard, Bibliothèque de la Pléiade, 1955.

VILLEBOIS, DE. *Mémoires secrets pour servir à l'histoire de la cour de Russie.* Paris: Dentu, 1853.

VOCKERODT, JOHANN. *Russia under Peter the Great* (in Russian, translated from the German). 1737.

WEBER, FRIEDRICH CHRISTIAN. *Nouveaux mémoires sur l'état présent de la Grande Russie ou Moscovie.* 2 vols. Paris, 1725. [English version: *The Present State of Russia,* anonymous translation from the High Dutch (including "Manifesto of the Criminal Process of the Czarewitz Alexei Petrowitz," translated from the French). 2 vols. London: W. Taylor, 1723; reprinted London: Frank Cass & Company, 1968.—TRANS.]

ZHELYABUZHSKY, IVAN. *Memoirs, 1682–1709* (in Russian). St. Petersburg, 1840.

SECONDARY SOURCES

ALEXANDROV, VICTOR. *Les mystères du Kremlin.* Paris: Fayard, 1960.

ANDREYEV, A., ed. *Peter the Great: A Collection of Essays* (in Russian). Moscow-Leningrad: Academy of Sciences of the USSR, 1947.

BASHUTSKY, A. *Panorama of St. Petersburg* (in Russian). St. Petersburg, 1834.

BASSEVILLE, DE. *Récit historique sur la vie et les exploits de François Lefort.* Lausanne, 1786.

BODY, ALBIN. *Pierre le Grand aux eaux de Spa.* Brussels, 1872.

BOGOSLOVSKY, M. *Peter I* (in Russian). 6 vols. Moscow, 1946.

———. *Russian Society and Science Under Peter the Great* (in Russian). Moscow, 1925.

BRANTISCH-KAMENSKI. *Illustration de la Russie ou galerie des personnages les plus remarquables.* Paris, 1829.

BRIAN-CHANINOV, N. *Histoire de Russie.* Paris: Fayard, 1929.

BRÜCKNER. *History of Peter the Great* (in Russian). St. Petersburg, 1882.

CABANÈS, DR. *Fous couronnés.* Paris: Albin Michel.

CARTIER, RAYMOND. *Pierre le Grand.* Paris: Hachette, 1963.

FUNK AND NAZAREVSKI. *Great Soviet Encyclopedia,* article on Peter the Great (in Russian). Moscow, 1955.

———. *Histoire des Romanov, 1613–1913.* Paris: Payot, 1930.

GREKOV, B. *Peasants in Russia from Ancient Times to the XVIIIth Century.* Moscow-Leningrad, 1940.

GRUNWALD, CONSTANTIN DE. *La Russie de Pierre le Grand.* Paris: Hachette, 1933. [English translation: *Peter the Great,* translated by Viola Garvin. London: Douglas Saunders with MacGibbon and Kee, 1956.—Trans.]

———. *Trois siècles de diplomatie russe.* Paris: Calmann-Lévy, 1945.

GUICHEN, VICOMTE DE. *Histoire d'Eudoxie Feodorovna, première épouse de Pierre le Grand.* Leipzig, 1861.

HAUMANT, EMILE. *La Russie au XVIIIe siècle.* Paris.

HUBERT, JEAN. *Le czar Pierre le Grand à Charleville* (in "Mélange d'histoire ardennaise"). Charleville, 1876.

IKONNIKOV. *New Materials for the History of Peter the Great* (in Russian). 1887.

———. *The Russian Woman on the Eve and After the Reforms of Peter the Great* (in Russian). Kiev, 1874.

KARAMZINE, M. *Histoire de la Russie.* 11 vols. Paris, 1819.

KERSTEN, KURT. *Pierre le Grand* (translated from the German). Paris: Albin Michel, 1939.

KLUTCHEVSKI, V. *Pierre le Grand et son oeuvre.* Paris: Payot, 1953. [English version: Klyuchevsky, *Peter the Great.* Translated from the Russian by Liliana Archibald. Boston: Beacon Press, 1958. —Trans.]

KOVALESKI, PIERRE. *Histoire de la diplomatie,* 3 vols. Paris: Médicis, 1946–1947.

———. *Manuel d'histoire russe.* Paris: Payot, 1948.

KRAKOWSKI, ed. *Histoire de Russie.* Paris: Deux-Rives, 1954.

LABRY, RAOUL. *Pierre le Grand* (in "Les grandes figures"). Paris: Larousse.

LAMARTINE, A. DE *Pierre le Grand* ("Civilisateurs et conquérants"). Paris: Lacroix, 1865.

Leningrad, Encyclopedic guide (in Russian). 1959.

LEROY-BEAULIEU, A. *L'empire des tsars et les Russes.* 3 vols. Paris: Hachette, 1883.

LORTHOLARY, A. *Le mirage russe en France au XVIIIe siècle.* Paris: Boivin, 1951.

LUPPOV, S. P. *The Building of St. Petersburg* (in Russian). Moscow-Leningrad, 1957.

MAÏKOV, V. V. *Doings and Amusements of the Emperor Peter the Great* (in "The Monuments of Ancient Annals") (in Russian). 1895.

MÉRIMÉE, PROSPER. *Histoire du règne de Pierre le Grand.* Paris: Plon, 1929.

MIAKHOTIN. *History of Russian Society* (in Russian). 1902.

MILIOUKOV, SEIGNOBOS, and EISENMANN. *Histoire de Russie.* Paris: Librairie Ernest Leroux, 1932. [English translation: Miliukov et al., *History of Russia.* Translated by Charles L. Markmann. New York: Funk & Wagnalls, 1968. —TRANS.]

MOURAVIEFF, BORIS. *Le testament de Pierre le Grand.* Neuchâtel: La Baconnière, 1949.

NOUGARET. *Beautés de l'histoire de Russie.* Paris, 1814.

NOVIK and LLONA. *Pierre le Grand.* Paris: Plon, 1933.

OUDARD, GEORGES. *La vie de Pierre le Grand.* Paris: Plon, 1929. [English translation: *Peter the Great.* Translated by F. M. Atkinson. New York: Brewer and Warren, 1930. —TRANS.]

PASCAL, PIERRE. *Histoire de la Russie.* Paris: Presses universitaires de France, 1957.

PINGAUD, LÉONCE. *Les Français en Russie et les Russes en France.* Paris, 1889.

PIRENNE, JACQUES. *Les grands courants de l'histoire universelle.* 7 vols. Neuchâtel: La Baconnière.

PLATONOV, SERGEI. *Histoire de la Russie.* Paris: Payot, 1929. [English translation: *History of Russia.* Translated by Emanuel Aronsberg. Edited by F. A. Golder. New York: Macmillan, 1925. —TRANS.]

PORTAL, ROGER. *Pierre le Grand.* Paris: Club français du livre, 1969.

RAMBAUD, ALFRED. *Histoire de Russie.* Paris: Hachette, 1879.

RÉAU, LOUIS. *L'art russe de Pierre le Grand à nos jours.* Paris, 1922.

————. *Pierre le Grand.* Paris: Hachette, 1960.

REYNOLD, GONZAGUE DE. *Le monde russe.* Paris, 1950.

SAINT-PIERRE, MICHEL DE. *Le drame des Romanov.* Paris: Robert Laffont, 1967.

SCHAKOVSKOY, ZINAÏDA. *La vie quotidienne à Moscou au XVIIe siècle.* Paris: Hachette, 1963.

SCHMURLO, E. *Peter the Great as Judged by His Contemporaries and by Posterity* (in Russian). St. Petersburg, 1912.

SÉGUR, GENERAL COMTE DE. *Histoire de Russie et de Pierre le Grand.* 2 vols. 1829.

SEMEVSKY, M. J. *The Czarina Catherine Alexeyevna, Anna and William Mons* (in Russian). St. Petersburg, 1884.

SOLOVYOV, SERGEI. *Public Lectures on Peter the Great* (in Russian). Moscow, 1872.

STAEHLIN, M. DE. *Anecdotes originales de Pierre le Grand.* Strasbourg, 1787.

STOLPIANSKY. *How St. Petersburg Was Founded and Grew* (in Russian). 1918.

TCHEBALSKY. *The Regency of the Czarevna Sophia* (in Russian). Moscow, 1856.

TEIL, BARON JOSEPH DU. *Le czar à Dunkerque.* Dunkirk, 1902.

TOLSTOÏ, ALEXIS. *Pierre le Grand.* Paris: Gallimard, 1929.

TOURGUENIEV, ALEXIS. *La cour de Russie, 1725–1783.* Berlin, 1858.

USTRYALOV, N. G. *History of the Reign of Peter the Great* (in Russian). 6 vols. St. Petersburg, 1859–1863.

VALLOTTON, HENRY. *Pierre le Grand.* Paris: Fayard, 1958.

VANDAL, ALBERT. *Louis XV et Elisabeth de Russie.* Paris: Plon, 1882.

VERNET, GEORGES. *Pierre le Grand en Hollande et à Zaandam.* Utrecht: Broes, 1863.

VOLTAIRE. *Histoire de Charles XII.*

————. *Histoire de l'empire de Russie sous Pierre le Grand.* Paris: Firmin Didot, 1885. [English translation: *Russia Under Peter the Great.* Translated by M. F. O. Jenkins. London and Toronto: Associated University Presses, 1983. —TRANS.]

WALISZEWSKI, KASIMIERZ. *L'héritage de Pierre le Grand.* Paris: Plon, 1900.

———. *Pierre le Grand.* Paris: Plon, 1887. [English translation *Peter the Great.* Translated by Lady Mary Loyd. New York: Appleton, 1897; London: William Heinemann, 1898. —TRANS.]

WEIDLÉ, W. *La Russie absente et présente.* Paris, 1949.

YATSEVICH, ANDREI. *The St. Petersburg of Serfdom* (in Russian). Leningrad, 1937.

ZABELIN, L. *The Private Life of the Russian Czars and Czarinas in the XVIth and XVIIth Centuries* (in Russian). Moscow, 1872–1875.

Index